In this ground-breaking work, James Roberts examines the willingness and ability of British volunteer and conscript infantrymen of the Great War to perform the soldier's fundamental role: to kill or maim the enemy, and accept the attendant chance of being killed or wounded. The literature to date has been, paradoxically, somewhat silent on the soldier's part in the act of killing.

This study recovers this neglected narrative through the experiences of 19th (Western) Division, as recorded in their unit war diaries – a source generated primarily to record the experiences of combat. The study's findings offer testimony to the courage and endurance of the Great War soldier in circumstances of terrible hardship and suffering. But they also reveal much lesser known and understood aspects of the soldier's behaviour in combat. Many infantrymen were unable and/or unwilling to traverse the experiential divide between civilian life and the ultimate act of soldiery. This in itself indicates the immense psychological steps taken by those (perhaps the minority) who found themselves capable of killing. Those who did fight gravitated towards weapons (such as the machine-gun or Mills Bomb) that, primarily through visual distance, partially sanitised the act of maiming the enemy. The bayonet kill, a far more personal form of combat, was a rare act; despite the British Army's undiminished championing of the bayonet as the principal weapon of the infantryman. But neither were the pacifistic legions always pawns in the hands of their senior commanders. Upon the physical No Man's Land they discovered a behavioural grey area between complete obedience and absolute defiance, and were able to tacitly limit their commitment to combat through subtle passive behaviour such as 'straggling' or "going to ground". In doing so they successfully wrestled back a degree of control over their battlefield fate. From a number of conclusions drawn by the study one predominates: civilian mores and values were not always surrendered the moment the infantryman crossed the parapet; many soldiers during the Great War found themselves willing servicemen, but reluctant killers.

James Roberts was born in the Worcestershire town of Evesham in 1967. His interest in the Great War began at an early age, inspired by stories of his Great Uncle Frank's mercurial Western Front service with 'D' Coy., 1/8th Worcestershire Regiment. James studied History at the University of Worcester and was awarded his PhD in 2004. During his time as a lecturer in Modern History, he delivered and published a number of academic papers examining the motivations and behaviours of the First World War soldier. James now lives in the Highlands of Scotland where he works as a commercial copywriter.

KILLER BUTTERFLIES

This book is dedicated to the memory of Private Frank Roberts of the Worcestershire Regiment who served on the Western Front during 1915-16, and to Private William Salter of the Royal West Kent Regiment who died fighting in Southern Italy in 1944 – both fine civilian soldiers.

KILLER BUTTERFLIES

Combat, Psychology and Morale in the British 19th (Western) Division 1915-18

James Roberts

Helion & Company Limited

Helion & Company Limited
26 Willow Road
Solihull
West Midlands
B91 1UE
England
Tel. 0121 705 3393
Fax 0121 711 4075
Email: info@helion.co.uk
Website: www.helion.co.uk
Twitter: @helionbooks
Visit our blog http://blog.helion.co.uk/

Published by Helion & Company 2017
Designed and typeset by Mach 3 Solutions (www.mach3solutions.co.uk)
Cover designed by Paul Hewitt, Battlefield Design (www.battlefield-design.co.uk)
Printed by Lightning Source Limited, Milton Keynes, Buckinghamshire

Text © James Roberts 2017
Maps drawn by George Anderson © Helion & Company 2017

Every reasonable effort has been made to trace copyright holders and to obtain their permission for the use of copyright material. The author and publisher apologize for any errors or omissions in this work, and would be grateful if notified of any corrections that should be incorporated in future reprints or editions of this book.

ISBN 978-1-911512-24-0

British Library Cataloguing-in-Publication Data.
A catalogue record for this book is available from the British Library.

All rights reserved. No part of this publication may be reproduced, stored in a retrieval system, or transmitted, in any form, or by any means, electronic, mechanical, photocopying, recording or otherwise, without the express written consent of Helion & Company Limited.

For details of other military history titles published by Helion & Company Limited contact the above address, or visit our website: http://www.helion.co.uk.

We always welcome receiving book proposals from prospective authors.

Contents

List of Maps	viii
Acknowledgements	ix
Introduction	x
1 The First World War British Soldier and the Historian	17
2 Combat Psychology and the Historian	28
3 Methodology Explained	38
4 Battle of Loos	51
5 Cumulative Aggression	64
6 Battle of the Somme	81
7 From *Esprit de Corps* to *Esprit de Platoon*	128
8 Messines Ridge and Third Ypres	146
9 The German Spring Offensives	187
10 The Last Hundred Days	229
11 Lessons Learnt	247
Bibliography	269
Index	281

List of Maps

1	French Flanders, 1915-16.	52
2	Battle of the Somme, July 1916.	82
3	Messines, June 1917.	147
4	Menin Road Ridge, September 1917.	172
5	Somme, March 1918 (1).	188
6	Somme, March 1918 (2).	205
7	Battle of the Lys, April 1918.	211
8	Aisne-Marne, May-June 1918.	222
9	Advance to Victory, October-November 1918.	230

Acknowledgements

The author would like to thank the following people and organisations for their assistance in the research and writing of this monograph.

The University of Worcester was kind enough to sponsor the original PhD thesis upon which this work is based. Dr Frank Crompton's championing of the original idea and the unwavering support of my tutor Dr. John Peters allowed the thesis to come to fruition. Dr. Gerry Dowds and Professor Dil Porter offered encouragement and advice throughout my time at Worcester and the comradeship of University's History Department provided a constant source of succour.

I was fortunate enough to receive generous funding from the Western Front Association which very much smoothed the path of researching in distant archives. The hospitality of my friends Mark and Tanya Spilsbury made London an affordable and pleasant city to work in. The original research was also aided by the efficiency and professionalism of the staff at both the Public Record Office and the Imperial War Museum.

The early drafts of the thesis were given form and direction by Professor David French and Professor Peter Simkins. The methodological and theoretical underpinning of the work benefited greatly from the advice of Professor Leonard V. Smith. The historical rigour of the final text is, I hope, a testimony to the time and expertise expended by Dr John M. Bourne and Professor Gary Sheffield. I would also like to extend my gracious thanks to Duncan Rogers and the staff at Helion for their time and effort in putting *Killer Butterflies* into print.

Finally, I would like to thank my friend Elizabeth Spilsbury, without whose constant support and encouragement this monograph would have remained nothing more than an idea.

Introduction

> Man, were he not corrupted by Governments, is naturally the friend of Man, and that human nature is not of itself vicious.[1]
>
> (Thomas Paine 1792)

The fundamental and ultimate act of warfare is to kill or harm.[2] From the sabre to the H-bomb weapon design has sought to destroy human bodies as a means to achieving military victory. This may seem blindingly obvious, but the reader of military history could be forgiven for thinking war to be no more violent than a football match or a game of chess and the centrality of the act of killing to war has tended to be either ignored or downplayed. Through this admission historians have replicated the assumptions of the societies they study; namely, that most men (and women) have killed when their government (through the agency of the military) ordered them to do so. The literature has consequently declined serious consideration of how citizens born from Western societies in which the maxim 'thou shall not kill'[3] is sacrosanct, have historically carried out and coped with the act of killing a fellow human being. As a corollary, how the battle plans of military commanders have been affected by the killing capabilities of their soldiers has suffered similar neglect. These omissions seem all the more inexcusable given that the majority of soldiers who fought the two major wars of the twentieth century were civilians with little prior experience or inclination towards soldiery.

The need to write killing back into the pages of military history has been underlined by the evolving science of combat psychology. This discipline has procured two

---

1 Thomas Paine, *The Rights of Man: Part the second* (1792).
2 This is not to say that the ultimate *goal* of military strategy is necessarily to kill the other side's soldiers (or civilians). Invariably military tactics aim at forcing the other side's army to capitulate – which can entail surrender or retreat. Therefore, the mere threat of force may be enough to secure victory. The point being made is that the *act* of killing or maiming other human beings is central to the activity of warfare.
3 In Western society, killing, under normal circumstances (that is, beyond state sanctioned killing such as executions), is deemed by law to be illegal, and considered by Christian religion to be a sin. See the 6th Commandment, Exodus 20.13. *The Bible: Authorized Version* London (1954) p. 66.

vitally significant pieces of knowledge on the reactions of the 'average' soldier in combat. First, that many soldiers take no active (that is aggressive) part in combat.[4] Second, that almost all soldiers eventually breakdown mentally under the strain of combat.[5] Given that the serious study of combat psychology was born during World War Two, it is to be expected that the best historical literature dealing with that and later conflicts should demonstrate an awareness of the universally debilitating effects of combat.[6] There is still, though, a comparative paucity of literature dealing with the soldiers' potential pacifism.[7] The historically reconstructed soldier of the early twentieth century and before appears, however, to have suffered from neither malady. Certainly, there is an understanding that *some* individual soldiers suffered from 'shellshock',[8] but the notion that many soldiers would eventually suffer some form of mental breakdown is largely absent.[9]

Historians of earlier conflicts do not have access to the kind of evidence offered by combat psychology. However, his should not negate adopting an approach which is sensitive both to the great difficulty of surviving combat mentally (let alone physically) for any length of time, and to many soldiers finding themselves unable or unwilling to actively participate in combat. Rather than assume that a soldier ordered onto the battlefield to kill has historically tried to do so, this study supposes that he *may not* have done so; either because he was unwilling or because, regardless of his conscious thoughts on the matter, found he was unable to kill or maim a fellow human being. Put differently, in adopting a philosophical approach sympathetic to that propounded by Thomas Paine (quoted in the epigraph), that Man is essentially pacifistic and desirous of living in harmony with his fellow Man, it has *not* also assumed that Man can so easily be *corrupted* by governments.

Such an approach has underpinned this investigation into how British infantry volunteers and conscripts of the Great War experienced and reacted to the role of combat during major set-piece attacks. That is, how 'civilian soldiers' with little or no prior exposure to soldiery executed the profession's fundamental role – to kill and accept the attendant chance of being killed. Over the last thirty years military historians have done much to advance understanding of how the British and Dominion soldier coped with the physical hardships and dangers prevalent during front-line

---

4   S.L.A. Marshall, *Men Against Fire: The Problem of Battle Command in Future War* Peter Smith (1978) 1st ed 1947.
5   R.L. Swank & W.E. Marchand, "Combat Neuroses: Development of Combat Exhaustion" in *Archives of Neurology & Psychiatry* (1946) Vol. 55 pp. 236-247.
6   John Ellis, *The Sharp End: The Fighting Man in World War II* Pimlico (1990) 1st ed 1980.
7   For the exception see David A. Grossman, *On Killing: The Psychological Cost of Learning to Kill in War and Society* Little, Brown & Company (1995).
8   Ben Shephard, *War of Nerves: Soldiers and Psychiatrists 1914-1994* Jonathan Cape (2000).
9   For an example of the neglect of this notion see Earl J. Hess, *The Union Soldier in Battle: Enduring the ordeal of combat* University of Kansas Press (1997). For a rare example of understanding see Charles (Lord) Moran, *The Anatomy of Courage* The Keynes Press (1984) 1st ed 1945.

service.¹⁰ In doing so, these studies have shed light upon the more salutary aspects of life in the trenches, and the mind-set of the Edwardian 'civilian soldier'. Progress in understanding what occurred once this soldier went 'over the top' – how the majority of soldiers behaved in combat, how they experienced and reacted to the act of killing and the very immediate fear of death – has been, however, comparatively leaden. We know a great deal about how the Great War soldier coped with the hardships and horrors of war (appalling conditions, fear of death and/or killing), without knowing enough about what those experiences (attempting to maim the enemy) actually were.

This languor seems unjustified given that copious documentation dealing with the daily execution of combat has survived in the form of unit war diaries and appended post-battle reports. To date such sources have been largely the sole preserve of historians investigating military tactics and strategy.¹¹ Yet these sources also afford a qualitative record of the expectations, thoughts and appraisals of senior and junior commanders on the combat activities of their rank and file infantry. They record, in the immediate aftermath of the event, traces of the actuality of combat. Although these sources themselves require qualified interpretation, war diaries do partially circumvent the inherent subjectivity and individuality of private papers and memoirs, whilst also overcoming the problems of both socially imposed censorship and self-censorship. Because unit war diaries were not dependant upon the war service of any individual, they also provide a continuous source of evidence. This is particularly important when it comes to investigating the experiences of the much neglected largely conscript army that fought the war's last year.¹²

In order to fully realise the potential of these sources this study has forgone the typical analysis of an entire army in favour of examination of a single division. Such a unit of investigation is substantial enough to offer potentially useful generalizations, whilst remaining amenable to an intensive longitudinal study allowing *comparative*

---

10 Ian F.W. Beckett & Keith Simpson (eds), *A Nation in Arms: a social study of the British Army in the First World War* Tom Donovan (1990) 1st pub 1985; Hugh Cecil & Peter H. Liddle (eds), *Facing Armageddon: The First World War Experienced* Leo Cooper (1996); John G. Fuller, *Troop morale and popular culture in the British and Dominion armies, 1914-1918* Clarendon Press (1990); Peter H. Liddle (ed), *Home Fires and Foreign Fields: British Social and Military Experience in the First World War* Brassey's Defence Publishers (1985); Gary Sheffield, *Leadership in the Trenches: Officer-Man Relations, Morale and Discipline in the British Army in the Era of the First World War* Macmillan (2000); Peter Simkins, *Kitchener's Army: The Raising of the New Armies, 1914-16* Manchester University Press (1988);Dale Blair, *Dinkum Diggers: An Australian Battalion at War* Melbourne University Press (2001); Glyn Harper, *Massacre at Passchendaele: The New Zealand Story* Harper Collins (2000); Desmond Morton, *When Your Number's Up: The Canadian Soldier in the First World War* Random House of Canada (1993).
11 See for example Peter Simkins, 'Co-Stars or Supporting Cast? British Divisions in the "Hundred Days", 1918' in Paddy Griffith (ed), *British Fighting Methods in the Great War* Frank Cass (1996), pp. 50-69.
12 For a rare contemplation of the conscript's experience see Ilana R. Bet-El, *Conscripts: Lost Legions of the Great War* Sutton Publishing (1999).

checks and balances.¹³ The 19th(Western) Division has been chosen for the investigation based upon the rationale of typicality. The 'Butterflies', as they were nicknamed by their last Commanding Officer, Major-General G.D. Jeffreys, were raised as part of Kitchener's 'second hundred thousand' and therefore its rank and file was exclusively comprised of civilian soldiers, they were recruited from across a broad swathe of the country and served in all the major set-piece battles executed by the New Army upon the Western Front from 1915 onwards.

Reading the experiences of 19th Division through this methodological lens reveals a narrative sometimes at odds with the current historiography. The infantry's collective experience of 'active service' was one of change, yet underpinned by a number of fundamental continuities. The background and recruitment experiences of the men populating a 'Service' division changed significantly over four-and-a-half years of war. The young and disparately recruited army of conscripts that fought the war's last year bore only a passing resemblance to the locally raised volunteer army that first stepped out upon the battlefields of Loos and the Somme. The expected role of the infantryman similarly changed, in time with the British Expeditionary Force's (BEF's) ascent of the tactical and technological 'learning curve'. Since 1 July 1916 the packhorses advancing in orderly waves, armed with rifle and bayonet, burdened by a plethora of construction equipment, but nominally charged only with occupying the enemy's 'destroyed' trenches, had been an endangered species. By the Autumn of 1918 their successors often carried a semi-automatic weapon, advanced as part of a mobile and tactically autonomous platoon, and were protected by a largely dependable 'creeping barrage', occasionally supplemented by mines, tanks and aircraft.

These changes in the division's combat experiences signal that 19th Division gradually learnt from and adapted to the problems raised by superior defensive firepower and the subsequent emergence of trench warfare; in which combat was dominated by the defensive triad of artillery, barbed wire and machine-guns. These findings broadly correlate with the 'revisionist' literature of recent years which has sought to resurrect the tactical, operational and technological achievements of the BEF and Dominion forces on the Western Front.¹⁴ 19th Division's experiences of the ascent, however, suggests some minor qualifications to this generally upbeat portrayal. This study's closer focus upon the *human element* within this 'learning curve' – the subtle

---

13 For a good example of similar small unit case study see Leonard V. Smith, *Between Mutiny and Obedience: The Case of the French Infantry Division during World War I* Princeton University Press (1994).
14 For the BEF see: Paddy Griffith, *Battle Tactics of the Western Front: The British Army's Art of Attack 1916-18* Yale University Press (2000) 1st ed 1994; Albert Palazzo, *Seeking Victory on the Western Front: The British Army and Chemical Warfare in World War I* University of Nebraska Press (2000). For the Dominion forces see: Bill Rawling, *Trench Warfare: Technology and the Canadian Corps, 1914-1918* University of Toronto Press (1992); Tim Cook, *No Place to Run: The Canadian Corps and Gas Warfare in the First World War* UBC Press (1999).

interplay between tactics, weapons and the soldiers who were charged with both firing and surviving them – indicates that 'friction' caused by the division's interaction with certain weapons often hindered the climb. In particular, 'lessons learnt' by 19th Division in late 1916 were not fully implemented upon the battlefield until the autumn of 1918.

Whilst 19th Division's 'learning curve' undulated and developed, their chosen stimuli to persuade its civilians to adopt a soldiery mentality and perform these changing combat roles experienced less evolution. The essential stimuli remained a combination of obedience (or discipline), weapon competency, exemplary leadership, a degree of battlefield conditioning, loyalty to a cause or body higher than oneself, and, the bottom line, fear of punishment. In particular, 'Drill' and the 'Bayonet' remained the stalwart methods of inculcating obedience and conditioning respectively. However, unalleviated concerns over battlefield command forced the division to embrace the morale potency of 'loyalty to the primary group' and, as a consequence, the cause or body demanding the infantryman's loyalty descended from King, Country or regiment, towards the humble platoon and section. In keeping with this seismic shift from the sublime to the pragmatic, the methods by which this loyalty was inculcated adopted some decidedly 'civilian' working-class cultural traits; football, especially, becoming the division's new religion.

These various training ground and playing-field cultivated stimuli continually yielded ambiguous results throughout the war. Although precise figures are difficult to quantify, this research suggests that a significant number of the division's infantrymen took *no active part* in combat. Those that did engage the enemy did so mostly with semi-automatic weapons that partly sanitised the act of killing. Very few soldiers were either willing or able to fight when the enemy drew nearer and the killing became more personal. The charging line of bayonet toting infantrymen prepared to do battle with cold steel, allegedly so much a part of the Regular Army's art of attack, and ubiquitous throughout the fictional literature of the time, remained a rare breed within the ranks of 19th Division's civilian soldiers.

Yet neither were these infantrymen always the innocent victims of trench warfare prescribed by the war poets. On the Western Front, artillery was king and the infantry were often its pawns, but the division's infantrymen did hold some agency over their battlefield fate. Throughout the war infantrymen were able to tacitly subvert the more extreme expectations of their superior commanders. The opening of the attack signalled the closure of communication channels between front and rear. The moment infantrymen stepped across the parapet they subsequently descended into a 'fog of war' which obscured the realities of battle from their superiors long enough to deem their actions a *fait accompli*. Cloaked by this 'fog of war', infantrymen were able to decide an objective's worth largely unfettered by the chain of command. 19th Division's Great War was consequently marked by one significant continuity; infantrymen decided when an engagement was over, not generals.

Gauging the collective strength of the civilian soldier's morale during the major set-piece battles of 1915 to 1918 is this study's second line of investigation. A number of quantitative methods have been deployed, based around the division's battle casualties and disciplinary record. These methodologies suggest that there were a number of noticeable peaks and troughs in the civilian soldier's collective morale. High points were reached during the Battle of Messines Ridge and during the 'Last Hundred Days'. The muddy denouement to the Somme and the worse days of Third Ypres pushed the infantry's endurance towards the edge, whilst the German Spring Offensives of 1918, at times, pushed it over the precipice. The explanations for these combat nadirs lie less within the infantry's ranks, and more with the objective circumstances (that is, those beyond their control) of the battles they fought.

Although infantry combat morale remained a vital component of success or failure, it was not *the* deciding factor of battlefield victory. The reality of this increasingly industrialised war was that depersonalised killing was king and the greatest killers were artillerymen. Given sufficient expertise and supplies, both sides could destroy the body and morale of the other's infantrymen almost with impunity. Put simply, on the Western Front infantry morale was no substitute for superior artillery firepower. Nevertheless, there could be no victories without advance and occupation of contested territories and, consequently, although infantry morale was not the hinge-factor in success, it remained a necessary component of victory. In this increasingly industrialised war, fought between mass armies of civilian soldiers, the active participation in combat of around half its infantrymen was often enough to make 19th Division an effective fighting force. Yet it was also necessary that the passive majority remained on the battlefield and made a passive contribution – carrying ammunition, running messages, tending the wounded and so forth. Throughout the war the 'collective' morale of the Butterflies' remained good enough to fulfil these tasks, for most of the time. Consequently, the 'collective' morale of the division's infantrymen remained *good enough* to achieve final victory in the Great War.

In the narrative that follows infantrymen will often be described as 'going to ground', or 'limiting their commitment' to a certain objective, or of having a lesser or greater morale in combat than their comrades. It cannot be stressed deeply enough that this study holds no desire to denigrate or judge in any way the efforts of these infantrymen. The actions of soldiers under fire can only rightfully be judged by those who shared in their danger. But it is right that the historian should accurately *report* the behaviour of soldiers under fire. A century on it is time to investigate this issue free from the stifling subjectivity of precepts such as courage or cowardice. In doing so we may find that our grandfathers and great grandfathers were not always the powerless victims of trench warfare normally described.

James Roberts
Speyside Scotland
January 2015

1

The First World War British Soldier and the Historian

The First World War/Great War has inspired more published memoirs than any other war in Britain's (not overly pacifistic) history.[1] That this war was fought by a more literate generation – and a great number of that generation – partly accounts for this phenomenon. That the memoirs (and poetry) of one or two volunteer junior officers should inadvertently stand for half a century as *the* history of the soldier's experience of this war is less explicable. Graves, Owen, Sassoon, Aldington, Sherriff and Blunden all, to varying degrees, wrote of the Great War as an experience of endless suffering and futile slaughter which induced an insipid cynicism and disenchantment in those who survived.[2] In particular, this poets' war (with a few exceptions) delineated the infantryman as an innocent victim of war – a soldier sent to the front to be killed rather than to kill. Owen's *Dulce et Decorum est*, for example, portrayed infantrymen as wretched hollow men: 'Bent double, like old beggars under sacks, Knock-Kneed, coughing like hags…', crushed by the sheer weight of the war.[3] Despite these macabre

---

[1] Hugh Cecil calculates that around 400 works of British war fiction were published between 1918 and 1939. See Hugh Cecil, 'British War Novelists' in Hugh Cecil & Peter Liddle (ed) *Facing Armageddon: The First World War Experienced* Leo Cooper (1996) pp. 801-16, p. 801.
[2] Richard Aldington, *Death of a Hero* London (1929); Edmund Blunden, *Undertones of War* Penguin (1982) 1st ed 1928; Edmund Blunden (ed), *The Poems of Wilfred Owen* London (1931); Robert Graves, *Goodbye to All That* Penguin (1960) 1st ed 1929; Siegfried Sassoon, *Memoirs of a Fox-Hunting Man* Faber & Faber (1928); Siegfried Sassoon, *Memoirs of an Infantry Officer* Faber & Faber (1930); R.C. Sherriff, *Journey's End* Penguin (1983) 1st ed 1929. Equally influential, especially upon the popular imagination, has been Erich Remarque's nominally fictitious account of the German soldiers' war. See Erich Maria Remarque, *All Quiet on the Western Front* Vintage (1996) 1st ed 1929.
[3] 'Dulce et Decorum est' in *Rupert Brook & Wilfred Owen* Everyman's Poetry (1997) p. 68. The term 'hollow men' is borrowed from T.S. Elliot, and described the living dead. See *T.S. Elliot: Selected Poems* Faber & Faber (1954) pp. 75-80.

visions being challenged by an equal number of more salutary portrayals,[4] by the early 1930s this 'literature of disenchantment' had become established as 'the truth about the war'.[5] One possible answer for this occurrence being that to a nation that had fought a war lasting over four years and costing 750,000 deaths for no palpable gain (or at least only the *negative* gain of halting German aggression), this image of futile suffering made sense, and most dissenting voices were ignored.[6]

Interest in the soldiers' experiences of the Great War (with the exception of being taken up by the cause of pacifism) was dampened by the expectation and subsequent realisation of a second 'world war'. When scholars and the general public alike rediscovered the Great War in the late 1950s and early 1960s this image of futile suffering had endured.[7] Joan Littlewood's play *Oh What a Lovely War* rewrote futility for a new generation of theatre goers, whilst Leon Wolff's *In Flanders Fields* and (to a lesser extent) Alan Clarke's *The Donkeys* did likewise for a new generation of reading public.[8] Popular entertainments such as *The Monocled Mutineer* and *Blackadder Goes Forth* stand testimony to how deeply ingrained upon this nation's collective memory this image of futile martyrdom still lies.[9] As *The Guardian* wrote in the early 1990s: 'The popular view [of the Great War] is that it was a pointless, almost accidental, waste of life.'[10] As we have moved into the twenty-first century, the continuing antagonistic public reception (as seen through the media) to any historical work endeavouring to revise this image (along with other potent 'myths' of the Great War) suggests little has changed.[11]

It was not until the 1970s that professional historians began to challenge seriously some of the assumptions that underlay this 'popular' understanding. In both spirit and substance, the serious historical study of the *soldiers'* experience of the Great War

---

4   See for example, Charles Edmonds, *A Subaltern's War* (1929); Frederic Manning, *The Middle Parts of Fortune* Peter Davies (1929); and later J.C. Dunn, *The War the Infantry Knew 1914-1919* Abacus (1987) 1st ed 1938.
5   Brian Bond, 'British 'Anti-War' Writers and Their Critics' in Hugh Cecil & Peter Liddle (eds) (1996), op cit., pp. 817-30, p. 821.
6   Ibid., p. 827.
7   On the subject of the origins and endurance of the 'literature of disenchantment' see also Modris Eksteins, *Rites of Spring: The Great War and the Birth of the Modern Age* Bantam Press (1989); Samuel Hynes, *A War Imagined: The First World War and English Culture* Bodley Head (1990); Martin Stephen, *The Price of Pity: Poetry, History and Myth in the Great War* Leo Cooper (1996).
8   Alan Clarke, *The Donkeys* Pimlico (1991) 1st ed 1961; Joan Littlewood, *Oh What a Lovely War* Methuen (2001) 1st ed 1963; Leon Wolff, *In Flanders Fields* Greenwood(1984) 1st ed 1958.
9   Alan Bleasdale, *The Monocled Mutineer* TV series, 1st broadcast 1987; Richard Curtis & Ben Elton, *Blackadder Goes Forth* TV series, 1st broadcast 1989.
10   Norman Stone, 'The Reason Why' *The Guardian* 11th Nov 1993.
11   See, for example, Gary Sheffield, *Forgotten Victory: The First World War – Myths and Realities* Headline (2001), esp. 'Introduction'. Here Gary Sheffield records the antagonistic response his own 'revisionist' endeavours have elicited from the media.

essentially began with the publication of John Keegan's *The Face of Battle* in 1976.[12] Keegan was less concerned with the 'popular image' than he was the profession of military history. Keegan chastised his professional forebears and peers for obscuring the realities of battle behind literary artifice and romanticised hyperbole. Keegan suggested that even the best that military history could offer was, in this respect, flawed. Dissecting Michael Howard's "straight-forward' battle-piece narrative of the Franco-Prussian war, Keegan asked: 'Did the whole lot, every last *Grenadier* and *Fusilier*, stick where they crouched on the open hillside? Were the bonds of discipline and group loyalty so strong that no one made a bolt for the rear, or burrowed for cover between the corpses of his comrades?'[13] The answer, Keegan implied, was probably not. However, he contended that until military historians wrote about battle from the soldiers' perspective rather than the commanders', and as a value free event rather than as a win/lose contest, we would never find out.[14]

Keegan chose to pass over two preceding historical studies whose stated remit had been to examine how the front-line soldier (in this case, of the Great War) coped with battle. Both Charles Wilson's (later known as Lord Moran) *Anatomy of Courage* and John Baynes' *Morale: A Study of Men and Courage* were nominally based upon the experiences of a single 'regular' battalion serving on the Western Front, although both studies posited a number of theories applicable to all soldiers in battle.[15] Both concluded that 'pride in the regiment' had been the essential element holding 'regular' battalions together under fire.[16] Despite their individually ground-breaking approaches however, both studies said very little about what actually happened on the battlefield. Wilson, with great insight, posited that all soldiers were vulnerable to the gradual insidious mental and physical strain caused by months of endless exposure to the hardships

---

12   John Keegan *The Face of Battle* Pimlico (1999) 1st ed 1976.
13   See Michael Howard, *The Franco-Prussian War* Hart-Davis (1961). Quoted in ibid., p. 45. As a veteran of the Italian Campaign (1943-44) Howard can claim a firsthand knowledge of life 'at the sharp end'. In Keegan's opinion, however, this experience was not reflected in Howard's writings on the subject.
14   Ibid., p. 52 & pp. 75-7.
15   Lord Moran *The Anatomy of Courage* The Keynes Press (1984) 1st ed 1945 & John Baynes *Morale: A Study of Men and Courage: The Second Scottish Rifles at the Battle of Neuve Chapelle 1915* Cassell (1967). Wilson's study was based upon his first hand observations serving as R.M.O. with the 1st (Regular) Battalion of the Royal Fusiliers on the Western Front 1914-17, and informed by his time spent lecturing aircrews of Bomber Command during the Second World War. John Baynes' study was based upon the experiences of the 2nd Scottish Riffles at the Battle of Neuve Chapelle, 1915. At the time of publication in the late 1960s Baynes was the battalion's C.O.
16   Wilson, in typically elegant prose, stated: 'The difference between a battalion of the professional army of 1914 and a Kitchener unit was … that they had implanted in the very marrow of men the creed of the regiment, which blossomed into a living faith till nothing else mattered.' See Lord Moran, op cit., p. 28 & p. 136, quote from p. 136; John Baynes, op cit., p. 88, p. 103, p. 169 & pp. 253-4.

of the front-line.[17] But he then simplified the soldier's behaviour under-fire down to those who did their duty, and those who shirked.[18] Similarly, Baynes gave a rather perfunctory summary of the 2nd Scottish Rifles' reaction to combat: 'There was no bitterness afterwards, and the survivors were again ready for anything after a few days' rest.'.[19] Baynes' seeming reluctance to contemplate any behaviour beyond the paradigm of 'courage' revels the limitations of military history written by insiders, and is well signalled by the following passage: 'It is obvious that in some units on that night nothing did happen…there must have been some battalions who had come to the stage of virtually refusing to move. These failures are not worth labouring, however.'[20] But surely these 'failures' were worth labouring? Why did these soldiers decide not to fight when others around them seem to have done so? How did these soldiers avoid battle? Were their officers complicit, or did they attempt to censure them?

Having interrogated the British Army's recorded past with a similar line of questioning, Keegan ventured the general hypothesis that once the arrows, cannons or bullets started firing, the objectives of the commander slipped from the minds of most soldiers, and their own personal survival, and that of their immediate comrades, became the priority.[21] Thus, in explaining Kitchener's Army's 'will to combat' on 1 July 1916, Keegan suggested that a combination of good leadership and a desire to do their duty got them over the top, but it was the desire to reach the (very) relative safety of the German front-line trenches that primarily motivated those few left standing to continue.[22]

Two studies promptly followed which went some way to 'Keeganising' the Great War.[23] Whereas *The Face of Battle* had been primarily directed towards academics and the 'specialist' reader, John Ellis' *Eye-Deep in Hell* was clearly intended to capture the imagination of the 'general reader'.[24] Moreover, Ellis attempted to paint a much broader canvas of the front-line soldiers' experience of the Western Front. The result was a gritty portrayal of 'life at the sharp end' – largely devoid of generals and battle plans – stripped down into a number of singular experiences: the setting, routines, conditions, equipment; the various facets of combat, rest and leave. It was also, like the popular image, an unrelenting portrayal of suffering and misery, in which the

17 Lord Moran, op cit., pp. 17-23.
18 Ibid., p. 4 & p. 140.
19 John Baynes, op cit., p. 89.
20 Ibid., pp. 93-4.
21 John Keegan (1976) op cit, p. 48.
22 Ibid., pp. 272-6. Keegan also included 'cohesion, sense of mission, mood of self sacrifice, local as well as national patriotism' in the list of motivations. Quote from p. 272.
23 The phrase is used by John Ellis to describe his part in the historiography of the Second World War, but it is equally applicable here. See John Ellis, 'Reflections on the 'Sharp End' of War' in Paul Addison & Angus Calder (ed) *Time to kill : the Soldier's Experience of War in the West, 1939-1945* Pimlico (1997), pp. 12-18, p. 15.
24 John Ellis, *Eye-Deep in Hell: The Western Front 1914-18* PSB (1976). This point is borne out by the number of full page photographs, and recourse to much famous poetry.

infantryman was the innocent victim of trench warfare. The front-line soldier faced a life of uninterrupted mud, rain, rats, corpses, flies, lice, guns and gas, shell fire and shortages.[25]

Denis Winter's *Death's Men* similarly evinced sensitivity to the insidiously destructive effects of combat, saying of the soldier that 'the majority ceased to fight except in a shadow-boxing way after a few months on the front line.'[26] However, Winter's study was more tightly focused – dealing only with the British volunteer soldiers' experience – and dealt at greater length with the process of recruitment and training, and the mentalities of Kitchener's men. Possibly for these reasons, *Death's Men* offers a slightly more balanced account. Winter suggested that 'most men did find a satisfactory home within the army.'[27]

Neither *Eye-Deep in Hell* nor *Death's Men* tell us all we need to know about the soldiers' experience of the Great War. The qualities of detail and precision found in *The Face of Battle* were somewhat lost in the broad canvas. Such an approach necessitated an over-reliance upon the literary memoirs of a few 'famous' junior officers, and a few not so famous. The upshot being that whilst they certainly wrote about battle from the soldiers' perspective, it was a very narrow view; in essence, a number of vignettes of war in 1915-16 drawn by predominantly upper middle-class volunteer officers.[28] The working-class volunteer's war, the conscript's war, and the war's last years were somewhat overlooked. Moreover, it is little wonder, given this reliance upon literary memoirs, that their historically reconstructed infantryman should be essentially a *victim* of the Great War – men sent to be killed rather than to kill.

The following twenty years have witnessed an exhaustive assault upon these imbalances, and a general re-writing of the soldiers' experiences of the Great War. Explaining such historiographical evolutions, especially one so recent, is a inexact art. The original historical enquiry will often mine near the surface, to get at the immediately available material, leaving those that follow to dig a little deeper. The unearthing of new types of evidence does not fully resolve the emergence of a 'revisionist' strand of historiography from the mid 1980s onwards; although a greater reliance upon private diaries, correspondences and memoirs certainly helped spread the historical cannon. Possibly of greater influence has been a change in the philosophical approach to war and society. The tendency to treat war in isolation, something apart from society, has given way to a readiness to witness war as an event occurring within the continuum of a society. This philosophical turn has caused a sensitising of the historical imagination which, in turn, has encouraged a tendency to understand all aspects of the Great War

---

25 Ibid., pp. 9-59.
26 Denis Winter *Death's Men: Soldiers of the Great War* Allen Lane (1978), p. 140.
27 Ibid., p. 51.
28 Although never made explicit, most of the accounts of life in the front-line are drawn from 1915-16, and the accounts of combat are evidently from the Battle of the Somme, 1916.

within the context of the society and times in which it occurred.[29] This is arguably an approach that is only realisable once an event becomes 'history', and is subjected to a more objective, emotion free, analysis.

The arrival of this revisionist strand of historiography was announced in 1985 by the publication of two texts offering a collection of likeminded essays on the British social and military experience of the Great War: *Home Fires and Foreign Fields* and *A Nation in Arms: a social study of the British Army in the First World War*.[30] In *Home Fires and Foreign Fields* Keith Simpson, in a essay summarising all things concerning the Western Front, confronted the supposed failings of the literature: 'There is a tendency sometimes to place too much emphasis on the horrors faced by the British soldier on the Western Front. Danger and fear were not necessarily the continuous or universal experience of all British soldiers, and many of them thought at the time, and later, that it had been 'the great adventure'.'[31] Simpson pointed to the numerous collections of unpublished and privately published contemporary letters and diaries as a means of sourcing the wider experiences of the soldier on the Western Front.[32] Simpson cautioned that 'It would be wrong to assume that the majority of British battalions or for that matter British soldiers were the passive victims of trench warfare...Within battalions, many junior officers, NCOs and soldiers relished the prospect of small unit combat against the enemy, and were willing to volunteer to go on raids or take part in bombing parties.'[33]

Few if any historians had previously found the mentalities of the British soldier quite so aggressive and few since have contended that the British soldier experienced and reacted to combat with such equanimity and enthusiasm. One notable exception is Peter Liddle, who, through a impressive array of monographs, articles and editorials, has been tireless in stressing that 'in a majority of cases men respond[ed] resiliently and with a measure of cheerfulness rather than otherwise to even prolonged strain.'[34] Liddle's interpretation of the British soldiers' resilience rests partly on the endurance of (what might be termed) certain Edwardian mentalities. The Somme and

---

29 It is also worth considering that a simpler explanation might be that historians, by inclination and training, have a predisposition towards reacting against their previous generation's interpretations of the past.
30 Peter H. Liddle (ed) *Home Fires and Foreign Fields: British Social and Military Experience in the First World War* Brassey's Defence Publishers (1985), Ian Beckett & Keith Simpson (eds) *A Nation in Arms: A Social Study of the British Army in the First World War* Tom Donovan (1990) 1st pub 1985.
31 Keith Simpson 'The British Soldier on the Western Front' in Peter H. Liddle (ed) op cit., pp. 135-158, p. 155.
32 Ibid., pp. 152-3.
33 Ibid., p. 149.
34 Peter Liddle, 'British Loyalties: The Evidence of an Archive' in Hugh Cecil & Peter H. Liddle, (ed) op cit., pp. 523-38, p. 525. See also Peter H. Liddle (1985) (ed) '*Home Fires and Foreign Fields*' op cit; Peter H. Liddle, *The 1916 Battle of the Somme: A Reappraisal* Leo Cooper (1992); Peter Liddle, 'Passchendaele Experienced: Soldiering in the Salient during

Passchendaele did not, he suggests, prove the final resting place of faith in (or even love for) the institutions of King, Country, Parliament and Empire, or the righteousness of England's cause.[35] In this sense at least, Liddle's work fits well within the 'revisionist' model of continuity over change. However, most 'revisionist' historians have tended to stress the continuation of less 'high-minded' ideals, with particular attention being given to continuity in the realms of social relationships and cultural experience.

Alongside Simpson and Liddle at the forefront of this re-evaluation of the British soldiers' experience of the Great War stands Peter Simkins, whose *Kitchener's Army* remains the seminal text on the volunteer soldiers' experiences of recruitment and training in England.[36] Simkins' consultation of copious amounts of contemporary sources has inspired a portrait of the Kitchener volunteer rich in subtle shades and nuances. Gone is the one-dimensional 'patriotic lemming of 1914'. In its place Simkins has drawn a multi-faceted individual potentially motivated to enlist by many things: unemployment, the chance to escape mundane and poorly paid labour, a simple youthful exuberance, peer pressure, a young girl holding a white feather, and yes, patriotism and a belief in the cause.[37] Once in the colours, Simkins contends, continuity in experience helped the newly enlisted volunteers cope with the hardships of the training camp. 'For the majority of working-class recruits [he argues], accustomed to long hours and poor conditions, being in the army simply substituted one set of hardships for another, and even offered certain compensations.'[38] Once 'on active service' it was, Simkins argues, *esprit de corps* that held the New Army together. Significantly, Simkins also sees continuity in civilian experiences operating here. He contends that this potent *esprit de corps* was founded upon *existing* community relationships.[39]

Gary Sheffield has likewise stressed the importance of the survival of civilian social relationships in the BEF's endurance, but with a studied focus upon the beneficial impacts of civilian norms upon officer-man relations.[40] The bond of loyalty forged

---

the Third Battle of Ypres' in Peter H. Liddle, (ed) *Passchendaele in Perspective: The Third Battle of Ypres* Leo Cooper (1997) pp. 305-323.
35 See esp. Peter Liddle (1992) op cit., p. 65 & p. 144.
36 Peter Simkins, *Kitchener's Army: The Raising of the New Armies, 1914-16* Manchester University Press (1988).
37 Ibid., pp. 169-75. The most important 'cause' being the defence of 'little Belgium'.
38 Ibid., p. 203.
39 Ibid., p. 317.
40 Gary Sheffield, *Leadership in the Trenches: Officer-Man Relations, Morale and Discipline in the British Army in the Era of the First World War* Macmillan (2000), esp. pp. 135-164; Gary Sheffield "A very good type of Londoner and a very good type of colonial': Officer-Man Relations and Discipline in the 22nd Royal Fusiliers, 1914-18' in Brian Bond et al *'Look To Your Front': Studies in the First World War by The British Commission for Military History* Spellmount (1999) pp. 137-146, p. 137; Gary Sheffield, 'Officer-Man Relations, Discipline and Morale in the British Army of the Great War.' in Hugh Cecil & P.H. Liddle (ed) (1996), op cit., pp. 413-424.

between junior officers and other ranks, Sheffield contends, played a major part in the BEF's willingness to fight.[41] At the heart of successful officer-man relations, Sheffield suggests, stood the 'deference in exchange for paternalism' relationship upon which Edwardian society itself was bonded. 'The peacetime experience of the working-class male soldier thus prepared him for military life. The officer-man relationship of the army reflected to an exaggerated degree the reciprocal deferential/paternal relationship of civilian society.'[42] The Edwardian working man's obedience to servitude rested upon the understanding that his master would care for his material welfare. Likewise, for the same reasons, the working-class ranker obeyed his middle-class officer.[43]

In explaining the endurance of the BEF, John Bourne has placed greater emphasis upon the social and cultural continuum experienced by the second half of this equation – the 'men'.[44] Bourne contends that: 'Working-class culture provided the army with a bedrock of social cohesion and community on which its capacity for endurance rested. [This was primarily because the] existential realities from which this culture evolved were remarkably similar to those of military life, both in the army and on the battlefield.'[45] Working-class life was marked by boredom, tedium, material hardship (sometimes danger) and subordination. So was the life of a front-line soldier. Survival came through a remarkable degree of mutuality: unions, friendly societies, the co-operative movement, the community of the yard, the pub and the club. On the front-line this 'mutuality' took the form of the comradeship derived from membership of the primary group – the platoon or section.[46] It was this comradeship that gave soldiers the courage to face the fear of mutilation or death, and the loss of that comrade that motivated the soldier to kill.[47]

John Fuller, like Bourne, also locates the endurance of the BEF in the successful transposition to the front-line and survival of working-class social and cultural norms.[48] Fuller however, places greater onus upon a continuation in cultural experience: 'The fact that there was a large degree of continuity in enthusiasms and attitudes from civilian life to military life is significant not only in its effects but also in what it says about the nature of the war experience. It suggests that for many men the war was not quite the chasm, cutting across individual and collective experience and sundering

---

41 Gary Sheffield (2000), op cit., pp. 146-8.
42 Gary Sheffield (2000), op cit., p. 72.
43 Gary Sheffield (1996), op cit., pp. 418-9.
44 John M. Bourne, *Britain and the Great War 1914-1918* Edward Arnold (1989) esp. Chap. 9 'Comradeship, Discipline and Morale' pp. 199-224 & John Bourne, 'The British Working Man in Arms' in Hugh Cecil & Peter H. Liddle, (eds) op cit., pp. 336-352.
45 John Bourne (1996), op cit., P. 341.
46 John M. Bourne (1989), op cit., p. 220 & John Bourne (1996), op cit., pp. 342-9.
47 John M. Bourne (1989), op cit., pp. 220-1. 'The result was hatred of the enemy and a thirst for revenge.' P. 221.
48 John G. Fuller, *Troop morale and popular culture in the British and Dominion armies, 1914-1918* Clarendon Press (1990).

past from future, that it is sometimes depicted.'⁴⁹ The main leisure activities of the working-classes – football, music hall, gambling and the excursion – were played out, at the behest of the rank and file, just behind the front-line.⁵⁰ As a consequence, the civilian mores and attitudes that both reflected and upheld these activities – a culture of consolation – flourished within the BEF.⁵¹ The rank and file were, therefore, able to defend against the hardships and horrors of war in the same way they tackled the trials of Edwardian working-class life; through a potent cultural cocktail of fatalism, escapism and a (often rather self-depreciating) sardonic humour.

Elucidating the 'behind the line' activities of the BEF has given a valuable insight into the wider experiences of the front-line soldier, whilst also acting as a useful corrective to the earlier literature's macabre portrayal of endless suffering. We now have a much fuller picture of the soldier's experience of the Great War. The same cannot be said, however, of our understanding of the same soldier's potential obduracy – whether expressed tacit or overtly – to the orders of higher command. Put differently, the operation of command within the BEF has tended to be accepted uncritically. Questions were raised over the perceived 'plastic qualities of the British soldier' in the late 1970s by David Englander and James Osborne, but their own enquiry was hampered by the 'closed' status of many relevant official documents.⁵² In the mid 1980s Gloden Dallas and Douglas Gill contended that the Etaples 'mutinies' represented a re-writing of the rule book: 'not by generals but by the army's other ranks.' However, the author's offer very little evidence of the apparently far-reaching affects of the Etaples mutiny on the Army whilst the war still raged, especially anywhere near the front line.⁵³ Therefore, as Gerald Oram admits, the subject of command authority within the B.E.F 'remains an area relatively neglected by historians.'⁵⁴

This sentiment is echoed with greater resonance by Leonard V. Smith who contends that 'the history of power-relations within the British army remains largely to be

---

49   Ibid., p. 154. Fuller's rather tentative conclusion that a continuation in cultural experience 'may have played a part in upholding the morale of the British and Dominion troops' is belied by a study which summarily dismisses (or at least underplays) all other motivations. Quote p. 175.
50   Ibid., pp. 81-110.
51   Ibid., pp. 114-30.
52   David Englander & James Osborne, 'Jack, Tommy, and Henry Dubb: The Armed Forces and the Working Class' in *The Historical Journal* Vol. 21 No. 3 (1978) pp. 593-621.
53   Gloden Dallas & Douglas Gill, *The Unknown Army: Mutinies in the British Army in World War I* Verso (1985), esp. pp. 72-98, quotation p. 76. Most historians have tended to dismiss events at Etaples as a 'storm in a teacup'. Gerard J. DeGroot, for example, states that: 'Much has been made of the British revolt at Etaples in 1917, when soldiers briefly rioted over conditions at a training camp. But that incident is significant only because, in the wider picture, it is insignificant.' See Gerard J. DeGroot, *The First World War* Palgrave (2001) p. 177.
54   Gerald Oram, op cit. p. 29.

written.'[55] Smith is well placed to make such a judgement. His *Between Mutiny and Obedience* has persuasively challenged the historiography of command authority within the French Army of the Great War. The French infantryman has traditionally been portrayed as a sacrificial 'lamb to the slaughter'. Audoin-Rouzeau for instance argues that throughout the war the *poilus* 'saw themselves as convicts condemned to wait for death or mutilation in the prison of the trenches', the 'feeling of being crushed, [and] the uselessness of any resistance' only served to deepened the malaise.[56] Smith suggests otherwise, arguing that the rank and file were gradually able to assert some control over the material conditions under which they served, and the circumstances in which they fought. The engendering of 'live and let live' tacit truces during 'trench warfare' represented one salient facet of this process; the mutinies of 1917 were its most profound demonstration.[57] Moreover, the morale of the French Army rested upon this reversal of command authority.

The self-confessed inspiration for Smith's study is Tony Ashworth's *Trench Warfare*.[58] Ashworth, like Smith, proposes a reversal of the traditional historical understanding of the (in this instance) British Army's command structure and authority. Ashworth contends that 'soldiers strove with success for control over their environment and thereby radically changed the nature of their war experience.'[59] The main method by which this renegotiation was achieved, he suggests, being the evolution of tacit truces during the long periods of static trench warfare. Ashworth delineates how these tacit truces ('live and let live') evolved from fragile and unpromising beginnings as breakfast time truces of convenience, to day and night long exchanges of peace. For Ashworth, however, these tacit truces were transient and effectively brought to an end by the higher command's policy of trench raiding. Moreover, his study assumed that passive activity (or at least the potential for passive activity) ceased during major 'set-piece' battles.

As with command authority within the BEF, so has our understanding of what occurred once the soldier went 'over the top' – how the majority of soldiers acted in combat, how they carried out and coped with *the act of killing* – suffered from studied neglect. This can partly be attributed to the earlier literature's over-reliance upon published memoirs, and partly to the academic imbalance in attention given by the 'revisionists' to the (albeit temporally more common-place) continuations in the frontline and behind the lines life of the soldier, against the discordant experiences of

---

55   Leonard V. Smith, *Between Mutiny and Obedience: The Case of the French Fifth Infantry Division during World War I* Princeton University Press (1994) p. 250.
56   Stephane Audoin-Rouzeau, *Men at War 1914-1918: NationalSentiment and Trench Journalism in France during the First World War* Berg (1992), p. 90 & p. 56.
57   Leonard V. Smith, op cit., especially p. 14 & p. 98.
58   Tony Ashworth, *Trench Warfare, 1914-1918: The Live and Let Live System* MacMillan (1980).
59   Ibid., pp. 14-15.

combat. This latter state of affairs is well illustrated by Ilana R. Bet-El's *Conscripts*.[60] As the title suggests, this is a much needed and in many ways excellent study of the largely neglected fifty percent of British soldiers who fought the Great War through compulsion.[61] Yet, it is less a narrative of 'life at the sharp end' than 'life at the supply end'. According to Bet-El 'food, clothing and cleanliness [were] the most crucial in determining their attitude to being conscripts.'[62] Combat in the narrative is portrayed only as a much feared and ever present back drop to the conscripts' day-to-day life at the front. It is unsurprising therefore that Bet-El should conclude that throughout the war 'the conscripts still saw themselves as working men, in the civilian sense of the word, employed by the army for a specific job – at an unsatisfactory rate of pay...'[63]

But this surely doesn't tell us all we need to know about the conscripts' experience of war? Admittedly, as Gerard J. DeGroot states, 'the drudgery of trench life had much in common with the monotonous dehumanisation of the factory. Except for the killing, war was not much different from work.'[64] But it is the act of killing that sets the prescribed role of the front-line soldiery apart from almost all other human activities. Therefore, we cannot properly understand the Great war soldiers' experience of war (or any soldiers' for that matter) without fully contemplating the act of killing. It is on the subject of killing that the historian can usefully learn from the study of combat psychology.

---

60 Ilana R. Bet – El *Conscripts: Lost Legions of the Great War* Sutton Publishing (1999).
61 Bet-El argues that the fundamental difference that set volunteers and conscripts apart was their experiences of enlistment. Volunteers, in his portrayal, were all motivated (in some way or other) to fight, and were willing participants in the enlistment process. Conscripts, on the other hand, were the hapless victims of bureaucracy; 'his life was disrupted for him by the external force of an army summons while he remained passive.' See ibid., p. 29.
62 Ibid., p. 109.
63 Ibid., p. 140.
64 Gerard J. DeGroot (2001), op cit., p. 162.

2

Combat Psychology and the Historian

Combat psychology has fairly recent origins.[1] The pre-war British Army gave little attention to the effects of combat upon the common soldier.[2] As part of a society that gave precedent to the values of 'manliness' and believed in the 'assumption that it was normal for men to act extremely aggressively', this was wholly understandable.[3] It was considered that a combination of loyalty to the regiment, strict discipline and strong leadership would ensure that the soldier fought.[4] This philosophy seems to have been vindicated by the Army's success in garrisoning the Empire and fighting a number of short wars against (albeit) technically inferior opposition. Warfare on the *veldt* challenged some of these certainties.[5] Exposure to the realities of protracted

---

1 Peter Watson suggests that: 'The military uses of psychology were first taken seriously during and immediately following the Second World War. Only in the early 1960s, however, did the subject really take off…' See Peter Watson, *War on the Mind: The Military Uses and Abuses of Psychology* Hutchinson (1978) p. 22.
2 Anthony Kellett, 'Combat Motivation' in Gregory Belensky (ed) *Contemporary Studies in Combat Psychiatry* Greenwood Press (1987) pp. 206-32 p. 206.
3 Joanna Bourke 'Effeminacy, Ethnicity and the End of Trauma: The Suffering of 'Shell-shocked' Men in Great Britain and Ireland, 1914-39', in *Journal of Contemporary History* Vol. 35(1) (2000) pp. 57-69 p. 59. See also George L. Mosse 'Shell-shock as a Social Disease' in *Journal of Contemporary History* Vol. 35(1) (2000) pp. 101-108, for a discussion upon the dominance of the ideal of manliness in Edwardian society and culture.
4 See for example *Infantry Training 1914* General Staff War Office H.M.S.O. IWM. The manual stated that the soldier should to be motivated to fight by the following methods. 'The soldier should be instructed in the deeds which have made the British Army and his regiment famous…The privileges which he inherits as a citizen of a great Empire should be explained to him, and he should be taught to appreciate the honour which is his, as a soldier, of serving his King and country…Drill in close order is of first importance in producing discipline, cohesion, and the habits of absolute and instant obedience to the orders of a superior…' pp. 2-3. For a good summary of the pre-war British Army's methods of achieving 'high morale' see John Bourne (1996), op cit., pp. 337-8.
5 See for example John Baynes' comments upon the experiences of the pre-war 2nd Scottish Rifles. John Baynes, op cit., pp. 15-50. For a good description of pre-war British Army see

industrial warfare, however, forced the Army and its paymasters towards the realisation that modern warfare would produce both demoralisation and a significant number of psychiatric casualties.[6] This awakening was painful and slow, as the high command railed against recognising 'emotional shock', fearing that the whole army might end up in hospital.[7] Some of the lessons learned by both Britain and her allies were recorded by the 1922 Home Office enquiry into 'Shellshock'.[8] One portentous discovery was that shellshock was more often occasioned by the psychological impact of shelling rather than actual physical damage to the brain.[9] The evidence of demoralization and psychiatric breakdowns from the Great War forced military establishments, both in Britain and the United States, to formally address issues of morale and motivation in the next world war.[10]

The lead was taken by the United States Army who, through the agencies of the Research Branch of the 'War Department's Information and Education Division', and the 'Army Historical Team', conducted a multitude of studies dealing with the American enlisted soldiers' experiences; especially the problems of adaptation to army life and motivation in combat.[11] These studies procured two pieces of previously un-comprehended knowledge. First, that many soldiers would take no active (that is

    Gloden Dallas & Douglas Gill, op cit., esp. pp. 13-25.
6   Steven Paul MacKenzie, *Politics and Military Morale: Current-Affairs and Citizenship Education in the British Army 1914-1950* Clarendon Press (1992) esp. pp. 12-15, pp. 33-4 & p. 224. MacKenzie suggests that the motivation underlying the creation of an education scheme – one which would stress war aims and post-war reconstruction – was a concern with flagging morale. Censor's reports had begun detecting a significant amount of 'war weariness' in the troop's correspondence during 1917. Haig had also been alarmed by the mutinies in the French Armies. Moreover, evidence of subversive rumblings at Etaples (September 1917) and Calais (April 1918) seemed to hasten the need for reinforcing the needs and benefits of continuing the war. By the Autumn of 1918 the 'Educational Training Scheme' had been inaugurated.
7   See for example, Ben Shephard, *A War of Nerves: Soldiers and Psychiatrists 1914-1994* Jonathan Cape (2000), esp. pp. 39-71. Shephard's book is the best single volume study of the troubled relationship between the professions of soldiery and psychiatry. See also Peter Leese, *Shell Shock, Traumatic Neurosis and the British Soldiers of the First World War* Palgrave Macmillan (2002).
8   Lord Southborough et al, *Report of the War Office Committee of Enquiry into 'Shell Shock'* H.M.S.O. (1922). Other influential reports were made by John T. MacCurdy, *War Neuroses* Cambridge (1918) & E.E. Southard, *Shell-Shock and Other Neuro-Psychiatric Problems Presented in Five Hundred and Eighty Nine Case Histories from the War Literature, 1914-1918* Boston (1919). (These texts have not been consulted by the study).
9   Gregory Belenky & Franklin D. Jones 'Introduction: Combat Psychiatry – An Evolving Field' in Gregory Belensky (ed) (1987), op cit. pp. 1-7 p. 2.
10 Anthony Kellett, *Combat Motivation: The Behaviour of Soldiers in Battle* Kluwer-Nijhoff Publishing (1982) pp. xiii-xiv, pp. 4-5 & p. 13.
11 For a summary of their work see Charles C. Moskos, *The American Enlisted Man: The Rank and File in today's Military* Russell Sage Foundation (1970), pp. 1-30.

aggressive) part in combat. Second, that almost all soldiers would eventually breakdown mentally under the strain of combat.

Arguably the most influential (and infamous) of these works was S.L.A. Marshall's *Men against Fire*, which offered the first systematic study of how frontline soldiers react in combat.[12] The study was based upon face-to-face interviews conducted with American G.I.s returning from the battlefield. It was undeniably dialectical: an evocation of the military benefits of 'primary group loyalty' (or 'small unit cohesion' to use the American idiom).[13] Marshall's most shocking revelation was that '75 per cent [of soldiers] will not fire or will not persist in firing against the enemy and his works.'[14] This figure appeared all the more astounding given Marshall's fairly permissive definition of a 'firer', which included anyone who fired their weapon once in any direction. This figure remained unchanged regardless of the length of the engagement, the experience of the unit, the terrain or the nature of the enemy. Moreover, it was always the same fifteen to twenty five percent who *did* take an active part in combat.[15] Marshall attributed the phenomenon of the 'non-firers' to the American soldiers' lifelong indoctrination into the maxim 'thou shall not kill'. American culture, schooling, religion and social values had conspired to make aggression and the taking of life prohibited and unacceptable. American society had created pacifistic citizens and: 'The Army cannot unmake him.'[16] As a result of this socialisation, Marshall argued, when faced with killing another man, even in self defence, most soldiers become 'a conscientious objector'.[17]

Although Marshall's vision of an inherently pacifistic American GI have never been wholeheartedly shared by historians or military planners, his calculations over the American infantrymen's 'ratio of fire' during the Second World War have become accepted as almost axiomatic. Chinks have been found in Marshall's armour. In 1988 Roger J. Spiller contended that Marshall's 'combat after-action interviews', whilst certainly groundbreaking, were not executed with the methodological assiduity required to substantiate such a hard and fast rule.[18] Spiller concluded that 'S.L.A. Marshall's ratio of fire cannot be proved.'[19] Interestingly, Spiller made no mention

---

12   S.L.A. Marshall *Men against Fire: The Problem of Battle Command in Future War* Peter Smith (1978) 1st ed 1947.
13   ibid., p. 23, p. 42 & p. 138. For contemporary studies on close unit cohesion see: Edward A. Shils & Morris Janowitz 'Cohesion and Disintegration in the Wehrmacht in World War II' in *Public Opinion Quarterly* 12 (Summer 1948) pp. 283-86; Roger W. Little, 'Buddy Relations and Combat Performance' in Morris Janowitz, (ed) *The New Military: Changing Patterns of Organization* Russell Sage Foundation (1964) pp. 195-223.
14   Ibid., p. 50.
15   Ibid., pp. 57-9.
16   Ibid., p. 78.
17   Ibid., p. 79.
18   Roger J. Spiller, 'S.L.A. Marshal and the Ratio of Fire' in *R.U.S.I. Journal* Vol. 133 pt. 4 (winter 1988), pp. 63-71, esp. pp. 68-9.
19   Ibid., p. 69.

of Marshall's 'conscientious objector' thesis in his critique, but did suggest that 'non-firing' may have been due to problems of terrain or local tactical expediency, contending that 'Marshall should have known that there are times in combat when one should *not* fire his weapon [original emphasis].'[20] This approach arguably signals the reluctance of many military historians to countenance the idea that realising killing in combat is anything other than a problem of discipline and weapons competency.

Perhaps the most vociferous criticism of the basic premise of Marshall's thesis has come from the historian Joanna Bourke. In *An Intimate History of Killing* Bourke argues that soldiers throughout the twentieth-century have often found the act of killing erotic, aesthetic and empowering.[21] She further suggests that 'in the writings of combatants from all three wars [two world wars and Vietnam], we read of men's (and women's) enjoyment in killing.'[22] The antithesis of Bourke's thesis is found in Dave Grossman's *On Killing*. Grossman argues that 'throughout history the majority of men on the battlefield would *not* attempt to kill the enemy, even to save their own lives or the lives of their friends [original emphasis].'[23] Grossman attributes the conspiracy of silence over this phenomenon to a number of occurrences: the male ego's penchant for a 'selective memory, self-deception, and lying' over issues of love and war; the fact that most of pre twentieth-century military history was written by 'good killers'; and the understandable predilection of good soldiers to deny the futility of his or her profession.[24] Grossman also suggests that psychologists have been complicit in this conspiracy through their misapplication of the 'fight-or-flight' model of animal aggression to human aggression.

Grossman rehearses the theory that during 'intraspecies' aggression animals have two further innate reactions – 'posturing' and 'submission' – and without this inbuilt recourse to 'mock battle' or surrender behaviour the species (any species) could not survive. However, Grossman uniquely appropriates this element of animal psychology to human intraspecies aggression. He contends that frightened humans think with their mid-brain, which is essentially indistinguishable from the animal's brain, rather than the forebrain, which is the part of the brain unique to humans. Consequently, he proposes, when humans are scared they invariably think and act like animals and

---

20   Ibid., pp. 68-9.
21   Joanna Bourke, *An Intimate History of Killing: Face-to-Face Killing in Twentieth-Century Warfare* Granta Books (1999), pp. 13-16. Bourke bases this contention upon the experiences of American, Australian and British troops during both world wars and Vietnam.
22   Ibid., p. 30.
23   Dave Grossman, *On Killing: The Psychological Cost of Learning to Kill in War and Society* Little, Brown & Company (1995), p. 4. Grossman is a soldier by (20 years) trade, a historian by first degree, and a psychologist by higher degree. He draws upon his own personal experiences, interviews with veterans (mostly of Vietnam), studies such as Marshall's, and secondary material that covers similar ground (i.e. Keegan etc.).
24   Ibid., 31-6, quote p. 31.

either posture or submit.²⁵ The advent of gunpowder and especially muskets and rifles afforded the soldier the ultimate 'posturing' weapon, he suggests. The soldier can make an awful lot of terrifying noise yet fire high or wide. Moreover, he indicates that the modern isolated battlefield affords every opportunity for the soldier to 'submit'; not necessarily through surrender, but rather by carrying out passive activities such as tending to the wounded or running messages.²⁶

Without wishing to state the obvious, clearly a great deal of killing has taken place in warfare (especially in the twentieth-century). Therefore, historically, some soldiers must have overcome their (alleged) innate and nurtured resistance to killing. 'Distance' is Grossman's primary explanation. It is the advent of machines capable of propelling missiles over great distances that has allowed Man to kill his fellow Man in increasingly vast numbers. He cites the example of the aircrews of Bomber Command who were able to kill 70,000 women, children and elderly in Hamburg in one night. This was 'depersonalised killing': they couldn't see their victims, they couldn't hear their screams; the pilots could deny the act emotionally even though they were all too intellectually aware of their culpability.²⁷ Grossman persuasively appropriates the same argument towards other 'distance killers' – artillerymen, naval gun crews, and so forth, and adds 'automation' and 'teamwork' (two factors often concomitant with 'distance' weapons) to the list of weaponry elements which have sanitised the act of killing, and consequently upped Man's killing potential. For example, the machine-gun, although often employed at close range during both world wars, allowed the act of *en masse* killing to be performed at the press of a button, and shared the culpability of the act amongst its operators.²⁸ To further substantiate this line of argument, Grossman shows that the bayonet kill – the antithesis of the aforesaid 'impersonal' and 'sanitised' acts of combat – has been beyond almost all soldiers throughout history.²⁹

Grossman finds some support on this issue. David French contends that during World War Two: 'Troops in combat rarely crossed bayonets, probably because the mere threat of hand-to-hand combat was sufficient to make one side or the other flee.'³⁰ Similarly, Richard Holmes suggests that historically, 'one side or the other

---

25 Ibid., pp. 5-8.
26 Ibid., pp. 9-16.
27 Ibid., p. 59 & pp. 99-106.
28 Ibid., pp. 107-8 & 153-5. Grossman terms the sanitising intervention of automation 'mechanical distance'. Discussing the influence of teamwork, he states that the two man crew typical of the Roman chariot 'was all that was needed to provide the same accountability and anonymity in close-proximity groups that in World War II permitted nearly 100 percent of crew-served weapons (such as machine guns) to fire while only 15 to 20 percent of the riflemen fired.' Quote p. 153.
29 Ibid., pp. 120-6.
30 David French '"You Cannot Hate the Bastard Who is Trying to Kill You…" Combat and Ideology in the War Against Germany, 1939-45' in *Twentieth Century British History* Vol. 11, No. 1, (2000), pp. 1-22, p. 11.

usually recalls an urgent appointment elsewhere before bayonets cross.'[31] To summarise, Grossman contends that the closer (in distance) a combatant gets to his or her victim, and the more physical the act of violence becomes, the less achievable the act has been – for 'most' human beings, throughout history.

Whilst man's (and woman's) ability to kill remains somewhat contentious amongst psychologists, there is something approaching a consensus over the second piece of knowledge to emerge from World War Two: that almost all soldiers subjected to combat will breakdown eventually. Roy L. Swank's and Walter E. Marchand's seminal study of American troops during the Normandy campaign, *Combat Neurosis: Development of Combat Exhaustion*, found that whilst most soldiers could fight 'efficiently' (becoming 'battle-wise') for between ten and thirty days, beyond this point deterioration set in and a near vegetative stage was reached by all but two percent of soldiers after sixty days.[32] They concluded that: 'Practically all infantry soldiers suffer from a neurotic reaction eventually if they are subjected to the stress of modern combat continuously and long enough.'[33] A similar study conducted by Lieut-Col. J.W. Appel and Capt. G.W. Beebe found that: 'Each moment of combat imposes a strain so great that men will break down in direct relation to the intensity and duration of their exposure.'[34] Eli Ginzberg's study of the American enlisted soldiers' combat efficiency also found that 'no soldier ever becomes acclimated to war. No matter how brave he is, no matter how deeply he believes in the righteousness of his country's aims, the passage of every day wears thinner his protective armor so that the time may come when he can no longer face the morrow.'[35] Such an understanding of the universally debilitating effects of combat has since become almost axiomatic within the study of combat psychology.

If the First World War engendered the (reluctant) acceptance that *some* soldiers would suffer a psychological reaction to combat, then the second brought about the realisation that *almost all* would mentally breakdown.[36] The idea that soldiers 'get used

---

31 Richard Holmes (1986), Richard Holmes, *Acts of War: The Behaviour of Men in Battle* The Free Press (1986), p. 377-8.
32 Roy L. Swank and Walter E. Marchand, 'Combat Neurosis: Development of Combat Exhaustion' in *Archives of Neurology and Psychiatry* Vol. 55 (1946), esp. pp. 237-43, quote p. 239. The two psychiatrists went into battle with a U.S. Infantry battalion serving in France.
33 Ibid., p. 243.
34 Quoted in Richard Holmes (1986), op cit., p. 215.
35 Eli Ginzberg, *The Lost Divisions* Greenwood Press (1975) 1st ed 1959, pp. 127-8. Elmar Dinter records that 389,159 American soldiers had to be sent home between 1942 and 1945 because of psychiatric problems. See Elmar Dinter, *Hero or Coward: The Pressures Facing the Soldier in Battle* Frank Cass (1985) p. 63.
36 It would seem that the symptoms and manifestations of battle induced mental illness are manifold. Most common is extreme mental and physical exhaustion; causing the sufferer to isolate themselves away from comrades, crying fits, anxiety fits, hypersensitivity to sound, and palpitations. This is only the beginning, and without rest things will inevitably get worse. Psychotic dissociation from reality, delirium, and manic depressive mood swings can follow. Then maybe amnesia, convulsive attacks, obsessive fears of death or

to combat', for anything more than a few weeks, was shown to be a fallacy. This understanding has encouraged two other related beliefs. First, neither individual personality nor ethnicity appears to make much difference to the soldier's ability to cope. Rather, the soldier's place on the continuum between effective performance and collapse is primarily decided by the intensity and longevity of combat.[37] Second, it appears that military establishments cannot do much about how aggressive or otherwise a soldier will be. As Elmar Dinter observed: 'Activity or passivity are a matter of inheritance, the influence of background and of education ... [they] are almost unchangeable, and the process of education is virtually complete by the time a young man is called up.'[38] The implication being that a relatively pacifistic civilian upbringing will produce a decidedly reluctant combat soldier.

Something approaching broad agreement also exists over the fundamental causes of the universal malady of 'shellshock'.[39] The major cause of anxiety is *fear*, and the greatest fear faced during combat is that of mutilation or death.[40] Though a number of studies have indicated that 'letting the side down' is also a major cause of fear, but one more prevalent amongst 'virgin' soldiers.[41] It is also agreed that physical fatigue brought on by exposure to the elements, lack of rest and nourishment can accelerate the soldiers' demise.[42] At the polar extremes however, those who consider that 'killing is easy' (even pleasurable) contend 'that more men broke down in war because they

      failure, stammers, tics, hysterical reactions and finally degeneration into a psychotic altered personality. See Dave Grossman, op cit., p. 45-8.
37 Gregory Belenky & Franklin D. Jones (1987), op cit. p. 5. Elmar Dinter, op cit., p. 11 & p. 66.
38 Elmar Dinter, op cit., p. 20.
39 There are a number of idioms used to describe the psychological effects of combat upon the soldier. Shellshock was the common term used during the Great War. Hence why it is used by this study. The United States Army and most psychologists have since preferred the term 'battle fatigue', 'combat stress' or simply 'exhaustion'.
40 See for example, Samuel A. Stouffer et al, *The American Soldier: Combat And Its Aftermath – Volume II* Princeton University Press (1949), p. 86; Elmar Dinter, op cit., p. 60; Richard A. Gabriel, *The Painful Field: The Psychiatric Dimension of Modern War* Greenwood Press (1988). Gabriel attributes the unusual battlefield discoveries in the aftermath of the Battle of Gettysburg (used by Grossman to support his thesis) to amnesia brought on by fear of dying. See esp. p.122. Peter Watson indicates that most 'stress' testing procedures conducted by military psychologists aim only to recreate the fear of injury or death, not of killing. He also discusses a number of battlefield studies (for example, John Dollard's first hand observations of Spanish Civil War soldiers in combat) which have also found that fear of injury or death is the primary fear. See Peter Watson, op cit., pp. 193-212 & pp. 213-14.
41 See for example Ben Shalit's analysis of Israeli soldiers during the Arab-Israeli conflict. Ben Shalit, *The Psychology of Conflict and Combat* Praeger (1988), pp. 10-13. See also Richard Holmes (1986), op cit., p. 206.
42 See for example Anthony Kellett (1982), op cit., esp. pp. 329-30.

were *not* allowed to kill than collapse under the strain of killing [original emphasis].'⁴³ Whereas those who witness a victory for the maxims of 'thou shall not kill' argue that: 'Resistance to overt aggressive confrontation...the need to kill, eventually drives the soldier so deeply into a mire of guilt and horror that he tips over the brink into that region that we call insanity.'⁴⁴ A divergence in interpretation which aptly indicates that the psychology of combat is a far from exact science.

An awareness of the universally debilitating effects of combat upon the soldier is well demonstrated within the historical literature dealing with the soldiers' experiences of World War Two and beyond. For instance, John Ellis' ground-breaking *The Sharp End* talks of the prevalence of the 'two thousand yard stare' amongst the soldiers of 1939-45.⁴⁵ Ellis describes how combat 'stresses were working on most front-line soldiers most of the time. Hardly any of them have any equivalent in civilian life and thus they make untoward demands on the soldier's mental resilience such that, in the long run, *any* soldier will break down [author's emphasis].'⁴⁶ This phenomenon is however still largely understated in the literature dealing with the Great War.⁴⁷

Richard A. Gabriel's *The Painful Field* makes a similar if more far-reaching observation, criticising the tendency of military historians to assume that recent generations were the first to suffer this malady.⁴⁸ Calling upon a vast array of battlefield accounts traversing the Roman siege of Syracuse (211 B.C.) to the Israeli incursion into the Lebanon (1982), he argues that: 'Fear and madness have been man's companions in war since the beginning of recorded history and, most probably, before that.'⁴⁹ Gabriel's psychoanalytical methodology – placing diagnoses drawn from late twentieth-century psychiatry upon symptoms described in historical accounts – has not always drawn favour from historians; military or otherwise. For example, it might be questioned whether the common soldier at Agincourt reacted to combat in the same way as the American G.I. in Normandy. Putting issues of the objective circumstances of combat to one side, it would seem possible that a number of changes that have taken place within twentieth-century western society which have affected the soldiers' reactions to combat. Advances in medicine and in life expectancy, a decrease in religious belief, and the growing perception of control over the environment have

---

43 Joanna Bourke (2000), op cit., p. 58. The same argument is forwarded in Joanna Bourke (1999), op cit., pp. 248-50.
44 Dave Grossman, op cit., p. 54. See also S.L.A. Marshall, op cit., p. 78.
45 John Ellis, *The Sharp End: The Fighting Man in World War II* Pimlico (1993) 1st ed 1980 esp. pp. 234-55.
46 Ibid., p. 248.
47 The earlier literature was better on this issue than the revisionists. See esp. John Ellis (1976), op cit. & Denis Winter, op cit.
48 Richard A. Gabriel, op cit., pp. 1-5.
49 Ibid., p. 7.

almost certainly changed Man's conscious attitudes towards accepting physical pain, suffering and the prospect of death.[50]

But the fundamental principles of shellshock offer some efficacy to such an approach. Combat psychologists (and psychiatrists) broadly agree that the outward symptoms of shellshock are usually the result of a *physiological* reaction to continued stress.[51] Whilst the objective circumstances of any given combat situation expose all soldiers engaged to the same external stressors, the levels of stress experienced by the individual soldier are largely dependant upon their *perception* and *appraisal* of that situation.[52] It cannot be proved therefore whether the Great War soldier suffered from a greater or lesser degree of stress than his later counterparts. However, given that the physiological construction of the human body has not changed significantly in the past one hundred years, it can reasonably be conjectured that all Great War soldiers were vulnerable to eventual mental collapse. The influences of cultural and social differences upon perception and appraisal could only delay or accelerate this collapse. These influences are arguably of greater moment when considering Great War soldiers' potential battlefield pacifism. The Victorian and Edwardian precepts of manliness, courage, bravery, and duty perhaps made the act of killing in warfare more permissible to the soldier of the early twentieth-century. Yet, to reiterate, these influences were countered by a civic society that deemed killing a crime, and a religious teaching that deemed killing a sin.

As this delineation of the findings of latter twentieth-century combat psychology suggests, the real obstacle faced by the historian wanting to understand how the Great War soldier experienced and reacted to combat is not so much one of theory, but rather of method. One consequence of the Edwardian military establishment's misunderstanding of the nature and significance of 'shellshock' was a tendency to deny the problem existed. As a consequence, there is a shortage of both statistical evidence and qualitative accounts. However, this does not prevent the historian adopting an approach which is sensitive to the *proven* great difficulty of surviving combat mentally (let alone physically) for any length of time. Similarly, even though qualitative evidence of the type (purportedly) recorded by Marshall's study is unavailable, it would be instructive to approach the subject mindful that, historically, many soldiers

---

50   Anthony Kellett (1987), op cit., p. xvii. John Baynes suggested that 'soldiers of the earlier days needed less sympathy, comfort, and interest than their modern counterparts, and perhaps most important of all, less explanation of why they should carry out certain actions.' See John Baynes, op cit., pp. 107.
51   See for example, Jon A. Shaw 'Psychodynamic Considerations in the Adaptation to combat' in Gregory Belenky (1987) (ed), op cit., pp. 117-32. Shaw writes that: 'Stress refers to an external stimulus impacting on the individual's nervous system in such a way as to evoke neuroendocrine and neurophysiological responses of arousal. The individual experiences stress internally as anxiety.' Quote p. 118. See also Elmar Dinter, op cit., esp. pp. 13-15.
52   See for example, Ben Shalit, op cit., esp. p. 10; Elmar Dinter, op cit., esp. p. 17.

may have found themselves unable to actively participate in combat. It will be argued in the following chapter on methodology that a number of 'traditional' sources can yield such evidence if examined in the light of this theoretical conceptual framework.

3

Methodology Explained

Sourcing the events of the twentieth-century battlefield is a most inexact science. At best the historian working from traditional sources can only hope to synthesise a number of disparate and extremely individualist and impressionistic accounts of combat. The proposed methodology, although far from being untroubled by censorious influences, partly circumvents these pitfalls by offering a continuous and detailed narrative of combat behaviour, whilst, at any given time, providing a number of indicators as to the combat morale of around 10,000 volunteer and conscript infantrymen.

The unit of study has been a single 'Service' division of the BEF – the 19th (Western) Division. Combat expectations, or what was expected of the combat soldier in battle, have been established from the written orders emanating from the chain of command (from brigade upwards). The prescribed methods of training infantrymen to perform these roles have been drawn from a combination of salient 'official' military publications (for example, *S.S.143 Instructions for the Training of Platoons for Offensive Action* (1917)) and the division's own recorded thoughts on the subject (for example, *Standard Organisation* (1917)).[1] The infantry's responses to these combat roles have been largely derived from a qualitative analysis of the reports of combat activities recorded in, or appended to (in the form of post-battle reports), unit war diaries. Two quantitative analyses have been utilised to compliment this qualitative approach. The first examines the number of casualties a unit was willing and/or able to sustain in the pursuit of a given objective. The second examines the occurrence of military offences directly related to the infantrymen's willingness and/or ability to fight; offences such as desertion, self-inflicted wounds and so forth.

The infantrymen's actions in combat have been described as *combat behaviour*, whilst their willingness and ability to carry out this role has been defined by the term

---

1 *S.S.143 Instructions for the Training of Platoons for Offensive Action, 1917* issued by the General Staff February 1917 IWM &0 G. 717/2. 'Standard organization of the "trench to trench" attack: The battalion in attack', issued by DHQ 1 Feb 1917. WO95/2054 General Staff 19th Division War Diary (Feb 1917) PRO.

combat morale. The term 'aggressively inclined' is used to denote an infantryman who was prepared to volunteer for an activity which planned to engage and kill the enemy, no other assumptions are made regarding the man's character. The terms 'pacifically inclined' or 'less aggressively inclined' have been used to denote infantrymen who preferred, on a given occasion, to assist the attack in a non-combat role, again no other assumptions are made regarding the man's character. It is suggested that if this decision was left to the infantrymen's junior officer or senior NCO, then suitably inclined men could be selected for either roles.

Defining Combat Morale

As John Fuller perceptively states: 'Morale is an elusive subject …'[2] Yet it is surprising, given the abstract nature of the subject, the number of studies relating to 'the soldier's experience' that use the term without clearly defining the entity under discussion.[3] A sample of the key definitions forwarded illustrates the need for precision. Lieutenant Colonel J.H. Sparrow, author of a 1949 War Office study into British Army morale during the Second World War, argued that 'it was the attitude of the soldier towards his employment as a soldier.'[4] One weakness with this definition is that it ignores the possibility that the soldier's 'attitude' may be dependant upon a multitude of factors, some of which may have little to do with the here-and-now of soldiery.

Lord Moran's contention that morale should define 'the product of his [the soldier's] whole thought' at least embraces this possibility.[5] S.L.A. Marshall offered a definition sensitive to the multitude of attitudes and feelings that comprise 'the whole complex body of an army's thought:' the list included the cause, politics, friends, commanders, food, pay, sex, God and the devil.[6] Whilst probably accurate – in the sense that all these concerns can affect the soldier's feeling of well being at some time or other – this typological definition fails to relate conscious thought to actual behaviour.

Samuel Stouffer's definition makes this connection, being sensitive to both the task orientation and collaborative nature of soldiery. Stouffer suggested that morale 'might be thought of as an inference from group behavior, verbal or nonverbal, as to

---

2   John G. Fuller, *Troop morale and popular culture in the British and Dominion armies, 1914-1918* Clarendon Press (1990), p. 21.
3   For example, the recent collection of essays 'Facing Armageddon' devoted a whole section to 'morale', yet no contributor forwarded a definition. See Hugh Cecil & Peter H. Liddle (eds), *Facing Armageddon: The First World War Experienced* Leo Cooper (1996).
4   Lt-Col. J.H. Sparrow, *Morale* London (1949) p. 1. Quoted in David French "Tommy is No Soldier': The Morale of the Second British Army in Normandy, July-August 1944.' in *The Journal of Strategic Studies* Vol. 19 No. 4 (Dec 1996) pp. 154-178.
5   Lord Moran, *The Anatomy of Courage* The Keynes Press (1984) 1st ed 1945, p. 158.
6   S.L.A. Marshall, *Men Against Fire: The Problem of Battle Command in Future War* Peter Smith (1978) 1st ed 1947, p. 158.

[the] cooperative effort toward some common goal.'[7] For the purposes of this study however, 'some common goal' is too general. After all, the infantry's commitment to fatigues is not the study's first concern. The more precise elucidations of the combat psychologist can usefully be employed to overcome such ambiguity. Ben Shalit argues that morale, in a military context, operates in a two stage process. In the first stage the soldier's morale is reflected by their 'willingness to engage in battle ...', whilst in the second stage the soldier's morale is reflected by their 'resilience' to combat – that is, their 'coping potential'.[8] Thus Shalit defines morale as 'the [soldier's] willingness to fight, and to persevere in fighting.'[9] With some fine-tuning, this can stand as the study's definition.

In order to indicate this study's more exacting focus upon the infantry's experience of combat (the fundamental role), rather than the infantry's whole experience of soldiery, it would seem appropriate to prefix 'combat' to the subject under discussion. Hence the study will use the phrase 'combat morale' rather than simply 'morale'. For the study to be sensitive towards Man's potential innate and nurtured resistance to killing a fellow human, the aggressive (to kill) and passive (to be killed) components of 'fighting' will need to be separately drawn out. The definition also needs to indicate that the study is primarily concerned with detailing the behaviour of infantrymen acting as a group, rather than explaining the motivations of individuals. Moreover, that the study is concerned with detailing the group's commitment to the objectives set by their senior commanders (who were themselves invariably acting upon the demands of high command). With these considerations in mind the following definition can be forwarded.

> Combat morale defines the degree to which infantrymen, as inferred from either individual or group behavior, were willing to kill and accept the concomitant possibility of death or injury, and persevere in this action, in order to achieve the objectives set by their senior commanders.

This maybe a little cumbersome, but it appositely defines the subject this study primarily aims to investigate.

Defining between 'Infantrymen' and 'Senior Commanders', 'Specialists' and 'Non-Specialists'

Within the BEF's command structure the following differentiations have been made between soldiers of various ranks. Officers and staff of brigade and division

---

7   Samuel A. Stouffer et al, *The American Soldier: Adjustment During Army Life – Volume I* Princeton University Press (1949), p. 83.
8   Ben Shalit, *The Psychology of Conflict and Combat* Praeger (1988) p. 35 & p. 36.
9   Ibid, p. 135.

have been defined as *senior commanders*, whilst officers and staff of corps and above have been given the term *high command*. On occasions the more specific title General Headquarters (GHQ) has been used to denote orders or ideas emanating directly from this source. This distinction (between senior and high commanders) has been made because the division was a permanent source of authority for the infantry, whilst corps and army changed regularly (see below). Moreover, it is a distinction that is sensitive to the potential autonomy of divisional and brigade commanders within this command structure. Where both levels of command are under discussion the term *chain of command* has been frequently utilised for the sake of succinctness. All regimental soldiers (that is soldiers serving within a battalion) have been given the nomenclature *infantry*. This definition covers all regimental officers including the battalion commanding officer (CO). This is based on the understanding that regimental officers were also combat soldiers like their men, and shared many of the dangers, if not all of the hardships, of their men. The term *officer commanding* (OC) has been used to define a junior regimental officers permanently in charge of a sub-unit of the battalion (company or platoon), or temporarily in charge of a operational unit such as a raiding party or patrol.

Within this broad definition the nomenclature 'specialist' has been given to infantrymen permanently engaged in handling weapons beyond the ordinary rifle. These 'specialists' being snipers, machine gunners, grenadiers (later named 'Bombers') and trench mortar gunners. This term does not include infantrymen temporarily engaged in such activities. For instance, most infantrymen carried bombs of some description during the battles of 1916, but in the normal course of duty were not expected to engage in this form of combat. The remainder, the non-specialists, have been labelled 'riflemen'. These delineations in the infantrymen's combative role, however, play little part in the post-1916 thesis, when, as we shall see, 'everyman' (more-or-less) became a 'specialist'.

The Rationale behind the Analysis of a Single Division

This research has concentrated upon a single division of the British Army 1914-1918 because such a unit of investigation is substantial enough to offer potentially useful generalizations, yet remains amenable to an intensive longitudinal study of official military documentation, and especially unit war diaries and appended reports. A division was also the largest operational unit within the BEF to provide a constant source of welfare, authority and (arguably) identity for the front-line infantryman. Whereas allocation to the larger units of corps and army changed continually throughout the war.[10] War diaries – this study's primary source of evidence – do not lend themselves

---

10 See for example, John Lee, 'The British Divisions at Third Ypres' in Peter H. Liddle (ed) *Passchendaele in Perspective: The Third Battle of Ypres* Leo Cooper (1997) pp. 215-26. Lee argues that 'The units were organised as divisions, were moved about as divisions and

to a cursory reading. As with personal diaries and correspondence, their assorted contents need to be read in entirety if the thoughts and observations of their various writers are to be properly comprehended. Moreover, this source has the advantage of being continuous – recording every day of combat, from the war's start to the war's finish. To make best use of this asset, the war diaries and their appended reports themselves also need to be read from start to finish. Only then can any subtle shifts in the infantrymen's combat behaviour and willingness and ability to fight, those experienced between major set-piece battles, be recognised. To carry out this task for a division involves reading at least seventeen sets of diaries and their appended reports, and represents many months work.[11] For an army, it would represent the work of many lifetimes.

For the study to be amenable to guarded generalisations, therefore, the division in question needs to be as 'typical' as possible. The 19th (Western) Division, by and large, fits this criteria. A brief rehearsal of purposes will help to illustrate why. The essential aim of the study is to examine how 'civilian soldiers' – that is volunteer and conscript infantrymen with no pre-war experience of soldiery, or prior relationship with the British Army – responded to combat. This brief therefore excludes a study of a Regular or Territorial unit. It could be argued that the moulding of all various types of units into amorphous 'national service' formations by 1917 makes this divide rather artificial. But there is compelling evidence that the individual identities and ethos of pre-war units survived the arrival of citizen soldiers.[12] So the essential aim of the study decrees that the unit investigated must be a New Army division. Certainly, a 'typical' New Army division was a mythical beast. Differences in where they fought, who they were commanded by, and the nature of initial recruitment, gave diverging shape to their service experience. There were, however, a number of facets to active service common to the majority of civilian soldiers. Most served on the Western Front, and most fought in at least one of the major set-piece battles this theatre of war witnessed. Tried against this criteria, the war service of the 19th Division was reasonably common.[13] Moreover, the 19th Division was (originally) drawn from a broad swathe of the British Isles; encompassing the industrial North and Midlands, as well as the rural Welsh valleys and Cotswolds. This made the divi-

---

    committed to battle as divisions … the division was a fairly stable organization, which men could think of as 'their own'.' p. 224.

11 One corps (constantly changing throughout the war), one division, three brigade, twelve battalion diaries, equating to seventeen. Later formations added to the division, including Machine Gun Corps and Trench Mortar Battery have also been examined.

12 See for example Gary Sheffield, "A very good type of Londoner and a very good type of colonial': Officer-Man Relations and Discipline in the 22nd Royal Fusiliers, 1914-18' in Brian Bond et al *'Look To Your Front': Studies in the First World War by The British Commission for Military History* Spellmount (1999) pp. 137-146.

13 The division spent its entire war on the Western Front, and was involved in the battle of the Somme, Third Ypres, the German 'Spring Offensives' and the last 'Hundred Days'.

sion more geographically representative than say a 'Pals' formation drawn from one location or single occupation. There were then a number of commonalities in the 19th Division's experience of active service which deem it a unit of investigation amenable to guarded generalisations.

Applying the Theories and Terminology of Combat Psychology

Although this study is grounded in historical, rather than psychological analysis, a number of ideas derived from the study of combat psychology have been drawn upon. These theories centre upon the impacts of certain weapon groups and/or methods of combat upon the infantryman's willingness and/or ability to kill. A distinction has been made between combat behaviour in which the aggressor specifically targets his victim, and witnesses the consequences of his actions, and modes of combat in which the effects of aggression were in some way *sanitised*.

The term *interpersonal combat* has been used to define combat executed at a close visible range,[14] in which the full (or almost full) effects of the aggressor's actions upon the target could consequently be witnessed, and fear of a concomitant act on behalf of the target was ever present. (It is this mode of combat that certain commentators claim has historically beyond the capabilities of most soldiers). The Edwardian military lexicon usually defined such combat episodes by the idiom *hand-to-hand fighting*. This term essentially defined fighting in which the aggressor used weapons which required physical application in order to harm their intended victim; the *bayonet* being the BEF's chief (and much lauded) *interpersonal* weapon. However, a broader definition of *interpersonal combat* has been utilised here, one that includes the use of semi-automated weapons (such as the rifle or bomb) *at close range*.

It will be contended that episodes which lay outside of *interpersonal combat* introduced a number of *sanitising* elements into the execution of combat; these being *distance*, *automation* and *teamwork*. The term *distance killers* has been applied to weaponry that allowed the infantryman to aggress his victim beyond a close visible range. The Lee Enfield Rifle, when used at distance, fits into this description, but the main protagonists were the machine-gun and light trench mortar. Essentially, these weapons could be employed beyond visible range, in the general direction of the target, without their effects being witnessed, and largely free from the fear of concomitant *interpersonal combat* on behalf of the target.

The term *distance killers* has also been applied to weaponry employing *teamwork* and/or *automation*: the former partly *sanitising* the act of combat by sharing out responsibility for the act, the latter by divorcing the act of firing from the act of harming the

---

14 No specific range has been used within this definition, but reports of combat in which the participants were between zero and 10 to 20 yards has usually been defined as interpersonal range.

target. Again, both the machine-gun and the light trench mortar were the infantry's ultimate expression of these modes of combat.

Combat Behaviour and Morale and the Problems of Evidence

The historian wishing to investigate how the Great War soldier experienced and responded to the fundamental role of combat is denied some of the methodological advantages open to historians of the other wars of the 'industrial' era. The soldier of the American Civil War has left behind a voluminous archive of 'uncensored' diaries and letters recording his first-hand accounts of battle.[15] Whilst the soldier of World War Two and beyond has frequently found his views on combat being chronicled by camp following journalists, psychiatrists, psychologists and so on.[16]

In the absence of these source materials the historian of the Great War has invariably turned to published memoirs and 'official' histories.[17] For instance, even Tony Ashworth's *Live and Let Live*, for all its ground-breaking theoretical underpinning, largely depends upon such sources of evidence.[18] However, asides the issue of typicality (how typical a literary middle-class officer was of the BEF as a whole), a number of historians have questioned the reliability of veteran's recollections when examining the role of combat. Richard Holmes has shown how the individual's view of battle is often narrow and fragmented and only takes on some form of meaning after the event, in discussions with fellow veterans and through consultation with 'official' transcripts.[19] Eric Leed sees this process of remembering as even more problematic. Leed argues that in order to survive within a society that paradoxically defined 'war as an abnormal state of existence', the civilian soldier was forced 'to set aside his soldierhood and expunge the sites of his imminent death and survival from his mind'; forced to rewrite his memory of war to correlate with his regained 'civilian' identity.[20] The

---

15   See for example, Earl J. Hess *The Union Soldier in Battle: Enduring the ordeal of combat* University of Kansas Press (1997), esp. p. xi.
16   See for example, Samuel A. Stouffer et al (1949) op cit.; Roger W. Little, 'Buddy Relations and Combat Performance' in Morris Janowitz (ed), *The New Military: Changing Patterns of Organization* Russell Sage Foundation (1964) pp. 195-223; Charles C. Moskos, *The American Enlisted Man: The Rank and File in Today's Military* Russell Sage Foundation (1970). The process began however during the Russo-Japanese war of 1905.
17   The acceptance of 'oral testimony' as a valid historical methodology came too late to record the recollections of most Great War veterans. However, Lyn MacDonald's perception and hard work has resulted in a priceless archive of material collected in six works (to date). See bibliography for texts consulted. The Sound Archives at the Imperial War Museum also contain the testimonies of a number of Great War veterans.
18   Tony Ashworth, *Trench Warfare, 1914-1918: The Live and Let Live System* MacMillan (1980).
19   Richard Holmes, *Acts of War: The Behavior of Men in Battle* The Free Press (1985) pp. 154-5.
20   Eric Leed, 'Fateful Memories: Industrialized War and Traumatic Neuroses' in *Journal of Contemporary History* Vol. 35(1) (2000) pp. 85-100, esp. p. 85 & p. 88.

upshot being that veterans rarely discussed the act of killing or maiming in their memoirs. Perhaps the best example of this alleged 'rewriting of memory' can be found in the pacifistic treaties of 'Mad Jack' Captain Siegfried Sassoon.[21] A similar social censorship can also be witnessed impacting upon the contemporary correspondence between soldiers on the battlefront and their families on the home front. At the other extreme lie the atypical 'good soldiers', such as Graham Greenwell, whose 'love of war' cannot be allowed to speak unreservedly for the unpublished masses of the volunteer and conscripted army.[22]

Stephane Audoin-Rouzeau also witnesses a significant problem in reconstructing the French soldiers' experience around memories affected by post-war civilian identities. In order to circumvent this problem Audoin-Rouzeau has turned to 'trench journals'. He suggests that because 'trench papers...respond[ed] little by little to the concerns, interests, grievances and hopes of their readers, and echoing them', they offer an 'authentic' voice for the French front-line soldiers' experiences.[23] John G. Fuller similarly claims that, in the British case, 'trench journals' capture both the 'spirit of the army' and the 'collective culture' of the BEF.[24] This methodological approach has certainly done much to further our understanding of the soldiers' whole experience of the Great War, including time spent behind the lines. Yet 'trench journals' had little or nothing to say about how the soldier felt about, or carried out, combat. In stark contrast, war diaries did record (amongst other things) the day-to-day combat activities of the unit.

This raises the question of why war diaries and their appended post-battle reports have been largely over-looked in the literature to date – their use being almost wholly confined to the study of tactics and strategy. This can partly be explained by the historiographical preoccupation with elucidating the morale of entire armies. To reiterate, war diaries do not lend themselves to a cursory reading. Time constraints alone, however, do not fully explain the neglect of war diaries as a potential source. The veracity of the accounts of combat activity recorded within their pages have also been questioned. Tony Ashworth unequivocally states that 'official war diaries were not used as sources since...they could not record the type of behaviour and events [the engendering of tacit truces] which are the subject of study here.'[25] Trench fighters, he argues, kept their passivity from the eyes of higher command by submitting bogus accounts of aggression. This behaviour is well exemplified by Richard Holmes' account of one company commander who, in response to his brigadier's insistence upon solid

---

21 Siegfried Sassoon, *Memoirs of an Infantry Officer* Faber & Faber (1930). It is evident that Sassoon was considered a competent, perhaps even dangerously enthusiastic infantry officer by his battalion. This understanding is somewhat at odds with his later memoirs.
22 Graham H. Greenwell, *An Infant in Arms* Allen Lane (1972), 1st ed 1935.
23 Stephane Audoin-Rouzeau, *Men at War 1914-1918: NationalSentiment and Trench Journalism in France during the First World War* Berg (1992) p. 34 & pp. 185-7.
24 John G. Fuller, op cit., p. 4.
25 Tony Ashworth, op cit., p. 10.

proof that patrols were traversing No Man's Land, 'kept a roll of the [barbed] wire in his dugout, and amused himself by forcing subalterns to sit on it until the blood came: those who did so were rewarded by a short length which enabled them to avoid their next patrol.'[26]

Yet it is a mistake to reject *passim* the reports of aggression found within war diaries upon this basis. Firstly, combat executed (or otherwise) during major set-piece attacks was far less open to fabrication. Moreover, a number of interpretive approaches can be (and have been) employed to partly answer concerns over potential invention and falsehoods.

War Diaries: Authorship and Audience

The official proclamations guiding the writing of war dairies during the Great War were set down in the *Field Service Regulations* of 1914.[27] Every military unit – from a Field Ambulance to GHQ – was required to keep a daily record of events. The diarist would be a designated officer; usually the CO or adjutant for a battalion, and a staff captain for higher commands.[28] The rationale behind keeping a daily diary were twofold: '1) To furnish an accurate record of the operations from which the history of the war can subsequently be prepared. 2) To collect information for future reference with a view to effecting improvements in the organisation, education training, equipment and administration of the army for war.'[29] These designs may have been in conflict – a didactic account of battle not always making the most sanguine offering for posterity. It is apparent however that officers further down the chain of command – senior commanders and their subordinates – were often too concerned with the present to worry over their place in history. A stronger censorious influence was probably provided by the diarist's more immediate audience: the next link up in the chain of command.[30] But here also the didactic rationale could overcome the diarist's concerns over possible chastisement. Battalion commanders, for instance, often wrote candidly (but respectfully) on failed combat operations in order to avoid a repeat performance. For example, following the division's faltering attack on the German Switch Line on 23 July 1916, the 7th Loyal North Lancashire Regiment (Loyals) recorded that their CO had sent a 'report on recent operations to Brigade with view to avoiding

---

26   Richard Holmes, op cit., p. 319.
27   *Field Service Regulations Part II: Organisation and Administration* War Office (1909) Reprinted 1914, Section 140 'War Diaries' pp. 174-7.
28   Ibid., p. 175.
29   Ibid., pp. 174-5.
30   The *Regulations* stipulated that 'The original copy will be forwarded on the last day of each month, unless otherwise ordered, direct to the officer in charge of the A.G's [Adjutant General's] office at the base, for the transmission to the military authorities concerned.' Ibid., p. 175. It would seem however that battalion war diaries usually took the more immediate route direct to brigade and then division.

similar situation in future.'³¹ From 1916 onwards, 19th Division, evidently under pressure from high command,³² insisted that its battalions provide detailed accounts of *all* combat operations, including their thoughts upon 'lessons learnt'. For example, orders for a raid to be executed by the 10th Worcestershire Regiment (Worcesters) on the night of 11 February 1917 insisted that 'A full report will be sent in by the 1st Post on the morning of the 12th.'³³ It was in the 'lessons learnt' section of post-battle reports especially that candidness seemed to reign.

The Field Service Regulations also stipulated the types of information solicited. The war diary was to record: 'All important orders, despatches, instructions, reports and telegrams issued and received, and decisions taken' relevant to the unit.³⁴ The collected unit diaries of a division consequently offer voluminous evidence on the thoughts, desires and concerns of both its battalion and senior commanders, as well as detailed discussions over proposed attacks (particularly formal orders) and proposed training methods. The combat expectations of the divisions senior commanders – in respect to both the major set-piece battles and the day-to-day execution of 'trench warfare' – have been drawn primarily from the written orders issued by division, and their replication down the chain of command. For example, '19th Divisional Order No. 9' sketched out the expectations of the General Officer Commanding (GOC) for his division in the forth-coming 'set-piece' offensive on the 25 September 1915 (Battle of Loos), whilst 'Battalion Order No. 1' outlined the 9th Battalion Royal Welsh Fusiliers Regiment (Fusiliers) CO's more exact rendering of these expectations for his battalion.³⁵

Of equal moment for the aims of this study, war diaries were also required to record: 'Detailed account[s] of all operations, noting connection with other units in the neighbourhood, formations adopted, ranges at which fire was opened, &c.'³⁶ It was

31 WO95/2080 7th Battalion The Loyal North Lancashire Regiment War Diary (July 1916) PRO.
32 On February 1st 1916 GHQ issued a general complaint regarding the terse recording of combat activities. 'He [Haig] is aware that it is not possible to be precise in every case, but considers that the use of such expressions as 'hostile patrol accounted for' or 'disposed of', 'hostile trenches successfully shelled' etc. convey little information of use.' See WO95/672 General Headquarters III Corps War Diary (June 1916) PRO. Report dated 1 Feb 1916.
33 'O.O. for Raid on German Line to be carried out by 10/Worc.R.' in WO95/2083 Headquarters 57th Brigade War Diary (Feb 1917) PRO.
34 *Field Service Regulations Part II* op cit., p. 176.
35 WO95/2052 General Staff 19th Division War Diary (July-Dec 1915) PRO. Order issued Sept 22nd. WO95/2092 9th Battn. The Royal Welsh Fusiliers War Diary (Sept 1915) PRO.
36 *Field Service Regulations Part II* op cit., p. 176. The *Regulations* foresaw that 'In the case of important actions, of which a detailed account may cover much space, a short reference to the occurrence should be made in the body of the diary, and a complete report on the action added as an appendix.' During trench warfare however these accounts were often provided in the form of Tactical Progress Reports (TPRs).

also required that any resultant casualties be recorded.[37] Consequently, the war diaries and appended reports often provide evidence of both the actualities and human costs of a combat operation, as witnessed *first hand* by the junior commander leading the unit, and recorded in the *immediate aftermath* of the operation by the CO or adjutant.

This is not to say that war diaries are free from methodological shortcomings. It would seem apt to begin by countering Tony Ashworth's rejection of unit war diaries as a viable source of combat behaviour and morale, particularly for the study of major set-piece attacks (which was, to be fair, not Ashworth's main brief). To reiterate, Ashworth dismissed the source on the grounds that reports of combat activities in war diaries were frequently spurious. Although this study does not deny the possibility that frontline soldiers made bogus reports in order to avoid dangerous combat activities during static 'trench warfare', it contends that this form of deception was far less prevalent during set-piece attacks. This was primarily because the author of these post-battle accounts (typically the battalion CO) and his main witnesses (typically junior officers) almost always had a high degree of initial commitment to the objective. Consequently, the combat episode being reported invariably took place.

It is suggested, moreover, that two (admittedly basic) checks can be made to further guarantee veracity. Firstly, it can reasonably be conjectured that an account of a combat activity in which the division's infantry suffered casualties was *not* a fictional account. Secondly, given that senior commanders and above wanted to hear about aggression and high combat morale, there would seem no reason to doubt the veracity of reported *pacifism* (non-aggressive activity during combat). For example, a TPR compiled by the 7th South Lancashire Regiment (South Lancs) which read: 'Not a shot fired by either side for abnormal considerable time. Probably owing to many meteorological conditions', would seem a fairly honest account of a tacit 'stand off'.[38] Whilst, on the same grounds, the consistent evocation made in the 'lessons learnt' columns that 'men must use their rifles' would seem to be a fairly honest admittance of widespread 'non-firing'.

Upward of half-a-dozen 'post-battle reports' have survived for each set-piece battle engaged in by 19th Division (normally located appended to the relevant brigade war diary). This number allows for in-depth comparisons and contrasts in combat behaviour and morale to be made; revealing both the commonplace and atypical episodes of the battlefield. Certainly there were censorious influences acting upon the writer. In the interests of the battalion's reputation especially, any combat behaviour falling well outside the Edwardian precepts of 'gallantry' and 'honour' would have probably been passed over. Yet an equally compelling influence was countering this desire to paper over the cracks. It was literally a matter of life or death that battalion commanders

---

37   Ibid., p. 177. Details of casualties were to include 'the names and ranks of officers, and number of other ranks...' Some battalion diaries went beyond this requirement and recorded the names of all OR casualties.
38   WO95/2081 7th Battn. The South Lancashire Regiment War Diary (Sept 1915) PRO. TPR dated 29 Sept 1915.

honestly recounted the combat behaviour their infantrymen were able to execute *and* cope with; and in doing so, potentially influence future plans and objectives.

Quantitative Methodologies

These qualitative methods of examining combat behaviour and morale have been bolstered by two quantitative 'measures' of the division's combat morale. The first is based upon the number of casualties individual battalions were willing to suffer before sacrificing the objective to safety. This measure is based upon the following interpretative construct: the higher the 'casualty rate' a unit was willing to suffer in pursuit of their objective, the higher their collective combat morale. Concomitantly, the lower the casualty rate, the greater the constraints a unit was placing upon their commitment to the objective.[39] In essence, this measure only offers a guide to a unit's 'passive' combat morale; their willingness to become a casualty, not their willingness to inflict casualties. This interpretive approach has some noted authority. Samuel Stouffer's World War Two study utilised the amount of 'nonbattle casualties' experienced by a unit in action (soldiers who left the battlefield physically unwounded but did not reach their objective) to indicate the unit's 'collective' commitment to combat: the lower the amount the higher the unit's commitment.[40] Significantly, Stouffer recommended this quantitative method because he felt it had the advantage of circumventing the subjective interpretations of both combatants and their senior commanders.

The second quantitative measure (or guide) is based upon the number of infantrymen found guilty by Field General Courts Martial (FGCM) of either Desertion, Absence or Self-Inflicted Wounds. Again, it only offers a guide to a unit's 'passive' combat morale, indicating the number of infantrymen who had descended to the lower reaches of, what this study calls, the combat morale/behaviour spectrum. This construal is based upon the following interpretative construct: an infantryman found guilty of such crimes had shown himself to be either unwilling or unable to execute the passive element of his role as a combat soldier; whether that be by deserting the battlefield, absenting himself from the frontline, or disabling himself. This method has been borrowed, in part, from David French's study of the British Second Army's morale during operations in Northern France in 1944. French uses incidences of desertion, absence without leave (AWOL), self-inflicted wounds and 'battle-stress' within Second Army to calculate their collective morale: all of these behaviours being interpreted by French as manifestations of the soldier's inability or unwillingness to

---

39 Most battalion and brigade war diaries gave detailed estimations of their battle casualties; including numbers of killed, wounded, and missing. A number of diaries also recorded their 'fighting strength' going into battle. It has therefore been possible to estimate the percentage of casualties suffered each time a battalion engaged in combat: this has been called their *casualty rate*.
40 Samuel A. Stouffer et al (vol. 2), op cit., p. 6.

cope with battle.⁴¹ There are insufficient records of shellshock (to use the idiom of the time) occurring within the division to allow an exact replication of this method. However, the FGCM registers provide a complete record of those infantrymen serving with the division convicted of either desertion, absence, or incidences of self-inflicted wounds.⁴²

To reiterate, this study is primarily concerned with investigating how British infantry volunteers and conscripts of the Great War experienced and reacted to the role of combat. That is, how 'civilian soldiers' with little or no prior exposure to soldiery executed the profession's fundamental role – to kill and accept the concomitant chance of being killed. With an understanding of the studiy's methodology in place we can know turn to the evidence itself, organised in chronological order and covering the division's entire war service.

---

41   David French, op cit., esp. pp. 157-63. It is worth noting that French also recommends this quantitative method because it overcomes the reliance upon a number of 'unrepresentative samples'.

42   WO213/5 to WO213/29 Judge Advocates General's Office: Field General Court's Martial and Military Courts, Registers. (July 1915-May 1919) & WO90/6 & WO90/8 Judge Advocates General's Office: General Court's Martial Registers, Abroad. (1900-1943), both PRO. These registers record the 'factual' details from the trials of soldiers on active service: this information includes the date of the trail; the soldier's name, rank, number and unit; the charge; the findings; the sentence; and details of any remittals or commuted sentences. Soldiers accused of purposely wounding themselves were charged with 'S.18.1 or 2' which the *Manual of Military Law* described as 'Malingers, or feigns or produces disease or infirmity; or Wilfully maims or injures himself or any other soldier...' *Manual of Military Law* War Office (1914) IWM, pp. 396-7. However, a later memorandum issued in 1916 on Courts Martials stated that 'It is usually impossible to obtain a conviction under Section 18 for 'Maiming,' as the special 'intention' has to be proved. Consequently, such cases should be tried under Section 40, 'Neglect to the prejudice, etc.' Which may indicate that many incidences of self-inflicted wounds are hidden behind the cover all S.40. See 'Circular Memorandum on Courts-Martial: For the use of Convening and Staff Officers, and Officers giving instructions on this subject' (Printed April 1916) IWM.

4

Battle of Loos

Overview

19th Division arrived in France late July 1915 and came under the command of Indian Corps, First Army.[1] Their GOC was Major General Charles Grant Mansell Fasken C.B.(1855-1928), an ex-Indian Army officer, formerly CO 52nd Sikhs and GOC Ferozepore Brigade: in the parlance of the times, a 'dug out' who had retired on 2 Jan 21914.[2] The nine months prior to embarkation spent by the division training in England mirrored that of so many New Army formations.[3] Dispiriting winter months spent under canvas on Salisbury Plain dressed in 'civvies' and training with dummy ('D.P.') rifles, giving way to happier times spent in comfortable billets on the North Somerset coast, the arrival of Khaki service dress and, by March 1915, the real impedimenta of war.[4] Once in France the division gained 'experience of the conditions, and... learn[ed] the geography of the front line [around Merville]' alongside the Meerut and Lahore Divisions of Indian Corps.[5] On 31 August the division assumed control of a four thousand yard sector of the front line system around Merville.[6]

Following two months of relatively 'quiet' trench warfare, 25 September 1915 wrought a violent but short-lived disjuncture in 58th Brigade's experience of 'active

1 WO95/2052 General Staff 19th Division War Diary (July 1915) PRO. Most of the division's units had reached France, via Southampton, by 21 July 1915.
2 See Everard Wyrall, *The History of the 19th Division 1914-18* Edward Arnold & Co (unknown), p. 2.
3 See esp. Peter Simkins, *Kitchener's Army: The raising of the New Armies, 1914-16* Manchester University Press (1988); Clive Hughes, 'The New Armies' in Ian Beckett & Keith Simpson (eds), *A Nation in Arms: a social study of the British Army in the First World War* Tom Donovan (1990) 1st pub 1985 pp. 100-126.
4 G.D. Jeffreys, *A Short History of the 19th Western Division 1914-1918* John Murray (1919) IWM, pp. 3-6.
5 WO95/2052 (July & Aug 1915), op cit. Diary entry July 1915.
6 Ibid., (Aug & Sept 1915).

52 Killer Butterflies

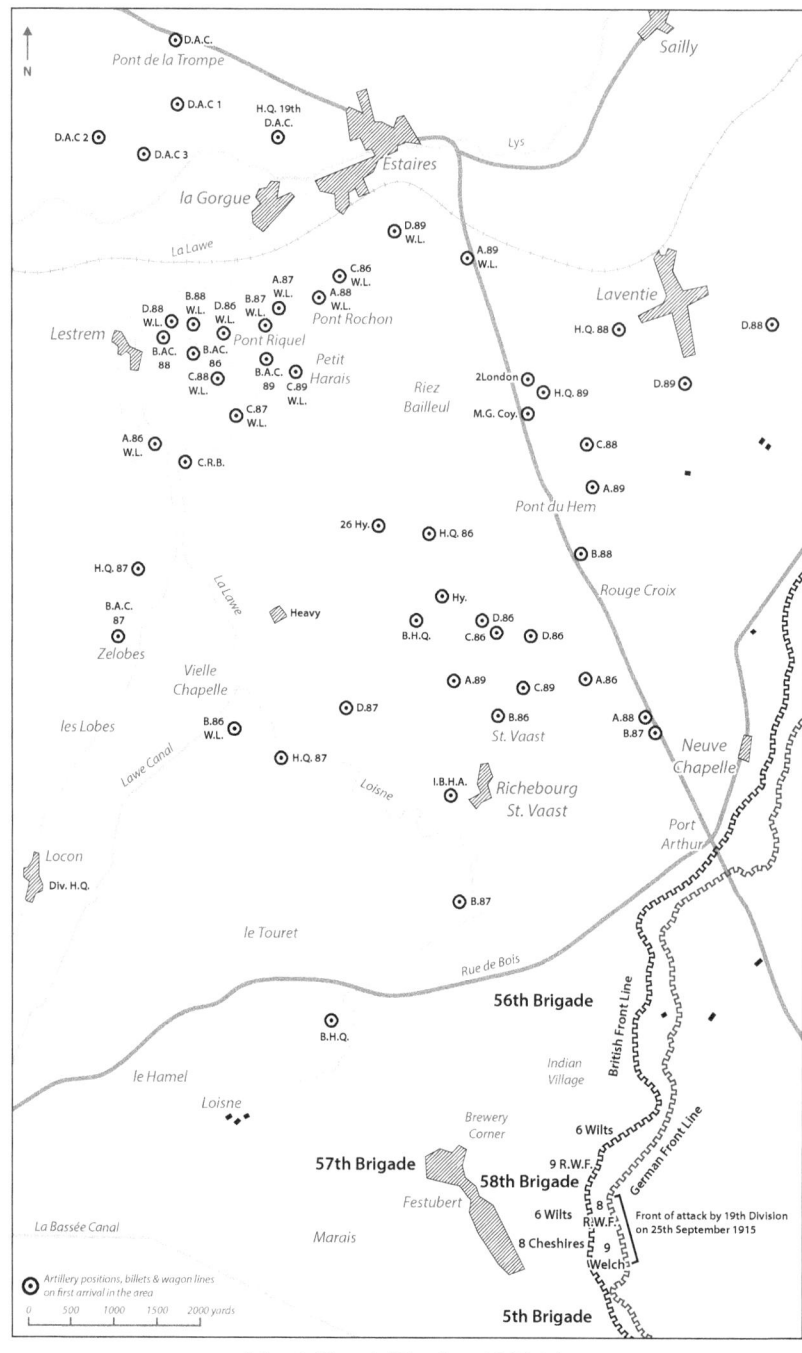

Map 1 French Flanders, 1915-16.

service'. In little over two hours of fighting the brigade suffered 654 casualties.[7] These infantrymen were added to a BEF casualty list that stretched to 60,000 by the battle's close. Yet despite this horrific toll of dead and wounded, the BEF was only performing a *subsidiary* role in Joffre's planned two-headed assault from Artois and Champagne.[8] 19th Division, for their part, were charged with performing a supporting role in First Army's already subordinate involvement within this subsidiary attack. The expectations of high command consequently did not stretch beyond the infantry being 'prepared to extend any success gained by the 2nd Division.'[9]

A general breakdown in communications and one terrible piece of miss-information, however, threw 58th Brigade amongst the leading waves smashed against a wall of German machine-gun fire. Faced with this metallic barricade, and surrounded by fallen comrades, most infantrymen directly went to ground; sacrificing the objective to survival. A few isolated parties – motivated and guided by their surviving junior commanders – managed to struggle to within sight of the German defences, but realising they were vastly outnumbered, likewise chose survival over the objective. Later the same day, and throughout the night, the motivation of saving their comrades lives compelled many infantrymen to chance similarly wretched chances of survival. The only infantrymen who had opportunity to respond in kind to this aggression were the machine-gunners; but even these specialists were essentially acting in desperate self-defence.

Whether or not their combat morale could have been sustained within this inferno was not tested. This was to be the division's first and only appearance in the BEF's last major set-piece battle of 1915. For the remainder of 1915 the division held various sectors of 'the line from Laventie past Neuve Chapelle to the marches below Festubert.[10] But one enduring facet of the Butterflies' combat morale did emerge during this brief but bloody encounter. The suffering of one casualty for every three infantrymen in the assault signalled the end of the attack – not at the behest of senior commanders, *but by the infantrymen's own hand.* Throughout the subsequent set-piece attacks of 1916-18 this (approximately) thirty percent casualty rate was often to delineate the limits of the infantry's collective 'passive' combat morale.

Composition and Training

The infantrymen of 19th Division belonged to a New Army unit that had been formed as part of Lord Kitchener's 'Second Hundred Thousand' in September 1914. As Major

---

7   WO95/2087 Headquarters 58th Brigade War Diary (Sept 1915) PRO.
8   Robin Neillands, *The Great War Generals on the Western Front, 1914-1918* Robinson (1999), p. 196. The French expected the BEF to cooperate with a subsidiary attack between La Bassee Canal and Lens, on the left flank of their assault on Artois.
9   'Indian Corps Operation Order No. 82.' in WO95/1090 General Staff Indian Corps War Diary (1915) PRO.
10 G.D. Jeffreys, op cit., pp. 5-6.

A.F. Becke's *Order of Battles* succinctly stated: 'This New Army Division had no existence before the outbreak of the Great War.'[11] The overwhelming majority of its original strength – raised predominantly from the individual regiment's local area were volunteers with little or no experience of soldiering. This naivety in martial affairs also held true for the greater number of the division's junior battalion commanders. Only battalion commanding officers and a smattering of company commanders appear to have previously served with the Regular Army. For example, the diarist of the 56th Brigade complained that 'only 15 officers [have]…served in the Army before war broke out. Of these, only 3 are regulars. The rest have from 15 months to 3 months service.'[12] Moreover, many of the division's senior commanders, in addition to the GOC 19th Division, were brought out of retirement. The division's 'official' historian, Everard Wyrall, noted that 'although a number of the senior officers of the newly-formed 19th Division had seen service with the Regular Army, scarce one of the junior officers had any previous experience of soldiering. The number of experienced N.C.O.s was also extremely small.'[13] The potential significance of this huge influx of 'civilians' for the division's future combat behaviour and morale should not be over-looked. The stark equation of over 13,000 civilian volunteers entering a military society populated by only a handful of regulars and ex-regulars held great portents for a future victory for civilian sensibilities.[14]

The training received during August 1915 to equip the infantrymen for the 'special form of warfare now obtaining …' was essentially (to use the modern parlance) 'on the job'.[15] The 'green' troops of 19th Division learnt the ropes in 48 hours stints alongside the 'old stagers' of the Meerut and Lahore Divisions of Indian Corps. This first 'tour of duty' lasted 48 hours for the rank and file; officers received a further two days in the front line. The non-specialist riflemen divided their time between learning the arts of trench construction and repair, whilst also attending to physical fitness.[16] Meantime the emerging 'specialists' were sent off to 'School' for a few days instruction in their particular weapons competency.[17]

---

11 Maj. A.F. Becke, (comp) *History of the Great War: Order of Battles of Divisions, Part 3A New Army Divisions (9-26)* H.M.S.O. (1938), p. 92.
12 See WO95/2075 Headquarters 56th Brigade (Nov 1915) PRO.
13 See Everard Wyrall, op cit., p. 2.
14 These figures are drawn from ibid., p. 4. Wyrall puts the figure at 13,379 infantry excluding officers.
15 This was how 57th Brigade HQ described the 'unexpected' trench warfare. WO95/2083 Headquarters 57th Brigade (Aug 1915) PRO.
16 See: WO95/2078 7th Battn. King's Own (Royal Lancaster Regiment) War Diary (Aug 1915) PRO diary entry 4 Aug; WO95/2075 (Aug 1915), op cit., diary entries 20, 24 and 31 Aug.
17 See:WO95/2080 7th Battn. The Loyal North Lancashire Regiment War Diary (Aug 1915), diary entry 15 Aug; WO95/2079 7th Battn. The East Lancashire Regiment War Diary (Aug 1915) diary entry 21 Aug; WO95/2078 (Aug 1915) op cit., diary entries 5 &

An indication of the infantrymen becoming involved in this 'specialised aggression' is given by the Loyals' 'Weekly Fighting Strength Return', which for the first week in September recorded that one officer and forty men had formed its 'Grenadier Company', and two officers and sixty nine men had formed its 'Machine Gun' section.[18] Whilst around the same time the 7th East Lancashire Regiment (East Lancs) recorded that it had 'Started training 16 men as snipers.'[19] Beyond learning to use a new weapon, infantrymen joining specialist units also experienced a change in command. As 58th Brigade aptly stated: 'Machine Guns & Grenadier Company joined Brigade H.Q. after arrival, being now detached from their units & being directly under Brigade Commander.'[20] In sum, their orders now came *directly* from the division's senior commanders. This was part of the process Tony Ashworth describes as 'centralisation', in which control over aggression was passed up to brigade and divisional commanders, thus by-passing the (allegedly) recalcitrant battalion commanders.[21]

In addition to 'centralisation', the creation of these specialised units and tasks may have allowed the higher command to channel the more 'aggressively inclined' soldiers towards the more aggressive roles. It is a moot point whether or not a machine-gunner – although one of the most prolific killers on the Western Front – needed to be more willing or able to kill than his fellow riflemen. This was often depersonalised aggression, and distance, automation and teamwork sanitised the act. However, the same cannot always be said for the Sniper. If not always close-to-hand, then the 'victim' was at least often visible and the effects of the soldier's aggression harder to deny.

For all infantrymen, specialist or otherwise, training with the bayonet was the prescribed key to soldierly proficiency and high aggressive combat morale. The East Lancs for instance recorded that: 'Instructions received for Coys. to do half an hour's bayonet fighting every day.'[22] This emphasis on the fighting efficacy of the bayonet enjoyed a long lineage within the Regular British Army. *Infantry Training 1914*, the pre-war Army's infantry bible, stressed that: 'It will be explained to the soldier that victory can rarely be won by fire alone, that the object of fire is to prepare the way for the charge with the bayonet, and that decisive success can only be gained by closing with the enemy.' The manual also made clear the (perceived) relationship between the bayonet charge and the desired 'offensive spirit'. 'In a bayonet fight the impetus of a charging line gives it moral and physical advantages over a stationary line…Infantry on the defensive should, therefore, always be ready to meet a bayonet charge by a

---

    9 Aug; WO95/2087 (Aug 1915), op cit., diary entry 6 Aug; WO95/2079 (Aug 1915), op cit.
18 WO95/2080 (Aug 1915), op cit.
19 WO95/2079 (Aug 1915), op cit.
20 WO95/2087 (Aug 1915), op cit. Snipers remained under battalion command.
21 Tony Ashworth, *Trench Warfare, 1914-1918: The Live and Let Live System* Macmillan (1980). esp. p. 99.
22 WO95/2079 (Sept 1915), op cit.

counter-charge ... When it is made success will fall to the line which is best in hand and charges with most spirit and determination.'[23] As we shall wee, this belief in the morale efficacy of the bayonet was to remain undiminished throughout 3 ½ years of increasingly industrialised warfare.

25 September 1915

Indian Corps began September already holding the sector of line that fell on the extreme left flank of the proposed Artois offensive. This would seem to have decided the supporting role (to the main British assault) given to the corps: 'the[ir] objective [being], firstly, of preventing the enemy from detaching troops to other areas and, secondly, *if success* was obtained, of pushing forward in co-operation with the 3rd Corps on the North and with the 1st Corps on the South. [my emphasis]'[24] Corps handed the first task to the Lahore Division who were ordered to carry out a diversionary attack on the 25th. The second task was given to 19th Division who were instructed to 'be prepared to extend *any success* gained by the 2nd Division by advancing against the southern end of the RUE D'OUVERT. [My emphasis]'[25] It is significant to note the contingency of prior 'success' running through these orders. There was also a diversionary element to the division's role. The division was instructed to deploy a smoke barrage approximately thirty minutes before the main assault; the intention being to 'deceive the enemy as to the exact front on which the 'accessory' [poisonous gas] will be used ...'[26]

By 22 September the division's role had been ironed out with greater precision, but another contingency had also been introduced – the weather. GOC instructed that they would support the forth-coming offensive: 'If the weather is favourable, by cooperating with the attack by 2nd Division on its right. By taking advantage of any weakening in the enemy's resistance to push forward in the general direction VIOLAINES – SALOME.'[27] The same order stressed that if the weather did not permit the use of gas 'there will be no attack North of the Canal by the 2nd Divn.', and the division's role would subsequently be reduced to 'taking advantage of any favourable results of attacks to North and South [original emphasis].'[28] At this point (the 22nd) GOC also outlined the roles assigned to each brigade: 'the [56th] Brigade must be ready to take immediate advantage of any retirement of the enemy on its front to press forward on the left of 58th Bde ... The 57th Bde. in Army Reserve...will remain in readiness

---

23 *Infantry Training 1914* General Staff War Office H.M.S.O. IWM, p. 80 & p. 222.
24 See: 'Indian Corps Operation Order No. 82.'; 'Weekly Report on Operations' 1 Oct, WO95/1090 (Sept 1915), op cit.
25 'Indian Corps Operation Order No. 82.' Ibid.
26 WO95/2052 (Sept 1915), op cit.
27 '19th Divisional Order No 9'. WO95/2052 (Sept 1915), op cit.
28 Ibid.

for immediate movement.²⁹ In summary, if weather contingencies and success of 2nd Division proved favourable, then the infantry of 58th Bde. were expected to capture and consolidate the opposing front line trench system. For their part, the infantry of 56th and 57th Brigades were expected to capitalise on any general retreat by the Germans.

As for method of assault, nothing too complex was asked. The infantry would advance in 'Artillery Formation' (AF). 'Each Battalion will attack in 4 lines, companies being distributed in depth on a frontage of 1 Platoon, with 50 yards distance between Platoons. Frontage for each Battalion 350 yards.'³⁰ Having traversed No Man's Land the infantry were to engage at 'close quarters, bomb & then charge with the bayonet.'³¹ This stratagem suggested a mixture of the old (the bayonet) and the newly discovered (the bomb). The division's senior commanders feared, however, that their infantrymen – after a few months of 'quiet' subterranean warfare – might lack the necessary 'fighting spirit' for such a close encounter. For example, the GOC warned his brigadiers that: 'All commanders are reminded that, if we get an opportunity … of fighting in the open once more, any tendency to get into communication and other trenches and to work up them…must be checked. Such action would only delay our advance and give the enemy time to reform: and the importance of a bold and rapid advance must be pointed out to regimental commanders.'³²

These then were the chain of command's 'official' expectations prior to 'zero hour' on the 25th. Despite all the official caveats regarding favourable weather conditions, the 2nd Division's inchoate assault was strangled by a gas attack launched upon a fickle breeze. This same turbid pall of gas and smoke obscured the realities of the battle from artillery observation, and led to GOC receiving the erroneous communiqué that: 'First Corps reports Fifth Bde. [2nd Div.] advanced unopposed…In view of this your right Brigade should cooperate by advancing.'³³ Blinded by this literal and very toxic 'fog of war', over optimistic imagination took the place of sound observation. The 9th Royal Welsh Fusilier Regiment's (Fusiliers') acting CO later acerbically commented that: 'The artillery observation officer who had wired down that the attack had commenced, about this time surpassed himself by phoning that the 9th R.W. Fus. had taken the first line if trenches. This must have been an effort of the imagination on his part as owing to the smoke, nothing could be seen.'³⁴ The consequences for 58th Brigade were to prove dire.

29 Ibid.
30 WO95/2087 (Sept 1915), op cit. Order issued on 21 Sept.
31 Notes taken by GOC at a conference held by First Army 7 Sept. WO95/2052 (Sept 1915), op cit.
32 Ibid. Order issued 15 Sept.
33 Telegraph sent by Indian Corps and received by 19th Division at 7.20am. WO95/2052 (Sept 1915), op cit. 5th Bde. also appear to have telegraphed 58th Bde. direct stating: 'If your Right shoves on now we shall do a big thing.' WO95/2087 (Sept 1915), op cit.
34 WO95/2087 (Sept 1915), op cit. Post battle report.

The signal for the advance went up at 6.30 am on the 25th. The task of commencing 19th Division's initiation into open warfare fell to 9th Welch Regiment (Welch) and the Fusiliers. The moment the cocktail of gas and smoke was released from the British front lines it became apparent that, as Major C. Burrard (acting CO Fusiliers, replacing Major Madocks who had been killed within one hour of the commencement of the battle) laconically opined, 'the advance was not [to be] the walk over that had been expected...'[35] On the initiative of a junior commander, the Fusiliers 'leading platoon was already extended, lying down [in No Man's Land], in line with the head of the sap, ready to advance.'[36] The remaining platoons of both battalions were mustering in the saps and communication trenches. These pre-battle logistics had been dogged by problems. Burrard later recorded that: 'There was considerable confusion & delay getting the men through the saps, but most of this was unavoidable. The trenches are very narrow, there was great congestion & the mud & slippery state of the ground militated against speed.'[37] Very soon this minor disorder was to deteriorate into turmoil as these grid locked infantrymen were enfiladed by machinegun fire and bombarded by howitzer shells. Whilst to compound matters, the recently discharged 'smoke hung low, and it was difficult to see what was going on [on] either flank.'[38]

The bleak portents of these preliminaries were realised the moment both battalions stepped out into No Man's Land. Possibly believing the communications trenches to be full of poisonous gas, the Welch rejected the relative safety of initial cover in favour of a immediate assault, across the open, from their own parapet.[39] The decision proved academic because: 'The leading and supporting platoons as soon as they were over the parapet were met by the most intense rifle and machine gun fire and suffered heavy casualties without being able to make ground. By about 6.45 am the casualties were already well over two hundred and all outside the parapet were exposed to a deadly fire from shrapnel, machine gun and rifle fire.'[40] Lieut-Col. Young (CO Welch) later wrote that: 'Nothing could have exceeded the gallantry of the whole Battalion but nothing could live in such fire.'[41] Taking the conventional route (through the saps) only led many Fusiliers to the same murderous end. It was reported by the supporting battalion that: 'The saps appear to have been marked down by MG (enemy's) ...'[42] The Fusiliers themselves also reported the 'saps being choked with wounded.'[43] As the

35 Ibid.
36 WO95/2092 9th Battn. The Royal Welch Fusiliers War Diary (Sept 1915) PRO.
37 WO95/2087 (Sept 1915), op cit. Post battle report.
38 Ibid. Post battle report made by CO Welch. See also WO95/2092 9th Battn. The Welch Regiment War Diary (Sept 1915) PRO, diary entry 25 Sept.
39 See WO95/2087 (Sept 1915), op cit. Post battle report.
40 WO95/2092 Welch (Sept 1915), op cit. Diary record for 25 Sept.
41 WO95/2087 (Sept 1915), op cit. Post battle report.
42 WO95/2090 9th Battn. The Cheshire Regiment War Diary (Sept 1915) PRO.
43 WO95/2087 (Sept 1915), op cit. Post battle report by the Fusilier's acting CO.

following account suggests, this method of assault may have however inadvertently spared many Fusiliers from the carnage of the battlefield. Burrard reported that: 'It was subsequently known that the men attempting to deploy were further impeded by men who had become casualties in the sap…[and that] 1 platoon of D Company which had not been able to deploy owing to the congestion caused by the wounded had returned intact.'[44]

The supporting wave of the 6th Wiltshire Regiment (Wiltshires) and 9th Cheshire Regiment (Cheshires) were faced with the same terrible odds as those who had gone before. Yet many more of their infantrymen were saved from the full ferocity of the German fire by the congestion in the saps and communications trenches. During the brief battle the Cheshires telegraphed brigade stating: 'The Welch are trying to get back to man the parapet and reform…the Cheshire companies are at the front parapet but could not get further blocked by 9 Welch.'[45] A few hours later Col. Jeffreys (CO Wiltshires) reported that 'our attack has absolutely checked. Only some of the R.W.F's and 1 Company of ours got out … As far as I can discover the process of getting through the sap was much too slow and perhaps could not have been quicker. I do not know how it happened that some of the Wiltshires got out before the Welch Fusiliers, I do not think the wire was properly cut or the enemy's M.G. on the enfilading salient on our right were silenced by the artillery. Our men were enfiladed directly they advanced.'[46] As this report reaffirms, the original plan (based upon the *success* of the 2nd Division) had gone badly wrong, leaving the 19th Division's immediate preparations and execution in disarray.

As all the above accounts attest, although the passive element of the infantry's combat morale was severely challenged, no riflemen of the 58th Brigade had the chance to aggress the enemy on the 25th. It seems that the role of infantry aggression fell primarily to the 'specialists'. There is only one account – a telegraph sent to brigade by Lieut. Thomas, a Machine Gun Officer of the Fusiliers – but it captures something of the combat behaviour of machine-gunners on the 25th: 'Re Lt Locke who was killed while serving a gun. I think the following facts should be known. He had been wounded in the chest but after he had been bandaged up he returned to his guns. What he saw in front to make him do what he did I don't know, anyhow he took the gun round through a sap-head and was killed while firing it. Personally I am inclined to think he may have spotted the M Guns that did so much damage to our advance … [he then mentioned his own role] [I] had my own two guns mounted … with orders to play on the German parapet and try to cover the retirement of our men…I should like to call the behaviour of the Wilts team to your notice. They have been serving all night and were fairly worn out but they kept up their fire as long as

---

44 Ibid.
45 Ibid. The message was sent sometime around 8am on the 25th.
46 Ibid. This post battle report appears to have been written on the 25th.

and whenever it seemed necessary.[47] In broad terms this was depersonalised aggression; distance, teamwork and automation all coming between the machine-gunners and their targets. It was also originally in frantic self-defence of his comrades. The desperate 'life or death' nature of the machine-gunner's situation tells us that this was not posturing combat behaviour.

Reports of the events of the 25th do give the impression that 58th Brigade's infantry responded uniformly to this terribly uneven encounter. The thoughts of Young over 'the gallantry of the whole Battalion' have been detailed. His sentiments were echoed by Jeffreys who stated: 'I am satisfied that he [Capt. Wykes] and his company [D Coy.] behaved with the greatest gallantry and did all that was humanly possible.'[48] Putting aside the subjective interpretation of gallantry, it is reasonably clear however that some groups of infantrymen found they possessed (if only momentarily) a greater combat morale than some of their comrades. DHQ's summary account of the 25th stated: 'Welsh Regt. and Royal Welsh Fusiliers advanced for 200 yards and were then held up by artillery fire and by heavy machine gun fire from German SUNKEN ROAD Trench.'[49] Yet the battalions typically reported less success in terms of ground advanced. The Welch for instance informed brigade that: 'Our firing line and support companies advanced over parapet at 6.30.a.m. but heavy casualties by H.E. shrapnel and M.G. and are held up one hundred yards in front of our parapet.'[50]

Clearly precision was impossible, but the difference does not seem to be entirely due to miscalculation. Some infantrymen *did* get beyond 100 yards of the jump off point. Young reported that: 'No one succeeded in getting more than about 80 yards forward except a small party collected by 2nd Lt A.J. Williams who being near an old German communication trench managed to crawl within 80 yards of the German line … A gallant feat in the face of such a fire.'[51] Burrard similarly wrote: 'I have also to report that, in spite of all the obstacles, several men reached the German wire but were unable to affect anything owing to the smallness of their numbers.'[52] Jeffreys likewise reported: 'At or nearly at 6.30 am D Coy under the command of Captain Wykes went over the parapet in support of the Royal Welsh Fusiliers … The company got out to a distance of about 50 yards *and some of it got into an old German trench*. The Company suffered 50 casualties and lost all its officers. It was brought out of action by 2nd Lieut Trueman, my Grenadier Platoon Commander who had accompanied it with some bombers [my emphasis].'[53]

These three reports, combined with the other accounts presented, illustrate the spectrum of combat morale/behaviour experienced within 58th Brigade on the 25th.

---

47   Ibid. Telegraph sent to the 58th Brigade Machine Gun Officer on 26 Sept.
48   WO95/2087 (Sept 1915), op cit. Post battle report.
49   WO95/2052 (Sept 1915), op cit. Report dated 25 Sept.
50   WO95/2087 (Sept 1915), op cit. Telegraph sent approx 8.30 am 25 Sept.
51   Ibid. Post battle report.
52   Ibid. Post battle report.
53   Ibid. Post battle report.

Most of the infantry who went over and survived managed to advance around fifty yards; some managed to make the cover of 'an old German trench', a very few (aided by the terrain) advanced to the German wire.

These latter reports also signal the apparent determining factor in deciding the poles of this spectrum: leadership. The small group who reached the German wire were 'collected' and led by a junior commander. The company that 'lost all its officers' mostly went to ground, and remained there until 'brought out' by a junior commander. This paralysis of leaderless Other Rank infantrymen is well illustrated by Lieutenant Colonel W.B. Wauntesey's (CO Cheshires') account of the faltering advance: 'Lieut Watts (since questioned) having formed out his plat[oon] could see nothing: move forward to find Welsh. When found they said their Officers were down & did not know what to do. He found Capt Hughes dead & then Capt McHeugie wounded. Lieut Watts asked if he should take over Welsh. McHeugie said yes & called out 'Forward the Welsh & the Cheshires, 3 cheers for the Welsh', Lieut Watts signalled forward his platoon, in doing so he was shot.'[54]

The actions of these junior commanders (and their fellow officers in 58th Brigade) would seem a consummate demonstration of high combat morale. To a man they seemed willing to die in pursuit of the objectives set by their senior commanders. Inspired by their example a few small groups of other rank infantrymen demonstrated a similarly heightened combat morale. It is also important to note that without their junior officers, most Other Ranks were largely unaware of the 'objective' – regardless of their 'collective' combat morale' – and therefore 'knowledge' was also an important morale component of leadership. For the remainder of those who survived the first fifty yards advance – denied the inspiration and guidance of leadership by the death or wounding of their officers – the survival of their comrades and themselves became the first priority. Faced with the stark choice between attempting the objectives of their senior commanders and almost certainly dying or being maimed in the process, or going to ground and *possibly* living to fight another day, they chose the latter.

It could, of course, be countered that all of those infantrymen who went to ground were already dead or seriously wounded. Therefore, to talk of 'choice' (however stark) is nonsense. Yet both a number of reports and the final casualty list indicate that many infantrymen did return from the battlefield physically unscathed. The Welch recorded that: 'As no progress could be made the word was carried down the line that the advance should stop and that those outside should endeavour to regain our parapets and reform. At about 7 am *the unwounded men commenced to come back* either through the saps or over the parapet and from this time until midday the Battalion was being reformed and the 9th Cheshires manned the parapet in case of a counter attack [my

---

54 Ibid. Post battle report. 58th Brigade recorded 15 officers dead and 15 wounded. The Fusiliers recorded 13 officers killed or wounded out of 25 officers committed to the assault. A casualty rate of over 50%.

emphasis].'⁵⁵ The 58th Brigade recorded that on the 25th the Welch suffered; 4 officers and 57 Other Ranks killed; 9 officers and 140 Other Ranks wounded; 24 Other Ranks missing, out of a total of around 800 men committed to the assault, and similar figures were recorded for the Fusiliers.⁵⁶ That left around 550 infantrymen physically unwounded. Just after Zero the adjutant of the Welch had informed 58th Brigade that: 'Message from Captain Nicholl says crater still held by enemy so impossible to advance further. 20 per cent casualties many killed.'⁵⁷ This would seem to confirm this estimation.

It has been shown that some of these infantrymen were unable to deploy owing to congestion in the saps. It is also possible that a few of them were amongst those who reached the German wire. But even so, this still means that the *majority* of infantrymen, at some point, prioritised their comrades and their own survival over the objectives set by higher command. The casualty rates suffered by the Fusiliers and Welch during these desperate hours were approximately thirty percent. This offers some indication as to how many casualties these 'green' infantrymen were willing to suffer, as a unit, before sacrificing the objective to survival. As has been suggested, it was to remain a reasonable guide to the division's collective combat morale for the remainder of the war.

In the immediate aftermath of the failed advance Brigadier General D. Mackenzie-Stuart (58th Brigade CO) was fulsome in his praise for his men, informing Fasken (GOC) that: 'It is gratifying to be able to report that the behaviour of all ranks under very trying circumstances, and in their first action was excellent ...'⁵⁸ This would seem to indicate that the combat behaviour and morale of 58th Brigade on 25 September 1915 was in alignment with the expectations of their senior commanders. It is worth noting that men such as Fasken and Mackenzie-Stuart, all 'dug-outs' that would be pensioned off before 1 July 1916, were no martinets. They were as keen not to throw their men's lives away on as futile attack as their men were themselves.

The Fusiliers and Welch survivors were withdrawn from the front line around midday. Most of the seriously wounded of the brigade had to await nightfall for rescue.⁵⁹ In the absence of any compassionate truces, this brought a continued strain upon the passive combat morale of both wounded and rescuer alike. Young wrote that: 'The enemy snipers and M. Guns continued to fire all day at the wounded whenever they saw one move. The dead recovered during the night are riddled...'⁶⁰ It is evident however that the desire to save the lives of their comrades helped to briefly

55 WO95/2092 Welch (Sept 1915), op cit. Diary entry 25 Sept.
56 WO95/2087 (Sept 1915), op cit. Post battle reports. Fusilier's initial casualties recorded as 7 officers 24 ORs killed; 4 officers 137 ORs wounded; 79 ORs missing. Ibid.
57 WO95/2087 (Sept 1915), op cit. Appended hand written message dated 8.25am 25 Sept.
58 'Reports on the Operations of Loos' (probably written 26/27 Sept). WO95/2087 (Sept 1915), op cit.
59 See WO95/2087 (Sept 1915), op cit., diary entries 25 & 26 Sept.
60 Ibid. Post battle report.

inure many infantrymen to this all pervasive danger. Wauntesey reported that: '"B" Company were occupied throughout forenoon in bringing in many wounded, in some cases going out nearly 100 yards. These actions were most gallant ... The labour of carrying the dead & wounded in the sticky mud was hard to realise unless seen ... The determination to save the wounded was very strong, men of No. 5 platoon went out several times to try & bring in Lieut Watts. He would not allow them to come near owing to M.G. fire. which opened each time. I understand that finally he threatened to fire with his revolver on the next man that came out.'[61]

Yet such endeavours were possibly eroding the combat morale of the Cheshires. Wauntesey wrote on the evening of the 25th that: 'I am anxious that my conditions may be recognized: officers and men have had little sleep 2 nights – they have been on the alert all day & 3 Cos will be so all tonight. They are wet through. They have all been working hard in repair of trenches & wire ... carrying wounded & burying dead. They have, moreover, been in surroundings of serious casualties. I have been carefully around them all & hear no word of complaint or discouragement ... [I] think that in an immediate attack – leading – *they could not do themselves justice* ... To give a young battalion so hard a trial will not, I hope, be necessary [my emphasis].'[62] It is evident that the Cheshires' CO was witnessing the *mental* impact of combat upon his troops, as well as the physical effects. Wauntesey's hopes were realised, and the Cheshires, alongside the rest of 58th Brigade, were withdrawn into reserve on the 29th without further engagements.[63]

The 19th Division's disciplinary record indicates that the infantry's longer term 'passive' combat morale was sustained in the aftermath of this first barren exposure to the major set-piece attack. Prior to embarkation a small smattering of soldiers had attempted to avoid the 'future' role of combat.[64] No infantrymen deserted or absented themselves from 'active service', or were convicted for 'self-inflicted wound' between July and October 1915.[65] This provides an 'ideal' figure from which the formations subsequent combat morale can be evaluated.

61 Ibid. Post battle report.
62 Ibid. Letter written by Cheshires to GOC 58th Bde. 25 Sept.
63 WO95/2087 (Oct 1915), op cit.
64 61 in total between the division's formation and arrival in France, but 45 of these were ABC. See WO86/63-5 Judge Advocates General's Office: District Court's Martial Registers, Home and Abroad. (Aug 1914-July 1915) & WO213/4 Judge Advocates General's Office: Field General Court's Martial and Military Courts, Registers. (July 1915), both PRO.
65 See WO213/4 (July-Oct 1915), op cit.

5

Cumulative Aggression

Overview

Throughout the period winter 1915 to spring 1916 the 19th Division remained in the familiar surroundings of Neuve Chapelle. DHQ was located at Lestrem until February, moving to La Gorgue until April, from whence the division was withdrawn from the line and proceeded to the 1st Army Training Area at St Venant. The division did not return to the frontline until 30 June, when they completed the journey from Artois to the Somme.[1]

The stage may have stayed the same, but significant changes were being made to the script. Whilst the infantry toiled in the November mire, 19th Division joined XI Corps; they were now in the company of professional soldiers, and under the command of the 'thrusting' Lieut-Gen. Richard Haking.[2] Meantime, the reverberations of a change in Commander-in-Chief had began to rattle down the chain of command. Control over the infantry's combat activities was tightened, greater aggression was demanded, and the genial GOC Fasken and a number of his 'dugout' colleagues were replaced, and a new GOC, Maj-Gen. G.T.M. Bridges arrived.

By the spring of 1916 the high command's continued drive towards greater specialisation and control had begun to bite, stimulating changes in the infantrymen's experience of trench warfare. Given the nomenclature 'cumulative aggression',[3] Haking's own particular enactment of this process signalled the burgeoning of attritional warfare. The enemy's defences, manpower and morale would be gradually worn down by daily artillery and trench mortar bombardments, supported by strafing machine-gun and

---

1   WO95/2053 General Staff 19th Division War Diary (Jan-June 1916) PRO.
2   The other divisions in XI Corps were the newly formed Guards Division and the Territorials of 46th (North Midland) Division.
3   A summary of morale penned by XI Corps for First Army during February stated that: 'The morale of the Corps seems to have been good. Gen. R. Haking continuously inculcated his policy of 'cumulative aggression'...' WO95/881 General Staff XI Corps War Diary (Feb 1916) PRO.

rifle fire, and punctuated by trench raids. The design of this latter enterprise being to 'penetrate their front line and to kill and capture as many Germans as possible.'[4]

This policy of 'cumulative aggression' effected a significant upturn in the amount of depersonalised combat experienced by the machine-gunners and trench mortars,[5] who increasingly shouldered the burden of delivering this attritional arsenal, whilst the inevitable blow-for-blow retaliation meant that *all* infantrymen endured a greater weight of hostile fire. Meantime, a small number of infantrymen were also exposed to *interpersonal* combat through the ultimate act of 'cumulative aggression' – the trench raid.

Matters of frequency, composition and technique, however, were left to the men on the ground. Battalion commanders responded by enlisting those best suited to the activity – predominantly the 'Grenadiers', now given the more appropriate title 'Bombers'.[6] These Bombers constituted the five to ten to per-cent of a battalion who had previously shown themselves willing (in the sense that they volunteered) to engage in interpersonal combat with the enemy (in so far as the 'bomb fight' brought combatants within five to ten yards of one another). These troops had been conspicuous by their absence during the division's first six months of 'active service'. Now their primary role in trench raiding helped elevate the Bombers (and the 'bomb') into the fighting vanguard of the infantry, a role they were to perform throughout the major set-piece battles on the Somme.

Sparing seventy to eighty per-cent of their strength more from trench raiding was not the end of the infantry's mild subversion of 'cumulative aggression'. Battalion commanders themselves did not pursue trench raiding with quite the vigour demanded by Haking. The upshot being that even the division's most committed raiders, the Welch, only executed four raids in the six month period (none of which realised their ultimate objective of actually violating the enemy's trenches). Moreover, the metaphorical 'fog of war' that hung with a stolid permanence over the frontline allowed these trench raider's to place meaningful limits upon their commitment to the objective.

4   WO95/2090 9th Battn. The Cheshire Regiment War Diary (Jan 1916) PRO. The Cheshire's diary for January included an appended report of a raid carried out by the Welch on the night of 10/11 Jan 1916.
5   Only the 'light mortars', or Stokes Mortars, were manned by the infantry. The medium and (later) heavy trench mortars were staffed by the artillery. It would seem that by this time around four officers and fifty Other Ranks made up a battery, one battery to each brigade.
6   This was to appease the sensibilities of *the* Grenadiers. Gary Sheffield notes that 'a vigorous bureaucratic campaign by the Guards succeeded in reserving the coveted name of the Grenadier Guards, and so the term 'bomber' entered the lexicon of the British army.' Gary Sheffield, *Forgotten Victory: The First World War, Myths and Realities* Headline (2001), p. 106.

Cumulative Aggression

During the days surrounding the 19th Division's arrival under his command Haking had outlined his plans for the 'Winter Campaign of 1915-1916'. Haking was eager to counter (what he perceived as) the intrinsic passivity of the infantry, stating that 'the natural desire of the troops to have a quiet time in the trenches must be discouraged in every possible way.' He also chastised the infantry for being 'apt to leave too much to the artillery ...', and the artillery for only firing when fired upon.[7] These criticisms were perhaps not unfounded. For example, DHQ began October reporting: 'No firing by our artillery to-day. Enemy have not fired at all.'[8] For the cure Haking prescribed for all ranks a healthy dose of 'fine offensive spirit';[9] a old Regular Army remedy for passivity, founded upon the belief that soldiers became more aggressive the more they fought. From now on the infantry (and artillery) would be compelled to take and uphold the initiative. Haking demanded that: 'All action by artillery, sniping, machine guns and trench mortars should be primarily offensive ... [and] that if the enemy does retaliate we at once swamp his efforts with heavy and rapid bursts of rifle, machine gun, trench mortar, and artillery fire.'[10] Patrols could no longer just observe, but must 'gain the mastery in the area separating our lines from those of the enemy.' (Note how Haking avoided the term 'No Man's Land' and all that it implied!). And then came the *coup de grace*, the infantry would carry out: 'The attack of small localities ...' – in the language of the infantry, 'trench raids'.[11]

It seems that high command believed this 'offensive spirit' would not flourish until the dead wood within the division's senior command was stripped away. All of the division's original senior commanders had been replaced by June 1916. GOC Fasken, Brigadier-General B.G. Lewis (56th Bde.) and Brigadier-General D.M. Stuart (58th Bde.) had all been replaced by January 1916. The eventual replacement GOC was Major-General G.T.M. Bridges, with Brigadier Generals C.C. van Straubenzee and G.D. Jeffreys taking command of 56th and 58th Brigades respectively. Twyford had also been replaced by July 1916; by Brigadier General C.C. Onslow. Similar purges across the BEF were creating promotion opportunities for the division's battalion COs. For example, in late November DHQ requested a 'report on all C.O.s & any other officer fit for promotion. Also for names of Reg[imental] officers fit for training as Staff Capt.'[12] This, in turn, created vacancies in battalion command that were filled

---

7   'Winter Campaign of 1915-1916' issued 4 Nov and 'Conference at Corps Headquarters' dated 23 Nov. WO95/880 General Staff XI Corps War Diary (Nov 1915) PRO.
8   WO95/2052 General Staff 19th Division War Diary (Oct 1915) PRO, TPR dated 1 Oct.
9   'Winter Campaign', WO95/880 (Nov 1915), op cit.
10 'Conference at Corps Headquarters' & 'Winter Campaign', ibid.
11 'Winter Campaign', ibid.
12 For example, in late November DHQ requested a 'report on all C.O.s & any other officer fit for promotion. Also for names of Reg[imental] officers fit for training as Staff Capt.' WO95/2075 Headquarters 56th Brigade War Diary (Nov 1915) PRO, diary entry 21 Nov.

by junior (but still Regular) battalion commanders. 56th Brigade recorded the impact: 'Battns all now commanded by young officers, & 3 of them are Regulars, one is an ex-regular.'[13]

The process of specialisation and control also continued apace, bring more infantrymen into its fold. In December each brigade added a 'Trench Mortar Battery' to its arsenal, and by June 1916 the strength of these units stood at around one hundred and twenty troops.[14] The turn of the year witnessed the creation of yet another specialist arm of the infantry, the Vickers Machine Gun Company, and the morphing of another '9 Officers, [and] 142 Other Ranks ...' into specialists.[15] These further pieces of specialisation brought the number of infantrymen handling specialist weapon to around twenty per-cent of a brigade's 'ideal' fighting strength. These evolutions in weapon technology were not always detrimental to the firepower under battalion command. During the same period the Lewis Gun sections had returned to their respective battalions, whilst the 'Grenadier' Companies had disbanded and reformed as 'Bomber Platoons' under battalion command.[16]

Cumulative aggression would ostensibly be underpinned by a lengthy four week period of training.[17] The proposed 'Winter Training' scheme was designed to cover every aspect of soldiery – both aggressive and passive. The long list included musketry, bayonet fighting, grenade throwing, patrol practice, physical training, RE work, wiring, communications, route marches and saluting.[18] 'Winter Training' was seemingly the first step in C-in-C Sir Douglas Haig's endeavour to 'shake up' the (allegedly) supine infantry in readiness for the big push. The adroit Burrard (acting CO Fusiliers) for instance commented that 'it might be called, a preparation for a future offensive. A very well worded memorandum was circulated by the C-in-C. to commanding officers personally, asking them to devote special attention to discipline and training and the inculcation of an offensive spirit in their men.'[19] Haig's opening salvo was, however, partially thwarted by the manpower demands of the frontline that necessitated 19th Division's return two weeks early.[20] As the aforementioned Burrard bluntly observed: 'This knock[ed] on the head battalion, brigade and Div training.'[21] Again,

13   Ibid. Diary entry 21 Dec.
14   See WO95/2075 (June 1916), op cit., diary entry 30 June.
15   WO95/2087 Headquarters 58th Brigade War Diary (Feb 1916) PRO, diary entry 14 Feb.
16   See: WO95/2081 7th Battn. The South Lancashire Regiment War Diary (Feb 1916) PRO, diary entry 13 Feb; WO95/2085 10th Battn. The Royal Warwickshire Regiment War Diary (Jan 1916) PRO, diary entry 16 Jan; WO95/2075 (June 1916), op cit., diary entry for 30 June.
17   The proposed 4 week period being mid-November to mid-December.
18   WO95/2081(Nov 1915), op cit., diary entries 26 Nov to 11 Dec.
19   WO95/2092 9th Battn. The Royal Welch Fusiliers Regiment War Diary (Nov 1915) PRO.
20   See: WO95/2052 (Dec 1915), op cit.; WO95/2081 (Nov 1915), op cit., diary entry 25 Nov.
21   WO95/2092 'Fusiliers' (Dec 1915), op cit.

any combative expertise the division hoped to acquire would be realised mostly 'on the job'.

The BEF's policy of specialisation and control was symptomatic of an increasingly industrialised war in which the types and number of machines capable of disabling the human body (and mind) were ever expanding. Yet Haking refused to let the cacophony of killing machines strangle the battle cry of the 'offensive spirit'. In February 1916 Haking informed: 'Divisional Commanders [that they] must use every endeavour to inculcate the offensive spirit in all subordinate commanders, down to Company and Platoon leaders. For the present time our offensive is limited to small raids and minor operations generally. The actual holding of a portion of the enemy's trenches is of no importance. Killing Germans, lowering the enemy's moral and raising that of our troops is the object to be kept in view.'[22] Haking offered a blueprint for killing more Germans: 'The infantry select points in the enemy's parapet which are favourable for a raid ... [Artillery then] cut the enemy's wire and destroy his parapet ... [the enemy is then faced with a dilemma] leave the gaps, thereby weakening his line and lowering the moral both of officers and men [or] repair his wire and give an opportunity of causing loss to the working parties.'[23]

Haking was similarly unswervingly in his belief that frequent exposure to combat spawned more aggressive and tenacious fighters. For example, Haking informed his divisional commanders in March 1916 that: 'We must get at least small parties of one or more platoons into the German trenches opposite the front of each Division in the line. This is absolutely essential if we are to maintain the offensive spirit that we have created and nourished during the last few months in the Corps. We must make our men realise that they have the power [of] getting into the enemy's trenches and driving him out; nothing short of that will render us fit for greater operations later on, when we shall end the war with one or two great battles.'[24]

Accounts of 'all arms cooperation' – nominally seeking to lacerate and bleed the enemy's frontline – infiltrated the war diaries during Haking's tenure. DHQ recorded in January 1916, for instance, that: 'Our artillery successfully cut the wire at [map ref] over a width of 30 to 40 yards and the parapet was levelled to the ground on a width of 20 to 30 yards; the expenditure of ammunition was 1999 rounds. Machine gun and rifle fire during the night was kept up at this point.'[25] The South Lancs recorded the immediate impact of 'cumulative aggression' upon the infantry's nocturnal habits: 'Organise[d] short rounds of fire during night of 9th/10th [Dec] – 3 rounds per man – at parts of enemy line fired on by our artillery today [the aim being to] breach the enemy's front line and to keep it as an open wound in his line of defence. To inflict

22 'Notes of a Conference held at Corps H.Q. on 13th February, 1916'. WO95/881 (Feb 1916), op cit.
23 Ibid.
24 'Notes on Conference at XI Corps Headquarters 10.30am 19th March 1916'. WO95/881 (March 1916), op cit.
25 WO95/2053 (Jan 1916), op cit. Diary entry 8 Jan.

casualties on the enemy.'[26] The impression given by such accounts is that Haking's 'cumulative aggression' had triumphed over 'the natural desire of the troops to have a quiet time in the trenches'. Haking certainly began 1916 believing this was the case, imploring his divisional commanders to consider 'the present situation and compare our offensive operations with the supine attitude adopted by the enemy. The importance of the comparison cannot be exaggerated, and all ranks are to be instructed as to what it means – our own moral improved and that of the enemy lowered.'[27]

Not all the division's battalion commanders were evidently so anxious to appease Haking, however. Battalion war diaries remained littered with 'quiet' days. The East Lancs, for instance, variously described the enemy as 'quiet', 'very quiet' and 'not very active' during one tour of duty in February 1916.[28] Likewise, the Loyals found the frontline during the following month 'quiet except for a little artillery activity in the afternoon', the 'Enemy [was] quiet', and the 'Enemy continued to be peaceful', allowing for 'Another peaceful day' and subsequently 'No Casualties during the four days.'[29] Poor weather could occasionally be the arbitrator of peace; Winter's parting offering provoking the East Lancs to record that: 'The weather again very bad, thick snow, trenches very unpleasant. Enemy fairly quiet…Very lucky in the last few days in line only 1 casualty altogether.'[30] Yet, as the same battalion reported, the onset of Spring did not always witness the blossoming of aggression: 'Enemy very quiet indeed scarcely a shot fired during the day.'[31] Evidently these battalion commanders, when not under direct orders to 'shake up' the frontline, were happy to let their infantrymen live a relatively 'quiet' life; perhaps even 'live and let live'.[32]

It is also worth considering that six battalions held the division's sector at any given time, and therefore only one out of these six need have been executing 'cumulative aggression' (by any means) to fill DHQ's war diary. The constrained temporal nature of aggression upon the division's sector of the frontline is well evinced by the following report made by the 7th King's Own Royal Lancaster Regiment (King's Own) in April 1916: 'Extremely quiet, hardly a shot fired. At 7pm considerable bombardment and rifle fire and MG fire heard to our N in the direction of Laventie; apparently just a little Sunday evening hate for all was quiet after an hour.'[33] The inference that sporadic bursts of 'hate' amidst long hours of 'quiet' were the norm is also surely telling. It is

26 WO95/2081 (Dec 1915), op cit. Diary entry 9 Dec.
27 'Notes of Conference at Corps H.Q., 15/1/1916.' WO95/881 (Jan 1916), op cit.
28 WO95/2079 7th Battn. The East Lancashire Regiment War Diary (Feb 1916) PRO. Diary entries 18 to 24 Feb.
29 WO95/2080 7th Battn. The Loyal North Lancashire Regiment War Diary (March 1916) PRO, diary entries 12 to 14 & 28 to 30 March.
30 WO95/2079 (March 1916), op cit., dairy entry 7 March.
31 Ibid. Diary entry 7 April.
32 See Tony Ashworth, *Trench Warfare, 1914-1918: The Live and Let Live System* Macmillan (1980).
33 WO95/2078 7th Battn. King's Own (Royal Lancaster Regiment) War Diary (April 1916) PRO, diary entry 2 April.

possible that 'cumulative aggression' was not being embraced with universal enthusiasm – some fronts were 'quieter' than others. No wonder then that Haking should be driven to complain in March 1916 'that the infantry have been relying a great deal – perhaps too much – upon the artillery to carry out our defensive and offensive operations.'[34]

If 19th Division's infantrymen were usurping 'cumulative aggression', then Haking had one further means of shaking up the front line – the most clandestine of weapons, the underground mine. The close control held over mining operations by high command and their senior commanders gave them a direct means of aggressing the enemy, and a method of aggression the infantry (on both sides) could not posture.[35] Consequently, from the moment the Germans blew a hole in the division's frontline they sparked off a mining war which briefly swept away any perfunctory aggression. Although this particular episode in trench warfare was sparked off by the Germans, the tit-for-tat exploding of mines that ensued between 14 and 25 March – 6 sets of mines were fired in total, 3 by each side – indicates that mining had long since infiltrated both the German's and BEF's tactical repertoire.

Not only did the exploding mines blow apart or burying those infantrymen who stood above them, but an accompanying fusillade of shellfire (and other ballistics) descended from the heavens to strafe the survivors. The human cost was appalling. Caught by one such explosion, the 8th North Staffordshire Regiment (North Staffords) reported that 'we had 6 men killed and 1 officer (2nd Lieut West) and 31 OR wounded by falling debris…'[36] The Gloucesters discovered that the blowing of a British mine brought little respite for the infantry. '[T]he enemy retaliated [to a British mine] by firing a mine just outside our wire opposite COLVIN STREET and opened machine gun and rifle fire on our parapet…enemy [then] opened an intense bombardment of our line with shrapnel and H.E…Considerable damage was done.'[37]

The carnage was short-lived. Underground mine construction was a lengthy business, and consequently neither side could blow the other up at such a breakneck speed *adinfinitum*. Moreover, Haking's espousals of 'swamping' the enemy were all very well, but in reality the artillery were running short of shells. The Gloucesters reported that: 'Retaliation [from the RA] was difficult to get and when attained was weak and ineffectual.'[38] The reason being, as the King's Own acerbically noted: 'Our artillery

---

34 'Notes of Conference held at Corps Headquarters 8th March 1916'. WO95/881 (Jan 1916), op cit.
35 The mines were constructed by the Mining Company Royal Engineers, under the auspices of Corps, and the decision to fire the mines seems to have been negotiated between divisional and high commanders.
36 WO95/2085 8th Battn. The North Staffordshire regiment War Diary (March 1916) PRO, diary entry 25 March.
37 WO95/2085 8th Battn. The Gloucestershire Regiment War Diary (March 1916) PRO, diary entries 20 to 21 March.
38 WO95/2085 'Gloucesters' (March 1916), op cit., diary entries 20 to 21 March.

under orders to economise ammunition so no support from them. We have to grin and bear it.'[39] The guns on both sides subsequently fell quiet during April. DHQ variously reported conditions along the whole sector of frontline as 'quiet and uneventful', 'Nothing noteworthy happened during the day', 'Desultory fire on both sides during the day' and 'the day was extremely quiet.'[40] Perfunctory aggression had seemingly re-emerged as the norm after two weeks of destruction from above the heavens and below the earth.

Trench Raiding

Trench raiding was the *tour de force* of 'cumulative aggression': the ultimate means by which infantry passivity would be broken, the 'offensive spirit' inculcated and the 'moral(e) ascendancy' seized and flaunted. Viewed from the other end of the chain of command, trench raiding threatened to expose every infantryman to the experience of interpersonal aggression. That the former did not eventuate, and the latter was kept voluntary, can largely be attributed to the chain of command's tactical inexperience over matters of trench warfare. The inability of trench raiding to 'shake up' the division's sector of the frontline perhaps also suggests the limits of command authority upon the Western Front.

Haking and his fellow senior commanders (and likewise the French and German Armies) had little or no experience of siege warfare on such a scale: no firsthand experience of two vast stagnating armies facing each other across 200 yards of barbed wire and bomb craters. How this great unforeseen stalemate was to be momentarily punctuated would have to be left largely to the men on the ground. So although Haking and his senior commanders had written trench raids into the division's 'art of attack', the finer details of timing, composition and technique were to be scripted by the infantry: usually by the CO or a 'thrusting' junior officer. For example, Lieut-Col. Tudor Fitzjohn (CO King's Own) wrote of how: 'On the night 11/12 [April] I arranged a raid on the German Trenches [map ref] for the purpose of obtaining a prisoner.'[41] It is also evident that ideas and reflections over 'intention, composition, orders, and the operations' of trench raiding were being written down by battalion COs, and disseminated amongst their fellow commanders. For example, the Cheshire's war diary had an appended detailed report (broken down into 'intention, composition, orders, operations and miscellaneous) written by the Welch's CO concerning a raid conducted by his battalion.[42]

---

39   WO95/2078 (March 1916), op cit., diary entry 25 March.
40   WO95/2053 (April 1916), op cit., diary entries 6 to 8 April.
41   WO95/2078 (April 1916), op cit. Account of a raid penned for 56th Brigade probably 12 April.
42   WO95/2090 (Jan 1916), op cit.

Being able to organise trench raiding unfettered by the chain of command had a black and white effect upon the infantry's experience of participation. Put bluntly, five of the division's twelve battalions did not plan and initiate a trench raid at all during this period. The slowest off the mark were the 57th Brigade, of which only one battalion executed a raid. Moreover, those battalions who *did* raid (excepting the Welch) limited themselves to one or two attempts. Haking's belief that: 'Raids should be looked upon as part of the ordinary duty of every battalion when it goes into the trenches' was clearly being hampered by the mildly recalcitrant 19th Division.[43]

Of equal significance, keeping the planning for trench raids 'in house' gave the keener battalion COs the freedom to form raiding parties around the nucleus of their Bombers. For example, a raid by the King's Own comprised: 'Lieut. Simpson + Batt and bombing platoons.'[44] These 'bombing platoons' comprised thirty or so infantrymen within the battalion who had already volunteered to specialise in and execute interpersonal combat.[45] Their central role in trench raiding helped elevate the Bombers (albeit transiently) into the fighting vanguard of the infantry. When the division was given the objective of capturing the labyrinth of La Boisselle on 3 July, it was to be the bombers, fighting trench to trench, who spearheaded the eventually successful assault.

If the size of the raid demanded it, these bombers would be joined by a number of (usually) volunteering riflemen. For example, the Loyals received orders on 15 December stating that: 'Each Battalion will submit the name of ONE Officer selected for a Bombing enterprise, and also the names of SIX men who volunteer for the work.'[46] The following account by the division's most prolific raiders, the Welch, indicates the composition of a larger raid: 'At 5pm two parties each of 2 Officers, 8 Grenadiers [Bombers], and 12 bayonet men, with a supporting party of 2 Officers and 40 other ranks left billets and proceeded to Rest House No. 5 LORETTO ROAD.'[47] Four officers and sixteen bombers were to spearhead the raid, alongside twenty four riflemen armed with bayonets. These troops – who comprised around five per-cent of the total battalion 'ideal' strength – were expected to engage in interpersonal combat behaviour. This point is emphasised by the objective, which was to 'attack the German line at [map ref], to penetrate their front line and to kill and capture as many Germans as possible'.[48] The supporting party – which comprised a similar proportion

---

43 'Notes on Corps Commander's Conference. Corps H.Q., 5pm 19/4/16'. WO95/881 (April 1916), op cit.
44 WO95/2078 (Jan 1916), op cit. Diary entry 11 Jan.
45 WO95/881 (March 1916), op cit. A report titled 'Disposition for night of 14th 15th March' recorded the strength of a bombing platoon as 28 men. This figure roughly correlates with the recorded strength of the 'Grenadier Companies' of August 1915.
46 WO95/2080 (Dec 1915), op cit.
47 WO95/2092 9th Battn. The Welch Regiment War Diary (Jan 1916) PRO, diary entry 10 Jan.
48 Appended report on raid conducted by the Welch on the night of 10/11Jan. WO95/2090 (Jan 1916), op cit.

of the battalion – were excused this duty, but faced a similarly heightened chance of wounding or death.

Battalion COs were able invariably to restrict participation to the willing minority because the battalions also invariably shouldered responsibility for deciding the objective of the raid, and consequently the method of assault. This responsibility also allowed battalions to limit the intensity and duration of the combat experienced by these infantrymen. Haking's minimum objective was 'get[ting] at least small parties of one or more platoons into the German trenches.'[49] The raiders of 19th Division generally adhered to this minimum, and contented themselves with 'forcing an entrance and killing Germans, destroying M.G. emplacements etc.' and then retiring.[50] Indeed, the exception tended to prove the rule: the one raid executed by the division that bore the imprint of Corps (the proposed raid included coordination with both underground mining operations and heavy artillery) exceeded the norm in terms of both objectives and composition.[51]

The infantry were also favoured by an element of control over trench raiding beyond the gift of the chain of command. One that came courtesy of frontline geography, and the jarring of early twentieth-century weapons technology with Victorian modes of communication. The passage of information between No Man's Land, the frontline and the rear were largely dependent upon a sluggish combination of 'runners', telegrams, and the occasionally errant pigeon. Consequently, the moment infantrymen stepped across the parapet they descended into a 'fog of war' which obscured the realities of battle from senior commanders long enough to deem their actions a *fait accompli*. 58th Brigade had already experienced this minor piece of succour during their hellish encounter at Loos. Trench raiding, however, provided a much greater opportunity for latitude; stretching from watering down the objectives to calling off the enterprise altogether.

Nine of the division's fourteen raids fell into this latter category: being either cancelled by their battalion CO prior to jump off; or, abandoned by the officer commanding (OC) the raid after Zero, but without engaging the enemy in any kind of combat. The decision motivated primarily by the belief that the prevailing circumstances were inimical to success. For example, a raid attempted by the South Lancs (the division's first endeavour) was halted before Zero because, in the opinion of their CO, the OCs 'did not know the ground [of the raid] and had never seen it in daylight or any other time. In consequence [he] ordered this party not to go out…[original emphasis]'[52] 58th Brigade recorded how the enemy, rather than poor reconnaissance,

---

49 'Notes on Conference at XI Corps Headquarters 10.30am 19th March 1916.' WO95/881 (March 1916), op cit.
50 WO95/2087 (Jan 1916), op cit.
51 See 'Scheme for an Offensive Operation to be carried out on 20/3/16.' WO95/2053 (March 1916), op cit.
52 WO95/2081 (Dec 1915), op cit. Report appears to have been written on 21 Dec 1915, the day after the cancelled raid.

had thwarted the Cheshires. 'The 9/Cheshire Regt. [had] renewed their attempt on enemy's trenches…a bombing party being drawn up in readiness at midnight. A patrol went out to the gap in enemy's wire and found a hostile working party there, also a little distance away, a lot of movement in the enemy's trenches. It was considered that any attempt that night was bound to result in failure and the enterprise was consequently abandoned.'[53]

The same evident equanimity on behalf of the raider's CO was, however, absent from the views of Lieut-Col. Winser (CO South Lancs) following his battalion's third abandoned attempt on the enemy's trenches:'Special operation attempted night 22/23 again tried night 28/29th. Only one torpedo was used on this occasion – heavier types than one used before. After the enemy's wire had been thoroughly patrolled, 2nd Lt O.C. Harvey and his party successfully carried torpedo to German wire, inserted it and fired it. Bombers who were waiting to enter the gap on hearing the torpedo explode were either seized with panic or else thought they were ordered to retire. In any case they retired to our lines. A great opportunity missed.'[54]

On further reflection Winser decided that his bombers *had* been 'seized with panic', and his peers and higher commanders agreed. On 7 March thirteen privates and one NCO of the South Lancs were court martialed for 'cowardice', found guilty and given an (eventually suspended) sentence of ten years penal servitude.[55] The actions of these bombers therefore provide a fine elucidation of how a group of infantrymen acting *on masse* could limit their commitment to the objective, once they had gone 'over the top'. They also provide a sobering reminder of the harsh consequences should this act be deemed too public or too demonstrative.

The vital element of control held by the infantry was rarely demonstrated in such audacious forms. Infantrymen could modify the objectives of a raid by more subtle means than retreat. Of the remaining five raids initiated by the division, two engaged the enemy in combat, yet still rejected the main objective (that of entering the enemy's trenches) in favour of immediate survival: the faltering raids being executed by the Welch[56] and King's Own. For example, Tudor Fitzjohn (CO King's Own) described the ambivalent successes of his battalion's debut trench raid. 'Previous artillery fire from our guns not good and only warned the Huns, attack took place at 4.30pm but the enemy's line was strongly held … We threw 130 bombs and then retired having only 3 men wounded slightly. Several Germans must have been hit.'[57] Evidently the raiders had lost the vital element of surprise. An account of the raid penned by DHQ (for XI Corps) however elaborated on the consequences of this lack of secrecy, reporting

---

53 WO95/2087 (Jan 1916), op cit., diary entry 3 Jan.
54 WO95/2081 (Feb 1916), op cit., diary entry 29 Feb.
55 WO213/8 Judge Advocates General's Office: Field General Court's Martial and Military Courts, Registers. (March 1916)PRO, p. 64.
56 See WO95/2090 (Jan 1916), op cit. Appended report on raid conducted by the Welch on the night of 10/11Jan.
57 WO95/2078 (Jan 1916), op cit., diary entry 11 Jan.

that 'a M.G. opened on the party at close quarters…bombs were also thrown…The party took cover, some under the parapet and some in shell holes, and replied to the bombers; they threw in all about 120 bombs. It was thought from the noise and the shouts that some of these fell well.'[58] These reports indicate that the artillery had failed to give the raiders some degree of parity in firepower. As a result, combat had quickly descended into a desperately uneven 'infantry versus machine gunner' conflict. Judging that the balance of firepower had swung viciously against them, these raiders eschewed the principle objective and went to ground. This decision presumably being taken by the OC, either in defence of his men's welfare, or response to their actions. Having found some cover they then engaged the enemy in a blind (the effects of their aggression remained unseen) and flurrying bomb fight. An experience of combat which briefly came very near to fulfilling the interpersonal combat expected of the raiders. They then retired.

Three of the twelve raids initiated by 19th Division avoided either cancellation, abandonment or modification to finally fight with the enemy in his trenches: the raids being executed by the North Staffords, Wiltshires and King's Own. Although the three raids were different in both scale and objective, they shared a number of commonalities in combat behaviour which indicate the nature of interpersonal combat as executed by the most committed trench fighters of the division. Of greatest import, combat was largely defined by the 'bomb-fight'; and it seems increasingly apparent that the hand bomb (or grenade) was yet another weapon that partially sanitized the act of killing and maiming, primarily by allowing the bomber to aggress his foe from some distance, and often blind. However, it is evident that a few infantrymen found themselves able to kill their foe 'face-to-face', possibly even by the much venerated (and practiced) 'bayonet kill'. It is also apparent that junior officers continued to provided the benchmark for high combat morale during these operations. These junior commanders were integral to the planning and successful initiation of these raids, they lead by example, and it would seem that their very presence was often (but not always) a crucial factor in motivating a party to fight.

The division's first taste of raiding success was provided by a large-scale raid executed by the North Staffords during the March 'mining war'.[59] The infantry's part in this operation was, according to Lieut-Col. W.J. Locker (CO North Staffords), 'ably organized' by a Capt. P.B. Purves of the battalion.[60] To realise the more stringent

---

58 WO95/ 2053 (Jan 1916), op cit. Report for XI Corps dated 12 Jan.
59 This raid was later to be given the title 'raid on the Birdcage'. For details of Wiltshire raid see: WO95/2093 6th Battn. The Wiltshire Regiment War Diary (April 1916) PRO, diary entry 9 April; WO95/2087 (April 1916), op cit., diary entry 9 April. For details of King's Own raid see: 'Account of Raid on enemy's trenches by 7th Royal Lancs. Regt. on 12/4/16' & 'Information gained from a Raid on German Trench near RICHEBOURG L'AVOUE 12/4/16'. WO95/2053 (April 1916), op cit.;
60 'Report on Raid carried out 20/3/16' WO95/2083 Headquarters 57th Brigade War Diary (March 1916) PRO.

objectives of this operation, the eventual 'scheme' was slightly more elaborate, and involved more infantrymen, than had heretofore been the norm. Two waves of raiders – consisting of: 'A bombing party of 1 Officer and 27 other ranks [and] A sweeping party of 1 Officer and 40 men' – were to attack the enemy's trenches, supported by: 'A covering party of 1 Officer and 30 men'. The close correlation in strength – approximately thirty – suggests this 'bombing party' was part of the battalion's official establishment. The 'bombing party' was to infiltrate the gap blown in the enemy's line, and 'bomb along the trenches from [map ref], bombing dug outs as they go…' Meanwhile, the 'sweeping party' were to search the resultant mine crater 'for wounded or demoralized Germans and will take as many prisoners as possible.' The 'covering party' were given the more passive role of shepherding back both prisoners and wounded.[61] We can see therefore that over half the party (around seventy infantrymen) were expected to engage in interpersonal combat behaviour – although it was preferable that the 'sweeping party' captured rather than killed its adversaries.

Neither their greater numbers nor their greater forethought, however, accounted for the raider's success (although they probably contributed, as did improved reconnaissance which avoided any unforeseen 'obstacles'). Rather, the critical element was evidently the weighty and thorough 'all arms cooperation' that accompanied the raid. A series of underground mines were to shatter or bury the German defenders, artillery and Trench Mortars would 'silence' known German strong points, while machine-gun and rifle fire would hit the flanks of the raid to deter counter-attacks.[62] The subsequent accounts of the OCs the raid attest that, on this occasion, design and reality married, and the raiders faced little initial opposition and were able to infiltrate the enemy's line.[63]

Locker reported that 'the men showed no hesitation in leaving our parapet or entering the German line.'[64] The OC the first wave described the events that followed: 'The Bombing Party reached the S. lip of the Crater L. without opposition, but over very heavy going at about 10-5pm. They entered the German trench just S. of this Crater and worked down it. They met 4 Germans who immediately bolted across the open, one of them was wounded by a bomb.'[65] Their next encounter with the enemy was, however, less one-sided. The OC reported that 'They reached the junction of

---

61 'Scheme for an Offensive Operation to be carried out on 20/3/16.' WO95/2085 'North Staffords' (March 1916), op cit.
62 See: 'Operation Order No. 24. Left Group 19th Divisional Artillery. Operation for Night 20/21st March 1916'; 'Action of Trench Mortar Batteries for Night 20th/21st March 1916'; 'Instruction and Information re Minor Operations to be carried out night of 20th'/21st March.' WO95/2085 North Staffords (March 1916), op cit.
63 See: WO95/2053 (March 1916), op cit., diary entry 21 March; WO95/2086 10th Battn. The Worcestershire Regiment War Diary (March 1916) PRO, diary entry 20 March.
64 'Report on Raid Carried Out 20/3/16.' WO95/2083 (March 1916), op cit.
65 Ibid. The accounts of the two parties were written under the title 'The reports of the officers concerned are as follows'.

[map ref] and were counter-attacked with bombs and rifle grenades.'[66] Reflecting upon the composition of this adversary, Locker noted that: 'The Germans appeared to have some organised party ready to repel a raid, as 5 minutes after our bombers entered the trench they were met by organised bombers with a plentiful supply of bombs.'[67] This indicates the extent to which the 'Bomber' was becoming an institutionalised facet of trench warfare. The OC gave an account of this 'Bomber verses Bomber' conflict. 'A bomb fight followed in which 5 of our bombers were wounded and casualties were certainly inflicted on the enemy, but the extent could not be ascertained, but the bombing Sergeant who was wounded early but continued to fight claims to have finished 4 himself and 2nd. Lieut. Cryan, the bombing officer confirms his story.'[68]

Having solicited the thoughts of the survivors of this encounter, Locker observed that: 'The bombers employed state that the Germans could throw quite as far as they could, but were not so accurate. Some of the German bombs burst outside the trench well behind our advanced throwers.'[69] The Bomber's own competence was also mildly criticised however, Locker complaining that: 'Our bombing party were too prodigal with their bombs when they first met the Germans. As a rule one bomb per traverse is sufficient to allow of an advance.' Locker also added that: 'All men taking part in the operation carried bombs. There was a certain amount of indiscriminate throwing when the party were fired upon.'[70] The impression then is one of a frenzied yet often blind exchange of bombs, possibly from behind the shield of a traverse, where every well aimed ballistic brought the combatants closer to instantaneous annihilation or mutilation. Thus this was a fight between highly motivated soldiers displaying a higher than normal aggressive (and passive) combat morale. The Bombing Sergeant, for example, was commended, 'though wounded in two places early in the affair and ordered back by his officer – continued to fight and only came in when the rest of the party withdrew.'[71] Moreover, this was also a fight in which the effects of their own aggression remained largely guesswork or supposition. Darkness threw an ambivalent cloak over the act, and the aggressors kept a partially sanitising distance away from their foe. It was an act of combat which shared some of the facets of depersonalised aggression; visual distance and, to some extent, automation.

Meanwhile, the 'sweeping party' had also 'reached the [enemy's] trench [map ref] without opposition except for some enfilade M.G. fire from the North which wounded 2 men.'[72] Unlike their fellow raiders, however, the 'sweeping party's' journey

66 Ibid.
67 'Raid on German Trenches, 20th March 1916'. WO95/2053 (March 1916), op cit. This report appears to be a duplicate of the "Report on Raid Carried Out 20/3/16' with an appended 'Lessons Learnt' section, from which this citation is drawn.
68 'Report on Raid Carried Out 20/3/16.' WO95/2083 (March 1916), op cit.
69 'Raid on German Trenches, 20th March 1916'. WO95/2053 (March 1916), op cit.
70 Ibid.
71 'Report on Raid Carried Out 20/3/16.' WO95/2083 (March 1916), op cit.
72 Ibid.

remained relatively unhindered; their OC noting that: 'Seven Germans only were seen unwounded and they were in full flight.' Yet they did endeavour to fulfil their objective of taking prisoners, but without success. The OC reported that: 'One prisoner was captured but would not come back across the Craters and had to be killed … A wounded under officer who would not surrender was killed by an officer [that is, by the OC] and his coat and the documents it contained are forwarded herewith.'[73] Despite its vapidity, this report details a singular moment in the division's history. This is the first account in almost nine months of 'active service' of the division's infantry engaging in an act of hand-to-hand killing – the reluctant prisoners being killed either by bayonet, a crack to the head with a knobkerries, or shot at close range: thus only in the latter case would the act of killing have been partially sanitised (by partial automation).

The 19th Division's second account of infantrymen engaging in an act of interpersonal (perhaps even hand-to-hand) killing derives from the successful raid executed by the King's Own. Tudor Fitzjohn (CO King's Own) noted that the party carried with them all the impedimenta of clandestine close-to-hand killing: 'The men had blacked faces, wore bombing jackets, carried about 6 to 8 bombs each, electric torches, wire cutters and knob kerries and bayonets.' One of the OCs the party, a Lieut. Simpson, also came face-to-face with the enemy: 'After entering the trench a sergeant and myself got cut off from the other party and encountered two Huns with rifles and fixed bayonets in inspection. The sergeant shot one with his revolver and I collared the other and endeavoured to bring him with me but he would not come and sat down and squealed. A German bomb dropped rather close to us so we killed him and passed on and came back to firing line round another traverse.'[74]

We can see here a scenario emerging in which interpersonal killing could occur. Both parties had a desperate choice to make, upon which their life, and the lives of their comrades depended. They could either retreat (flight), use their weapons (fight), act as if they intended to use their weapons (posture), or surrender (submit). The sergeant acted first and choice to fight, shooting his adversary at close range. Outnumbered, and with his dead comrade lying next to him, the lone German soldier then submitted, but refused to be taken prisoner. With their lives once more under immediate threat, the raiders again choice to fight, and killed their adversary – either with his revolver, the knob kerries or bayonet. Tudor Fitzjohn also recorded that during the same raid a: 'L/Cpl. H. Tite did extremely good work and bayoneted and bombed 3 Germans himself.'[75] This was therefore the only account of actual hand-to-hand combat behaviour (bayonet kill) during the raid.

73 Ibid.
74 'Account of Raid on enemy's trenches by 7th Royal Lancs. Regt. on 12/4/16'. WO95/2053 (April 1916), op cit. The report was written by Lt. Col. Tudor Fitzjohn (CO King's Own) for Col. C.V. Trower (CO 56th Brigade), and included 'reports from the two officers in charge of the parties.' The report was then passed up the chain of command to First Army.
75 Ibid.

These brief acts of interpersonal combat behaviour are thrown into stark relief by the lethal potency of the distance killers – especially the archetypal depersonalised aggressor, the 'Mining Co. R.E.'. To return to the North Staffords' raid, the OC the 'bombing party' reported how 'a small party specially detached investigated the new crater and looked over the lip and saw 9 dead Germans …' Likewise, the 'sweeping party' 'detailed to search the new Craters…report[ed] 14 German dead and some 5 or 6 who were half buried and could not be taken out.' Whilst both raiding parties noted 'the very effective co-operation of the T.M. Batteries … They must have caused many casualties to the enemy.'[76] A five minute bomb-fight executed by thirty or so bombers had inflicted around half a dozen casualties, and suffered similar loses. The second wave had killed two Germans, but not before sustaining two casualties themselves to enemy machine-gun fire. Whereas the 'all arms cooperation' had killed or wounded at least two dozen of the enemy, with no reported losses, this was yet another pertinent demonstration that depersonalised killing was king, and the infantry were often its pawns.

On hearing of the North Staffords' endeavours, First Army Commander General Sir Charles Monro wired XI Corps to say: 'Am delighted to hear of your successful raid last night. Please congratulate all concerned from me. *This is just what we want* [my emphasis].'[77] If this was so, then it is hard to imagine that the division had satiated the pugnacious desires of high command. The infantry had successfully clouded Haking's utopian vision of perpetual raiding. During the six months of the 'cumulative aggression' campaign, just over one hundred of their ranks (and those mostly Bombers) had collectively spent under one hour in the enemy's trenches. During these raids they had collectively suffered two men killed and fifteen wounded – deplorable losses, but only a short addendum to the casualty toll of trench warfare, and immaterial in comparison to the endless casualty lists produced by the major set-piece battle.

Had 19th Division shot itself in the foot by subverting 'cumulative aggression', and in particular, the ostensible policy of constant trench raiding? They had, after all, largely passed up the opportunity to practice a form of combat – bombing – that would proliferate throughout the Somme Offensive. The findings of later twentieth-century combat psychology would seem to posit ambiguous advantages to raiding. The participants would have experienced a degree of conditioning to the mental and physical challenges posed by 'the real thing'. But there was a fine line between useful conditioning and the first descents towards battle fatigue. Moreover, raiding always carried the unwanted caveat of losing a unit's most committed trench fighters before the main event. These concerns aside, the real problem with cumulative aggression lay in the fact that the balance of firepower swung in neither sides favour at this juncture. Whenever the division truly hurt their adversary, the Germans hit back equally hard.

---

76   'Report on Raid Carried Out 20/3/16.' WO95/2083 (March 1916), op cit.
77   'Copy of 11th Corps Wire No. 6.842. dated 21/3/16.' WO95/2085 North Staffords (March 1916), op cit.

This 'truth' of the firepower balance upon the Western Front in 1916 underlines that 'cumulative aggression', insofar as infantrymen were concerned, was at best problematic. It denied the reality of an industrialised war in which depersonalised killing was king, and the greatest killers were artillerymen. The infantrymen burrowing in the frontline trenches were decidedly more vulnerable to hostile shellfire than the artillerymen and their impedimenta. Moreover, it is abundantly clear that during this episode of trench warfare the artillery of both sides primarily targeted not each other, but the infantry. Consequently, it seems reasonable to argue that 19th Division's infantrymen were wise to limit their commitment to trench raiding and 'cumulative aggression' in general, and by doing so, nurture their precious combat morale for the battles that lay ahead.

6

Battle of the Somme

Overview

On 1 July 1916, almost a year to the day since embarkation, the division's apprenticeship in trench warfare – sometimes violent, always arduous, yet often 'quiet' – came to an abrupt end. During July the division was engaged in set-piece attacks upon La Boisselle (2nd to 6th), Contalmaison (7th to 9th), the 'Switch Line' (23rd) and the 'Intermediate Line' (30th). The chances of being killed or wounded during the month spiralled from 1 in 45 to 2 in 3. By July's close 6,575 infantrymen of the division had become casualties.[1] Whatever anticipations or fears the infantry held over combat, by 31 July most had faced them. After a much needed respite, the Division being sent to hold the line around Wytschaete and the River Lys in Flanders, came the attack on Grandcourt (Battle of Ancre 18 November). Lumping across this chilling snow covered wasteland the chances of becoming a casualty again descended towards 2 in 3, and the likelihood of success disintegrated into the icy morass along with them.[2]

The first day failure of artillery shells to destroy the German defences and defenders, and thus affect the decisive breakthrough, brought about an immediate tactical rethink. It is evident that 19th Division took its first tentative steps upon the 'learning curve' as early as 2 July 1916.[3] The division's post-1 July set-piece attacks were

1 III Corps recorded the following casualties for 19th Division during July 1916: officers killed 60, wounded 220, missing 22; ORs killed 393, wounded 4874, missing 1006; total 6575. This equated to roughly 70 % of the division's 'ideal' strength. WO95/673 General Headquarters III Corps War Diary (July 1916) PRO.
2 57th Brigade recorded 947 infantry casualties (all branches) for the attack of 18 November; almost exactly 1 in 3 of their 'ideal' infantry strength of 3000. Yet in reality the fighting strengths of most battalions was nearer 500, which suggests the chances of becoming a casualty had actually descended towards 2 in 3. WO95/2083 Headquarters 57th Brigade War Diary (Nov 1916) PRO.
3 For a comprehensive account of the British Army's assent of the 'learning curve' see Paddy Griffith, *Battle Tactics on the Western Front: The British Army's Art of Attack 1916-18* Yale University Press (2000), 1st ed 1994.

82 Killer Butterflies

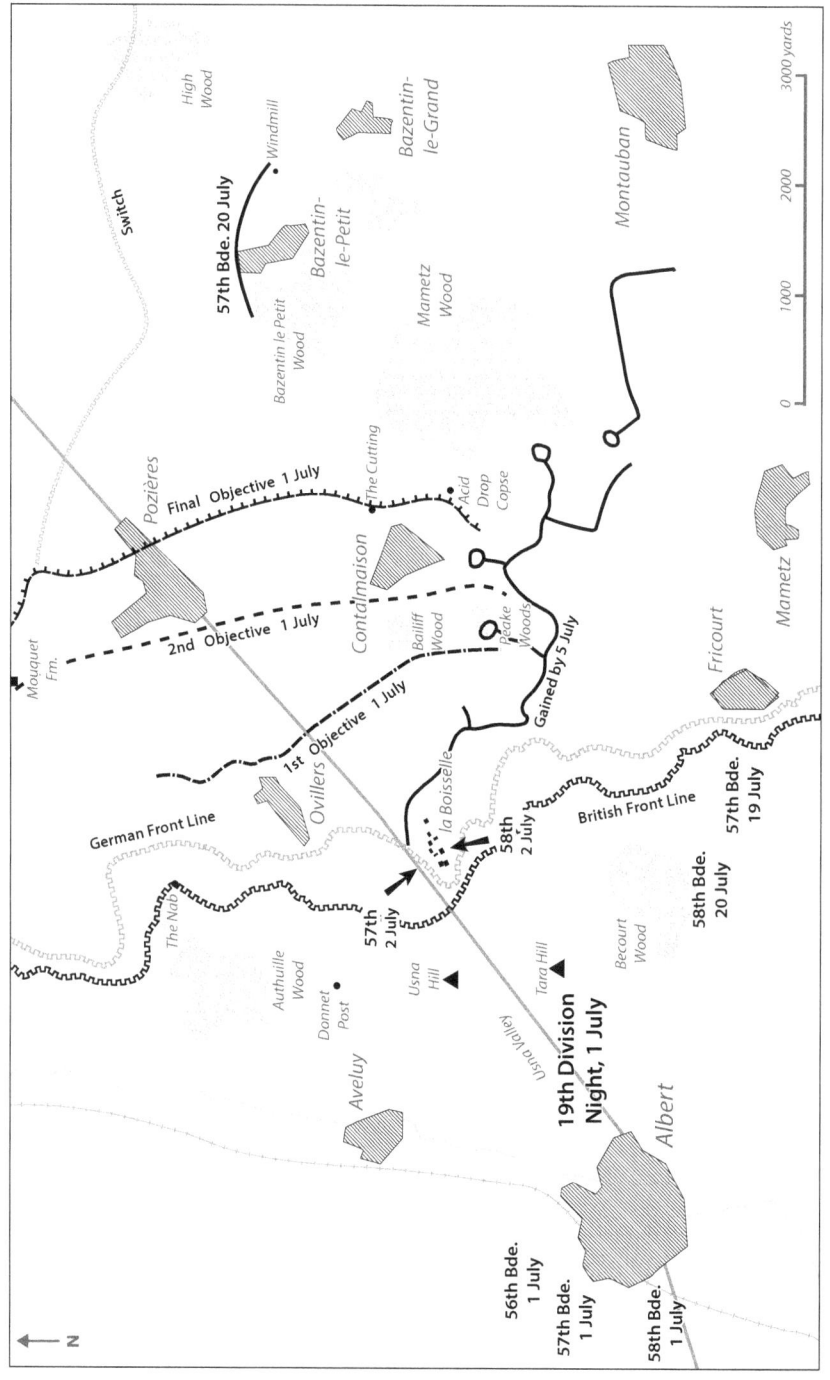

Map 2 Battle of the Somme, July 1916.

protected by an increasingly sophisticated artillery 'creeping barrage' in which the artillery's prime goal was to 'silence' rather than destroy the enemy's own gunners and machine-guns. There is continuing evidence of assent during the November assaults. The creeping barrage was growing in complexity and (to some extent) efficacy, as was the cooperation between the infantry specialists and artillery.

Although combat always threw up its singularities, there were a number of commonalities in the infantry's responses to the attack. If the 'creeping barrage' failed to 'silence' the enemy's machine-guns – the *bête noire* of any infantry assault – the advance would inevitably falter: the infantrymen choosing survival over the objective when casualties reached the 'critical' level of around thirty percent. This critical level was, however, occasionally breached if enough junior commanders remained standing to uphold the voice of command. Thus the Battle of the Somme was marked by one hugely significant piece of continuity: infantrymen still decided when an engagement was over, not generals. When design matched reality, and the creeping barrage did silence the enemy's fire, the majority of infantrymen would reach the targeted trench system. There are no reports of the much vaunted bayonet fight, but many accounts of the enemy either surrendering or retreating.[4] This suggests that most infantrymen (on both sides) were either unwilling or unable to execute close-to-hand interpersonal combat, and particularly the bayonet kill.

The most notable commonality, however, was the domination of the bomber and the bomb, particularly during the four day assault upon La Boisselle. It is clear why this was the infantry's preferred method of assault: the battlefield terrain often lent itself to a subterranean trench assault, it was comparatively less costly in lives, and this mode of attack passed the mantle of combat back to the infantry's fighting vanguard – the Bombers. The combat behaviour of the bombers closely mirrored that of trench raiding. Adversaries engaged in violent yet short-lived bomb fights, at a few yards distance, and often shielded by a parapet or traverse. Thus the bombers inched their way forward, trench by trench, until either superior firepower, casualties or sheer physical and mental fatigue brought the advance to a halt.

In scripting this (what might be termed) localised version of the 'bite and hold' method of assault, the division's senior commanders and battalion COs had effectively endorsed the collective combat morale and preferred combat behaviour of the infantry. Aggressive combat behaviour was the domain of the bombers – the core of the battalion's five to ten percent committed trench fighters – supported by the distance killers – the machine-gunners and trench mortars – leaving the majority of infantrymen to carry out the (nevertheless vital) passive combat behaviour role of keeping the attack

---

4   This of course does not discount the possibility that some infantrymen may have engaged in close-to-hand interpersonal combat (with the bayonet), but were killed, or their endeavours went unnoticed. The latter would seem unlikely however, given how much prestige was placed upon skewering the enemy.

fuelled with ammunition. This was an assaulting unit with a diminutive yet ferocious sharp end, and a very long tail.

The Days Leading Up to the 'Great Offensive'

The plans for July 1st 1916 were vast in detail and heroic in ambition. Haig informed Fourth Army's corps commanders that: 'He wished SERRE, MIRAUMONT spur, POZIERES, CONTALMAISON, and MONTAUBAN to be the objectives to be attained during the first day's operations.'[5] This represented a first day advance totalling roughly two to three miles on a fifteen mile front, stretching from Serre to Montauban. Every step taken by the infantry was to be choreographed in time with the artillery's destructive capabilities, and enacted as a prelude to the cavalry's triumphant breakthrough. Haig instructed his army commanders that: 'The depth to which the infantry can penetrate at each forward bound depends mainly on previous artillery preparation…Experience has shown that where the artillery preparation has been thorough the infantry advance should not be very difficult or costly … If the first attack goes well every effort must be made to develop the success to the utmost by, firstly opening a way for our Cavalry and then as quickly as possible pushing the cavalry through to seize BAPAUME.'[6]

It can be seen that High command had not anticipated that the infantry would have to sweat blood for every liberated yard of Picardy soil. Rather the opposite. The programme for the opening scenes of the show envisaged that the artillery and Royal Engineers (RE) would destroy, the infantry would advance in 'Artillery Formation' (AF) at an orderly pace to occupy and consolidate, and then the cavalry would then breakthrough and conquer. A subsidiary role for the infantry seen to befit: 'New Army troops [who were, according to General Sir Henry Rawlinson] unfortunately…not… imbued with the discipline of the Army and its great traditions.' 19th Division's own *déclassé* foot soldiers – now assigned to Lieutenant General Sir William Pulteney's III Corps, and part of 'Rawly's' Fourth Army, who were to spearhead the assault – were placed in reserve; ready to assist 34th and 8th Divisions should their advance falter.

The specific first day objective handed to III Corps was to 'seize and consolidate the line ACID DROP COPSE (inclusive) – THE CUTTING – POZIERES…';

---

5 'Conference held at Fourth Army Head-quarters 17th May, 1916'. WO95/672 General Headquarters III Corps War Diary (June 1916) PRO.
6 Remarks on artillery taken from: 'First Army No. GS405'. This document recorded: 'Extracts from Notes of the Conference of Army Commanders held by the Commander-in-Chief at Third Army Headquarters ST. POL, on Thursday, the 15th June, 1916.' WO95/881 General Staff XI Corps War Diary (1916) PRO. Remarks on cavalry taken from: 'Report of the Army Commander's remarks at the Conference held at Fourth Army Headquarters, 22nd June, 1916'. WO95/672 (June 1916) op cit. These were the 'orders from the Commander-in-Chief', but read out by Rawlinson.

roughly three miles in advance of their jump off point.⁷ As the Reserve Division, 19th Division were charged with capturing and consolidating between 1500 and 4200 yards of the enemy's trenches, depending upon the fortunes of 34th and 8th Divisions.⁸ Although it was expected that: 'Assaulting columns [would] go right through above ground' in classic AF, the division's senior commanders already envisaged that the infantry 'specialists' would do any necessary 'hard fighting'. DHQ ordered that: 'Bombing parties must be used for clearing communication trenches. In cases where a communication trench runs into the objective, a special party consisting of: Bombers, A Lewis Gun team, A Stokes Mortar detachment with the necessary carriers…will be told off by Brigades to the specific task of working up such a trench to engage any strong point in the objective.'⁹

The anticipated role for the remaining 'non-specialist' rifleman was more akin to a packhorse than a warrior. The North Staffords, for instance, noted that 'the 'fighting order' as carried by this Bn; showed that the men in the ranks carried <u>69 lbs</u> at the very least! [original emphasis]'¹⁰ Whilst DHQ went so far as to order that the 'two grenades carried per man are not to be used by the latter, except in an emergency, but are to form a reserve for the recognized bombers.'¹¹ Moreover, although DHQ had ordered that: 'Men in the ranks are not to fall out to assist back wounded men', they had sanctioned a number of other passive combat roles for the 'non-specialists'.¹² These included: 'Carrying parties of a minimum number of 6 Officers and 200 men from <u>each</u> of the 56th and 58th Brigades…[original emphasis]'¹³

The infantry were granted two months away from the frontline to prepare for these anticipated tasks; two months in which to bridge the lacuna of experience between 'trench warfare' and, what GHQ perceived as, a return to 'open warfare'.¹⁴ The infantry specialists concentrated upon adapting their *modus operandi* from defensive to offensive. For example, the machine-gunners were to practice 'rapid recognition of targets and laying …over distances of several hundred yards, and in conjunction with imaginary advancing infantry.' Meanwhile, for the 'non-specialist' riflemen, the time-honoured soldierly arts of 'steady drill', 'fire discipline', advancing in 'extended order'

---

7   '3rd Corps Operation Order No. 70'. WO95/672 (June 1916), op cit. Order dated 20 June. The planned attack by III Corps lay roughly in the centre of Fourth Army's approximately fifteen mile frontage.
8   '19th Division Order No. 51' issued 22 June. WO95/2053 General Staff 19th Division War Diary (June 1916) PRO.
9   Ibid.
10 WO95/2085 8th Battn. The North Staffordshire Regiment War Diary (July 1916) PRO, diary entry 1 July.
11 'Orders which will hold good for any attack which the 19th Division may be called upon to make', received from 19th Division on 17 June. WO95/2087 Headquarters 58th Brigade War Diary (June1916) PRO.
12 Ibid.
13 '19th Division Order No. 51' issued 22 June. WO95/2053 (June 1916), op cit.
14 '19th Division Training', issued 18 April. WO95/2053 (April 1916), op cit.

and 'bayonet fighting' were the mainstays of the training. Activities considered by DHQ to be 'well calculated to engender good discipline under arms...'[15] Or in other words, designed to inculcate the infantryman to advance and fire at the enemy when ordered.

The belief that 'Drill' created obedient fighters enjoyed a long lineage within the Regular Army. For example, *Infantry Training 1914* stressed that: 'Drill in close order is of first importance in producing discipline, cohesion, and the habits of absolute and instant obedience to the orders of a superior...'[16] The 19th Division then endeavoured to transpose these parade ground skills onto the battlefield by practicing the capture and consolidation of a mock fortified village.[17] The schemes involved all branches of the infantry cooperating (at brigade and then divisional level) to overcome a number of scripted scenarios. These included: 'An advance across the open [at night] and an attack at dawn', and 'rapid deployment from a wood [and] hasty entrenchment.'[18] The infantrymen of 19th Division therefore prepared to enter battle on 1 July having honed their musketry and bayoneting skills; having practiced the act of unquestioning obedience; and having been exposed to some of the *practical* difficulties awaiting them on the battlefield.

The rank and file of 19th Division who marched their way from Albert to the frontline in the dusk of 30 June still, by and large, comprised the division's original volunteers of 1914-1915. Twelve months 'on active service' had cost the division 882 infantrymen dead.[19] Their replacements, and those for the wounded and sick, had occasionally arrived from 'foreign' drafts; suggesting that the 'local character' of the division's battalions may have been mildly diluted by summer 1916. For example, the Wiltshires recorded in January 1916 that: 'A draft of 102 [was] received comprising men from 1st, 2nd, 3rd and 5th Battalions.'[20] Nevertheless, allowing for casualties, the 'class of 1914-15' still represented over two thirds of the division's strength. Regardless of origins, however, most infantrymen shared one common background. As Brig-Gen. C.C. Onslow (GOC 57th Brigade) astutely noted, 19th Division entered the Somme offensive 'with troops who were really participating on their first aggressive battle.'[21]

---

15 Ibid.
16 *Infantry Training 1914* General Staff War Office H.M.S.O. IWM, pp. 2-3 & p. 80.
17 'Divisional Scheme A', issued May 1916. WO95/2080 7th Battn. The Loyal North Lancashire Regiment War Diary (1916) PRO.
18 See WO95/2086 10th Battn. The Worcestershire Regiment War Diary (April/May 1916) PRO, diary entries 29 April, 1-4 May & 8-24 May.
19 *Soldiers Died in the Great War, 1914-19: A Complete and Searchable Digital Database* [CD ROM] Naval & Military Press (1998). This represented approximately 9% of the division's original infantry strength.
20 WO95/2093 6th Battn. The Wiltshire Regiment War Diary (1916) PRO, diary entry 5 Jan. See also: WO95/2086 (March 1916) op cit., diary entry 4 March; WO95/2087 (Jan-June 1916), op cit.
21 'Fighting of the 57th Brigade at LA BOISSELLE, from the 2nd to the night 5th/6th July'. WO95/2085 'North Staffords' (July 1916), op cit.

The composition of the division's brigades on entering battle had changed somewhat since the turn of the year; now reflecting an approximate 25/75 split between specialists and riflemen. Each battalion roughly comprised between 550 and 800 infantrymen.[22] Of these, around 100 were specialists. The North Staffords, for instance, recorded 56 Lewis Gunners and 34 bombers.[23] However, the same battalion also noted that: 'Each platoon had two bombing squads of 5 men each.'[24] This indicates that around 100 riflemen were expected to act as *pro tempore* bombers, alongside the official bombers.[25] These battalion specialists were accompanied by around 150 machine-gunners and 100 'Stokes' trench mortars serving under brigade command.[26] For the remaining riflemen there were a plethora of 'officially' designated passive activities: carrying parties, runners, signallers and so forth.[27] According to the North Staffords' CO, this only 'left a platoon roughly 20 men [out of 40] for purely fighting purposes.'[28] A small number of officers and NCOs from each battalion were also kept behind to form the cadre of a 'replenished' unit, in the event of heavy casualties.[29]

1 July 1916

The failure of the seven day artillery bombardment to destroy the German machine-gunners and their apparatus transformed the infantry's relatively straightforward task of 'occupation and consolidation' into a murderous struggle. 56th Brigade recorded how: 'The attack by the 8th Division on the left against OVILLERS was held up by terrific hostile machine gun fire…[causing] very heavy casualties in consequence.'[30] All was not lost, however. By midday '34th Division had penetrated the first and second lines South of LA BOISSELLE…'[31] At 4.30pm III Corps finally ordered 19th Division into the inferno – their objective to 'attack LA BOISSELLE and trenches S.E. of it … with 57th and 58th Brigades.' III Corps proposed to cover the assault with the archetypal preliminary artillery bombardment; 'Artillery [will]…bombard

---

22 Exact figures are only available for the 56th Brigade, which recorded that 'nos. of men actually fighting of units at commencement of operations: R Lanc R 21 off. 814 O.R. E Lanc R 16 off. 770 O.R. S. Lanc R 21 off. 636 O.R. N. Lanc R 14 off. 514 O.R. M.G. Coy 5 off 147 OR. TMB 2 off. 118 OR…' WO95/2075 Headquarters 56th Brigade War Diary (June 1916) PRO.
23 WO95/2085 'North Staffords' (June 1916), op cit. Diary entry 30 June. It would seem that no specialist role was 'officially' allocated to the 'snipers' during these attacks.
24 Ibid.
25 How typical this arrangement was, however, is difficult to surmise.
26 WO95/2075 (June 1916), op cit.
27 See WO95/2085 'North Staffords' (June 1916), op cit., diary entry 30 June.
28 Ibid.
29 See WO95/2086 (June 1916), op cit., diary entry 30 June.
30 WO95/2075 (July 1916), op cit., diary entry 1 July.
31 'III Corps Summary of Operations 1st to 31st July, 1916.' WO95/673 (July 1916), op cit.

the objective for 30 minutes starting from Zero. Minus 30. At zero minus 5 the fire will become intense. At Zero the fire will lift and the infantry will assault.'[32]

The North Staffords recorded that at 8pm 'orders were received to advance to the front line, and bomb out LA BOISSELLE, starting the attack at 10.30pm.'[33] The Cheshires were informed that: 'The object of the attack is to bomb and block all the trenches, to clear out all dugouts and to consolidate on a line between [map ref].'[34] The North Staffords recorded that the 'Bn was fallen in, and all the Bombers collected at the lead…'[35] Now the failures of the morning came back to haunt these attacking troops. The North Staffords continued that: 'We then started up the one communication trench, which was found to be blocked with wounded, and odd men…[of 34th Division] who had made an attack in the morning. As a result of this, our bombers did not get up till 12 midnight, and the 10th Worcesters, who were going to help us in this attack, were in the same plight. The 3 coys that were following…did not arrive up till 4.30A.M.'[36] The Worcesters offered their own account: 'In the communications trench confusion reigned. Wounded were being brought out, we were trying to get in, carrying parties were trying to go both ways, it was raining and the trench was knee-deep in mud.'[37]

Battalion HQ, judging that the chances of success were fading with the dawn, now called a halt. 'As a result of this [North Staffords recorded], we did not attack, because it was broad daylight then, and we were meant to attack in the dark…This was duly reported to 57th Bde. who approved of the action taken.'[38] The Cheshires and Fusiliers encountered similar chaos, and their CO responded on behalf of their men with similar foresight. As the Cheshires moved forward they found 'the trenches were very much knocked about and full of wounded and dead and the enemy was shelling them heavily.'[39] Stranded in these avenues of dead and dying, with darkness falling, and the blackening ether filled with screeching annihilation, the Cheshires became disorientated, disordered and then lost. Lieut-Col. R.B. Worgan (CO Cheshires) reported that 'I found CAPT WARD O.C. D Coy who told me the Bn had got separated and he did not know where the remainder were.'[40] It took Worgan two further hours to reorganise (some of) his battalion and send them forward towards the jump-off point.

32 '3rd Corps Operational Order No. 71.', issued 4.30pm 1 July. WO95/673 (July 1916), op cit.
33 WO95/2085 'North Staffords' (July 1916), op cit., diary entry 8pm 1 July.
34 'BM488', issued 7pm 1 July. WO95/2090 9th Battn. The Cheshire Regiment War Diary (July 1916) PRO.
35 WO95/2085 'North Staffords' (July 1916), op cit., diary entry 8pm 1 July.
36 Ibid.
37 WO95/2086 (July 1916), op cit. Diary entry 1 July.
38 Ibid.
39 'Personal narrative of events from 7pm 1st July to 3.30am 5th July', written by Lt-Col R.B. Worgan, CO 9th Cheshires. WO95/2090 (July 1916), op cit.
40 Ibid.

He concluded that 'it was then too late to carry out the original plan of attack and… [I] went back to report the position personally to the Brigadier.'[41]

Inertia then prevailed until 2.30am, when the Cheshires were 'order[ed] to attack the German front line without delay.'[42] Yet the Cheshires remained rooted to the British frontline. It would seem that a lack of specialists at the sharp end was now stalling the attack. The aforementioned Ward, endeavouring to reconnoitre the ground in front of his company 'went across to the captured German trenches and was informed by the Major in command [Maj. A. Carton de Wiart, the Gloucesters CO], that he was short of trained Grenadiers [bombers] and MG's … [Ward then] 'sent over [his] 2 MG's and attached Bn Grenadiers (about 12), followed by the whole of D Coy.'[43] Meanwhile, Ward himself moved forward to check the situation in the 'New Crater' (the proposed jump off point). He found the Crater 'occupied by about 40 or 50 officers and men [34th Division], dug in round the front edge and right flank. The officer i/c did not think there was room to move a Coy into it.'[44] Ward now made a decision which overrode his orders, and prioritised his men's safety over the objective. He reported that: 'By this time it was daylight and enemy snipers were very active. I decided that no good purpose could result by moving the Coy into the CRATER which was already quite strongly held …'[45] D Company subsequently prepared to defend their current position.

With the Cheshires digging in, the advance of the supporting unit, the Fusiliers, was likewise stalled. At this juncture Lieut-Col. R.A. Berners (CO Fusiliers) took steps to postpone the attack until more propitious circumstances could be arranged. 58th Brigade reported that: 'A consultation with O.C. 9 RW Fusiliers made it clear that no attack could be carried out until the afternoon…This scheme was approved by 19th Division…'[46] Fearing a massacre, battalion commanders had protected their infantrymen from merciless German machine-gun and sniper fire, and (with due deference) petitioned for a change of plan. In the chaotic atmosphere of battle, infantrymen were once again calling the shots.

With the attack halted most battalions were ordered to retire: many had seen nothing of the enemy, none had fired in anger. Lieut-Col. C.R.P. Winser (CO South Lancs) candidly summarised the effects of this ultimately barren 24 hours upon his troops: 'The whole movement had been exceedingly tiring, executed under a very hot sun, through crowded trenches, with constant halts: above all, with no achieved object.

41 Ibid.
42 Ibid.
43 'D Coy. narrative of events from about 5pm – 1.7.16 to about 2.30pm – 2.7.16.' WO95/2090 (July 1916), op cit.
44 Ibid. 58th Brigade recorded the following day 'pushed 3 Companies across to the CRATER which was already held by portions of 34th Division.' WO95/2087 (July 1916), op cit., diary entry 2 July.
45 Ibid.
46 WO95/2087 (July 1916), op cit., diary entry 7am 2 July.

Consequently, men + officers who had been fresh were rendered almost out of count for immediate fighting purposes by fatigue.'⁴⁷ Most of these weary troops, however, received a brief respite. The Loyals reported for instance: 'Relieved and marched back to Railway cottage [map ref] at 8.15am, slept in field and rested all day.'⁴⁸ Some were not so fortunate. 'D' Company of the Cheshires endured 12 hours of hostile shelling, and lost all their officers and NCOs bar one.⁴⁹ Despite this dire experience, Ward (himself a casualty) wrote that: 'The men were excellent and performed their duties with a willingness and cheerfulness that was deserving of the highest praise and made one feel proud of them.'⁵⁰ A glowing tribute which speaks of the high passive combat morale of the OR infantrymen on 1 July. Significantly, good leadership did not leave the battlefield when Ward himself fell. Ward noted that 'Sgt Boyd performed all his duties exceptionally well and I found him most reliable.'⁵¹

La Boisselle: 2-6 July

Over the following five days, following their brief stay of execution on 1 July, all units of 19th Division finally took their combative bow in the 'great offensive'. With 'Plan A' in disarray, the division's senior commanders set about devising other means by which the German's seemingly impregnable frontline could be penetrated. A preliminary bombardment of La Boisselle was rejected in favour of a 'feint' (or 'Chinese') bombardment upon Ovillers.⁵² Rather than attack in AF, the leading battalion would 'begin to gain ground by sending small bombing parties up the communications trench from [map ref] and parties to work along the frontline trench running East from this C.T.' Only once this objective was secured would the supporting battalion 'attack across the open from our front line trench.'⁵³ Despite such cautious overtones, these orders were still delivered with the menacing caveat of 'captur[ing] LA BOISSELLE this afternoon without fail and regardless of losses, as the success of the whole operations there depends on its capture.'⁵⁴ Yet it was largely because battalion commanders and their infantrymen could not completely disregard the lives of their comrades, nor their own lives, that this demand was not satiated for another two and a half days. The

---

47 WO95/2081 (July 1916), op cit., diary entry 1July. See also WO95/2086 (July 1916), op cit., diary entry 2 July.
48 WO95/2080 (July 1916), op cit., diary entry 2 July. See also WO95/2081 (July 1916), op cit. Diary entry 2 July.
49 'D Coy. narrative of events from about 5pm – 1.7.16 to about 2.30pm – 2.7.16.' WO95/2090 (July 1916), op cit.
50 Ibid.
51 Ibid.
52 'Operation Order No. 55', issued 2 July. WO95/2087 (July 1916), op cit.
53 'Operation Order No. 55', issued July 2nd. WO95/2087 (July 1916), op cit.
54 Ibid.

'fog of war' that hung across the battlefield allowed battalion commanders to modify the orders of their seniors in defence of their infantrymen's welfare.

Reflecting upon the ensuing attack on La Boisselle, Onslow (GOC 57th Brigade) recorded that: 'The case was exceptional, and as far as one knows outside the experience of any member of the Brigade. The fighting devolved into a struggle for the possession of a strong point, built in and round a small village…the whole being under-mined with subterranean passages connecting up mine heads and deep dug-outs, with numerous lateral and longitudinal communication trenches.'[55] The partial sanctioning of their superior commanders, and the subterranean nature of the battlefield, gave the infantry enough latitude to fight this unexpected battle largely in accordance with their prefered combat behaviour and collective combat morale. Consequently, as Winser (CO South Lancs) recognised, it was: 'The Battn. Bombers [who] did most of this fighting.'[56]

Leading the division into battle, the Cheshires found immediate reason to eschew the overland charge in favour of a subterranean bombing assault. Having 'commence[d] by sending small bombing parties up the communication trenches', Worgan (CO Cheshires) 'then decided to attack the support line proper [frontage 490 yards] over ground', as per orders, covered by their own Lewis Gunners.[57] However, Worgan reported that: 'Unfortunately the advance was stuck up by a deep and wide communication trench across our front.' He then decided upon a new plan of attack: 'This trench was entered and occupied. Bombing parties were formed and were ordered to work forward to the support line [the objective] and from there work out to the right and left.'[58] In their wake followed the Fusiliers and Wiltshires, supported by: 'A + B Coys [of the Welch, in reserve, who] were ordered to do duty as carrying parties and about 5pm commenced to form a line from our old front line trench across NO MANS LAND to the village of LA BOISSELLE…'[59]

By dusk, after four to five hours of combat, 58th Brigade's assault had faltered; still someway short of the objective. It would seem that the balance of firepower had eventually swung away from the brigade, persuading battalion COs to call a halt. Berners (CO Fusiliers) reported that 'bombing attacks were immediately initiated along the trenches…and considerable progress was made, but at some cost owing to bombing counter attacks delivered by the enemy in cooperation with his snipers, who

---

55 'Fighting of the 57th Brigade at LA BOISSELLE, from the 2nd to the night 5th/6th July'. WO95/2085 'North Staffords' (July 1916), op cit.
56 'Precis of Fighting 3rd – 9th July 1916.' Written by Lt-Col C.R.P. Winser and sent to 56th Brigade 13 July. WO95/2081 (July 1916), op cit.
57 WO95/2090 (July 1916), op cit., diary entry 2 July.
58 Ibid.
59 WO95/2092 9th Battn. The Welch Regiment War Diary (July 1916) PRO, diary entry 2 July.

proved to be very deadly.'[60] Worgan judged that these counter attacks had left the Cheshires too short of men to force the objective, reporting that: 'At about 8.30pm we had gone as far as I decided our strength permitted, in fact we were holding the line rather weakly …'[61] Perhaps, however, the Cheshire's primary problem was a lack of commanders. 58th Brigade recorded that 'casualties, considering the severity of the fighting, had not so far been excessive. Although the 9 Cheshire was left at the end of the day with only the Commanding Officer and one officer.'[62] Whether the infantry would concur with their senior commander's interpretation of 'excessive' is questionable. The Wiltshires, for instance, suffered 315 casualties – a casualty rate of around forty five percent – before their CO chose consolidation over the objective.[63] It is worth reiterating that battalion COs made these decisions fully aware that their orders were to capture the objective 'without fail and regardless of loss.'[64] This indicates that this uncompromising order was open to some tacit renegotiation.

Whilst 58th Brigade were being repulsed from La Boisselle, '2 Companies (C & D) and two sections of Regimental Bombers' belonging to the East Lancs, in conjunction with 101st Brigade, executed a conspicuously successful bombing attack upon 'Heligoland Redoubt'.[65] Capt. H.W. House's (OC C Company) account of the attack offers some insights into the combat behaviour of bombing parties attempting to 'clear out' (to use the contemporary military euphemism) the deep chambers and dark corridors that encompassed La Boisselle.[66] The bombing parties initially experienced little resistance; encountering outnumbered pockets of German troops who either retreated, or chose surrender over being blown apart by a bomb slung surreptitiously into their

60 WO95/2092 9th Battn. The Royal Welsh Fusiliers War Diary (July 1916) PRO, diary entry 2 July.
61 'Personal narrative of events from 7pm 1st July to 3.30am 5th July', written by Lt-Col R.B. Worgan, CO 9th Cheshires. WO95/2090 (July 1916), op cit.
62 WO95/2087 (July 1916), op cit. Diary entry 2 July.
63 WO95/2093 (July 1916), op cit. Casualties for 2 July were recorded as follows: 4 officers 35 ORs killed; 4 officers 237 ORs wounded; 35 ORs missing. The CR was 45%, based upon an estimated strength of 700. Casualty rates for the other attacking battalions are less accurate because they are based upon the period up to 4 July, and not individual operations. The Fusiliers recorded 186 casualties (8 officers): a CR of 27% based upon the same estimated strength. WO95/2092 'Fusiliers' (July 1916), op cit. The Cheshires recorded 307 casualties (13 officers): a CR of 44% based upon the same estimated strength. As a mark of their heavy casualties, the diary recoded on the 6th that 'The Battalion was reorganised into two platoons per Coy…'WO95/2090 (July 1916), op cit.
64 WO95/2090 (July 1916), op cit., diary entry 2 July.
65 WO95/2079 7th Battn. The East Lancashire Regiment War Diary (July 1916) PRO, diary entry 2 July.
66 'Report on operations of two Coys (C&D) during a period of time from 12 noon July 2nd till 3am July 4th 1916, assisted by half the Regt. Bombers.' Compiled 14 July by Capt. H.W. House, OC C Coy during operations. Ibid.

dugout.⁶⁷ House reported that the 'Regt. Bombers, under Lieut. E.G. Edwardes, cleared from [map ref] in which portion they captured 5 prisoners and accounted for approximately the same number ...'⁶⁸ Meantime the following C Company liberated some wounded of the 34th Division 'who were prisoners in the deep dug outs.' A detachment of C Company then 'captured 8 Germans about [map ref] and accounted for a considerable number in dugouts.' The balance of firepower was now momentarily wrestled from the East Lancs by the entrance of enemy machine-guns. House reported that 'C Coy pushed along the old German front line, bombing most of the way, to [map ref] at which point the Germans retired up a communication trench to [map ref]. Half C Coy followed and were held up at [map ref] by enemy block and 2 M.G.s.' The machine-gun was a less potent a killer below ground, however (which is largely why the infantry preferred subterranean attacks to overland charges), and the intuition of Edwardes, allied to the high combat morale of his bombers, succeeded in out-flanking the 'block' and 'bombing out the M.G. and party who withdrew...' D Company 'had meantime cleared the main German support line to this point and taken 17 more prisoners, and accounted for quite as many.' With dusk falling the East Lancs then consolidated. They had taken 58 prisoners yet suffered only 14 wounded; which underlines the impression that their superior numbers had declined their adversary against much interpersonal combat, and moreover, indicates the East Lancs' willingness to accept the surrender.⁶⁹

Dawn on the 3rd saw 57th Brigade ordered to 'join hands' with 58th Brigade in a redoubling of the division's struggle to capture La Boisselle.⁷⁰ Plans were now changing by the hour, upon a battlefield where communications also travelled by the hour, leaving already stressed battalion commanders precious little time for organisation. The North Staffords reported the damaging effects of such delays: 'Even this time, the whole scheme was too hurried, no time was allowed to explain to the men what was required of them.'⁷¹ Yet these communication problems delivered a small but precious boon to the infantry: the 'fog of war'. As 56th Brigade later realised, this stolid 'fog' ensured that senior commanders 'were rather left in the dark as to how the

67 On 31 June the East Lancs' recorded strength was 786 infantrymen, therefore two coys. and half the Bombers would have equated to around 375 officers and ORs. In House's account the German defenders were only ever counted in tens and twenties. WO95/2075 (July 1916), op cit.
68 'Report on operations of two Coys (C&D) during a period of time from 12 noon July 2nd till 3am July 4th 1916, assisted by half the Regt. Bombers.' Compiled 14 July by Capt. H.W. House, OC C Coy during operations. WO95/2079 (July 1916), op cit.
69 Ibid.
70 '[E]ntries from my Battn War Diary July 1st – 6th for Brigade War Diary', sent by Lt-Col R.A. Berners to 58th Brigade on 6 July. WO95/2087 (July 1916), op cit.
71 WO95/2085 'North Staffords' (July 1916), op cit., diary entry 3 July. See also WO95/2087 (July 1916), op cit., diary entries 3 July.

attack was proceeding.'[72] Battalion commanders were at liberty to modify the orders of their seniors to protect the welfare of their infantrymen.

As the following accounts indicate, the infantry were quick to override orders and turn to their preferred method of assault – the subterranean bombing attack – partly to avoid suffering high casualties. The North Staffords began the attack cautiously; only sending forward one platoon to secure the ground for their bombers: 'The first party to go over was one platoon of D Coy under 2nd Lt C.J. Hunter. They went over about 4.5A.M. and seized the crater in front of the La Boisselle salient, before the Bombers entered…[From here] all 24 bombing parties entered the village before the other troops.'[73] Meantime, the Cheshires and Wiltshires had 'decided to bomb down the two saps towards the second line…[and] Bombing and carrying parties were [subsequently] organised.'[74] Worgan (CO Cheshires), explaining the reasoning behind this decision, later informed 58th Brigade that 'it would have been impossible to attack this line over ground as one flank were in the air and the front was held by machine guns…further there were four rows of strong uncut wire in front *and we should have been wiped out*…[my emphasis]'[75] We can see that, in taking this course of action, Worgan overrode his orders in defence of his men's welfare. Bombing their way along the subterranean approaches to La Boisselle, the assaulting battalions initially enjoyed the same success (and seemingly same firepower advantage) as the East Lancs the previous day. The North Staffords reported that: 'The Bn swept up the village and trenches fairly easily at first, up to a point about ¾ way up…By this time, about 100 of the enemy had surrendered.'[76]

Capturing the village itself proved less 'easy'. La Boisselle afforded little concealment for the attacking infantry, but the half destroyed hamlet provided a haven for the German snipers; the fortified village strained the infantry's supply lines, but housed (in some safety) abundant German reinforcements. Consequently, the balance of firepower swung like a pendulum in time with the infantry's entry and exit from the village. The North Staffords reported that 'the bombs ran short, in spite of a party of Glosters helping in the carrying; so a local counter attack by the enemy succeeded in driving us back to a point about ¼ way up the village.'[77] The sound of retreating infantrymen momentarily drowned out the voice of command, which, due to enemy snipers, was already becoming rather faint. Confusion and disorder ensued. 'Just when

72 WO95/2075 (July 1916), op cit., diary entry 8 July.
73 WO95/2085 'North Staffords' (July 1916), op cit., diary entry 3 July.
74 WO95/2090 (July 1916), op cit., diary entry 3 July. See also WO95/2092 'Welch' (July 1916), op cit.
75 'Personal narrative of events from 7pm 1st July to 3.30am 5th July', written by Lt-Col R.B. Worgan, CO 9th Cheshires. WO95/2090 (July 1916), op cit.
76 WO95/2085 'North Staffords' (July 1916), op cit., diary entry 3 July. See also WO95/2092 'Fusiliers' (July 1916), op cit. Diary entry 3 July.
77 WO95/2085 'North Staffords' (July 1916), op cit., diary entry 3 July. See also WO95/2086 (July 1916), op cit. Diary entry 3 July.

this withdrawal was taking place [the North Staff recorded], at about 6 A.M., the C.O. (Major C. WEDGEWOOD. D.S.O.) and Major Carnegy (cmdg B Coy) were killed by enemy snipers; who were plentiful, and claimed many officers. At this point, many officers had been killed or wounded, and the B[att]ns were mixed up in the line (it was afterwards found that about 150 men had been fighting in a party well away to the right flank) …'[78] Having retreated to the outer edges of the village the North Staffords were able to regroup, reinstate command, reinstate the supply lines and reinforce their beleaguered troops. Consequently, 'an advance was made well beyond the C.T. leading to OVILLERS. A block was established in this trench as we passed.' The pendulum then inexorably recoiled. 'The advance was continued, but a counter-attack on our left unfortunately succeeded in forcing this block, and as a result of this and more men arriving to re-inforce [sic] the enemy, the whole line fell back, and finally consolidated about ½ way through the village.'[79] The time was now noon; the battalion had been fighting for eight hours and suffered a casualty rate of thirty six percent.[80]

The Cheshires endured a similar reversal of the balance of firepower. Worgan recorded that: 'The Bombing party of the 9th Cheshires under Lieut Watts [Loos veteran], bombed right down the sap into the second line, working to the right and left.' As they neared the centre of the village, however, 'the enemy put in a strong bombing counter attack and drove us back again to our original position which we managed to hold and block.'[81] We have seen how battalion commanders invariably attributed these reversals to a shortfall of manpower and firepower. We can also look beyond the views of these commanders and witness that the infantry were *willing* to sustain between thirty and forty percent casualties before surrendering the objective to safety. The combat morale of the infantry therefore also held a salient influence over the outcome of this battle. This is not, of course, to deny that manpower and firepower (and success) themselves influenced the infantry's combat morale. It would

78   WO95/2085 'North Staffords' (July 1916), op cit., diary entry 3 July. See also 'Fighting of the 57th Brigade at LA BOISSELLE, from the 2nd to the night 5th/6th July'. Ibid.
79   Ibid. See also 'entries from my Battn War Diary July 1st – 6th for Brigade War Diary', sent by Lt-Col R.A. Berners to 58th Brigade on 6 July. WO95/2087 (July 1916), op cit.
80   WO95/2085 'North Staffords' (July 1916), op cit., diary entry 3 July. Casualties for 3 July were recorded as follows: 4 officers 28 ORs killed; 8 officers 210 ORs wounded; 34 ORs missing. CR 36%, based upon a recorded strength of 790. The Gloucesters recorded 302 casualties – including 4 officers killed and 6 officers wounded – CR around 40% based upon an estimated strength of 700. WO95/2085 8th Battn. The Gloucestershire Regiment War Diary (PRO) 1916. The Royal Warwicks, in reserve, suffered 2 officers killed 1 wounded (the CO), 27 other casualties. WO95/2085 10th Battn. The Royal Warwickshire Regiment War Diary (July 1916) PRO, diary entry 3 July. The Worcesters recorded a higher casualty list of 362 – including 10 officers killed or believed killed, and 5 officers wounded – CR around 50% based upon an estimated strength of 700. The Worcesters recorded that 'a heavy shrapnel fire was opened [upon them whilst they lay out in the open, waiting to advance] causing considerable casualties.' Which might account for the higher CR. WO95/2086 (July 1916), op cit.
81   WO95/2090 (July 1916), op cit.,Diary entry 3 July.

seem reasonable to assume that a well stocked, equipped and confident unit stood a greater chance of also being a *willing* unit. Worgan was the first battalion commander, however, to break ranks and suggest that *fatigue* (or, put differently, the infantry's *ability* to fight) had also played a part. The Cheshires' CO observed that after 10 or so hours of sporadic but intense combat, with very little rest: 'Our men were so tired that the enemy could easily out throw them.'[82]

By the end of the battle for La Boisselle, an understanding of the influence of fatigue had reached the division's senior commanders. Reflecting upon these operations, Onslow (GOC 57th Brigade) wrote that: 'In this style of fighting it was found that nearly all the Regimental Bombers of all four battalions were drawn early into the battle and after an hour or twos' fighting were *quite worn out and could advance no more*. Every effort was made to relieve these men by any other bombers who could be found, and these were then able to force an advance for a short distance. These in turn required relieving and this was found to be a very difficult matter...[Therefore] bombing parties must be relieved frequently, they advance a certain distance, and then *being tired and worn out, they block and remain stationary* throwing a large number of bombs unnecessarily [my emphasis].'[83]

Onslow's observations clearly attest that even the infantry's most 'committed trench fighters' (the bombers) could only withstand aggressive combat *physically* for a 'few hours'. Perhaps, however, more can be drawn from these remarks. We have already witnessed the chain of command's (especially battalion commander's) increasing willingness to accept 'commotional' shellshock as a genuine malady, and justification for leaving the battlefield. It is possible that Onslow was in fact diagnosing what later armies would call 'battle fatigue'; yet could either not understand the malady in these terms, or could not report it with such candour. These bombers, for instance, were still *physically* capable of 'throwing a large number of bombs' *beyond* the point of their becoming 'tired and worn out', but this aggression was now evidently shorn of concentration and composure. It could be inferred therefore that *mental fatigue* was undermining the bomber's ability to fight.

With 57th and 58th Brigades depleted and fatigued after two days of aggressive combat, the division's part in capturing La Boisselle now passed onto the marginally fresher reserve unit, 56th Brigade. Despite unpropitious beginnings, 56th Brigade experienced a slightly deeper 'bite' and more tenacious 'hold' than their forerunners, and finally overwhelmed this most obdurate of strongholds. The initial assault was once again bedevilled by communication troubles and rapidly changing orders. The Loyals recorded being: 'Sent up to Old British front line without guides or any instructions, except to act as support to 7/R Lanc. Rgt. [King's Own] who were in old

---

82 Ibid.
83 'Fighting of the 57th Brigade at LA BOISSELLE, from the 2nd to the night 5th/6th July'. WO95/2085 'North Staffords' (July 1916), op cit.

front line German trench.'⁸⁴ Lieut-Col. W.J.M. Hill (CO Loyals) was later to bemoan that: 'There was still no communication between Brigade and Battalion H.Qrs…Only means of communication was by pigeon.'⁸⁵ The King's Own themselves were less in the dark, recording that: 'At 8.30am the Battalion was ordered to attack and consolidate a line S of the village giving an advance of 500 [yards].'⁸⁶ News that 'this attack was delayed for one hour' did not however reach the South Lancs in time to prevent B and C Companies advancing in keeping with the original Zero.⁸⁷ The artillery were also apparently blind to latest developments, because the King's Own reported that: 'The preliminary artillery bombardment did not take place …'⁸⁸

Despite these initial setbacks the King's Own experienced some moderate success, reporting that 'the Batt launched the attack up 3 communication trenches leading to the objective … The advance was finally held up by strong machine gun positions to the N.E. of the village[,] consequently a line was taken up and consolidated giving an advance of about 300 [yards]'⁸⁹ Winser (CO South Lancs) later detailed why the enemy's machine-guns were invariably the *bête noire* of any overland infantry assault, recording that 'I have no suggestions to offer as to how to overcome hostile Machine Guns. So far as my experience goes they had no flanks to get round, i.e., as soon as one tried to get around the flank of one gun one came under close fire of another.'⁹⁰ Prior to coming up against these hostile machine-gunners, the King's Own had found: 'The enemy largely occup[ying] their deep dug outs from which they were ejected [presumably meaning surrendered or retreated] or killed.'⁹¹ A lack of recorded opposition suggests the enemy's snipers and reinforcements had vacated the village, leaving the bombers (and supports) to 'clear up' by means of stealthily executed bombing raids. However, although the battalion took 27 prisoners, they themselves suffered 86 casualties; which indicates the toll taken by the enemy's machine-guns before the infantry sacrificed the objective to safety.⁹²

---

84 WO95/2080 (July 1916), op cit., diary entry 3/4 July.
85 Ibid. Diary entry 7 July. See also 'Precis of Fighting 3rd – 9th July 1916.' Written by Lt-Col C.R.P. Winser and sent to 56th Brigade 13 July. WO95/2081 (July 1916), op cit.
86 WO95/2078 7th Battn. King's Own (Royal Lancaster Regiment) War Diary (July 1916) PRO, diary entry 4 July.
87 'Precis of Fighting 3rd – 9th July 1916.' Written by Lt-Col C.R.P. Winser and sent to 56th Brigade 13 July. WO95/2081 (July 1916), op cit.
88 WO95/2078 (July 1916), op cit., diary entry 4 July.
89 Ibid.
90 'Precis of Fighting 3rd – 9th July 1916.' Written by Lt-Col C.R.P. Winser and sent to 56th Brigade 13 July. WO95/2081 (July 1916), op cit.
91 WO95/2078 (July 1916), op cit., diary entry 4 July.
92 Ibid. The breakdown was 16 ORs killed, 2 officers and 66 ORs wounded, 2 ORs missing. Some of these casualties were also probably caused by 'the enemy's artillery [which] was [according to 56th Brigade] both active and accurate throughout the day.' WO95/2075 (July 1916), op cit. Diary entry 4 July.

The division was not always on the wrong end of the one-sided 'infantry versus machine-gun' conflict. Their own machine-gunners were also exacting a high toll on the German defenders during the capture of La Boisselle. For example, 57th Brigade Machine Gun Company reported that a '2nd Lt PHILLIPS [had] observed Germans moving across gaps in communication trenches towards LA BOISSELLE, fire was opened and good effect obtained, one of the gaps was afterwards seen to be blocked by 9 dead bodies.'[93] The infantry's own distance killers were also endeavouring to make a more direct intervention in the 'infantry versus machine-gun' conflict, transforming the battle into a 'machine-gun versus machine-gun' duel. The same company reported that: 'Some Germans and two M.G.s and possibly a third M.G. were seen at [map ref]…2nd Lt PHILLIPS opened fire and assisted by an Artillery Observation Officer succeeded in killing two men and putting one gun out of action, the remainder disappeared.'[94]

In the intervening time the South Lancs' bombers were seemingly experiencing a more arduous fight. 'The enemy made a very stout resistance in the houses which were fortified [Winser (CO) noted], and in numerous shell craters and small traverse trenches…A house at [map ref] proved a particularly formidable obstacle and nearly two hours were occupied in outflanking and capturing it. This turned out to be the Battalion Commander's house, and was in a very strong state of defence.'[95]

Winser inadvertently indicated the partially 'depersonalised' nature of this combat behaviour, recording that: 'Officers and all my men who did any bombing are unanimous in stating that they could out throw the enemy by about 5 yards.'[96] This suggests that 'bomber versus bomber' conflicts were often executed at a distance of at least ten yards, often being executed from behind barricades. The adversary was often a shadowy figure whose fate could only be guessed at; giving to the hand bomb the sanitising elements of visual distance and automation. Just to underline the infantry's axiom 'bombers fight, riflemen carry', Winser also noted that this unwavering 'attack was carried out by the Company bombers under 2nd Lieut. W.E.C. Sturman, the remainder of the Company feeding them with bombs and supplying replacements to casualties.'[97] However, Winser's observation also indicates that, as the battalion's five to ten percent most committed trench fighters became casualties, replacements had to be found (in the immediate short term at least) from amongst the previously less aggressively inclined majority. Perhaps, therefore, their elevation to the 'sharp end' was another factor in the eventual faltering of these bombing attacks.

93 WO95/2086 57th Brigade Machine Gun Company War Diary (July 1916) PRO, diary entry 5 July.
94 Ibid.
95 'Precis of Fighting 3rd – 9th July 1916.' Written by Lt-Col C.R.P. Winser and sent to 56th Brigade 13 July. WO95/2081 (July 1916), op cit.
96 Ibid.
97 Ibid. See also WO95/2080 (July 1916), op cit.

With La Boisselle now in British hands, the German artillery were at liberty to bombard the already decimated village. The South Lancs recorded that: 'During the afternoon the enemy bombarded LA BOISSELLE heavily. The night was fairly quiet and consolidation went well… [But next day] There was a considerable amount of shelling all day and night and a lot of casualties.'[98] Whilst the South Lancs consolidated, a 'short conference' between 56th Brigade's senior commanders decided that their fellow Lancastrians would 'push on again in the afternoon [of the 5th] and make good a further line of trenches.'[99] This once again gave the leading battalion, on this occasion the East Lancs, little time to receive, digest and disseminate these new instructions.

The resultant attack underlines just how important junior officers were in deciding eventual success or failure: partly because their presence stimulated a greater combat morale from their ORs; partly because, with orders changing by the hour, there was precious time to 'enlighten' the ORs, who were consequently 'in the dark' without their junior officers.

The 56th Brigade reported that the attack was 'carried out by means of bombers who bombed up the communication trenches supported by trench mortars.'[100] The advance then floundered upon the infantry's perennial adversary, the machine-gun. 'The Battalion gained its objective on the left [the East Lancs reported] but owing to the right being held up by heavy machine gun fire it had to fall back to its original line.'[101] The 90 casualties suffered in this reverse included 4 officers killed and 10 wounded: a staggering ratio of 1 officer to every 6 ORs, in a unit where only 1 in 50 of the strength were officers.[102] Robbed of the voice of command, the East Lancs fell back in some disarray and went beyond their 'original line', 56th Brigade reporting, with some circumspection, that the East Lancs had 'apparently received orders from C.O. of the Sherwood Foresters (under the command of 57th Brigade) to retire.'.[103] It then passed to the Loyals to partially save the day. "C' Coy [the battalion recorded, was] at once ordered to charge to regain lost ground: they went over the open in very good order, and retook the line vacated by the East Lancs.'[104] This 'very fine performance' was seemingly precipitated by very few (if any) officer casualties.[105] But not

---

98 'Precis of Fighting 3rd – 9th July 1916.' Written by Lt-Col C.R.P. Winser and sent to 56th Brigade 13 July. WO95/2081 (July 1916), op cit.
99 WO95/2075 (July 1916), op cit., diary 5 entry July.
100 WO95/2075 (July 1916), op cit., diary entry 5 July.
101 WO95/2079 (July 1916), op cit., diary entry 5 July.
102 Ibid. The breakdown was 4 officers 31 OR killed; 10 officers 49 OR wounded; no missing. The battalions strength on June 31st was 16 officers 770 ORs. WO95/2075 (July 1916), op cit.
103 WO95/2075 (July 1916), op cit., diary entry 5 July.
104 WO95/2080 (July 1916), op cit., diary entry 5 July.
105 Ibid. The diary made no mention of any officer casualties on this day. During the entire La Boisselle operation the battalion recorded 2 officers killed and 5 wounded, out of a compliment of 14 – half that suffered by the East Lancs. WO95/2075 (July 1916), op cit.

only was the voice of command sustained. The high combat morale of one junior officer, and particularly his willingness to engage in an act of ferocious depersonalised combat behaviour, turned the tables in the 'infantry versus machine-gun' conflict. The Loyals reported that 'Lieut. Wilkinson on the left held up some Germans with a Machine Gun as they were advancing down a trench, and in spite of the retirement of the East Lancs, by his prompt action he stopped a determined rush by the Huns.'[106] The Loyals then promptly re-imposed command upon the briefly errant East Lancs, reporting that: 'Captain Maule rendered great assistance in getting the East Lancs up again from the Old British front line back to their trenches.'[107]

Despite these salutary accounts, it seems that some of the gains of 4 July were still surrendered. With plans for the 'contemplated general advance' of the 7th resting upon the status quo of the 4th, 56th Brigade 'decided that the line which had been taken by the 7/R. Lanc. R. and then apparently lost should be made good *at all costs* by the night of July 6th [my emphasis].'[108] The East Lancs were subsequently given the chance to redeem themselves. The infantry's preferred method of attack initially brought about a stuttering advance. 56th Brigade recorded that: 'The attack commenced at 7-30pm but did not by any means meet with immediate success. The advance of the bombers was very slow, the enemy putting up stout resistance. About 10pm…considerable advance had been made but that the main objective was still untaken.'[109] With the proposed Zero for the next large-scale offensive looming, 56th Brigade lost patience with the subterranean bombing attack, and a 'message was then sent to O.C. 7/E. Lan. R. to make good the objective by a direct assault.'[110] Cloaked by darkness, this 'was eventually done and the position was taken, the Battn. killing about 40 Germans and destroying a machine gun.'[111] The loss of only one officer (missing), allied to the relatively small number of OR casualties (46), indicates that the voice of command was on this occasion sustained, and, moreover, that the enemy's machine-gun was 'silenced' before it could inflict the heavy casualties.[112]

Contalmaison: 7-9 July

With high command determined to push on, there was to be no immediate rest for the division's infantrymen. III Corps' next objectives were 'THE CUTTING,

---

106 WO95/2080 (July 1916), op cit., diary entry 5 July.
107 WO95/2080 (July 1916), op cit., diary entry 5 July.
108 WO95/2075 (July 1916), op cit., diary entry 6 July.
109 WO95/2075 (July 1916), op cit. Diary entry 6 July. The East Lancs' Bombers were being assisted by '2 Lieut Wigley and 16 bombers' of the King's Own. WO95/2078 (July 1916), op cit. Diary entry 6 July.
110 WO95/2075 (July 1916), op cit., diary entry 6 July.
111 Ibid.
112 The breakdown was 6 OR killed; 40 OR wounded; 1 officer missing (believed killed). WO95/2079 (July 1916), op cit., diary entry July 6th.

CONTALMAISON, BAILIFF WOOD.'[113] The 19th Division was given the task of capturing 'the trenches running West of BAILIFF WOOD towards LA BOISSELLE.'[114] 56th Brigade noted that their objective in this 'big attack' equated to 'a German Trench some 350 yards to its front.'[115] A visible indication of how far high command's expectations for a major set-piece battle had fallen since 1 July. The method of artillery cover was also changing. Although III Corps still proposed: 'An intensive artillery bombardment' prior to Zero, this particular fusillade would 'lift back gradually through CONTALMAISON and will continue at a deliberate rate on the line BAILIFF WOOD ... [The] Attacking troops will approach each objective as near as possible before the bombardment lifts.'[116]

Destruction therefore remained central to the artillery's method, yet the idea of simply keeping the enemy tied down in his trenches was entering their stratagem. The infantry were witnessing the growth pangs of the 'creeping barrage'. The infantry were, to begin with, understandably dubious over the wisdom of following a line of exploding shells, and DHQ gave 58th Brigade a choice: they could either 'creep up behind the receding artillery barrage, or so time a continuous advance, as to reach their objective at the time the barrage lifts from there...'[117]

Moreover, despite these evolutions in artillery tactics, the division's senior commanders kept faith with the preliminary subterranean bombing assault. DHQ ordered that: 'At Zero hour...9 Welch Regt will begin to bomb up the trenches running from [map refs]. Points [map ref] to be consolidated, and blocks established. At 10 minutes after Zero hour 9 Welch Regt will attack overground, and will capture enemy's line from [map ref] ...'[118] With the (albeit finite) acquiescence of their senior commanders, the Bombers consequently remained the vanguard of the infantry attack. The division's senior commanders were also scripting an enhanced role for the infantry's own distance killers, DHQ ordering that '4 M.G.s of 58 M.G. Coy and 4 Stokes Mortars...' were to support the attack.[119]

Measured against the splintered yardstick of the Somme offensive, 19th Division's attack on Contalmaison was relatively successful. Pinned down by a wall of fire from the artillery's creeping barrage, hit by infiltrating bombing parties, and faced with a wall of infantry emerging from the shroud of ballistics, many German defenders either surrendered or retreated. As a result, most of the objectives were captured (and subsequently held) a few hours after Zero, with marginally fewer casualties than had previously been suffered.

---

113 III Corps Operation Order No. 79', issued 6 July.
114 'III Corps Summary of Operations 1st to 31st July, 1916.' Ibid.
115 'B.M.265', WO/952075 (July 1916), op cit., diary entry 7 July.
116 'III Corps Operation Order No. 79', issued 6 July. WO95/673 (July 1916), op cit.
117 '19th Divisional Order No. 56', issued 6 July. WO95/2075 (July 1916), op cit.
118 '19th Divisional Order No. 56', issued 6 July. WO95/2087 (July 1916), op cit.
119 '19th Divisional Order No. 56', issued 6 July. WO95/2087 (July 1916), op cit.

The attack was delivered by 56th and 58th Brigades.[120] As with the assaults on La Boisselle, the infantry attacked Contalmaison with a diminutive sharp end supplied by a hefty tail. For example, 58th Brigade employed the entire strength of the Fusiliers (minus specialists) to fuel their advance.[121] For those at the sharp end – on this occasion the King's Own and Welch – the first steps behind a 'creeping barrage' did not auger well. The King's Own reported that: 'The attack began at 8am but our artillery had not lifted and at least 30 men were hit by our own shells…'[122] This indicates that the 'creeping barrage' did not wholly relieve the strain upon the infantry's passive combat morale during the advance. Nevertheless, the Bombers spearheading the attack were partially successful in paving the way for the infantry's overland charge. The King's Own recorded that: 'The right company (C) bombed up to point [map ref] and then the whole battalion charged across the open and carried the trench which was the objective.'[123] Whilst 58th Brigade were informed that 'various German communication trenches leading towards the enemy [had] been made good by bombing parties…' before 'the 9 Welch advanced over the open and gained its objectives, supported by the 6th Wiltshires …'[124]

The attack yielded a large haul of German prisoners. The King's Own, for instance, netted: '1 Major, 1 Captain, 5 Lieutenants, 400 [other ranks] prisoners [and] 3 machine guns (1 of which was turned on the enemy)…'[125] The capture of what amounted to an entire German battalion by a similar number of British infantrymen, is suggestive of the combat behaviour executed during this attack. A curtain of spitting death threatened destruction for any German foolish enough to raise his head above the parapet, whilst belligerent bombing sorties had already flushed out those seeking safety in the outlying communication trenches and dugouts. For once, a charging line of infantrymen were handed the firepower initiative, and subsequently reached the enemy's frontline largely unmolested. The successful capture or defence of the objective now rested upon the execution of interpersonal combat; either down the barrel of a gun, or at the point of a bayonet. We can assume that some of the antagonists were willing and able to engage in these acts. The plethora of German captives indicates, however,

---

120 At this time 56th Brigade also had command of the 13th Royal Fusiliers and 13th Rifle Brigade, in addition to the North Staffords. The King's Own were the only unit normally serving under the brigade to be involved in the attack on Contalmaison on the 7th, although the Loyals' bombers were 'lent out' to assist in the attack. WO95/2075 (July 1916), op cit. Diary entry 7 July.
121 WO95/2092 'Fusiliers' (July 1916), op cit., diary entry 7 July.
122 WO95/2078 (July 1916), op cit., diary entry 7 July.
123 Ibid. The Loyals noted that their 'Battalion Bombers helped attack of 7/R. Lanc. R.' WO95/2080 (July 1916), op cit., diary entry 7 July.
124 WO95/2087 (July 1916), op cit. Post battle report written by Berners (CO Fusiliers). The Welch reported receiving assistance from: 'A party of bombers from the 5th Battn. South Wales Borderers…' WO95/2092 9th Batt. The Welch Regiment War Diary (July 1916) PRO, diary entry 7 July.
125 WO95/2078 (July 1916), op cit, diary entry 7 July.

that the mere threat of this violence was enough to court the surrender. Of equal significance, the greater mass of King's Own infantrymen were more than willing to accept this surrender. When the battlefield was stripped of its depersonalised killers, posturing the act of interpersonal combat could often be enough to win the day.

Although III Corps observed that '19th Division [had] reached objective at 9.30am', the division's part in the fighting was far from over.[126] Despite recording conspicuous success, the King's Own admitted that: 'The centre and left companies [had] made slower progress.'[127] The Wiltshires were less charitable in their interpretation, recording that '56th Brigade on our right attempted to attack BAILIFF wood and CONTALMAISON but were driven back thereby leaving our line in the 'air' with a gap of 600 yards. In the afternoon front line suffered casualties from German snipers on our right.'[128] This was probably too harsh a judgement upon the 56th Brigade, because 24th Division had also been 'driven out of CONTALMAISON and intermediate line', further exposing 58th Brigade's right flank.[129] Moreover, the 'clearing' operations executed by their own bombers had not been entirely successful. The Welch reported that: 'During the afternoon a number of casualties were caused by snipers from the rear and it was found that some Germans were still in the trench between [map ref].'[130] If the Bombers of 58th Brigade were partially culpable for the suffering of their fellow infantrymen, then they were soon to make amends, as the burden of killing the enemy once more became their own. Berners (CO Fusiliers) reported that: 'During the night of the 7th July the enemy communications trenches were again cleared and held by bombers and the party of German snipers which had harassed our line was successfully accounted for.'[131] Long (CO Wiltshires) recorded that: 'These snipers however were killed by our bombers late in the evening.'[132] Shrouded by darkness, the infantry's most 'committed trench fighters' had infiltrated the enemy's lines and destroyed this foe.

In capturing and holding the environs of Contalmaison the infantry had been willing to suffer between twenty and thirty percent casualty rate. For example, the King's Own recorded that: 'Our losses were 1 Officer killed and 6 wounded. Other ranks 14 killed 122 wounded, 13 missing', which represented a casualty rate of around twenty percent.[133] Whilst the Welch suffered 224 casualties, including 7 officers,

---

126 WO95/673 (July 1916), op cit., diary entry 7 July.
127 WO95/2078 (July 1916), op cit., diary entry 7 July.
128 WO95/2093 (July 1916), op cit., diary entry 7 July. See also WO95/2087 (July 1916), op cit., diary entries 7 July.
129 WO95/673 (July 1916), op cit., diary entry 7 July.
130 WO95/2092 'Welch' (July 1916), op cit., diary entry 7 July. See also WO95/2092 'Fusiliers' (July 1916), op cit., diary entry 7 July.
131 WO95/2087 (July 1916), op cit. Post battle report written by Berners (CO Fusiliers).
132 WO95/2093 (July 1916), op cit., diary entry 7 July.
133 WO95/2078 (July 1916), op cit., diary entry July 7th. 156 casualties in total and a overall CR of 21% (based upon their strength on June 30th, minus the casualties of the 4th).

which represented a total casualty rate of approximating thirty to forty percent.[134] Although officer casualties were still high in proportion to their actual number, we can see the voice of command continued to resound upon this battlefield. We can also see that the casualty rate did not strongly puncture the critical point of thirty percent, suggesting that this (what amounted to) relatively rapid success was achieved partly because the battle for Contalmaison fell within the limits of the infantry's present 'passive' combat morale.

Yet exposure to 48 hours of the worse nature and man could throw at them had plainly taken its *physical* toll on the infantry. On the 7th the Wiltshires reported that: 'Our men were in a very exhausted condition – the night was a very wet and trying one but the enemy did not attempt any counter attack.'[135] Leaving the frontline on the following day the Cheshires recorded that: 'The appalling state of the trenches and the exhaustion of the men made progress [to billets] very slow.'[136] We can again postulate that this physical fatigue may also, for many or some have been matched by *mental* fatigue.

The 'Switch Line', 23 July

When 19th Division returned to the battlefield on 19 July, Fourth Army's attention had turned to a 'new German trench known as 'SWITCH' line'.[137] The line ran between the Bapaume road and the north of High Wood, and the division's task was to 'capture … and [then] to construct a line of trenches between our present right and HIGH WOOD'.[138] The method of assault mirrored that of the attack on Contalmaison: an AF overland charge, led by the infantry specialists, and covered by a 'creeping barrage'.[139] The division's senior commanders' faith in the efficacy of this itinerant wall of artillery fire had, however, grown somewhat in the preceding fortnight, and they now considered that success hinged upon near faultless coopera-

---

134 The breakdown of casualties suffered by the Welch was: 1 officer, 13 ORs killed; 6 officers, 178 ORs wounded; 1 officer, 25 ORs missing; total casualties 224. This represented a CR of 32% based upon a approximate strength of 700. It is therefore likely that the actual strength was lower, and therefore the CR was higher, probably nearer 40%. WO95/2092 'Welch' (July 1916), op cit. The Fusiliers suffered 44 casualties (3 officers), the North Staffords 60 casualties (4 officers). WO95/2092 'Fusiliers' (July 1916), op cit & WO95/2085 'North Staffords' (July 1916), op cit.
135 WO95/2093 (July 1916), op cit., diary entry July 7th.
136 'Appendix IX' Narrative of events 'A' Coy July 8th/9th. Written by Capt. Jenns. WO95/2090 (July 1916), op cit.
137 'III Corps Summary of Operations 1st to 31st July, 1916.' WO95/673 (July 1916), op cit.
138 'Addendum No.2', issued July 22nd, to 'III Corps Operation Order No. 91', issued 19 July, ibid. See also WO95/2075 (July 1916), op cit., diary entry 22 July.
139 See: WO95/2087 (July 1916), op cit; 'Order BN361' dated 21 July and appended to WO95/2080 (July 1916), op cit; 'III Corps Operation Order No. 91', issued 19 July WO95/673 (July 1916), op cit.

tion between infantry and artillery. '[S]uccess of the attack will probably depend on the promptness with which the infantry follow up the artillery…the leading line is to creep up as close as possible under cover of the artillery barrage and rush the position at the exact time laid down by the artillery to lift from the objective…It is better that the infantry should have to lie down in front of the position and wait for our guns to lift than that there should be a pause between the artillery preparation and the assault sufficient to allow the enemy to bring his machine guns into action.'[140] As this order illustrates, the nature of this infantry/artillery cooperation had evolved significantly since 1 July. The simple maxim that artillery would conquer and infantry occupy was losing ground to a new principle: the artillery would *quell* the enemy's machine-gun and artillery fire sufficiently long enough to allow the infantry to advance unscathed towards the enemy's trenches.

During a ten day hiatus the depleted ranks of the division were boosted by the arrival of 'fresh' infantry drafts. Yet, although III Corps had promised that, 'Lots of new drafts were coming', the numbers did not add up.[141] For example, 58th Brigade had suffered 1167 (recorded) casualties, but received only 584 reinforcements.[142] The net result being that the majority of battalions were reduced to a fighting strength of less than 500. The Loyals, for instance, reported on 21 July that 'we are now to hold 1000 yrds with only 480 men.'[143] Compounding this numerical shortfall, many of these 'fresh' drafts were returning wounded who, according to the Worcesters, 'were useless owing to wounds being improperly healed.'[144] The Loyals similarly complained that a 'draft of 109 other ranks contained several men who had been slightly wounded in the first few days of the battle. These men are not fit after 10 days to return to a battalion which is just going to take part in active operations. They should have been given a longer rest or else sent to a battalion which were merely holding the line.'[145] Of the 306 reinforcements received by the Cheshires, 87 were rejected and sent to the 'Salvage Corps'!'[146] Besides having the walking wounded substituted for A1 soldiers, the arrival of 'foreign drafts' was also drawing the chagrin of battalion commanders. Winser (CO South Lancs) complained that: 'A draft of 78 men was received. All the men being drawn from other units – chiefly West Yorks and York and Lancaster Battalions. A draft of 90 men and NCOs had been waiting for this battalion at the Base Depot since the last week in June. This draft, however, was sent to the 17th

---

140 '19th Division Order No. 59', dated 20 July. WO95/2087 (July 1916), op cit.
141 WO95/2075 (July 1916), op cit., diary entry 13 July.
142 'Reinforcements received during period 5th to 13th July.' WO95/2087 (July 1916), op cit. See also: WO95/2080 (July 1916), op cit., dairy entry 11 July; WO95/2078 (July 1916), op cit., diary entries 11 & 17 July; WO95/2085 'North Staffords' (July 1916), op cit.
143 WO95/2080 (July 1916), op cit.
144 WO95/2086 (July 1916), op cit., diary entry 8 July.
145 WO95/2080 (July 1916), op cit., diary entry 17 July. See also WO95/2078 (July 1916), op cit.
146 WO95/2090 (July 1916), op cit., diary entry 11 July.

Manchesters Regt. The oddity of these arrangements was pointed out to Brigade Headquarters for a representation to be made on the subject.'[147]

The honest answer was that the BEF could not be allowed to decimate the male population of a single community in a single battle – from now on the dead of each battlefield would be drawn from across the nation. Consequently, the 'local character' of the 19th Division – still fairly concentrated on 1 July – was turning decidedly watery. For example, the Worcesters recorded that they had: 'Received a draft of 206 men chiefly from Bedfordshire Regt. (also Essex Regt.).'[148]

It was not only the ORs that were causing 19th Division manpower headaches, the atrophy of battalion commanders was also a major concern. Some of the battalions were able to make good their losses. For example, the 10th Royal Warwickshire Regiment (Royal Warwicks) received 7 new officers to replace 6 casualties.[149] But the heavy casualty toll amongst junior commanders was motivating a serious revaluation of their battlefield role by the division's senior commanders. Bridges (GOC 19th Division) 'addressed all Officers and Sergts. [of the Worcesters and]…bade us remember that as trained Officers and N.C.O's we must not throw away our lives and should *rather direct operations than fight ourselves* [my emphasis].'[150] Bridges' concerns were clearly well founded; the Worcesters had lost 15 officers in the assault on La Boisselle alone. Yet the implication was that the GOC no longer wanted his officers and senior NCOs to lead from the front – by example – but to 'direct' the battle from the rear. We have witnessed throughout the division's 'active service' to date how vital exemplary leadership by junior commanders (and to a lesser extent senior NCOs) was to the collective combat morale of a company or platoon in combat. To stem the flow of officer casualties, the division's senior commanders were apparently prepared to gamble on the infantry's collective combat morale, and place a much greater responsibility for battlefield success upon junior NCOs and private soldiers.

As it was, any effort on behalf of 19th Division to prepare itself once again for battle was largely wasted. III Corps reported how the attack 'failed to gain its objectives, being met by heavy machine-gun fire from the front and by machine-gun and artillery fire from the two flanks.'[151] The muddy and shell strewn morass of the Somme battlefield encumbered the infantry's attempt to keep their appointment with the creeping barrage; exposing them to the full force of the enemy's fire. However, a report from the R.F.C. illustrates how fine the line between success or failure could potentially be during an advance protected by a 'creeping barrage.' 'He saw the German machine-gunners leave their dug-outs and cellars directly the bombardment lifted. They ran down the trenches to their fire stations and opened fire at once. It appears that the

---

147 WO95/2081 (July 1916), op cit., diary entry for 10-19 July.
148 WO95/2086 (July 1916), op cit., diary entry July 11th. See also: WO(5/2085 'North Staffords' (July 1916), op cit; WO95/2093 (July 1916), op cit.
149 WO95/2085 'Royal Warwicks' (July 1916), op cit., diary entries 2-21 July.
150 WO95/2086 (July 1916), op cit., diary entry 8 July.
151 'III Corps Summary of Operations 1st to 31st July, 1916.' WO95/673 (July 1916), op cit.

infantry had not got close to the position as was possible during the bombardment, which gave the German machine-gunners the chance of doing more damage than would have been possible had the infantry been close up.'[152]

For 19th Division the attack provided was straight from the Loos anthology, and they acted accordingly. With the casualty rate rapidly spiralling towards thirty percent most infantrymen surrendered the objective to survival, and went to ground. A few isolated pockets of their fellow comrades, led by junior officers, made greater headway before making the same decision. There was however one salient variation. For the first time in the division's short history, a significant number of its infantrymen – through either force of circumstance, loss of officers, or diminishing combat morale – surrendered to the enemy. For those who survived the enemy's fire or avoided his prison camps, another agonising 48 hours of hostile shellfire lay install to drain their already beleaguered combat morale.

The 19th Division's part in the attack on the 'Switch Line' was enacted by 56th Brigade, with support from the Gloucesters and Royal Warwicks of 57th Brigade. The dissemination of orders was typically rushed. Zero was set for 12.30am, yet the Loyals' CO was not 'summonsed to Bde H.Qrs for [a] conference' until 9pm, and was subsequently unable to 'issue final orders for Coys' until 11.15pm.[153] This appears to have undermined the division's attempt to devolve greater responsibility onto the individual soldier. Communications were also predictably troubled. 56th Brigade complained that: 'As usual during heavy artillery bombardments all telephonic communication soon ceased and runners between Battalions and Bde. H.Q. were the only possible means of getting any information. No news of any kind was received as regards the progress of the operations until 2-6am [one and a half hours 'in the dark'].'[154] The upshot being that senior commanders could once again do little to effect events on the battlefield once the infantry had 'gone over the top'. Thus decisions over the objective's final worth were essentially left to the men on the ground.

Faced with charging blind and defenceless into a fusillade of enemy machine-gun fire, the infantry were soon to judge the 'Switch Line' a lost cause. First over were the Loyals, who were 'held up by M. gun fire' moments after leaving the cover of the Bapaume Road.'[155] Called to their assistance, the East Lancs swiftly reported back: 'Huns putting up stout resistance please order intense bombardment of SWITCH LINE. Have suffered heavy casualties.'[156] Meanwhile, the South Lancs were thrown

---

152 Ibid.
153 WO95/2080 (July 1916), op cit., diary entry 22 July. 56th Brigade reported that: 'Owing to the short notice given us to get out orders the Brigadier sent for all Officers Comdg Units, and held a conference at Bde H.Qrs. at 9pm.' WO95/2075 (July 1916), op cit., diary entry 22 July.
154 WO95/2075 (July 1916), op cit., diary entry 23 July.
155 WO95/2080 (July 1916), op cit., diary entry 23 July.
156 WO95/2075 (July 1916), op cit., diary entry 23 July. The brigade war diary, in keeping with normal practice, recorded the timing and details of each message sent and received from the frontline.

into the fray, but could only offer the same dour communiqué: 'We are having many casualties from Machine Gun Fire, from right flank and front, all the Officers except one in the two leading Coys are reported hit. The 57th Bde. have not yet attacked …'[157] The Royal Warwicks later accounted for this delay, and their all too familiar fate: 'Owing to the Worcesters' guides not knowing the way, and also to the heavy shelling, we were not in position till 1.5am, by which time the barrage had lifted. The companies all went over, but owing to the heavy machine gun fire, were forced to withdraw to their original trench.'[158] It is worth noting that upon this exposed battlefield, striped of subterranean trenches and interlinking dugouts, the bomb was a decidedly impotent weapon.

Even though the experience of intense hostile machine-gun fire was universal, where the voice of command survived, a greater (if ephemeral) advance was sometimes achieved. As the above account from the South Lancs attests, and as Winser (CO) was to reiterate a few hours later, 'the majority of [his] Officers [were] out of action.'[159] Around the same time Winser also informed the Loyals that 'my Battn. has not in any place got to the first objective and only a few detached parties have made any appreciable advance.'[160] At the head of these 'detached parties' (seemingly ignoring their GOC's advice) were junior officers. Winser related how: 'A wounded officer has just reported that he got close to the 1st Objective but that his men were mown down by an enemy machine-gun.'[161] The Loyals forwarded a similar account. 'Report received from 2 Lt. TOVANI that CAPT. THOMPSON and 2 Lt. HOYLE were killed. The Coy. had got within a few yards of the German front line trench, but again held up by M. Guns. Being unable to get on 2 Lieut TOVANI withdrew the remainder of the Coy. (about 50 men) to our front line.'[162] On returning to the frontline, 2nd Lieutenant Tovani recorded the immense combat morale shown by himself, and shared by fifty or so ORs of D Company: 'We attacked and got within 30 yds from German lines. We suffered heavy casualties and *after 3 or 4 attempts to take the line* still suffering heavy casualties we withdrew to our original position to reorganise [my emphasis].'[163]

It is evident, however, that the presence of a junior officer did not always motivate a platoon or company to continue the advance. Lieutenant Porter (OC 'C' Company Loyals) reported that 'his Coy. [only 45 ORs strong] had suffered heavily. They had got within 20 yards of German trench, but were then held up by M. Gun fire. He was left alone with 2 men one of whom was hit. He then managed to crawl down

---

157 Ibid.
158 WO95/2085 'Royal Warwicks' (July 1916), op cit., diary entry 23 July.
159 WO95/2075 (July 1916), op cit., diary entry 23 July.
160 WO95/2080 (July 1916), op cit., diary entry 23 July; the message was times at 3.10am.
161 WO95/2075 (July 1916), op cit., diary entry 23 July.
162 WO95/2080 (July 1916), op cit., diary entry 23 July.
163 Ibid. Hand written message sent at 3.15am.

the road.'¹⁶⁴ Although Porter's company were under-strength, it would seem unlikely that they had *all* become casualties during this advance. Besides the casualty statistics (discussed below) there is some qualitative evidence of infantrymen leaving this battlefield very early on. The Loyals reported that: 'By this time [12.45am, 15 minutes after Zero] several men of 'B' Coy were back in our line: reported that enemy held trench very strongly and that their M. Guns caused very heavy casualties.'¹⁶⁵ Faced with such terribly one-sided odds, not all infantrymen were evidently willing (or perhaps able) to sacrifice their lives or limbs *at all cost*.

With the battlefield littered with casualties, the survivors crawling back to the (marginal) safety of the frontline, and with the OsC the isolated and under-strength parties that had made some headway deciding to withdraw, battalion COs called a halt to the attack. Two hours after Zero, Hill (CO North Lancs) 'ordered [A Coy.] NOT to attack but to consolidate the frontline and hold against counter attack… [original emphasis]'¹⁶⁶ A few minutes later the South Lancs informed brigade 'are withdrawing to their original trench, they have not got their first objective. O.C. would like enemy's line shelled as soon as possible to prevent Machine Guns being used further.'¹⁶⁷ Lieutenant Colonel P.O.W. Goodwyn (CO East Lancs) then told brigade: 'Have seen O.C. 7/S. Lan. R. who is back holding his original trenches and says cannot get on, and secondly that his line as he has it, is strongly held. I am therefore getting my Battalion…back to its original position on the edge of BAZENTIN-LE-PETIT WOOD.'¹⁶⁸ Apparently with little choice, 56th Brigade then rubber-stamped the decisions of their battalion COs, ordering the leading unit (Loyals) that 'in view of the 1st Bde. and 7/S. Lan. R. having moved back to their original position, that they must also withdraw and gain touch on their flanks.'¹⁶⁹ The only other subsequent battlefield communiqué was a call from DHQ stating '58th Bde. would relieve the 56th and 57th Bdes. in the evening.'¹⁷⁰

The number of casualties the infantry were willing to sacrifice in pursuit of the 'Switch Line' diminished with each succeeding wave. This suggests (perhaps expectedly) that knowledge of what lay ahead lessened the combat morale of the later attackers. The Loyals reported on 24 July: 'Casualties now corrected to 11 Officers and 290 Other Ranks for the four days'; a so far uniquely high casualty rate upward of sixty percent of those 480 troops alive and well on the 19th.¹⁷¹ The South Lancs

---

164 Ibid.
165 Ibid. B Coy. had been in the first wave, alongside D Coy., 'going over' at 12.30am. C Coy. had followed immediately in their wake.
166 Ibid. Message sent 2.35am.
167 WO95/2075 (July 1916), op cit., diary entry 23 July. Message received 3.58am.
168 Ibid. Message received at 3.58am.
169 Ibid. Message sent 4am.
170 Ibid. Message received at 7.15am.
171 WO95/2080 (July 1916), op cit., diary entry 24 July. The battalion had reported a 'few men gassed' on the 21st, so a few of the 480 had already become casualties before 23/24 July.

recorded 237 casualties; a casualty rate of around forty five percent.[172] Following in their wake, the Gloucesters and Royal Warwicks recorded casualty rates of forty and twenty six percent respectively.[173]

However, these higher figures may be slightly deceptive. The 302 casualties suffered by the Loyals included 65 ORs and 5 officers reported 'missing'. Some of these men may have been amongst the dead yet to be accounted for. In the final reckoning, another 40 or so troops would be added to the 35 ORs initially declared killed on 23 July.[174] Yet it seems highly likely that the final death toll would have been swelled by some of the 191 OR infantrymen initially reported 'wounded' that day.[175] Although no officers were amongst the initial count (despite Tovani's eye-witness account), 5 would eventually be declared killed. Reports of Captain Thompson's demise were seemingly exaggerated, but 2nd Lieutenant Holye was amongst the final toll; so it is possible the other 4 were drawn from the 5 officers initially reported missing.[176] Again though, the final officer death toll may have included some of the 6 officers initially reported 'wounded'. The implication of these casualty figures is, therefore, that 2 (depleted) platoons of the Loyals, with OsC still standing, were compelled to surrender. The casualty figures recorded by the South Lancs – which included 1 officer and 61 ORs initially reported as 'missing' – and their later amendments, suggests a similar occurrence in this battalion.[177]

Some qualitative evidence of a possible outbreak of surrendering is provided by the Worcester's faltering attempts to capture a German machine-gun post prior to Zero. Two attacks executed on the 21st by 'strong patrols…supported by Bombers and Lewis Gun' had been 'heavily fired upon and forced to retire', with the result that their own 'gun was lost'. The following day: 'Another attack was made on the Machine Gun

---

172 WO95/2075 (July 1916), op cit. This CR is based upon an estimated strength of 500 (the battalion had 418 survivors up to July 13th, and subsequently received 78 drafts).
173 The Gloucesters CR is based upon 200 recorded casualties, and an estimated strength of 500. WO95/2085 'Gloucesters' (July 1916), op cit., diary entry 23 July. The Royal Warwicks CR is based upon 130 recorded casualties, and an estimated strength of 500. WO95/2085 'Royal Warwicks' (July 1916), op cit., diary entry 23 July. The East Lancs, who sent forward at least 1 company in support of the Loyals, recorded 107 casualties; a CR of 21% based upon an estimated strength of 500. WO95/2075 (July 1916), op cit.
174 67 infantrymen were recorded 'killed in action' on 23 July, and another 12 were recorded 'died of wounds' in the following few days. *Soldiers Died in the Great War*, op cit.
175 WO95/2075 (July 1916), op cit. The full breakdown of casualties recorded by the Loyals on July 23rd was as follows: 13 ORs killed; 6 officers, 191 ORs wounded; 5 officer, 65 ORs missing; total casualties 302.
176 *Soldiers Died in the Great War*, op cit.
177 WO95/2075 (July 1916), op cit. The full breakdown was as follows 5 officers, 10 ORs killed; 11officers, 149 ORs wounded; 1 officer, 61 ORs missing; total casualties 237. The final death toll of ORs for July 23rd would total 33. Again, it seems highly likely that many of these 23 additional fatalities would have been infantrymen who died of their wounds later that day. *Soldiers Died in the Great War*, op cit.

by 2 platoons of C Coy...and 2 platoons of B Coy ...' Significantly, it was a 'Sergt. who was in charge of the leading platoon of C Coy...' This suggests the Worcesters *were* acting upon the advice of their GOC. The battalion reported that: 'The attack was a failure and the greater part of the 2 platoons of C Coy were missing believed prisoner.' The senior NCO leading C Company, however, avoided capture and spent 2 days 'in a dugout in side of road about [map ref] and was bombed by our own men (58th Bde) before he got back, his companion being killed.'[178] The Worcesters recorded 161 casualties between July 21st and 23rd, 64 of which were ORs reported 'missing'.[179]

If these incidences of surrender were indicative of a deterioration in the division's collective combat morale then it is hardly surprising. Interminable days of exposure to hostile fire, witnessing their comrades being killed or mutilated, fearing for their own lives and limbs and faced with yet another 'hard fight' (their third or fourth in twenty days), left the infantrymen prey to psychological breakdown. The Cheshires recorded that 'MAMETZ Wood as we found it consisted of gaunt trunks of trees, with broken tops and dead branches littering the ground. All life seemed to have ceased to exist. Shell holes made anything but foot transport impossible. The smell of dead bodies pervaded the place.'[180] On 23 July 'O.C. 8th North Staffords report[ed to his brigadier] that his men are very shaken owing to the heavy shelling.'[181] Having witnessed: 'A number of men [being] buried and then were literally blown to pieces by a large H.E. shell which dropped in the middle of them', Fitzjohn (CO King's Own) atoned that this was a 'most unpleasant day and the men were considerably shaken.'[182]

The 'Intermediate Line', 30 July

Fourth Army returned to the offensive on 30 July 'attacking the enemy's positions between DEVILLE WOOD and POZIERES...'[183] III Corps' had been temporarily excused the elusive 'Switch Line', and were to concentrate instead upon the 'Intermediate Line'; which (as the name suggests) lay between them and their former objective.[184] The 19th Division's specific objective being 'to capture the German Intermediate line between POZIERS and HIGH WOOD.'[185] The division's senior commanders were now granted a greater degree of latitude over planning; including the

178 WO95/2086 (July 1916), op cit., diary entry 21 July.
179 Ibid. The full breakdown was as follows: 3 officers 18 ORs killed; 5 officers 71 ORs wounded; 64 ORs missing; total casualties 161. In the final reckoning, another 9 ORs were added to the final death toll. *Soldiers Died in the Great War*, op cit. This suggests that at least 50 infantrymen had been compelled to surrender – or 2 under strength platoons.
180 WO95/2090 (July 1916), op cit., diary entry 24 July.
181 WO95/2083 (July 1916), op cit., diary entry 23 July.
182 WO95/2078 (July 1916), op cit., diary entry 25 July.
183 '57th Brigade Preliminary Order No. 22', issued 28 July. WO95/2078 (July 1916), op cit.
184 'III Corps Summary of Operations 1st to 31st July, 1916.' WO95/673 (July 1916), op cit.
185 WO95/2078 (July 1916), op cit., diary entry 30 July.

timing, and artillery support.[186] GOC responded by scripting an enhanced 'covering' role for the trench mortars and machine-gunners, whilst keeping the Bombers in their leading role. But the main event remained the AF overland charge supported by a 'creeping barrage'[187]

The task of capturing the 'Intermediate Line' fell to 57th Brigade, with support from the King's Own of 56th Brigade. Seemingly because the division's objective was a single but long trench system, the battalions attacked simultaneously, side-by-side, rather than in waves. In contrast to the previous assault's midnight rendezvous, Zero for this attack was set by DHQ for the unusually bright hour of 6.10pm. This suggests the possibility that the division's senior commanders were willing to sacrifice the cloak of darkness in order to avoid the concomitant chaos that ensued from navigating in the dark. They also tried to give their battalions time to digest and disseminate the plan of attack; 'the Brigadier General [57th Brigade] had a conference of all Officers and told them the scheme for the attack' as early as July 28th.[188] The preliminary bombardment had also apparently done its job. 'During the night of the 29th/30th [the Royal Warwicks reported] a patrol went out to ascertain the amount of wire the enemy had in front of his line. The patrol returned safely and reported that the wire was well cut.'[189] On this occasion, then, the battlefield preliminaries augured well for the division's infantrymen.

The advance of the King's Own upon the 'Eastern' half of the 'Intermediate Line' largely realised this promise. 'At 6.9pm the Field Artillery opened an intense bombardment on the hostile trenches and under cover of this bombardment our front line advanced in one wave and lay down close under the hostile position. The second line advanced and lay down simultaneously in rear. At 6.10pm the artillery lifted and both lines got up and rushed the position immediately. It was taken *almost without opposition* and it was obvious from the subsequent examination of an officer prisoner that the success of the operation was due to our following up so closely on the artillery barrage that the enemy had no time to get his machine guns out and man his parapet before our men were on top of him [my emphasis].'[190]

The testimony of the said 'officer prisoner' (even allowing for a demoralised and ingratiating captive) certainly did substantiate the battalion's claim that success was realised through near faultless cooperation between artillery and infantry. The interrogation of L.T. Everling (a company OC) also suggests that the advancing infantry significantly outnumbered their German counterparts, and moreover emphasises the impression given by the King's Own that this 'officer prisoner' was far from alone in quickly surrendering. Everling 'stated that the Intermediate Line was held by 3

---

186 III Corps Operation Order No. 96', issued 28 July.
187 '57th Brigade Preliminary Order No. 22', issued 28 July. WO95/2078 (July 1916), op cit.
188 WO95/2085 'Royal Warwicks' (July 1916), op cit., diary entry 28 July.
189 Ibid. Diary entry 30 July.
190 WO95/2078 (July 1916), op cit., diary entry 30 July.

companies…at the time of our assault with a large proportion of machine guns.' Which suggests a conflict between one (albeit under-strength) battalion against one (potentially likewise diminished) company. Given Everling's foreknowledge of the attack – he told his captures that: 'Instructions had been given…that a British attack was to be expected at any time – it would seem that defending the line lightly regards *Landers*, but fairly heavily regards machine-gunners, was part of the German's *intended* method of defence. If so, then clearly the key to capturing the German front-line lay in silencing his machine-guns. As it was, Everling was effusive in his praise for the way in which the King's Own (with the aid of the creeping barrage) overcame the *bête noire* of the infantry assault; telling the battalion that 'our infantry attacked with great dash and determination and that they moved across the open to the assault so close up under our artillery barrage that as the artillery fire lifted the infantry were on top of the hostile parapet and this gave the garrison no chance to man the parapet or place their machine guns in position.'[191]

Although the number of *Landsers* accompanying their commanding officer was not recorded, the impression is of a company of German infantry caught in their dugouts, many of whom subsequently offered or accepted the surrender. The lack of recorded 'opposition', or indeed record of any fighting whatsoever underlines this impression. The 120 casualties suffered by the battalion, 18 of which were fatalities, indicates however that this was no walkover. Perhaps a number of these casualties were caused by the German distant killers; the Royal Warwicks, for instance, reported 'that there was heavy shelling by both sides for quite one hour before the assault which rather upset things.'[192] But perhaps also some interpersonal combat was executed before the surrender was either elicited or accepted. A casualty rate of around twenty percent, however, indicates that the battle for the 'Intermediate Line' fell well within the limits of the division's present 'passive' combat behaviour/morale spectrum.[193]

The attack upon the centre of the line experienced a slightly more qualified success. The Royal Warwicks reported that: 'At one minute to zero the Coys, who were now all in the front line, crept out under the barrage: 'B' and 'C' making the 1st line, 'A' and 'D' Coys the 2nd line. 'A', 'B' and 'C' Coys reached their objective but 'D' Coy were stopped halfway by heavy M.G. fire and lack of Officers (casualties). Nevertheless they were led up with the line later.'[194] Evidently the creeping barrage had failed to deliver the firepower initiative to 'D' Company, and the subsequent loss of leadership ground

---

191 'Extracts from conversation with LT. Everling, commanding 4th Coy, 1st Battn. 75th R.I.R. Captured on night of 30/30st. in S.2.D Intermediate Line.' Received from III Corps intelligence on August 1st and appended to Ibid.
192 WO95/2085 'Royal Warwicks' (July 1916), op cit., diary entry 30 July.
193 The full breakdown of casualties was as follows: 2 officers 16 ORs killed; 5 officers 87 ORs wounded; 10 ORs missing; a total of 120 casualties. A casualty rate of 22% based upon the battalion's strength on 30 June, minus all casualties since, plus the two sets of drafts, which equated to 542. WO95/2078 (July 1916), op cit., diary entry 30 July.
194 WO95/2085 'Royal Warwicks' (July 1916), op cit., diary entry 30 July.

the advance to a halt. The battalion recorded 9 officer amongst the 157 casualties suffered, which evinces that the voice of command had been somewhat subdued.[195] A casualty rate of around thirty percent also suggests that this attack pushed the Royal Warwicks towards the limits of, but not beyond, the division's 'passive' combat morale/behaviour spectrum.[196]

The Gloucesters and Worcesters, making up the left (western) flank of the attack, experienced an absolute reversal. The Gloucesters recorded that they had: 'Attacked the German intermediate line, A+B Coys in front line, C+D Coys in second line. Our attack was held up by enfilade Machine Gun fire and concealed snipers from the right. Our men returned to their original front line at 9.30PM…the C.O. [acting] Major Thymme was wounded in the body while urging on the second line.'[197] 9 officers were amongst the 169 casualties suffered, which suggests a loss of command was also elemental in this reverse.[198] Their casualty rate was also rising beyond the 'critical' thirty percent when they surrendered the objective to safety.[199]

Likewise, the Worcesters reported that: 'The attack as far as the Battalion was concerned was a complete failure.' However, although the Worcesters accepted that 'our right flank [was] exposed', Battalion HQ placed most of the blame for the loss of the firepower initiative at the feet of their own infantrymen, complaining that: 'Each Coy of the Battalion appeared to wait for each other and did not follow up the Barrage sufficiently.'[200] This indictment was collaborated by the enemy; Everling testifying 'that the British troops which attacked the right [the western end] of the intermediate line were slower in the assault and did not go forward under the barrage so well as the other assaulting troops as he knew that the Coy. on his right had not been broken in upon like this.'[201]

Hesitancy on behalf of the Worcesters had lost them the advantage of superior firepower, leaving them at the mercy of unmolested machine-gun fire. The Worcesters, however, suffered conspicuously low casualties in relation to their fellow attackers during this faltering advance: 2 officers and 82 ORs, of which 14 were fatalities – a

---

195 The full breakdown was as follows: 3 officers 17 ORs killed; 6 officers 116 ORs wounded, 15 ORs missing; total casualties 157. Ibid.
196 A CR of 31% based upon estimated strength of 500.
197 WO95/2085 'Gloucesters' (July 1916), op cit., diary entry 30 July.
198 The full breakdown (reported by the Gloucesters) was as follows: 3 officers killed; 3 officers wounded; 3 officers missing; OR casualties 160. Ibid. In the final reckoning the Gloucesters suffered 54 OR fatalities – considerably higher than either the King's Own or Royal Warwicks'. *Soldiers Died in the Great War*, op cit.
199 The Gloucesters suffered a CR of around 35% based upon estimated strength of 500.
200 WO95/2086 (July 1916), op cit., diary entry 30 July.
201 'Extracts from conversation with LT. Everling, commanding 4th Coy, 1st Battn. 75th R.I.R. Captured on night of 30/30st. in S.2.D Intermediate Line.' Received from III Corps intelligence on August 1st and appended to WO95/2078 (July 1916), op cit.

casualty rate of less than twenty percent.[202] The Worcesters had begun July willing to suffer upwards of fifty percent casualties in the pursuit of La Boisselle. By July's close that willingness had evidently been shorn in half. Although the Worcesters' deteriorating casualty rate was, to date, singular, it does suggest that the infantry's 'passive' combat morale could not be sustained in battle indefinitely – especially on a diet of 'partial' successes.

We have seen that the corrosive ferocity of the July Somme offensives may have eroded the willingness or ability of some infantrymen to cope with combat – as seen by the Worcesters' falling casualty rate, the ubiquity of fatigue, evidence of unwounded soldiers leaving the battlefield early, and surrendering. Yet the weight of evidence suggests a collective 'passive' combat morale marked by far more resilience than disintegration. This impression is given even greater clarity by the division's disciplinary record. Only a smattering of infantrymen were found guilty of absenting themselves from duty, and only two unfortunate soldiers were sentenced for desertion, between July and the division's return to the Somme in October 1916.[203] So, even though a number of infantrymen were almost certainly finding it increasingly difficult to cope with the Somme battlefield, very few were driven into attempting to escape the role of combat (by either self-mutilation, absence or desertion) completely. The infantry were, albeit briefly, less willing to adhere to the rules, however. The overall number of disciplinary offences increased threefold in August. A quick and lasting return to the pre-1 July norm indicates that this was hardly the nascent beginnings of a rebellion. Indeed, one third of the 31 offences recorded in August involved the charge of 'drunk'. Evidently, therefore, a few of 19th Division's infantrymen had chosen to escape briefly the Somme through a less dangerous route – the bottom of a glass.[204] The sparing of the death sentence in the case of the division's two deserters also suggests that high command considered there was little need to chasten the infantry with the ultimate example.[205]

The Battle of the Ancre, 18 November

The 19th Division entrained back to the Somme in late October, joining II Corps under the command of the Reserve (Fifth) Army. During this battlefield interregnum questions had been raised over the operations of the chain of command during the

---

202 The full breakdown was as follows: 1 officer 13 ORs killed; 1 officer 59 ORs wounded; 10 ORs missing. A CR of 17% based upon a estimated strength of 500. WO95/2086 (July 1916), op cit. In the final reckoning one more OR joined the ranks of the killed. *Soldiers Died in the Great War*, op cit.
203 WO213/10-12 Judge Advocates General's Office: Field General Court's Martial and Military Courts, Registers (July – Oct 1916) PRO.
204 The majority of offenders were NCOs, suggesting that 'drunkenness' was a wider malaise amongst the ORs, but less acceptable in men who were supposed to set an example. Ibid.
205 See WO213/11-12 (Sept/Oct 1916), op cit.

preceding offensives. At least one corps commander felt that things had not run as smoothly as desired. 'The conduct of chain of command was discussed [at a IX Corps conference held in mid-September]. The Corps Commander pointed out that *a change of control had been brought about by altered conditions*, partly due to trench warfare, and partly due to increase of Army and large number of inexperienced officers [my emphasis].'[206] Throughout the 19th Division's active service to date we have glimpsed the one ace tentatively held by the infantry – the ability to tacitly subvert the more 'thrusting' expectations of the chain of command. During trench warfare 'cumulative aggression' had been partially undermined, and in major set-piece battles it was the infantry who decided an objective's worth. The normally smooth operations of the chain of command were being ground down by persistent bouts of Clausewitzian 'friction'; and the high command's patience was severely tested during the process.[207] To overcome the civilian soldier's apparent recalcitrance greater vigilance was demanded from senior commanders: 'It is not sufficient merely to issue an order. Steps must be taken to see they are carried out.'[208]

Poor weather had delayed the opening of the last act of the Somme offensive until 13 November, and the division finally took their bow on the 18th; their objectives 'GRANDCOURT TRENCH and GRANDCOURT ...'[209] The infantry were not to take a step upon this battlefield without the protection of (what DHQ was now calling) the 'rolling barrage'. Two battalions were to lead the attack; 'advanc[ing] in two waves of extended lines, 50 yards distance between the waves, and, closely following the barrage [they would] assault and capture GRANDCOURT TRENCH ...' A second wave of two 'battalions [would then] pass through the leading battalions and keeping close to the barrage [would] assault and capture GRANDCOURT VILLAGE ...'[210] Judging by the complexity of planning, weight of targets, and precision of infantry cooperation, the 'creeping' or 'rolling' barrage had grownup somewhat since its troubled birth in July 1916.[211] Yet the artillery were not the only unit evolving, the infantry's own specialists were experiencing a degree of elevation. The machine-gunners were to assist the artillery by 'forming barrages in front of the attack on the first and

---

206 'Conference held at Headquarters., IX Corps on 13th September 1916' WO95/835 (Sept 1916), op cit.
207 Carl von Clausewitz, *On War* Penguin (1968), 1st ed 1832, pp. 164-7. Although Clausewitz stressed the potentially fatal consequences of infantry friction, he saw it as a transient phenomenon, without organisation, direction or durability, and likened infantry friction to any other chance variable, such as the weather.
208 'Conference held at Headquarters., IX Corps on 13th September 1916' WO95/835 (Sept 1916), op cit.
209 '19th Division Operation Order No. 90', issued 14 Nov. WO95/2053 (Nov 1916), op cit.
210 '58th Brigade Order No. 87' issued 25 Oct, amended 12 Nov. WO95/2088 (Oct/Nov 1916) op cit.
211 See 'Division Operation Order No. 92', issued 16 Nov, with additional amendments added 17 Nov. WO95/2053 (Nov 1916), op cit.

second objectives', and then 'keep the line BAILLESCOURT FARM – QUARRY [the third objective] under fire until the attack upon it is pushed home ...'[212]

This was essentially a extension of the machine-gunner's trench warfare role – a depersonalised strafing of the enemy. Nevertheless, some of their ranks were to get a little closer to their victims; eight gun crews of each brigade being ordered to 'accompany or follow the attacking troops [and to] engage any counter-attack which may develop.'[213] Likewise, in order to keep the attack moving, the trench mortars were also being pushed closer towards their victims. 'Stokes mortar batteries will be placed as far forward as possible in assembly trenches [DHQ ordered], and will follow the last wave of their respective brigades to central positions...They will there be in readiness to send guns forward on demand by battalion commanders to deal with any points which are holding up the attack.'[214] The advancing infantrymen were also to receive some help from a recent debutant to the battlefield; DHQ informing its brigades that 'Tanks will be used to assist the infantry attack.'[215] Evidently the tank was yet to impress the high command, because II Corps Commander warned his troops 'not however [to] depend too much on the assistance which will be given to them by the Tanks...Whatever happens the infantry must not wait for tanks.'[216]

The bomb and the bombers remained elemental to the planned assault. The advancing infantry were carrying rifle and bayonet, but the bomb was undoubtedly considered the foremost 'cleaning' tool. DHQ for instance ensured that a stockpile of the weapon was to hand. 'The 56th Brigade will arrange to send a large supply of grenades with the attacking battalion and to establish and supply a bomb store near the western end of GRANDCOURT VILLAGE, to be used by both brigades [56th and 57th].'[217] This of course meant that many infantrymen were designated the task of carrier. 56th Brigade for instance ordered that: 'Three platoons [from the attacking battalion] will furnish a carrying party ...'[218] Meantime the task of 'cleaning', particularly where enemy 'strongpoints' were anticipated, evidently remained the domain of the Bombers. 58th Brigade for example ordered that: 'Half a company with a proportion of bombers will be specially detailed by O.C. 6th Wilts to capture and clean up BAILLESCOURT FARM.'[219]

---

212 '58th Brigade Order No. 87' issued 25 Oct, amended 12 Nov. WO95/2088 (Oct/Nov 1916) op cit.
213 Ibid.
214 '19th Division Order No. 76', issued 8 Oct. WO95/2053 (Oct 1916), op cit.
215 'Division Operation Order No. 92', issued 16 Nov, with additional amendments added 17 Nov. (Nov 1916), ibid.
216 'Minutes of Conference held by GOC II Corps on 23rd October 1916.' (Oct 1916), ibid.
217 'Division Operation Order No. 92', issued 16 Nov, with additional amendments added 17 Nov & '19th Division Order No. 76', issued 8 Oct. (Oct 1916). Ibid.
218 '56th Brigade Order No. 132', issued 17 Nov. (Nov 1916), ibid.
219 '58th Brigade Order No. 87' issued 25 Oct, amended 12 Nov WO95/2088 (Oct/Nov 1916) op cit.

Admittedly this order opened the door to *pro tempore* bombing. Yet it would seem likely that the division's senior commanders were neither expectant nor particularly keen on this eventuality. DHQ for instance ordered that each man would carry 120 rounds of ammunition and '2 Mills grenades', yet cautioned that this latter weapon was 'not to be used by the [rifleman] except in an emergency, but are to form a reserve for the *recognised bombers* [my emphasis].'[220] The implication was that only those men who had previously volunteered themselves willing to execute interpersonal combat, and had subsequently trained for the role, could be entrusted with the task. So although the intended 'AF assault' gave the infantry a rather opaque front end, the battle plans still envisaged a speedy transformation into a diminutive yet ferocious sharp end, supplied and supported by a hefty tail.

High command took a gamble on the weather on 18 November – and lost. Brigadier-General G.D. Jeffreys (GOC 57th Brigade) reported that: 'In the early hours of the morning of 18th November the weather changed and the hard frost gave way to snow and sleet, which made visibility very bad and caused the good going of the previous night to become very bad through mud and slush. It was very dark at zero hour.'[221] The bleak outcrop of rubble and sludge that was once Grandcourt Village subsequently remained little more than a chilling mirage to the footsloggers of 19th Division. The 'rolling barrage' jumped from trench to trench, unaffected by the icy morass, whilst its human cohorts stumbled and flailed and fell prey to the enemy's remorseless fire. A few isolated platoons made a transient advance to the first objective, but most hardly got started, and a few 'disappeared' altogether. Perhaps rather unnecessarily, Jeffreys concluded that: 'Had it been fine weather, and light, I feel sure they would have succeeded.'[222] But then an attack launched at 6am in late November was always going to struggle to deliver such prerequisites.

II Corps recorded that: 'At 6.10AM [on the 18th] the assault was launched. The morning was very dark, and sleet and snow was falling.'[223] The division attacked on a four battalion front: 'The 8/N Staffs were on the right, the 10/R Warwicks in the centre + the 8th Gloucesters on the left of the 57th Bde', the South Lancs (supported by the East Lancs) formed the left flank, the Cheshires were later committed to the right flank, 'the cleaning up battalion being the 10/ Worcesters.'[224] The dissemination of orders to the men on the ground was again rushed – primarily because objectives were being altered at the eleventh hour. The South Lancs recorded that 'at 11.30.p.m., 1 copy of orders [received]. These were the original orders for taking the first objective and were read out to Company Commanders hurriedly by the C.O…'[225] Meantime,

220 '19th Division Order No. 76', issued 8 Oct. (Oct 1916), ibid.
221 'Operations on the Ancre October – November 1916' (Nov 1916), ibid. This document was compiled by DHQ from accounts given by both brigade and battalion COs.
222 Ibid.
223 WO95/639 (Nov 1916), op cit., diary entry 18 Nov.
224 Ibid.
225 CO's account of the battle sent on 22 Nov. WO95/2081 (Nov 1916), op cit.

two further objectives were added by 56th Brigade. Consequently, it was not until '5.20.a.m., [that] Coy Commanders left Bde H Qrs to rejoin [sic] their Companies at the jumping-off point and explain the scheme to them.'[226] The South Lancs' CO was later to recommend that 'Battalion Commanders should receive their orders from Brigade at least 24 hours before zero hour for a 'Set Piece'. If these orders are subsequently altered at short notice a certain amount of confusion and possible failure will be the result.'[227] This was sound advice based upon empirical learning.

The infantry faced a difficult enough task without being metaphorically 'in the dark' as well as literally. DHQ summarised the situation thus: 'It was very dark at zero, and sleet was falling…direction was soon lost, as landmarks previously noted could not be seen, and some confusion resulted.'[228] Snow turning towards sleet signalled a thaw that was rapidly transforming the battlefield into a quagmire, causing immediate delays to the infantry's appointment with the creeping barrage. The South Lancs reported that although 'A and B Coys were extending into 4 waves as they advanced towards their objective. A Coy found it impossible to deploy to the left, owing to the marshy conditions of the ground.'[229] As the hours wore on constant shellfire churned this marsh into a impenetrable morass, making conditions underfoot unbearable. The Cheshires reported that: 'The going was very bad and before reaching our kicking-off place a thick fog came down…After reaching STUFF TRENCH direction was lost, it was impossible to pick up any landmarks. The mud was knee-deep and clinging, men were bogged and could not pull themselves out.'[230]

As the infantry struggled over the top they descended into a 'fog' that was both real and figurative. The Royal Warwicks reported '6.10am barrage opened and groups forward. By time leading wave had advanced 50 yards in BATTERY VALLEY it became invisible to Battn. Headqts owing to the darkness which was intensified by falling snow.'[231] The North Staffords recorded the consequences of this blindness: 'After commencement of operations all touch seemed to have been lost with the Battn.'[232] Jeffreys (GOC 57th Brigade) was later to complain that: 'It was not until 5 am on 19th [almost 24 hours later] that I knew the location (approximately) of the various units.'[233] The dense 'fog of war' that continued to engulf the First World War battlefield added further woes to the infantry's already burgeoning list of troubles. Every time a junior officer was hit the advance would invariably falter; partly due (as we have seen) to the loss of exemplary leadership, but also because further orders could not be communicated to the leaderless ORs. It was also nigh on impossible to

---

226 Ibid.
227 'New Lessons Learnt and Old Ones Emphasised' Ibid.
228 WO95/2053 (Nov 1916, op cit., diary entry 18 Nov.
229 CO's account of the battle sent on 22 Nov. WO95/2081 (Nov 1916), op cit.
230 WO95/2090 (Nov 1916), op cit., diary entry 18 Nov.
231 WO95/2085 'Royal Warwicks' (Nov 1916), op cit., diary entry 18 Nov.
232 WO95/2085 'North Staffords' (Nov 1916), op cit., diary entry 18 Nov.
233 'Operations on the Ancre October – November 1916' WO95/2053 (Nov 1916), op cit.

coordinate artillery support if the infantry became waylaid or lost direction, which meant that the infantry were often left at the mercy of enemy fire, or worse, strafed by their own artillery.[234] Yet the 'fog of war' continued to offer the infantry a minor boon. By the time news of this attack had traversed No Man's Land and travelled along the chain of command, decisions taken on the battlefield had become a *fait accompli*. Consequently, infantrymen still decided when an engagement was over, not generals.

The decision to abandon the objective of Grandcourt was not, however, immediately universal. The South Lancs had managed to make some headway before their CO, acting in accordance with his infantrymen, called a halt. By 7am the South Lancs had captured their first objective and were 'penetrat[ing] the Western end of the village.'[235] Although their CO later reported that: 'There were numerous casualties in gaining this objective from snipers and M.G. fire from the N.W ... and GRANDCOURT', the coda: 'Several prisoners surrendered freely' suggests that the South Lancs initially fell upon their beleaguered adversary in great enough numbers to provoke an outbreak of submission.[236] With whispers of failure seeping back to DHQ, the South Lancs then became the victims of their own success when the creeping barrage was hauled back onto the first objective. The CO detailed how 'our own artillery opened a second barrage of shrapnel and H.E. over the objective just gained, causing many casualties here and along railway. It lifted after half an hour onto GRANDCOURT.' Undeterred, the South Lancs determined to push on to their second objective, but the advance was halted when hostile fire teamed up with this 'friendly fire'. 'During this barrage attempts were made by bombing parties from D Coy to enter the village but were prevented by this barrage, and hostile M. Guns [their CO reported].' It was seemingly a lack of officers, more so than a lack of men, that was undermining the advance. The CO reported that: 'At this period there was only one Officer left in the front line in command of all three companies, all the rest having become casualties by 9.30.a.m.'[237]

Yet the presence of a junior officer did not always compel the advance forward. The much diminished East Lancs (down to two Coys.) were following on behind their fellow Lancastrians, charged with the 'capture [of] BAILLESCOURT FARM after the 1st and 2nd objectives had been gained.'[238] Although the second objective remained elusive, the South Lancs' CO was anxious to keep the East Lancs moving forward. 'At 9.45.a.m. one Company E. Lan. R. under Captain HUNT had taken up

---

234 Jeffreys recorded for instance that 'I was very doubtful about the situation on the right, parties of our men being several times reported in different trenches opposite our right, so that I was very loth [sic] to have these shelled.' Ibid.
235 WO95/2075 (Nov 1916), op cit., diary entry 18 Nov. See also CO's account of the battle sent on 22 Nov. WO95/2081 (Nov 1916), op cit.
236 CO's account of the battle sent on 22 Nov. WO95/2081 (Nov 1916), op cit.
237 Ibid.
238 'Narrative of Operations during 18th November – 7th East Lancashire Rgt.' WO95/2079 (Nov 1916), op cit.

a position alongside HANSA ROAD in rear of objective just gained. At 10.a.m. the C.O. [South Lancs] sent a verbal message to Captain HUNT to push on, as this Coy was due to attack BAILLESCOURT FARM at this hour.'[239] Hunt however declined, replying that 'he was held up at the corner of the village by M.G. fire and unable to do so.' Shortly afterwards Hunt received orders from his own BHQ to 'dig in'. Meantime nothing had been heard of the second company of East Lancs until '11.55am when the O.C. the Coy reported that he had been held up by machine gun fire just outside the village and was now digging in ...'[240] Either in disregard or absence of orders, these junior officers of the East Lancs had called a temporary halt to the advance, prioritising the welfare of their men over the objective. Faced with inertia from both led and leaderless men, the South Lancs' CO concurred that 'further advance through GRANDCOURT was at present impossible', and gave the order to consolidate.[241]

The Gloucesters also reported that their: 'First objective [was] reached and carried.'[242] Yet even the division's normally buoyant senior commanders considered that 'so many casualties were sustained in either killed or prisoners that the advantage was nullified.'[243] It would seem that the Gloucesters' circumscribed success was achieved partially at the expense of the Royal Warwicks' unqualified failure. 'About 7.20am one or two wounded men of 'C' and 'D' Coys [Royal Warwicks] reported that these Coys had borne to the left at the bend in BATTERY VALLEY, and gone with the 8/ Gloucesters 'C' and 'D' and about 22 men of A and B Coy [and] appear to have pushed through with the Gloucesters and endeavoured to consolidate beyond O.G.2 in neighbourhood of [map ref], but ultimately compelled to withdraw and hold on to O.G.1.'[244] Waylaid troops had gravitated towards the Gloucesters' front, allowing the battalion to muster a strong enough force to get through the German wire and machine-gun fire and seize their first objective. Yet even these greater numbers were soon overcome by a potent cocktail of mud, machine-gun fire and 'friendly' barrages.

The 19th Division's first 18 months experience of combat have unequivocally shown that surrendering the objective to safety, in the face of heavy hostile fire, was commonplace infantry combat behaviour. By such means the infantry decided an objective's worth, and lived to fight another day – saving their lives for a more propitious battlefield. The division's attack on the 'Switch Line' (23 July) had witnessed the emergence of a far more 'black or white' piece of combat behaviour: infantrymen surrendering the objective, but also themselves with it – living, but not to fight another day. The number of reports filed by 57th Brigade of infantrymen 'disappearing' or 'vanishing'

239 CO's account of the battle sent on 22 Nov. WO95/2081 (Nov 1916), op cit.
240 'Narrative of Operations during 18th November – 7th East Lancashire Rgt.' WO95/2079 (Nov 1916), op cit.
241 COs account of the battle sent on 22 Nov. WO95/2081 (Nov 1916), op cit.
242 WO95/2085 'Gloucesters' (Nov 1916), op cit., diary entry 18 Nov.
243 WO95/2083 (Nov 1916), op cit., diary entry 18 Nov.
244 WO95/2085 'Royal Warwicks' (Nov 1916), op cit., diary entry 18 Nov.

(and the direct reference made to 'prisoners' quoted above) indicates that the malaise resurfaced with greater virulence during the Battle of Ancre.

Jeffreys gave a apocalyptic account of the fate of the North Staffords. 'Nothing more has been heard of the 8th North Stafford Regt. which appears to have been absolutely cut off. No message ever came from them and the CO and Battalion HQ are missing.'[245] The North Staffords themselves reported that the: 'Total number returned who had taken part in the attack were 1 officer 171 O.R.'; of the 16 officer casualties, 12 were reported 'missing'.[246] Jeffreys gave a similarly doomed account of the Royal Warwicks. 'About 30 to 40 men of this battalion came back together with 70 North Staffords above mentioned, otherwise the two right companies are completely vanished.'[247] 57th Brigade HQ were able to offer a more specific account of disappearances amongst the Worcesters. 'Of the two platoons detailed to deal with dugouts in bank at [map ref] not a man returned. A considerable number of our men were distinctly seen being marched off as prisoners from a trench on Eastern slope of BATTERY VALLEY.'[248] Both the Royal Warwicks and Worcesters reported estimated 'missing' totals of 3 officers and upward of 50 OR infantrymen; which equated to roughly two platoons each.[249] In the final reckoning however, a number of the 'missing' of 18 November were added to the legions of the dead.[250] In particular, of the 300 or more North Staffords originally unaccounted for, a staggering 9 officers and 155 ORs were eventually recorded as 'killed'.[251] Nevertheless, it would seem likely that upward of six platoons surrendered to the enemy on the 18th.

Were these incidences of surrender indicative of deterioration in 19th Division's collective combat morale? The same morale sapping ingredients that were present on 23 July were in attendance here – endless days under hostile fire, comrades falling like shattered nine pins, the constant fear for their own lives and limbs – and there was now

---

245 Jeffreys to DHQ, written on 18 Nov. Included in 'Operations on the Ancre October – November 1916' WO95/2053 (Nov 1916), op cit.
246 WO95/2085 'North Staffs' (Nov 1916), op cit., diary entry 18 Nov.
247 Jeffreys to DHQ, written on 18 Nov. Included in 'Operations on the Ancre October – November 1916' WO95/2053 (Nov 1916), op cit.
248 WO95/2083 (Nov 1916), op cit., diary entry 18 Nov.
249 The Royal Warwicks recorded 3 officers and 65 ORs missing. WO95/2085 'Royal Warwicks' (Nov 1916), op cit., diary entry Nov 18th whilst the Worcesters recorded 3 officers and 50 ORs missing. WO95/2086 (Nov 1916), op cit., diary entry 18 Nov.
250 The Worcesters reported the following breakdown of casualties: 1 officer, 5 ORs killed; 1 officer, 41 ORs wounded; 3 officers, 50 ORs missing; total estimated casualties 101. In the final reckoning, 3 officers and 26 ORs were recorded as killed or died of wounds in the immediate aftermath of 18 Nov. WO95/2086 (Nov 1916), op cit., diary entry 18 Nov. The Royal Warwicks initially reported the following breakdown of casualties: 2 officer, 17 ORs killed; 7 officer, 121 ORs wounded; 3 officers, 65 ORs missing; total estimated casualties 215. In the final reckoning, 5 officers and 67 ORs were recorded as killed or died of wounds in the immediate aftermath of 18 Nov. WO95/2085 'Royal Warwicks' (Nov 1916), op cit., diary entry Nov 18th. *Soldiers Died in the Great War*, op cit.
251 WO95/2085 'North Staffords' (Nov 1916), op cit., diary entry 18 Nov.

the added ingredient of insufferable cold and damp. Perhaps, therefore, these groups of infantrymen had lost their willingness to fight and readily chose surrender. In the minds of the division's senior commanders the primary cause was not low morale, but a rapid recoil in the balance of firepower allied to no means of escape – all brought about by poor 'cleaning'. DHQ reported, for example, that: 'The 8th N. Staff. Regt. on the right got over the first German line without serious opposition, but the cleaning up party allotted to this trench went astray, and as this was held by the enemy, the battalion was cut off…'[252] However, the correlation between intense and relentless hostile fire, high casualties, poor conditions, and the recording of troops surrendering *on masse* is, at the very least, suggestive.

If infantrymen (either as individuals or in groups) were finding their combat morale unequal to the bloody Somme battlefield, then combat (aggressive or passive) could be avoided by less overt means than flight or submission. The mist and the mire provided a degree of opportunity for infantrymen to slip away from the advance, and re-join their battalions when the fighting was over – an act described by the military as 'straggling'. The Cheshires' advance was particularly conspicuous for its large number of stragglers. Having jumped off, the whole battalion was almost immediately waylaid. The CO informed 57th Brigade 'that owing to the fog the battalion lost direction and found themselves across Lucky Way before they could recognise their position. They there swung half right and at this moment the barrage opened. The going was very heavy indeed and officers and men were dead beat, they however attempted to overtake the barrage but at 5.15 had only reached our newly dug front line.'[253] At this juncture a group of officers endeavoured to realise the objective, but found that 'the men by this time had thinned out considerably…'[254] Nonetheless '4 Officers and *a handful of men* charged O.G.1 in the vicinity of FIGHT TRENCH. The enemy replied with bomb and M.G. fire. As the party were too small to be of any use they withdrew to the new trench picking up *the stragglers* on the way [my emphasis].'[255]

It is evident that many of the waylaid groups of infantrymen had every intention of keeping up with the advance and pursuing the objective. The battalion for instance reported that: 'Two platoons on the left who had become completely detached worked their way through the embankment in Battery Valley, bombed a dug-out and secured a machine gun.'[256] This group of 'lost' infantrymen were clearly not averse to combat. Moreover, we cannot discount the possibility that other errant platoons were similarly inclined. Nevertheless, at the point when the Cheshires reached the 'newly dug frontline' there must have been enough infantrymen present to convince the OCs that the objective was worth pursuing – indeed, 4 officers would suggest an entire company.

252 WO95/2053 (Nov 1916), op cit. Diary entry 18 Nov.
253 Hand written note from CO to 57th Brigade 18 Nov. Included in 'Operations on the Ancre October – November 1916' WO95/2053 (Nov 1916), op cit.
254 Ibid.
255 WO95/2090 (Nov 1916), op cit. Diary entry 18 Nov.
256 Ibid.

Neither can casualties account for the subsequent 'thinning out of the men'. The Cheshires only recorded '28 wounded and 15 missing', although they accepted that 'some of these missing may yet appear as wounded.'[257] Even so, this was an infinitesimal number compared to the legions of casualties normally suffered in such a reverse. The answer would appear to be, therefore, that a large number of infantrymen slipped away from the advance, and were either 'picked up' shortly afterwards, or 'found' a number of hours later. For example, a junior officer of the Cheshires went in search of errant infantrymen the following morning and 'found a large number of our fellows all mixed up with other units…I did not stop to count them exactly; but Lt Gadson estimates the lot to be between 100 and 150.'[258]

The post-operational reflections of DHQ provide some evidence that many infantrymen, whilst committed to staying with the advance, may have been either unwilling or unable *to fire* at the enemy. In discussions over the division's proposed training schedule for December 1916 DHQ recorded that: 'The Divisional Commander considers that musketry should receive increased attention…He considers that Infantry should be taught to fire whilst advancing as occasions have of late presented themselves in which the enemy, not subjected to our artillery barrage, has exposed himself during our advance and awaited the assault in comparative safety, owing to the fact that *no rifle or machine gun fire has been brought to bear on him* [my emphasis].'[259]

Perhaps Bridges (who, as a Regular soldier, certainly knew something about the strictures of 'fire and movement') was correct; this apt demonstration of 'non-firers' was simply a problem of inadequate training. But maybe the GOC's words also unintentionally contained a truth of infantry combat behaviour and morale. The majority of infantrymen possessed a passive combat morale high enough to sustain them through the advance, and, if the firepower odds were not stacked too steeply against them, achieve a victory. Yet the aggressive combat morale of *many* infantrymen was less vigorous. Certainly we have seen that a small number of infantrymen were willing and able to kill their enemy *face-to-face*. We have also seen that the hand thrown bomb precipitated interpersonal combat on a scale the bayonet could not deliver. Moreover, we have also witnessed that machine-gunners, with the act of killing partially sanitised by distance and teamwork, would fire upon the enemy; at least in desperate self-defence. But the possibility remains that many infantrymen were committed non-firers.

There is also a degree of evidence that the Battle of Ancre had taken its toll on the infantry's broader ability to cope with combat. Summarising the state of the returning survivors of 57th Brigade's attack, Jeffreys wrote that: 'Practically all the men of 8th

---

257 Ibid.
258 Letter written by junior officer of Cheshires to his CO, dated 8.20am 19 Nov, and appended to Fusiliers diary. WO95/2092 'Fusiliers' (Nov 1916), op cit.
259 'List of Courses at Divisional School of Instruction'. WO95/2053 (Dec 1916), op cit.

North Staffords, 10th R. Warwicks, and 10th Worcesters are very tired *and some of them are much shaken* [my emphasis].'²⁶⁰ The casualty rates suffered by 19th Division on 18 November further underline the impression that the closing episodes of the Somme was one act too far for many infantrymen to perform. Admittedly, the willingness to suffer casualties – as a consequence of partial success or absolute failure – of those battalions leading the line had showed no fall off from July 1916. The Gloucesters, Royal Warwicks and North Staffords all suffered casualty rates oscillating around fifty percent, although this figure falls towards forty percent if the 'missing' are removed.²⁶¹

The casualty rates indicate, however, that two equally tenacious foes – the German defenders and the Picardy winter – had withered the 'passive' combat morale of a number of battalions. The already battered and bruised East Lancs (down to two companies) surrendered the objective of 'Baillescourt Farm' when their casualty rate surpassed ten percent.²⁶² The mud laden Cheshires gave up Grandcourt before this figure was breached.²⁶³ Whilst the Worcesters abortive 'cleaning' operations resulted in a casualty rate below twenty percent; and this figure also falls to ten percent if the two surrendering companies are removed.²⁶⁴ One important qualification needs to

---

260 Jeffreys to DHQ, written on 18 Nov. Included in 'Operations on the Ancre October – November 1916' WO95/2053 (Nov 1916), op cit.
261 The Gloucesters recorded 12 officers and 283 ORs as casualties. This gave the battalion a CR of approx. 60%, based upon an estimated strength of 500. However, if the two companies of Royal Warwicks who assisted in their attack are added to their strength, then the CR falls to approx. 42%. WO95/2085 'Gloucesters' (Nov 1916), op cit. The full breakdown of casualties recorded by the Royal Warwicks is as follows: 2 officers, 17 ORs killed; 7 officers, 121 ORs wounded; 3 officers, 65 ORs missing; total casualties 215. This represented a CR of approx. 47% based upon a recorded strength of 455. If the missing ORs are removed the figure drops to approx. 33%. WO95/2085 'Royal Warwicks' (Nov 1916), op cit. The North Staffs recorded 17 officers and 317 ORs as casualties. This represented a CR of approx. 65% based upon a estimated strength of 500. This estimation is a reasonably accurate estimate, based upon the battalion reporting 172 infantrymen returning from the attack, and adding this figure to the reported casualties. If two surrendering platoons are removed the figure drops to approx. 55%. WO95/2085 'North Staffords' (Nov 1916), op cit. In capturing their first objective, but surrendering the second, the South Lancs recorded 132 casualties. This represented a CR of approx. 40% based upon a recorded strength of 324. WO95/2081 (Nov 1916), op cit.
262 The full breakdown of casualties was as follows: 1 officer, 3 ORs killed; 1 officer, 12 ORs wounded; 4 ORs missing; total casualties 21. This represented a CR of approx. 12% based upon a recorded strength of 180. WO95/2079 (Nov 1916), op cit.
263 The Cheshires suffered 43 casualties, none of which were fatal. Their CR was approx. 9%, based upon an estimated strength of 500. This would appear to have been the mean fighting strength of the battalions by November 1916. WO95/2090 (Nov 1916), op cit. Diary entry 18 Nov.
264 57th Brigade recorded that the Worcesters had suffered 106 casualties. Their CR was approx. 18% based upon an estimated strength of 600. This is a reasonably accurate estimate, based upon the Worcesters reporting that: 'The battalion marched 500 strong' on

be placed upon these low casualty rates; all of these battalions were following in the wake of the initial assault, and were therefore somewhat conscious of the carnage that lay ahead. Even so, these casualty rates were rock bottom when compared to those of July 1916.

Although the evidence of this chapter points towards a diminishing of 19th Division's collective 'passive combat morale', the division's disciplinary record for late 1916 reveals that the number of infantrymen who felt compelled to remove themselves (by whatever means) from active service remained very low. The one minor change was the number of infantrymen found guilty of 'Desertion', as opposed to the lesser charge of 'Absence'. Sentences for 'Desertion' had been running at one per month since September, but rose to three during November.[265] This slight rise was, however, numerically insignificant in comparison to the number of infantrymen who were staying in the firing line, and it is perhaps more remarkable that these few were not joined by many more.

The reactions of DHQ and above to these mild breakdowns in discipline does not suggest they were overly fretful of the Butterflies' collective combat morale. During the Spring of 1916 the chain of command had executed one soldier: Pte. J. Cuthbert of 9th Cheshire Btn, a man with a previously poor disciplinary record who had refused an order to join a working party in No Man's Land.[266] Four of the division's five deserters from the Somme were treated with greater leniency; two of the men *were* sentenced to 'Death', but their sentences were later commuted to 'Penal Servitude' by high command, one of which was suspended.[267] Following the attack of 18 November three infantrymen from the North Staffords were also sentenced to 'Death', but for 'Disobedience', and their sentences were likewise commuted and then suspended.[268] One veteran of the Somme was, however, granted no mercy: L. Corp. GE Hughes of the 7th King's Own Royal Lancasters was executed for Desertion.[269]

If these isolated executions were carried out, partly at least, *for the sake of example*, to dissuade other infantrymen of the division from acting likewise, then it does not seem symptomatic of any growing fear over 19th Division's collective combat morale. Evidently the chain of command was willing to spare the rod, and it seems unlikely

  25 Nov. If the reported 50 missing ORs are removed from this equation the CR falls to 9%. WO95/2083 (Nov 1916), op cit & WO95/2086 (Nov 1916), op cit.
265 See WO213/12 Judge Advocates General's Office: Field General Court's Martial and Military Courts, Registers. (Nov/Dec 1916) PRO & WO90/6 Judge Advocates General's Office: General Court's Martial Registers, Abroad. (1916) PRO.
266 See WO71/464 'Proceedings of F.G.C.M. of Pte. J. Cuthbert, Pte. J. Dineen and Pte. Bate of 9th Cheshire Bttn. April 9th 1916' Cuthbert was executed, Dineen and Bate were reprieved.
267 See WO213/12-13 (Nov/Dec 19160, op cit.
268 See WO213/12 (Nov/Dec 1916), op cit.
269 WO71/521 'Proceedings of FGCM of L. Corp. GE Hughes 7th King's Own Royal Lancasters, dated Nov 9th' PRO.

that the threat of 'Penal Servitude' would have much effect upon a man faced with a 1 in 3 chance of losing his life. Moreover, it seems reasonable to assume that had DHQ and above wanted to quash what they perceived as a breakdown in discipline and morale amongst their troops, they would have taken the opportunity to make an example of more than just the unfortunate L. Corp. GE Hughes.

7

From *Esprit de Corps* to *Esprit de Platoon*

Overview

The winter of 1916-17 was evidently a period of troubled reflection in the BEF. 1916 had not been the promised year of victory. It was time for a tactical rethink. The tactics and training schemes outlined in *Infantry Training 1914* had served the old professional army well enough during the mobile battles of 1914, but had been considered too complex and beyond the grasp of the amateur New Army.[1] The alternative – 'artillery destroys, infantry occupies' – had proved a naïve and abysmal failure on 1 July 1916. For the next five months commanders at all levels of the BEF had, by bloody trial and error, sought a new and more efficacious 'art of attack'. Over the winter GHQ endeavoured to collate and disseminate (what appeared to its eyes) the most striking forms of this art. The results were *S.S.135 Instructions for the Training of Divisions for Offensive Action* and *S.S.143 Instructions for the Training of Platoons for Offensive Action*.[2] If the infantrymen of 19th Division were successfully ascending a 'learning curve', however, then it was partly a 'self-learning curve'. 19th DHQ, not content to await proclamations from on high, had concurrently issued the conclusions of its own tactical introspections – *G. 717/2. 'Standard organization of the 'trench to trench' attack: The battalion in attack'*.[3]

One big idea, insofar as the infantry were concerned, ran through these various tactical deliberations; the need to make the *platoon* the primary formation of the infantry assault. The belated acceptance that generals and even battalion COs could not wrestle back control over the Great War battlefield, allied to changes adopted

---

1 *Infantry Training 1914* General Staff, War Office. H.M.S.O. (1914) IWM.
2 *S.S.135 Instructions for the Training of Divisions for Offensive Action*, (DTOA 1917) issued by the General Staff December 1916, with minor revisions August 1917. IWM. *S.S.143 Instructions for the Training of Platoons for Offensive Action, 1917* issued by the General Staff February 1917 IWM.
3 G. 717/2. 'Standard organization of the "trench to trench" attack: The battalion in attack', issued by DHQ 1 Feb 1917. WO95/2054 (Feb 1917), op cit.

by the German defenders – holding the firing line lightly, but defending the ground behind with heavily fortified interlocking strong-points – had fed the crystallisation of *platoon based tactics*. The battalion/brigade organisation of attack – composed of a small vanguard of bombers, a long wave of 'non-specialist' riflemen, and a supporting cast of (largely off scene) machine-gunners and trench mortars, all commanded by a number of 'specialist' officers – had purportedly proved too cumbersome and intractable for the modern battlefield. From its battle-scarred cocoon emerged the lighter and more flexible 'autonomous fighting platoon', armed with every weapon currently available to the infantry.[4]

If the reconstituted platoon was to function as planned, every rank was required to shoulder a greater responsibility for combat. Not just the platoon's junior officer, who now held ultimate command over every weapon group; or the platoon's NCOs, to whom the mantle of exemplary leadership was passing; but to *every man* of the platoon, three-out-of-four of whom were now handling a specialist weapon (Lewis Gun, Rifle Grenade or bomb), and *all* of whom were required to be a *pro tempore* specialist.

The 19th Division spent the best part of December 1916 and March 1917 on the training camp. The frontline around Hebuterne was then held from 11 January until the German retreat to the Hindenburg Line beginning 24 February, during which time the division executed a largely uncontested advance through Serre. The Wytschaete Ridge, to the south of the Ypres Salient, was held during April. May found the division defending the BEF's very own *Voie Sacrée*, the Menin Road, and ensconced in the shadow of Hill 60.[5]

Platoon Tactics

One of the primary rationales behind this shift towards platoon based tactics has already been witnessed throughout this study thus far. *S.S.143* stated that the 'matter of control by even Company leaders on the battlefield is now so difficult that the smaller formations, i.e., platoon and section commanders must be trained to take the necessary action on their own initiative, without waiting for orders.'[6,7] We have seen time and again how the link in the chain of command fractured at platoon level the moment the infantry stepped over the parapet, leaving battlefield command solely in the hands of 'temporary' junior officers. Platoon tactics gave official commendation to this shift in command authority by proposing to make platoon commanders (and, to

4 With one exception, the Stokes Mortar remained a brigade weapon, but under the command of the platoon during the attack.
5 WO95/2054 (Jan-May 1917), op cit.
6 *S.S.143* op cit, p. 11.
7 Ibid., p. 11.

some extent, NCOs) responsible for the post-Zero battlefield; a command that would have been somewhat impotent without a concomitant increase in platoon firepower.

The German Army's decision to base the defence of their frontline upon a deep, interwoven line of lightly manned but heavily armed strongpoints, necessitated that this firepower equated to *every* weapon then at the infantry's disposal. *S.S.143* recognised that, with the Germans no longer holding the firing line linearly and in strength: 'Tactics of a Platoon in Attack…[in] either a Trench-to-Trench attack or in Open Warfare…resolve themselves in the majority of cases into the method of attack of Tactical Points … [which] may be described as a locality…[a] 'strong point'…'[8] The majority of these 'strongpoints' consisted of concrete blockhouses that were immune to even a direct artillery hit. The task of permanently silencing these fortresses, therefore, fell upon the infantry. A long line of rifle and bayonet touting troops attacking a blockhouse – *a la mode* 1 July 1916 – were little more than lambs to the slaughter. Forty or so men, armed with a plethora of specialist 'cleansing' weapons, commanded by one, autonomous, on-the-spot commander, and well practiced in the art of 'cleaning', appeared a far more encouraging proposition. *S.S.143* decreed that: 'The guiding principles of this organisation are that the Platoon shall consist of a combination of all the weapons with which the Infantry are now armed, and that specialist commanders for Infantry are undesirable.'[9] Thus the autonomous fighting platoon was born.

The first half of this new 'official' doctrine – *S.S.135* – dealt mostly with the organisation of higher formations, and was of greater interest to generals and brigadiers than platoon commanders. The document was an apostle of lessons learnt in the deployment of artillery, reserves, tanks and so forth, and the best use of technological innovations, especially in the realms of communications (the perennial bugbear).[10] Naturally, aspects of these developments touched closely upon the future experiences of the infantry. In particular, it is apparent that the role of the machine-gunner was (with the clear exception of the Lewis Gunners), moving closer to that of the artillery – both organisationally and experientially. *S.S.135* stated that the primary use of the brigade machine-gunner was: 'To provide covering fire for the attacking Infantry… there are now sufficient guns in a Division to supply covering fire, similar to the artillery barrage, along the whole Divisional front.'[11] Moreover, the inauguration of 'the Corps Machine Gun [unit] under the orders of the Corps Commander' signalled a further 'centralisation' of the arm, and meant that the majority of machine-gunners operating on the division's sector during an attack were now taking their orders from higher (and high) command.[12] The Stokes Mortars, meantime, both organisationally and experientially, kept a foot in both camps. Prior to the assault, the Stokes

8   Ibid., p. 8.
9   *S.S.143* op cit., p. 3.
10 See *S.S.135* op cit., pp. 33-42.
11 Ibid., p. 44.
12 Ibid., p. 44-5.

Mortars were under brigade command, and would form part of the barrage – albeit a more flexible part, and aimed primarily at the enemy's machine guns. With the first phase successfully completed, the Stokes Mortars came under battalion command, and joined the infantry assault, their primary task 'that of dealing with any enemy machine guns, or strong points, which may be temporarily holding up part of our advance.'[13]

S.S.135 also codified the lessons learnt by the artillery during 1916. The arch distance killer would remain king. The broad objectives assigned to the preliminary bombardment were to 'demolish the enemy's trenches and works as far as it is desirable to do so, to destroy wire entanglements and other obstacles that would impede the advance of the assaulting troops, to cause casualties and loss of morale among the garrison of the enemy's trenches…'[14] Yet the onus had moved from destroying, to *neutralizing* the enemy's defensive weaponry. For example, discussing 'counter battery work', *S.S.135* wrote that: 'At the moment of assault, all known hostile batteries which might interfere with the advance are subjected to an intense bombardment by long range guns and howitzers, with the object of destroying the actual guns *or of preventing the enemy detachments from serving their guns. This latter procedure is known as neutralizing fire* [my emphasis].'[15] The role of 'neutralization' was more overtly stated in the work of the '18-prs Field Artillery Barrage': 'Immediately the advance begins the 180prs. commence an intense bombardment, with the object of forcing the enemy to take cover and thereby prevent him manning his defences before the infantry reach the trench.'[16]

S.S.135, laying the groundwork for the arrival of the second half of the 'official' doctrine, unequivocally announced that the BEF's tactical response to this expanding battlefield role was to be the autonomous fighting platoon. 'The ultimate unit in the assault is the PLATOON. The platoon must be organised and trained as a self-contained unit capable of producing the required proportions of riflemen, rifle-bombers, bombers, carriers and runners trained to work in combination. One or two Lewis guns may also be added on occasion. On the resourcefulness and self-sufficiency of the platoon in dealing scientifically with every obstacle which it may meet, on its internal organisation into small parties trained to their particular tasks under their own leaders, and on the skill of the platoon leader and the hold which he has over his command, the success of the assault will largely depend.'[17]

The 'ideal' reconstituted platoon would have a strength of 36 OR infantrymen, divided into four sections, three of which were to be based around an individual specialism: Lewis-Gunner, Rifle Grenadier or Bomber. The minimum strength was

---

13 Ibid., p. 50.
14 Ibid., p. 9. Complete destruction was unadvisable because it robbed the invading infantrymen of subsequent protection from counter-attack.
15 Ibid., p. 11-12.
16 Ibid., p. 12.
17 Ibid., p. 17.

set at 28, the maximum at 44. It was suggested that below the minimum would not produce the required firepower, above the maximum would prove too large to control.[18] The addition of the new specialism of Rifle-Grenadier effectively increased by a third the number of battalion infantrymen carrying 'distance' weapons; 9 Lewis-Gunners and 9 Rifle Grenadiers per platoon, 72 per company, 288 per battalion.[19] This brought the overall number of 'distance' specialists serving within a brigade to approximately thirty percent of its ideal strength (or forty percent of its actual strength).[20]

Platoon tactics did not, however, demand any significant increase in the number of infantrymen specialising in interpersonal combat. One section of dedicated Bombers per platoon represented a continuation of the 40 or so who had previously served under the battalion. Although there was one slight but nevertheless important change; 2 men of the Bombing section were also required to be 'Bayonet Men' – an unequivocal form of interpersonal combat specialism derived from trench raiding. Of the remaining 9 men serving with the 'non-specialist' 'Riflemen' section, 2 were similarly to be designated 'Bayonet Men', whilst two pairs of 'picked shots' (snipers) and 'Scouts' were also to be nominated.[21] If this multitude of officially designated specialists threatened to make the non-specialist riflemen an endangered species, then *S.S.143*'s entreaty towards pro tempore specialism spelt his extinction. 'Every man is a rifleman and a bomber, and in the assault, with the exception of the No. 1 and No. 2 of Lewis Gun, fixes his bayonet. Men in rifle sections must be trained either to the Lewis Gun or rifle bomb.'[22]

The development of the autonomous fighting platoon not only demanded that all infantrymen learn a specialism, but also that they grasp a greater degree of 'all arms' cooperation than hitherto experienced. The tactical deployment of the platoon outlined by *S.S.143* centred upon hitting the enemy strongpoint with a two-pronged enveloping attack. The Bombers would infiltrate one side of the strong-point, under the cover of a fusillade from the Rifle Grenadiers – described by *S.S.143* as 'the 'howitzer' of the infantry and used to dislodge the enemy from behind cover and to obtain superiority of fire by driving him underground' – whilst the Riflemen infiltrated the opposite

---

18 *S.S.143* op cit., p. 6.
19 The number of Lewis-Gunners per battalion during 1916 had been approximately 50. Although the distance element of combat would, during the proposed method of attack, be reduced to tens of yards, not hundreds, and the target was more likely to be witnessed, the elements of teamwork (in the case of the Lewis Gun) and automation remained.
20 This total is derived as follows: approx. 1000 Lewis-Gunners & Rifle-Grenadiers, approx. 100 Trench Mortars, approx. 175 Vickers Machine-Gunners (DHQ recorded a total of 531 officers and ORs serving with the Vickers Machine-Gunners in the division during April 1917), this equates to approx. 30% of an ideal strength of 4000 infantrymen. DHQ recorded an actual fighting strength of 9,300 Infantrymen for April 1917, this lower figure, 3100 per brigade, gives a distance specialist percentage of approx. 40%. WO95/2054 (April 1917), op cit.
21 Ibid., p. 13.
22 *S.S.143* op cit., 'Notes' to Appendix I, 'Formation for trench to trench attack'.

side, under the cover of a barrage from the Lewis-Gunners.[23] This 'art of attack' was conspiring to dethrone the Bombers from their position as vanguard of the infantry. For if the infantry attack of 1916 had the appearance of a snake – a diminutive sharp end with a long tail – with the Bombers forming the head, then the 1917 creation was more akin to an octopus – with a multitude of arms reaching out to simultaneously assault the enemy.

This level of 'all arms cooperation', together with the decision to withdraw specialist commanders, also necessitated a fundamental change in the platoon commander's battlefield role. The diagrammatic representations of the platoon's method of attack appended to *S.S.143* drew attention to 'The position of the Commander', which was alongside the Rifle Grenadiers, directing and coordinating the attack, not leading it. The role of exemplary leadership (during the attack) had devolved to the NCO; the 'Platoon Sergeant' assisted by his 'Section Commanders'.[24]

The 19th Division's own tactical response to the harsh lessons of the Somme – 'Standard Organization' – concurred with most of the sentiments and solutions laid out in the 'official' doctrines.[25] The autonomous fighting platoon was (no doubt under the influence of *S.S.135*) seen as the way ahead to resolving a intractable and dispersed battlefield, and 'deflect[ing] to either side and work[ing] around the flanks and rear of the resistance' the most efficacious tactical deployment of this platoon against the enemy's strongpoints.[26] Moreover, both agreed upon the vital importance of thorough 'mopping-up' (or 'cleaning' of captured trenches) to avoid counter-attacks from the rears, and suggested a similar improvement: dedicated units, following on immediately behind each attacking wave. For example, 'Standard Organization' stated that: 'Mopping up' parties will not be found from the battalion carrying out the assault of a trench, unless this trench is the final objective …'[27]

19th DHQ originally proposed to follow its own path, however, when it came to the formation and deployment of the infantry's distance weapons. 'Standard Organization' (in a move that foreshadowed German *Sturm* tactics deployed the following spring) witnessed a greater potential for the Lewis Gun and Rifle Grenade;

---

23   *S.S.143* did not outline the tactical deployment of the platoon quite so clearly, but the appended diagrams which accompanied the description – 'Appendix VIII Trench to Trench Attack: Platoon in First Wave meeting a point of resistance' & 'Appendix X Attack in Open Warfare: correct method of action of a Platoon in firing line, meeting a point of resistance.' – suggest the interpretation given here. *S.S.143* op cit., pp. 7-8.
24   Ibid. 'Appendix VIII Trench to Trench Attack: Platoon in First Wave meeting a point of resistance' & 'Appendix X Attack in Open Warfare: correct method of action of a Platoon in firing line, meeting a point of resistance.'
25   G. 717/2. 'Standard organization of the 'trench to trench' attack: The battalion in attack', issued by DHQ 1 Feb 1917. WO95/2054 (Feb 1917), op cit. The document bore the signature of Lt-Col. R.M. Johnson, an officer of the General Staff, and the division's G.S.O.1.
26   G. 717/2. 'Standard Organization', WO95/2054 (Feb 1917), op cit.
27   Ibid.

not just as weapons to cover the attack, but weapons that could *spearhead* the attack. Rather than placing these distance weapons in discrete units behind the first wave, a team of Lewis Gunners and 6 Rifle Grenadiers would advance with the leading wave, as part of 'interdisciplinary' sections. 'Standard Organization' was particularly optimistic that the Lewis Gun could be transformed into a semi-mobile weapon capable of increasing the firepower of the leading wave; especially during the advance across the open, when the infantry were particularly vulnerable to hostile fire. 'Pending the introduction of some form of light automatic rifle, 2 Lewis guns per company in the front line will accompany the first wave. One of these guns, with two men of its team, will move in the centre of each platoon in the first wave. One of the men will carry the gun and a crutch (19th Division pattern) for firing from a kneeling position, whilst the other will carry ammunition drums. Fire will be opened from these guns on any of the enemy who show themselves in or in front of the trench to be assaulted, but the advance must not be delayed.'[28]

As we have seen, DHQ had previously raised concerns over the 'non-firing' of riflemen in the leading wave. Placing a sanitised distance weapon at the sharp end (the sanitising elements of distance being reduced, but teamwork and automation still present) was their response. DHQ, in agreement with GHQ, however, also witnessed the death-knell of the 'specialist, stating that 'regards bombers, every Infantry man should understand their use, and be a potential bomber.'[29]

Although 'Standard Organization' presents a reasonable facsimile of the 'official' doctrines, DHQ was adamant that it had something unique, and worth guarding. Major-Gen. Bridges unequivocally informed his battalion COs that: 'A copy of the G.H.Q. standard form of attack has been received. It is not proposed to follow it, and the Divisional standard form will be followed.'[30] Perhaps Bridges, as a pre-war Regular, was pursuing the traditional military axiom of claiming success as one's own, whilst blaming failure on someone else (a maxim that was to rule during the German spring Offensives). What is certain, however, is that DHQ had given the division the necessary tools to draw their own learning curve. No 'minor operation' was allowed to pass without the 'lessons learnt' being recorded and disseminated throughout the division. For example, DHQ recorded how "Lessons learnt from the raid'[executed by the

---

28 Ibid. In contrast, *S.S.135* envisaged no part for the Lewis Gun in the leading lines. 'If the attack goes through without check, Lewis guns are not required with the leading lines; but in order to give the leading troops some means of dealing with machine guns, which may have escaped the bombardment and barrage, Lewis guns must be close at hand…as a rule it has been found convenient for the guns of each assaulting Company to move on the flanks of the second wave.' *S.S.135* op cit., p. 46.
29 'Outline of training programme for 19th Division during period of rest'. WO95/2053 General Staff 19th Division War Diary (Dec 1916) PRO.
30 'Notes on Battalion Commanders' Conference at 19th D.H.Q. 4th March 1917.' WO95/2054 (March 1917), op cit.

Worcesters had been] issued to Bdes, R.A., R.E., 5th S.W.B. [pioneers] & School.'[31] This 'Divisional School' had opened on 1 December 1916, and was, according to DHQ, designed 'for the all-round training of young officers and NCOs ...'[32] By such means, therefore, the division's young charges were also schooled in 19th Division's way in war.

In defence of Bridges' claims to originality, the division was organising for platoon tactics before the arrival of *S.S.143*. For example, in early January, 58th Brigade reported that: 'The GOC [Brig-Gen. Glasgow] and Bde Major went to HEUZECOURT to witness a demonstration by the specially trained platoon of the 9th Welch Regt. Major Gen Bridges was present. [And three days later]...The GOC and Bde Major went to GEZAINCOURT to see a demonstration by the special platoon 8th Gloucester Regt of the 57th Bde.'[33] Evidently one battalion from each brigade had been requested to organise and practice (a version of) platoon tactics, and then demonstrate the new 'art of attack' to their fellow infantrymen and commanders.[34] By March platoon tactics dominated the division's training programme; DHQ, for instance, gave precedence to practicing the: 'Attack and seizure of a strong point by a platoon – holding attack – enveloping and flank attack – development of all weapons with which the platoon is armed.'[35] It is also apparent that battalions were reorganising towards autonomous fighting platoons prior to *S.S.143*. For example, the Loyals reported on 1 January 1917: 'Started organization of bombing sections in each platoon.'[36] As has been alluded, *S.S.135* had announced the arrival of platoon tactics prior to this time. But it would seem that DHQ took the idea and ran with it. Rather than charge Bridges with plagiarism, therefore, it might be fairer to conclude that the lessons of the Somme had forced most (but not all) senior commanders who served there along the same learning curve.

The BEF had a plan – the autonomous fighting platoon – time to learn that plan, and the weapons to put the plan into action. But one very large and glittering spanner threatened the works: every man could be handed a specialist weapon, but could every man, or enough men, be trained, inculcated or conditioned to use that weapon on the enemy? As Bridges bluntly informed his troops: 'If they don't learn how to kill Huns, the Huns will kill them.'[37]

31 WO95/2054 (Feb 1917), op cit. Diary entry 11 Feb.
32 WO95/2053 (Dec 1916), op cit., diary entry 1 Dec.
33 WO95/2088 Headquarters 58th Brigade War Diary (Jan 1917) PRO. Diary entries 3 & 5 Jan.
34 See: WO95/2085 10th Battn. The Royal Warwickshire Regiment War Diary (Jan 1917) PRO, diary entry 5 Jan; WO95/2080 7th Battn. The Loyal North Lancashire Regiment War Diary (Jan 1917) PRO, diary entry 4 Jan.
35 'Notes on Battalion Commanders' Conference at 19th D.H.Q. 4th March 1917.' WO95/2054 (March 1917), op cit.
36 WO95/2080 (Jan 1917), op cit., diary entry 1 Jan 1917.
37 'Notes on Battalion Commanders' Conference at 19th D.H.Q. 4th March 1917.' WO95/2054 (March 1917), op cit.

Both GHQ and DHQ viewed overcoming this fundamental problem of combat as relatively uncomplicated, largely because they witnessed killing as primarily a problem of discipline and training, and the individual's disposition towards combat very much a secondary, but not inconsequential concern. *S.S.135* repeated the mantra that the key to 'combat morale' was discipline, and the key to discipline was 'Drill': 'The morale of the unit must be improved by attention to saluting, turn out, clothing, and by close order drill.'[38] *S.S.143* joined in the chant: 'Steady drill and ceremonial are necessary to inculcate discipline, of which cleanliness, smartness and steadiness are the bedrock.'[39] DHQ added its voice: 'Discipline to be tightened up. Soldierly bearing to be insisted upon. Officers to check slovenliness and lack of soldierly bearing in any unit of the Division.'[40] DHQ also witnessed the importance of weapon competence, demanding that 'musketry should receive increased attention…especially the art of 'fir[ing] whilst advancing'.[41] The Cheshires 'Syllabus of Platoon Training' similarly emphasised musketry, and the infantryman was to undergo 'Standard tests in: Rapidity of loading. Aiming, Firing. Judging Distance … Practice over 30 yd range.'[42]

The psychological, or human, aspect of combat was not entirely neglected; both GHQ and DHQ recognised the need to inculcate the desire to fight. DHQ pinned its hopes upon the bayonet: 'Bayonet fighting and physical drill most important. Confidence in and ability to use the bayonet has a stimulating effect on will power and morale.'[43] DHQ also saw a place for cap-badge loyalty, suggesting that: 'Cheering requires attention – Perhaps the shouting of the name of the regiment – 'Hurrah the ——— shire' would be a good institution.'[44] Whilst GHQ reiterated the belief that exposure to combat spawned more tenacious trench fighters: 'Obtaining complete command of No Man's Land. This is of special importance [*S.S.135* suggested], especially from the point of view of moral[e], both for cultivating an offensive spirit and for the resulting feeling of confidence created among the troops about to attack. The greater the number of men who have been 'over the top' on patrols, the greater the confidence of a unit.'[45]

As we have seen, these tried and tested axioms had yielded ambiguous results during 1916. A number of infantrymen took no active part in combat and even less participated when fighting descended towards interpersonal combat. It may have been that

---

38 *S.S.135* op cit., p. 4.
39 *S.S.143* op cit., p. 12.
40 'Notes on Battalion Commanders' Conference at 19th D.H.Q. 4th March 1917.' WO95/2054 (March 1917), op cit.
41 'Outline of Training Programme for the 19th Division during period of rest.' WO95/2053 (Dec 1916), op cit.
42 WO95/2090 9th Battn. The Cheshire Regiment War Diary (April 1917) PRO.
43 'Notes on Battalion Commanders' Conference at 19th D.H.Q. 4th March 1917.' WO95/2054 (March 1917), op cit.
44 Ibid.
45 *S.S.135* op cit., p. 49.

the BEF could do little more to overcome twenty or so years of social conditioning, or perhaps an even more immovable innate resistance to killing. If so then the BEF was not going to accept the status quo, and new innovations were being advanced. DHQ attempted to capitalised upon their troop's obsession for football as a novel means of inculcating the *esprit de corps*. Each occasion the division was resting its battalions would compete in a knockout tournament, at stake the honour of being the divisional champions; '73 footballs and 20 spare bladders…Shorts, shirts or jerseys…[and] 31 sets of goal-posts' were requisitioned accordingly.[46]

The inspirational potential of cap-badge loyalty was also preoccupying GHQ, who now proposed a seismic shift in its source – from *esprit de corps* to *esprit de platoon*. *S.S.143* stated that: 'True soldierly spirit must be built up in Sections and Platoons. Each section should consider itself the best section in the platoon, and the platoon the best in the battalion.' *S.S.143* ventured that: 'The Platoon Commander should be the proudest man in the Army. He is the Commander of *the* unit in the attack [original emphasis].' The emergence of *esprit de platoon* also promised to make the 'temporary' junior officer the most important man in the BEF – on and off the battlefield. The platoon commander was, from this point on, responsible for the training, discipline, welfare and combat morale of his unit. High standards in all departments would be achieved principally by 'setting an example'. *S.S.143* stated, for instance, that: 'The confidence of his men can be gained by: Being the best man at arms in the platoon, or trying to be so…[and by] Example, being himself well turned out, punctual, and cheery, even under adverse circumstances.' *S.S.143* also reiterated the tenets of *noblesse oblige*, just in case the working-class ranker officer had not grasped the principles of the old feudal spirit when he'd been on the wrong side of the deal: 'The confidence of his men can be gained by: Looking after his men's comfort before his own and never sparing himself.' *S.S.143* concluded bystressing that: 'He [the Platoon Commander] can, if he is so disposed, establish an esprit de platoon which will be hard to equal in any other formation.'[47]

By nurturing the *esprit de platoon* the BEF had discovered, either by design or accident, the morale potency of 'loyalty to the primary group' (or 'close unit cohesion'). The suspicion is that the devolution to platoon tactics naturally suggested a concomitant emphasis upon the morale of the platoon, rather than GHQ recognising that comradeship provided a potent morale force upon the battlefield. Nevertheless, the BEF had now tapped into, and was endeavouring to enhance, 'loyalty to the primary group'. Yet, as far as aggressive combat morale was concerned, the 'primary group' was a double edged sword. As we have seen, comradeship could inspire infantrymen to incredible feats of bravery to *save another man's life*. But the collective power of

46 '19th Division No.G.304' "Committee Meeting was held at D.H.Q. today to discuss the procedure as regards the Recreational Training Period', dated 29 Nov 1916. WO95/2053 (Nov 1916), op cit.
47 *S.S.143* op cit., p. 14.

this compulsion as often as not motivated the group to sacrifice the objective to safety. The task now facing the BEF was to give comradeship an aggressive element. *S.S.143* considered that 'example' had a function here also; the platoon commander was encouraged to be 'blood-thirsty, and forever thinking how to kill the enemy, and helping his men to do so.'[48] How the commander himself was to attain this level of belligerence was not stated. In the final analysis, however, turning camaraderie towards violence still hinged upon the trusty bayonet: 'Bayonet fighting produces lust for blood [*S.S.143* opined]; much may be accomplished in billets in wet weather, as well as out of doors on a fine day.'[49] So the aggressive combat morale of the platoon largely rested upon the belief that skewering a sandbag would naturally drive the infantryman to skewer his fellow man.

The pre-war Regular commanders who lauded the steel tip were undoubtedly correct to view the bayonet charge as the epitome of the offensive spirit. A line of infantrymen prepared to pig-stick the enemy, and face the same disembowelling fate, were experiencing an aggressive combat morale that would be hard to better. In the abstract it was a sound philosophy. In reality, on a battlefield saturated by spitting shards of white hot metal, the bayonet charge was often akin to suicide. Moreover, the evidence gathered here suggests that many infantrymen were either unwilling or unable to execute this extreme form of interpersonal combat. Alternatively, the same evidence indicates that many infantrymen found firing a machine-gun within the spectrum of their combat morale, whilst those prepared to execute more interpersonal forms of combat found the bomb fight a far more viable form of combat than either close-up rifle fire-fights or the bayonet fight. If the BEF wanted to up the firepower of the infantry attack, therefore, the solution would seem to have been to load the platoon with more distance and sanitising weapons.

The evolution of platoon tactics suggests the BEF grasped this principle. Yet it is clear that there was a inner discord within the BEF over the embracing of new weapons technology; a conflict no more apparent than in the philosophical battle raging between the bomb and the 'rifle and bayonet'. *S.S.135's* treatise against the bomb splendidly captures the prejudices of the pre-war Regulars. 'At the present time there is a great danger of the importance of the bomb being unduly emphasized at the expense of the rifle and bayonet. It must be impressed upon all ranks that the rifle and bayonet is, and always will be, the infantryman's principal weapons, and that they cannot be too familiar with them or too expert in their use. Attacks over the open with the rifle and bayonet, if vigorously pushed home, will always succeed in making progress when the co-operation between the Infantry and Artillery is good; bombing attacks along trenches, however vigorous and however well supported by Artillery, will never succeed in making any real progress. It may be taken for granted

---

48   Ibid., p. 14.
49   Ibid., p. 12. A remarkably bathetic sentence which mixed the brutal with the everyday travails of life.

that once the attack has come down to the bombing stage, the operation has come to a standstill.'[50]

This prejudice against the bomb clearly flew in the face of costly experience. 19th Division had captured La Boisselle with the bomb; apparently a method that 'will never succeed in making any progress'. Equally spuriously, *S.S.135* argued that the 'bombing attack' was more costly, both physically and mentally, than the overland charge. 'A bombing attack is very slow, it entails great fatigue, not only among the actual bombers, but also among the carrying parties who have to keep up the supply of bombs, and the casualties are usually out of all proportion to the gains realised.'[51] Bombers certainly did suffer from fatigue, but then so did almost every infantrymen who executed combat on the Western Front. Moreover, evidence clearly indicates that bombing attacks were *less* costly than the overland charge – this was why the infantry invariably resorted to them (that, and avoiding a bayonet fight). The answer to this unfounded prejudice against the bomb (and other sanitising weapons) was seemingly that many old Regulars feared that, amidst the growing impedimenta of industrialised killing machines, the humble infantryman was losing his traditional 'offensive spirit'.

Although Bridges shared this animus against the bomb – stressing that 'the rifle and bayonet are the first weapon of the infantry soldier'[52] – DHQ's own platoon tactics demonstrated a clear willingness to embrace and encompass the latest weapons technology. Bridges, however, was temporarily assigned to head a military mission to the United States during May and June 1917.[53] His replacement, Major-Gen. Cameron 'Tiger' Shute, although a general with a reputation for innovation, was less than impressed by the division's own improvements. A few days into his new tenure Shute expressed his chagrin at what he witnessed on the training ground. 'The G.H.Q. system of attack which I understand you have been practicing has got a lot of dodges; Moppers-up and such things…[and] the Battalion Commanders are rather inclined to introduce complicated things into the attack and to do away with simplicity which is necessary under fire.'[54] Shute's disapprobation stretched to DHQ's one genuine piece of innovation. 'The Army Commander asked me what I thought about firing from the hip. Well, I don't think much of it; men may shoot their own men down.'

'That shit Shute',[55] as A.P. Herbert famously described him, was not prepared to hold fire and be proved wrong, even though the battle was now only days away. On 26 May the South Lancs reported: 'Brigade was inspected in mass by Div. General on training ground. Addressed the Brigade with a very tigerly expression re forth-

50   *S.S.135* op cit., p. 52 'Action of Bombers'.
51   Ibid., p. 53.
52   G.123/24/2 dated 17 March. WO95/2054 (March 1917), op cit.
53   I am grateful to Dr. J.M. Bourne for providing this information. October 2002.
54   WO95/2081 7th Battn. The South Lancashire Regiment War Diary (May 1917) PRO.
55   A.P. Herbert was a British political activist, writer, humorist and a Member Parliament who had gained first hand experience of Major General Cameron Shute during his time under his command in the 63rd Naval Division.

coming offensive and announced many drastic changes.' It would seem that this obvious 'thruster' wanted a bit more 'offensive spirit' and a few less 'dodges'. The South Lancs candidly described the inevitable effects of such last-minute wholesale changes. 'G.H.Q. standard plans of organisation and attack, which after a great deal of changes and labour have been approaching perfection, have now been completely thrown to the wall. All plans for the offensive have also been changed, and the result is a chaotic whirl in the brains of the Battalion Staff and Company Commanders.'[56] One week later this 'chaotic whirl' led the battalion up the Messines Ridge and into the attack.

Trench Raiding Prior to Third Ypres

The experiential gulf between trench warfare and the set-piece attack was intermittently bridged by the division's own hands, at the insistence of the BEF's continuing policy of trench raiding. If there was still a moral(e) agenda to raiding then it went unrecorded. Rather, it would seem that reconnaissance and identification were increasingly becoming the primary concerns. This was especially the case on the Ypres Salient during the build up to the Messines offensive, when, as the South Lancs recorded: 'Patrols and small raids to obtain identification formed the chief feature. These were energetically demanded by Bde and Div. Staffs, and several were carried out nightly...'[57]

The wisdom of trench raiding had been somewhat further undermined by the recent change in German defence tactics. As one group of Worcester raiders observed: 'It appears that he [the enemy] holds a chain of posts just in front of WALTER Trench with M.G.'s, and has odd Listening Posts out well in front. There was not the least sign of either of his trenches being used.'[58] In March 57th Brigade reported that: 'The German front line in the HOLLANDSCHESCHUUR SALIENT was entered on several occasions but was always found to be unoccupied.'[59] Consequently, of the eleven raids/patrols executed by 19th Division during this period, only two resulted in unqualified success.[60] At best, 'no enemy were met and the party returned without any

---

56   Ibid., diary entry 22-29 May. The South Lancs were not afraid to name names: 'The forthcoming offensive was practiced. This varied daily, or rather hourly. The changes were principally due to the change in Divisional Commanders which has taken place. Major Gen. C.D. SHUTE C.B. C.M.G. has taken over command of the Division.'
57   WO95/2081 (May 1917), op cit., diary entry 18-20 May.
58   'Report of Raid carried out by one and a half coys. of 10/Worc.R. on night of 11/12th Feb', written by Lt. Col. D.M. Sole (CO) on 12 Feb. WO95/2054 (Feb 1917), op cit.
59   WO95/2083 Headquarters 57th Brigade War Diary (March 1917) PRO, diary entries 23-30 March. See also WO95/2090 (May 1917), op cit. Undated handwritten account.
60   See: 'Two accounts of a 'Raid 5/6/17' written respectively by 2nd Lt. Alf Smith and 2nd Lt. H.H. Backhouse'. WO95/2078 7th Battn. The King's Own (Royal Lancaster) Regiment War Diary (May 1917) PRO & WO95/2086 10th Battn The Worcestershire Regiment War Diary (May 1917) PRO, diary entry 25 May.

prisoners or identification.'⁶¹ At worst, raiders found themselves strafed by machine-guns or artillery safely ensconced well beyond their frontline objectives. For example, the Worcesters' reward for finding one dead German was '45 wounded … [and] about one dozen missing', all thought killed.⁶²

The lesson was seemingly clear. The wily 'Bosche' were no longer hanging around their frontline in large numbers waiting to be shelled or captured. Particularly on the ridges that surrounded Ypres, the Germans were holding the line with small bodies of troops housed in concrete dugouts hidden in the shattered woods that still clung to the slopes, protected by deep and dispersed machine-guns also ensconced in concrete blockhouses. This deemed the objective of reconnaissance and identification extremely problematic, whilst the object of killing Germans was more likely to result in killing Tommies.

The combat behaviour displayed during these faltering raids indicates that making every man a specialist would not compel every man to take an active part in combat. Raids continued to be marked by significant numbers of infantrymen declining interpersonal combat. Lt-Col. Sole (CO Worcesters) gave the following account of his battalion's troubled large-scale raid. 'As our troops advanced under the barrage, which was perfect, an enemy patrol was seen well in front of their line in a good strong post well sandbagged and with a dug-out, this post opened fire with rifles. The barrage appears to have been laid just behind the post. If our troops had shown more dash, this post could undoubtedly have been taken in my opinion, as it was, Capt. STUART went forward, but the men did not back him up close enough. The post which consisted of five men got out and ran the moment our barrage lifted, two of them throwing away their rifles as they ran.'⁶³ Evidently these Worcester raiders (in Sole's opinion) lacked the required combat morale (or 'dash') to advance into the enemy's rifle fire, and then face the prospect of interpersonal combat; despite the example set by their junior commander. The (admittedly heavily outnumbered) German defenders likewise chose the passive option the moment interpersonal combat threatened, and the chance to escape presented itself.

Such outright refusals were rare, however, and it remained more common for raiders, when apprehended close-up by the enemy, to engage in flurrying (and often blind) exchanges of bombs and rifle fire before retiring. The Royal Warwicks, for example, reported how: 'Just as the[ir] raiders had got through the wire and the barrage opened, enemy were seen moving along what was thought to be an unused piece of trench. As they threatened to cut the raiders off, the latter attacked them at once. In this they were greatly handicapped by shell holes filled with wire, and after an exchange of shots and bombs our men withdrew. 2nd Lt Butcher and 5 men were wounded but

---

61   WO95/2080 (Feb 1917), op cit., diary entry for 2 Feb.
62   'Report of Raid carried out by one and a half coys. of 10/Worc.R. on night of 11/12th Feb', written by Lt. Col. D.M. Sole (CO) on 12 Feb. WO95/2083 (Feb 1917), op cit.
63   Ibid.

were all brought back to our lines.' Rather unnecessarily the diarist added 'the raid was not an unqualified success.'[64]

An aversion to the act of killing did not alone account for the transient and frenzied nature of these conflicts. It is apparent that a more immediate and intense fear of death or mutilation also repelled infantrymen against interpersonal combat. This is certainly the impression given by the rarest of war diary specimens – the voice of the ORs. Lacking the cool hand of the public school educated junior officer, and stripped of any sense of the wider picture, L-Corp. Faulkner's (NCO South Lancs) account finely elucidates how the shock and intensity of fire at interpersonal range could quickly dissolve the aggressive intent of a raiding party into survival. Faulkner was the junior NCO of a patrol of 11 ORs led by a 2nd Lt. Burdett. The patrol had infiltrated the German line and was 'almost up to the second line when they [the Germans] started to bomb us…[Faulkner recounted that] Mr BURDETT said 'disperse' so we all scattered. Sgt YEADON shouted 'get back' and we all scrambled about. Bombs were flying and machine guns were firing from the point we had left.'[65] The East Lancs recorded (less vividly) a similar experience. 'When the party had almost crossed the bad ground a shower of bombs landed amongst them from the direction of the crater in [map ref] then lights were fired amongst the party…every one dived into the shell holes which were full of water and made their way back towards our own line.'[66]

These accounts of infantrymen sacrificing the objective during the first blows of interpersonal combat require qualification. The objective of a raid (or patrol/raid) weighed against heavy and sustained fighting. Without the goal of capturing and holding enemy territory, all levels of command considered high casualties (although they sometimes occurred) both undesirable and unwarranted. Moreover, these smaller raids/patrols largely depended upon stealth, and the moment cover was blown the raiders had little chance of recovering the firepower initiative without enlisting help, and thus turning a 'minor operation' into a mini battle.

If the infantry's continued disinclination towards interpersonal combat threatened to undermine the evolution of platoon tactics, there were some shards of light reflecting from these raids – although those pre-war Regulars who continued to champion the bayonet over the bomb may have preferred to avert their gaze. DHQ received some affirmation that placing a sanitised distance killer at the sharp end *would* up the firepower of the leading waves. Reflecting upon: 'The fact that we [a party of Welch raiders] had no losses', Godfrey (CO) recorded: 'The Lewis guns had it all their own way at times…This raid has undoubtedly pointed out the tremendous use of a Lewis gun handled by one man and a carrier – no hitch occurring in the

---

64 WO95/2085 'Royal Warwicks' (May 1917), op cit., diary entry 28 May.
65 'Patrol of 1 officer, 2 N.C.O.s and 9 O.Rks night of 18th May, 1917. Report of L/C Faulkner.' WO95/2081 (May 1917), op cit.
66 'Report on Raid on Nags Support Trench on Morning of 19th May, 1917' WO95/2079 7th Battn. The East Lancashire Regiment War Diary (May 1917) PRO.

supply of drums, over 400 rounds being fired. The withdrawal was covered solely by them …'⁶⁷ We might add that it *also* 'pointed out' the comparative ease with which infantrymen could use this weapon upon (or in the general direction of) the enemy, especially in self-defence, even when the range – 15 yards – was encroaching upon the interpersonal.

The bomb remained the raiders primary weapon of choice should they get close-up to the enemy. The following account of a raid executed by the King's Own reiterates the impersonal nature of combat involving the bomb. Four platoons were involved, each with a separate objective. Two of the platoon were observed, their respective commanders 'Capt. Openshaw and 2/Lt. Grant were wounded…', and the parties subsequently made no headway. However, the remaining platoons, commanded by 2nd Lt. Alf Smith and 2nd Lt. H.H. Backhouse respectively, could both report that: 'The enemy offered little resistance.' Both then met with the enemy. Smith reported: 'When we got about 70 yards from OBJECT SUPPORT we came across several concrete dugouts which we cleared with smoke bombs first, finally throwing in two or three bombs Mills…In one dugout the enemy refused to leave dugout. This was dealt with, the dugout was then entered, three men were found dead and two un-wounded.' Backhouse gave a similar account: 'I noticed concrete emplacements in trench in centre of wood, and immediately barrage lifted my platoon rushed in and proceeded to the left, where we found concrete dugouts occupied by small parties of the enemy. With two exceptions they willingly surrendered.' After around ten minutes 'cleaning' both parties retired, 'with no casualties in consequence.'⁶⁸

As the Butterflies clung onto the bomb, and readily embraced the Lewis Gun, they could at least offer one account which would have gladdened the hearts of the bayonet hugging pre-war Regulars. The Worcesters recorded how: 'Two raiding parties under 2/Lt Luckmann and 2/Lt Froggatt each of 11 O.R … [had] entered NAGS NOSE on either side of the crater. The crater was rushed. Two prisoners were taken, and *the rest of the post were bayoneted or clubbed to death, about 6 men*. Raiders returned at 1am with two prisoners and without having suffered a casualty [my emphasis].'⁶⁹ Doubtlessly the two prisoners were taken for identification, and it was down to their good fortune not to be skewered or bludgeoned to death.

A similarly rare combat episode had occurred during the division's extended respite from the Somme during the Autumn of 1916. A raiding party of the East Lancs, comprising Lieutenant Edwardes (OC Regt. Bombers and veteran of La Boiselle) and 32 ORs, under the cover of an 'all-arms' barrage, had successfully penetrated the enemy's line and 'found several HUNS bolting back to the enemy front line, Lieut

---

67 'Report on Raiding Party 9th Battalion Welch Regt.' written by Lt-Col W. Godfrey for 58th Brigade on 31 Jan 1917. WO95/2088 (Jan 1917), op cit.
68 Two accounts of a 'Raid 5/6/17' written respectively by 2nd Lt. Alf Smith and 2nd Lt. H.H. Backhouse. WO95/2078 (May 1917), op cit.
69 WO95/2086 'Worcesters' (May 1917), op cit., diary entry 25 May.

EDWARDES hitting two with his revolver fire.' There then followed a frenzied episode of interpersonal killing. 'Lieut. EDWARDES then left 4 men in observation taking the rest of his party to join Sergt. NERY'S which had taken full advantage of a long straight trench full of cowed Germans not recovered from their surprise. Cudgels were applied and bombs thrown on the demoralized crowd until the stock of bombs ran out, when (the party having passed back 5 prisoners) Lieut. EDWARDES ordered the return.'[70]

The raiders described this form of hand-to-hand combat behaviour as 'cudgel driving'. Edwardes reported that these 'cowed Germans' 'offer[ed] practically no resistance to our Raiders bombing and 'cudgel driving'...[the] enemy [being] demoralized by the raiders movements...' It is also possible that many of the German defenders, in the process of carrying out a relief, were unarmed; the CO noting that 'several fire steps had German packs fully equipped laid out on the fire-steps in the frontline trenches.' Edwardes claimed that 'at least 20 Germans [were] killed and an equal number wounded by his party', and clearly little or no attempt was made to elicit the surrender.[71]

It would seem wholly justified to grant these small raiding parties of the East Lancs and Worcesters – separated in time by the passage of eight months – the nomenclature committed trench fighters. Yet the numbers involved are telling. Taking the Worcester raiders first, if every infantryman took an active apart in this orgy of violence, then this still only amounted to two dozen men, or less than five percent of the battalion's strength. Turning to the earlier raid, we know that 33 infantrymen took part in the East Lancs raid; yet 10 of these men took no part in the killing (whether pleasurably or otherwise).[72] We can only say with any degree of certainty therefore that the East Lancs had 20 or so infantrymen, out of a battalion of 500 plus, that had carried out an act of interpersonal aggression in this eight month period.

The combat behaviour of the vast number of the 19th Division trench raiders suggests that the majority of infantrymen continued to experience an aversion to interpersonal combat. This is not just a posthumous judgement, but a facet of combat that at least one CO had been enlightened to by 1917. Reflecting upon his battalion's first faltering raid, Lt-Col. D.M. Sole (CO Worcesters) recorded that: 'It is more

---

70 'Narrative of Raid' written by East Lancs CO Lieut-Col. T.J. Torrie and based upon the report of the OC Lieut. Edwardes. Included in 'Report on Raid effected on night of 15/9/16' WO95/2075 Headquarters 56th Brigade War Diary (Sept 1916) PRO. See also 'Raids carried out by IX Corps during night of 15th/16th. Sept[embe]r'. WO95/835 General Staff IX Corps War Diary (Sept 1916) PRO.
71 Ibid.
72 The CO reported that 2 men remained to 'direct the party on its return', whilst 4 men guarded against a counter attack from the portion of firing line left un-raided, whilst 'Lieut. EDWARDES then left 4 men in observation'. 'Narrative of Raid' written by East Lancs CO Lieut-Col. T.J. Torrie and based upon the report of the OC Lieut. Edwardes. Included in 'Report on Raid effected on night of 15/9/16' WO95/2075, (Sept 1916) op cit.

apparent than ever, that if the rank and file are to take an *active part* in operations they must have more training at their work, and their own officers must get more chances of handling them, otherwise *the fighting all falls on a few gallant men and the bulk do not do their share* ... [my emphasis]'[73] If we substitute 'gallant men' for the less subjective 'committed trench fighters', then Sole's reflections candidly and unequivocally stated what the war diaries had heretofore only unwittingly pointed towards – that a number of infantrymen took no active part in combat, and the number grew the more personal combat became. Yet this jarring message was destined, for the time being, not to travel far along the chain of command. Each subsequent interpretation of Sole's original report failed to mention this 'spanner' in the infantry's works. Perhaps denial was the best form of coping with such unwelcome news – especially with the next 'big push' looming.

73 'Report of Raid carried out by one and a half coys. of 10/Worc.R. on night of 11/12th Feb', written by Lt. Col. D.M. Sole (CO) on 12 Feb. WO95/2054 (Feb 1917), op cit.

8

Messines Ridge and Third Ypres

Overview

Third Ypres and the preceding Battle of Messines Ridge thrust 'platoon tactics' onto the demanding stage of the major set-piece battle. The first act raised the prospect of victory in 1917. Messines delivered what 1 July 1916 had only promised – a near walkover. Vast superiority in artillery firepower and manpower allowed the division to capture the Ridge almost without a shot being fired or bayonet being thrust. This overwhelming success encouraged the belief that 1917 (like 1916 before it) could be the year of victory. Major-General Bridges told 56th Brigade on the eve of Third Ypres: 'Remember that you are taking part in the greatest battle that has ever been fought, that the enemy is now very shaky, and it is a psychological moment when a heavy blow has a very good chance of knocking him out.'[1] But this vision of impending victory proved a mirage. As the script for Third Ypres unfolded it began to read unerringly like episodes from the Somme. Pilckem Ridge (31 July) provided a rather sobering reminder that the balance of firepower had not been permanently grasped by the British, and that the Great War battlefield still held all the potential horrors of 1916. Moreover, the division found that they could still not step over the parapet without the skies collapsing. The battle of Third Ypres duly descended into the 'battle of the mud'.

Yet the 'learning curve', although it ached and bowed, struggled upwards throughout the battles of 1917. At the Battle of Menin Road Ridge (20-25 September) the division reaped some minor rewards from this continuing ascent. The 'creeping barrage' had developed and grown into a largely dependable form of infantry protection. DHQ had also expended great efforts in ensuring that the infantry behind this fusillade of shrapnel were 'fresh', and thus as mentally and physically capable of coping with combat as was achievable. A further devolution of command had placed battalion

---

1   'Notes on Conference given by the Divisional Commander to the Officers of 56th Brigade, 26/7/17'. WO95/2076 Headquarters 56th Brigade War Diary (July 1917) PRO.

Messines Ridge and Third Ypres 147

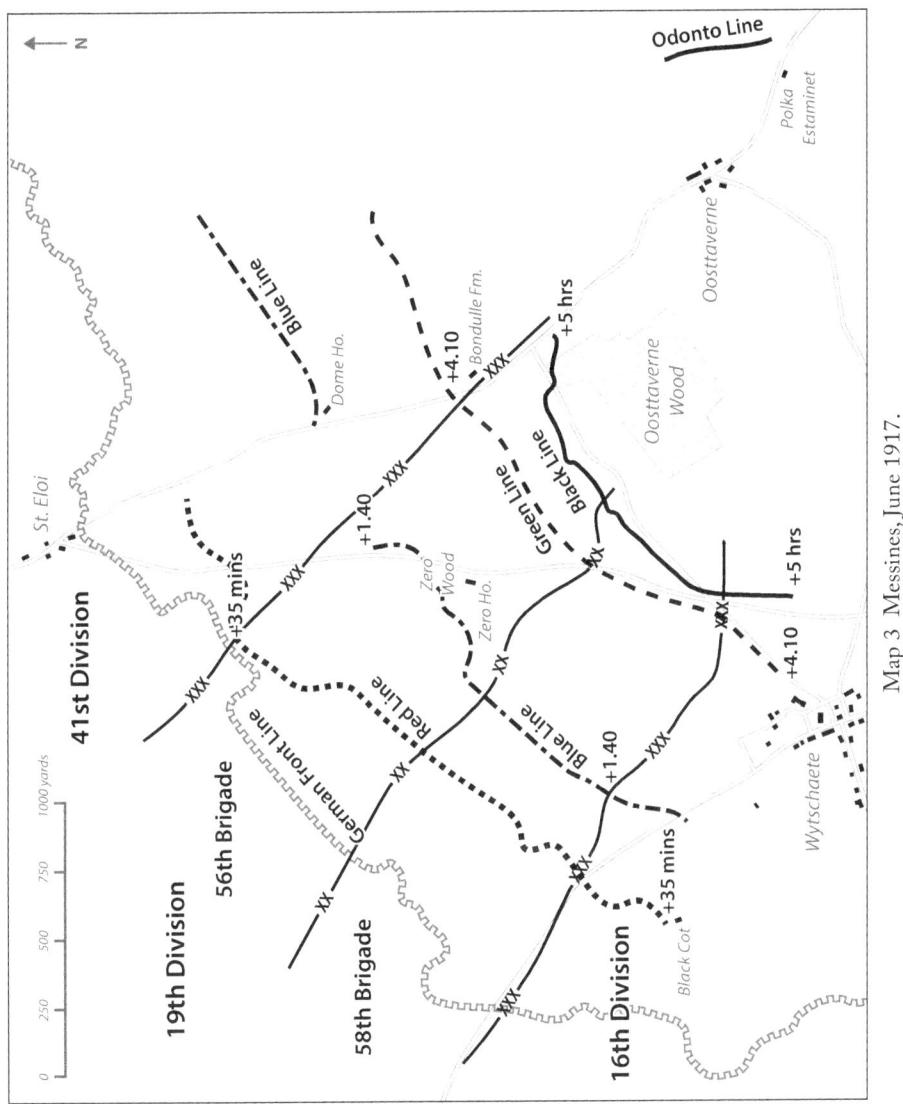

Map 3 Messines, June 1917.

commanders in (official) overall control of the battlefield they entered upon. So when the inevitable severing of communications caused the similarly inevitable rupture in the chain of command, the attack did not grind to a halt. Rather, battalion commanders pushed reserves forward to overcome localised resistance before the situation became critical, and the motion of the advance was sustained. And these recalcitrant strongholds were broken because the division finally demonstrated, after nine months of training and practice, that they could act as autonomous fighting platoons.

The battles of 1917, however, offered an ambivalent report upon the overall achievements of platoon tactics insofar as its effects upon combat behaviour and morale were concerned. One-in-three remained the critical casualties rate, and even this ceiling slipped out of reach amidst the mud and perpetual shellfire of 31 July. The division's combat morale, despite the importations of platoon tactics, remained a finite essence requiring lavish and considered protection from artillery. Neither did Third Ypres sooth the headache caused amongst senior commanders by the continuing philosophical battle between the bomb and bayonet. They clung determinedly to the belief that the bomb only caused delay and greater casualties, whilst the bayonet (and rifle) delivered a quick and clean resolution – and displayed the requisite 'offensive spirit'. The Butterflies remained unconvinced. Their ranks still held a small number of committed trench fighters willing to engage in close-up and personal combat (the 'few gallant men' of earlier description). The majority, however, remained reluctant interpersonal killers.

The Battle of Messines Ridge, 7-14 June 1917

The proposed breakout from the Ypres Salient first necessitated the capture of the high ground which lay to the south for whilst the Germans held Messines Ridge, they enjoyed a bird's eye view over the projected battlefield. 19th Division received confirmation on 4 June that 'IX Corps in conjunction with II ANZAC and X Corps will capture the MESSINES – WYTSCHAETE Ridge and the enemy trench system to the east of it as far as the OOSTTAVERNE Line…'[2] Zero was set for 3.10am on 7 June. The plan of attack had drunk heartily from the distilled wisdom of the post-Somme training doctrines. The ambitions of high command were tempered. Objectives were measured in yards not miles. The division was charged with the capture of five consecutive lines of enemy trenches (designated Red, Blue, Green, Black and Mauve), but on a narrow frontage of less than one thousand yards. This allowed the division to hit the enemy's frontline with deep and successive waves of

---

2   '19th Division Operation Order No. 136', dated 4 June 1917. WO95/2054 General Staff 19th Division War Diary (June 1917) PRO, diary entry 7 June.

'fresh' troops, and no battalion was burdened with capturing more than two reasonably closely positioned trench lines.[3]

One aspect of planning was unequivocal. Any inclination that an infantry advance was achievable without massive and sustained artillery support had now been erased from the plans. A intense preliminary bombardment lasting five days would precede the attack. At Zero the Divisional Artillery would then 'form (1) a creeping, and (2) a standing, barrage, covering the advance of the infantry ...', the design of the latter being to 'neutralize' the enemy's own machine-guns and artillery. A number of 'halts were built into the timing of the 'creeping barrage' to allow the infantry time to consolidate and assemble for the next stage of the attack.[4] The intensity and versatility of the barrage was to be enhanced by the division's own brigade machine-gunners, who were to 'form Corps Machine Gun Barrages...[to] cover the advance of the infantry until Zero plus 3.40. [the first two objectives].'[5] The infantry's own distant killers had joined the artillery partly to increase the human destructive capacity of the barrage. The division's 'Machine gun Arrangements' stated that: 'Guns [were] to establish a creeping barrage either direct enfilade, or oblique in front of the Artillery barrage. *The object of this barrage is to catch anyone running back from the Heavies or sheltering in shell holes or ditches between the trenches* [my emphasis].'[6] Just in case the message had somehow been lost upon the infantry, the plans for 7 June graphically restated that success rested upon near-faultless cooperation with this creeping cocktail of artillery and machine-gun fire. 'The main factor of success and in reducing casualties in the Infantry advance is for all ranks to advance close under the Artillery barrage. Failure to dash into the enemy's position the instant the barrage lifts enables the enemy to come out of his shelters and mow down the attackers with Machine Gun and rifle fire.'[7]

Two further weapons completed the triad of distance killers charged with protecting the infantry's advance. A deep underground mine was to sound a prelude to the division's advance: 'At Zero a mine will be sprung by 250th Tunnelling Co under the German trenches in the HOLLANDSCHESCHUUR.' (This rather benign statement hides the fact that the Royal Engineers planned to raise the Messines Ridge

---

3   See: '19th Division Operation Order No. 136', dated 4 June 1917. WO95/2054 (June 1917), op cit.; '9th Bn. The Cheshire Regiment Instructions for the Offensive'. WO95/2091 9th Battn. The Cheshire Regiment War Diary (June 1917) PRO; '57th Brigade Preliminary Instructions for the Offensive Part 1' issued 31 May. WO95/2083 Headquarters 57th Brigade War Diary (May 1917) PRO; 'Operational Order No. 42'. WO95/2081 7th Battn. The South Lancashire Regiment War Diary (June 1917) PRO.
4   '19th Division Operation Order No. 136', dated 4 June 1917. WO95/2054 (June 1917), op cit.
5   Ibid.
6   See: '19th Division Instructions for the Offensive. Part I, General Staff. Appendix I. Machine Gun Arrangements.' Issued 21 May 1917.; '19th Division Operation Order No. 136', dated 4 June 1917. WO95/2054 (June 1917), ibid.
7   '19th Division Operation Order No. 136', dated 4 June 1917, ibid.

to the ground with the simultaneous explosion of a further eighteen mines). Whilst the latter stages of the attack were to be accompanied by the mercurial Tank: 'One section of 'A' Bn., Heavy Branch, Machine Gun Corps (Tanks) will co-operate in the attack…[joining] when the infantry assault is made from the BLUE LINE [second objective] at Zero plus 3-40.'[8] The usual scepticism accompanied proposed infantry/Tank cooperation. The South Lancs, for example, were warned: 'Tanks will probably be co-operating on the Brigade front. On no account will Infantry wait for the tanks or crowd round them.'[9] Two fears are evident here: first, Tanks were prone to breakdown on route and would probably not show up; second, if they did, the infantry would naturally seek protection behind these metallic shields, and the rapid advance would be reduced to a cumbersome crawl. So whilst the infantry were becoming increasingly comfortable with the 'creeping barrage', and the mine was seen as a reasonable adjunct to the attack, the Tank remained, at least for senior commanders, a mistrusted and largely unwanted comrade in arms.

19th DHQ could not send its troops into battle without a final entreaty against 'non-firing', and another stab at the infantry's inclinations towards sanitised weaponry. 'Ensure that men use their rifles. Experience in all recent engagements prove that men who use their rifles, and who do not in emergency rely solely on Lewis Guns and bombs, invariably win the day, while men who do not use their rifles, but on emergency clamour for Lewis Guns and Bombs often get defeated.'[10] So the philosophical battle between the bomb (now joined by a new *bête noire*, the Lewis Gun) and the 'rifle and bayonet' continued to smoulder, signalling that the old-Regular's fears over the 'offensive spirit' of their troops remained unalleviated.

The proposed Messines Ridge offensive was the most 'infantry friendly' plan the Butterflies had yet experienced, and promised to assuage many of the failings that had blighted the battles of 1916. The *expectations* of high command and DHQ had retreated back some way towards the *reality* of their infantry's combat morale and behaviour (concerns over 'clamouring' for the bomb asides). Certainly, most of the tactical and technological ingredients ('creeping barrage', tanks, machine-gun support, deep and successive waves) had been deployed during the 'Battle of Ancre', and 19th Division had still suffered a bloody reverse. Yet a number of factors extant to the plan itself, particularly preparations and timing, had weighted the dice in the infantry's favour. The battalions were somewhere near full 'fighting strength'; averaging over 800 infantrymen per unit, allowing 25 percent to be 'left out' of battle.[11] Senior and battalion

---

8   Ibid.
9   'Operational Order No. 42'. WO95/2081 (June 1917), op cit.
10 '19th Division Operation Order No. 136', dated 4 June 1917. WO95/2054 (June 1917), op cit.
11 DHQ recorded the following strengths on 6 June: King's Own 598; East Lancs 642; South Lancs 621; Loyals 637; Gloucesters 642; Royal Warwicks 666; Worcesters 645 ; North Staffs 688; Cheshires 686; Fusiliers 681; Welch 647; Wiltshires 676; Machine-Gun Coys. 537; Left Outs 2041. WO95/2054 (June 1917), op cit.

commanders continued to change a pace, and junior officers continued to be moved around regiments, but a number of stalwart officers survived, and the men – allowing for a steady trickle of casualties, sickness and drafts – had had six months in which to gel. The infantry had spent a number of weeks on the training ground during this time together, grappling with the tenets of 'platoon tactics'. As the 'Z Day' approached, time was set aside to practice and prepare for the specific battle ahead.[12]

Early omens were good. The division was ordered to test the waters of the Messines battlefield two days prior to Zero, and found them surprisingly calm. Two raids were executed simultaneously by one company of the Fusiliers and King's Own respectively. DHQ later reported that: 'No difficulty was experienced in following the barrage. The enemy's trenches were found very much knocked about.'[13] Lt-Col J.F. Smeathman (CO Fusiliers) noted that, in marked contrast to the forays on the eve of the Somme: 'The wire was no obstacle anywhere…'[14] Whilst 2nd Lieut. H.H. Backhouse (OC No. 4 Platoon King's Own) observed that the: 'Enemy offered no resistance. Enemy retaliated very feebly…No machine Gun or emplacements were found.'[15] Nevertheless, further investigation 'found concrete dugouts occupied by small parties of the enemy.'[16] Knocked about both physically and mentally by three days of incessant bombardment, surprised and outnumbered, the enemy were only too willing to surrender. 'The enemy offered little resistance and were generally easily turned out by smoke bombs … The total number of prisoners taken 1 Officer and 76 Other Ranks.' The raiders, for their part, suffered '2 O.R. killed, 3 Officers and 18 O.R. wounded (several of whom are at duty), 2 O.R. missing.'[17] DHQ's philosophical battle between the 'bomb and the bayonet' also received a fillip, DHQ reporting to IX Corps that: 'The Royal Welsh Fus. claim to have killed 15 with the bayonet …'[18]

'The Battle of MESSINES RIDGE was opened by the exploding of numerous mines. The mine exploded under the HOLLANDCHESUR Salient was a great

12 See: WO95/2081 (June 1917), op. cit., diary entry 2-6 June; WO95/2091 (June 1917), op cit., diary entries 1-7 June; WO95/2083 (June 1917), op cit., diary entry 1-5 June. WO95/2075 Headquarters 56th Brigade War Diary (June 1917) PRO; WO95/2080 7th Battn. The Loyal North Lancashire Regiment War Diary (June 1917) PRO.
13 'Report on Raid carried out in conjunction with the practice barrage on the afternoon of 5th June 1917', written by GOC for attention of IX Corps on 6 June. WO95/2054 (June 1917), op cit.
14 See: 'Report on Raid' written by Lt-Col J.F. Smeathman (CO Fusiliers) for the attention of 58th Brigade. Ibid.; WO95/2075 (June 1917), op cit., diary entry 5 June.
15 'Report on Raid' written by 2nd Lieut. H.H. Backhouse (King's Own) for 56th Brigade on 6 June. WO95/2054 (June 1917), op cit.
16 Ibid.
17 'Report on Raid carried out in conjunction with the practice barrage on the afternoon of 5th June 1917', written by GOC for attention of IX Corps on 6 June. WO95/2054 (June 1917), op cit.
18 Ibid.

success' 57th Brigade triumphantly recorded.[19] The survivors on the Ridge were momentarily comatose and thrown into confusion by the explosion, and the immediate German response was restricted to a few badly aimed shells. DHQ informed IX Corps at 3.26 am that: 'The mines went up pretty well all right, not quite simultaneously, but nearly so. The men got over all right. The mine did not interfere with them. Nothing much coming over – a few whizz-bangs and gas shells.'[20] The Chief Liaison Officer (a Major Howard) informed DHQ at 5.50am that '57th Brigade was crossing our front line as I came back without a shot being fired at them.'[21] 57th Brigade later recorded that 'owing to the very slight barrage put up by the enemy, casualties had been practically nil.'[22] 'Friendly fire' often proved a rather more deadly foe. The East Lancs, for instance, reported that: 'There was little opposition so the barrage was too slow for the men, some of whom were hit in attempting to pass through our barrage to follow up the retiring enemy.'[23]

Infantry in the first wave found that 'A few Huns were sticking out but the majority [were] surrendering.'[24] The Fusiliers recorded that: 'Little resistance was encountered except in isolated cases, the Germans surrendering, on the whole, quickly. Eighty prisoners and five Machine Guns were captured by the time the 1st Objective had been taken. There was very little barrage fire from the Germans.'[25] The Wiltshires reported a similar catch of both material and human booty: '5 Machine guns, 3 Trench Mortars and 179 prisoners being captured and 50 of the enemy being killed during the advance.'[26] The second waves found that the Blue and Green lines gave way just as easily. The South Lancs reported how: 'The Battalion passed through the 7/N.Lan.R, who had taken the first objective without meeting any severe resistance.

19 WO95/2083 (June 1917), op cit., opening entry for 7 June.
20 Extract from 'Message Diary', a record of telegraphs sent and received by DHQ during the battle. WO95/2054 (June 1917), op cit.
21 'Message Diary' WO95/2054 (June 1917), op cit.
22 'Account of Operations carried out by 57th Brigade in the Battle of the Messines Ridge. June 7th – 10th 1917.' WO95/2083 (June 1917), op cit.
23 WO95/2079 (June 1917), op cit., diary entry 7 June. See also: 'Message Diary' WO95/2054 (June 1917), op cit.; WO95/2075 (June 1917), op cit., diary entry 7 June; WO95/2092 9th Battalion The Welch Regiment War Diary (June 1917) PRO, diary entry 7 June; A HWT from the Cheshires timed at 5.55am. WO95/2088 Headquarters 58th Brigade War Diary (June 1917) PRO; WO95/2085 10th Battn. The Royal Warwickshire Regiment War Diary (June 1917) PRO, diary entry 7 June; 'Account of Operations carried out by 57th Brigade in the Battle of the Messines Ridge. June 7th – 10th 1917.' WO95/2083 (June 1917), op cit
24 'Message Diary' WO95/2054 (June 1917), op cit.
25 WO95/2092 9th Battn. The Royal Welsh Fusiliers War Diary (June 1917) PRO, diary entry 7 June.
26 WO95/2093 6th Battn. The Wiltshire Regiment War Diary (June 1917) PRO, diary entry 7 June. See also: WO95/2080 (June 1917), op cit., diary entry 7 June; WO95/2078 7th Battn. King's Own (Royal Lancaster Regiment) War Diary (June 1917) PRO, diary entry 7 June.

During the 2 hours halt on the Blue Line the companies re-organised themselves and the advance was continued against the Green line. This was also taken to time and consolidation was carried out, about 100 yards in advance of the Green Line. The casualties suffered were very slight and such of the enemy as were found, surrendered very easily.'[27] Despite suffering early navigational troubles, the Cheshires could also report that 'the first objective allotted to this Battn…was taken without opposition… The GREEN LINE was [also] taken at [the] scheduled time.'[28]

The inner defence lines briefly offered a splinter of resistance, but soon crumbled with the same permeability under the advance of the third waves. The North Staffords reported that: 'At 8.10am the BLACK LINE was assaulted between [map ref]. This line was completely captured by 8.20am. Very few casualties and little resistance was offered by the enemy. The tendency of the enemy was to rush forward and surrender or retire, very few actually stayed in the trenches.'[29] The Royal Warwick gave a similar account: 'The BLACK LINE and the copse along the road just North of the house at [map ref] was occupied by the enemy, and there was a brief exchange of rifle shots. The resistance was, however, very short-lived and the enemy about 70 in number very soon threw down their arms, and came forward with their hands up (most of them were in a state of abject terror.)'[30]

Acting upon orders: 'Each battalion then sent forward one company to the MAUVE Line' to execute 'battle patrols'. Any resistance was again 'soon silenced and a number of prisoners taken…'[31] The North Staffords recorded how: 'Parties were pushed forward to search OOSTTAVERNE WOOD and in one or two cases good batches of prisoners were brought out. Patrols were sent out from the MAUVE LINE. One of which pushed through our barrage into OOSTTAVERNE VILLAGE and brought back valuable information.'[32] Similarly, 'A Coy. [of the Royal Warwicks] were ordered to search OOSTTAVERNE WOOD…A considerable number of enemy were in concrete dug-outs in the Wood and they surrendered freely. About 80 officers and men of the 44th I.R. including Lieut. Co. Freyberg of that Regt. were taken prisoner.'[33]

---

27 WO95/2081 (June 1917), op cit., diary entry 7 June.
28 WO95/2091 (June 1917), op cit., diary entry 7 June. See also WO95/2092 'Welch' (June 1917) op cit., diary entry 7 June.
29 WO95/2085 8th Battn. The North Staffordshire Regiment War Diary (June 1917) PRO, diary entry 7 June.
30 WO95/2085 'Royal Warwicks' (June 1917), op cit. Diary entry 7 June. At 9.30am DHQ had been informed that a 'wounded officer of Worcesters has just come back and says that we had a very easy time in getting into the BLACK LINE and captured between 50 and 60 prisoners.' 'Message Diary' WO95/2054 (June 1917), op cit.
31 'Account of Operations carried out by 57th Brigade in the Battle of the Messines Ridge. June 7th – 10th 1917.' WO95/2083 (June 1917), op cit.
32 WO95/2085 'North Staffords' (June 1917), op cit., diary entry 7 June.
33 WO95/2085 'Royal Warwicks' (June 1917), op cit., diary entry 7 June.

By midday 19th Division had captured all their objectives to timetable, but now paid the price of success – an extra objective. 'At 1.35pm orders were received from the Division that the 57th Brigade was to push on and capture the OOSTTAVERNE Line.'[34] The 'New Zero Hour [was] 3.10pm today.'[35] The perennial bugbear of faulty battlefield communications, seemingly mastered to this point, now threatened to trip up the 57ths. 'The signal communication, which up till now, had been good, became very bad…Visual was also a failure – in fact the only reliable means of communication now was the runners. Hence it was extremely difficult to write out Operation Orders to reach units in time…orders never reached some units till a few minutes before Zero.'[36] As 57th Brigade HQ later admitted: 'This advance was a great gamble …'[37]

In the division's previous experiences, gambling on the Western Front was usually a game of high odds and little return. But on 7 June the firepower odds were stacked heavily in their favour, and the gamble paid off. The Royal Warwicks detailed how 'Officers Commanding Coys. were hastily assemble, and Coys. were ordered to form up on the N.E. edge of the wood…The advance through the village and on to ODONTO TRENCH was carried out with practically no enemy opposition. About 40 prisoners were taken in the village, and in dug-outs in ODONTO TRENCH.'[38] The North Staffords experienced even more hectic preparations, but equal success: 'Owing to the 8th Glosters not having received orders till late it was found we were the front line on the Right and although in SUPPORT this Coy actually captured part of the objective…Very few casualties and very little resistance. 40 – 60 prisoners captured including two Officers also 3 Field Guns…'[39]

In the aftermath of the battle DHQ also made a significant observation on the collective mental state of infantrymen in the advance. 'A long halt may tend to cool the men's excitement which has been worked up to the highest pitch, and which if once lost is difficult to re-kindle.'[40] The suggestion being made here (albeit slightly unwittingly) is that the much desired 'offensive spirit' – whether in the passive form of an infantryman steeling himself to face potential death or maiming, or in the aggressive form of an infantryman fortifying himself to kill – was a transient and fragile state of consciousness. Evidently, even in a 'walkover' such as Messines, once the fire was extinguished it was extremely difficult to re-light.

34 'Account of Operations carried out by 57th Brigade in the Battle of the Messines Ridge. June 7th – 10th 1917.' WO95/2083 (June 1917), op cit.
35 These orders from DHQ had been sent at 12.40pm, so 30 minutes had already been lost. 'Message Diary' WO95/2054 (June 1917), op cit.
36 'Account of Operations carried out by 57th Brigade in the Battle of the Messines Ridge. June 7th – 10th 1917.' WO95/2083 (June 1917), op cit.
37 Ibid.
38 WO95/2085 'Royal Warwicks' (June 1917), op cit., diary entry 7 June.
39 WO95/2085 (June 1917), op cit., diary entry 7 June.
40 'Comments that may be useful as Lessons' WO95/2054 (June 1917), op cit.

As dusk approached on 7 June Shute warned his troops: 'You will have to do a little digging and wiring to-night. If you do not you will have a lot of casualties to-morrow.'[41] Now began the second half of the battle – holding on to the Ridge. Whilst the infantrymen were digging in supporting machine-gunners assumed the role of frontline defenders. The 57th Machine Gun Company details how: 'The 16 Guns of the Coy were placed in this [front] line: 2 on right flank, 2 at dividing point about [map ref], 10 distributed along the line (in front area) to best advantage, 2 forming dividing points on left flank.'[42] At dusk on the 8th the expected counter-attack commenced, but was easily thrown back by a combination of artillery and machine-gunners. At '8.15pm the enemy started to barrage on our whole system of trenches [the North Staffords recorded]…and a counterattack was anticipated. Our Artillery replied vigorously. At 9.30pm the enemy was seen to leave his trenches to attack but was repulsed by our Artillery and M/Gun fire.'[43]

The material and human bounty captured by 19th Division on 7 June signalled the almost total capitulation of the German defenders. The 57th Brigade boasted that: 'The 2nd Division (Prussian) must have been practically annihilated. The whole of the Regimental Staff of the 44th Regiment was captured, including Battalion Commander, as well as four batteries of artillery of the 1st Artillery Regiment. The actual number of machine guns, trench mortars and prisoners captured is unknown, but at least 500 of the latter were sent back.'[44] 58th Brigade counted a similar haul: 'The number of prisoners who passed through the Brigade Cage was one officer and 291 O.R. War material captured 18 Machine Guns, 7 Trench Mortars.'[45] In the final reckoning DHQ counted 1252 prisoners.[46] This bounty had been brought at a cost to the division of just over 1,000 casualties; most of whom were either wounded or missing.[47] This represented a 1 in 7 chance of becoming a casualty – comparatively favourable odds upon the First World War battlefield.

Commanders at all levels considered 7 June a day of unmitigated success for 19th Division. IX Corps Commander described the battle as 'a striking success', GOC Shute told his division that: 'You have done perfectly splendidly. I congratulate you', Brigadier-General. T.A. Cubitt boasted that: 'The operations carried out by [his] 57th

41 'Message Diary' 6pm WO95/2054 (June 1917), op cit.
42 WO95/2086 57th Machine Gun Company War Diary (June 1917) PRO, diary entry 8 June.
43 WO95/2085 'North Staffords' (June 1917), op cit., diary entry 8 June.
44 'Account of Operations carried out by 57th Brigade in the Battle of the Messines Ridge. June 7th – 10th 1917.' WO95/2083 (June 1917), op cit.
45 WO95/2088 (June 1917), op cit., diary entry 7 June.
46 'Narrative of Operations' for June 1917. WO95/2054 (June 1917), op cit.
47 Initial casualties were recorded at noon on 7 June as follows: 6 Officers, 81 ORs Killed; 27 Officers, 711 ORs wounded; 315 ORs missing; total casualties 1140. Fighting Strength (FS) minus MG Coys. 7986. This equated to a 1 in 7 chance of becoming a casualty. The vast majority of 'missing' were later accounted for, either as killed, wounded or returned. Ibid. Diary entry 7 June.

Brigade were highly successful', and Lt-Col. Hill concurred that 'The whole attack [by his Loyals] was a brilliant success.'[48] Although the word 'success' was often banded around rather liberally by Great War commanders, especially by Brigadiers and above, on 7 June its use seems highly justified. A stunned German infantry seemed to be suffering from a collective form of combat neurosis which had drained them of any will to resist. Consequently, each successive infantry wave rolled over the Messines defensive lines with the ease of a tidal wave smashing a beach hut.

In the aftermath of the battle the division's senior commanders were faced with the welcome task of explaining this success, rather than partial or outright failure. DHQ were adamant that the artillery had paved the way to victory. 'The plan of reducing the number of field guns in the creeping barrage and increasing those employed in depth on all trench lines and suspected machine gun emplacements and strong points for upwards of 1,000 yards in rear of the creeping barrage was most successful. It entirely prevented all distant machine gun fire on our advancing infantry and completely destroyed the moral of the enemy.'[49] 58th Brigade concurred: 'The success of the operation must be attributed to thorough preparation, and especially to the bombardment by the Heavy Artillery, which cleared the way completely for the advance of the infantry.'[50] Besides the observations of their own troops, the testimonies of captured German officers also fed the belief that artillery had triumphed: 'nearly all the cellars in WYTSHAETE were knocked in by our bombardment...' one such officer told DHQ.[51]

DHQ also considered that taming the perennial bugbear of communications had played a vital part in success. 'The communications were based on 'Forward Communications in Battle' (s.s.148). The arrangements worked admirably...' In particular, DHQ felt that: 'The liaison and reconnaissance made by Major HOWARD (G.S.O.2, 19th Division) were of the utmost value', and that 'good communication between Divisional and Brigade Headquarters, and between Brigade and Battalion Headquarters' had been maintained as a result.[52] Yet, in their commendation of communications on 7 June, senior commanders were arguably getting *effect* confused with *cause*. Good communications were maintained *because* the battlefield was largely devoid of enemy fire. This presented senior commanders with an uncomfortable paradox; quick and fulsome information was more urgently required, but far less achievable, when things went wrong. For whereas good news sped across the battlefield, bad news crawled.

The infantry themselves receive a certain amount of applause from above. Reflecting upon the successful capture of Oosttaverne Village, DHQ wrote '[that] the assault

48 'IX Corps No. g.221/218' dated 15 June. WO95/2054 (June 1917), op cit.; 'Message Diary' timed 6pm 7 June. Ibid. WO95/2080 (June 1917), op cit., diary entry 7 June.
49 'Comments that may be useful as Lessons' WO95/2054 (June 1917), op cit.
50 WO95/2088 (June 1917), op cit., diary entry 8 June.
51 'Message Diary' 6am & 8.40am 7 June. WO95/2054 (June 1917), op cit.
52 Comments that may be useful as Lessons' ibid.

succeeded reflects the greatest credit on all ranks of 57th Brigade as it was impossible to get any detailed orders to Company and Platoon Commanders in the time available.'[53] DHQ went on to offer broader praise for the: 'Excellent control of platoon commanders over their platoons' on 7 June.[54] Whilst 57th Brigade likewise observed, 'the very excellent leading by Battalion and Company Officers.'[55] Significantly, the 57ths attributed this 'excellent leading' to the emergence of 'platoon tactics': 'The advantages derived from practicing and training in the Standard Form of Attack were very evident, one of the chief being the superior leading displayed by platoon commanders.'[56]

There is nothing in the evidence to doubt that battalion command operated effectively on 7 June. It is certainly plausible that the advent of platoon tactics had improved the leadership qualities of junior officers, and the quality of 'officer-man' relations. But were the successes of 7 June evidence that the evolution of platoon tactics – with its plethora of specialist weapons, and its nurturing of the *esprit de platoon* – had lifted the collective combat morale of the division? The combat behaviour enacted during the battle offers an ambivalent reply. The small number of infantrymen reported genuinely 'missing' indicates that few if any surrendered.[57] Intentional 'straggling' also seems to have been a rare event; although during the advance Capt. Watts (Cheshires) did report that: 'There are probably many OR who got lost in the mist this morning and will probably rejoin [sic].'[58]

The 19th Division did experience a notable upturn in absentees and desertions in the aftermath of the battle; yet the ten convictions still represented a disciplinary drop in the ocean of infantrymen 'holding fast'.[59] The execution of one of these deserters, Pte. D. Blakemore of 8th North Staffordshire Battn, albeit for a second offence, nevertheless signalled that the chain of command still considered the occasional beating of the stick salutary for the division's combat morale.[60]

It is perhaps the casualty rates for 7 June which provide the most revealing statistic. The advance upon Messines Ridge resulted in casualties gravitating around fifteen

53 'Narrative of Operations' ibid.
54 'Comments that may be useful as Lessons' ibid
55 'Account of Operations carried out by 57th Brigade in the Battle of the Messines Ridge. June 7th – 10th 1917.' WO95/2083 (June 1917), op cit.
56 Ibid. Whose 'Standard Form' was not recorded! Nevertheless, this would seem to suggest that platoon tactics were executed in some form on 7 June.
57 See WO95/2091 (June 1917), op cit., diary entry 7 June.
58 HWT WO95/2091 (June 1917), op cit., diary entry 7 June. See also HWT WO95/2088 (June 1917), op cit.
59 Between 25 June and 1 July the Division had 4 'absentees' or 'ABC' and 6 'Desertions' recorded against them. May had brought about only 4 convictions. WO213/15-17 Judge Advocates General's Office: Field General Court's Martial and Military Courts, Registers. (May to July 1917) PRO.
60 WO71/569 Proceedings of F.G.C.M. of Pte. D. Blakemore of 8th North Staffordshire Battn. June 28th 1917, PRO.

percent.[61] This tends to confirm the impression given by the qualitative evidence: that the resilience of the Butterflies' passive combat morale was, in comparison to previous combat experiences, not greatly challenged. The same can be argued for the Butterflies' collective willingness to kill. The observations of the infantry tend to justify 57th Brigade's conclusion that: 'The enemy was in a completely disorganised state and the troops encountered by this Brigade put up a very poor resistance, preferring rather to surrender.'[62] Indeed, there are only two accounts deriving from the period 7 to 8 June of the enemy actually being killed. During the capture of the Blue Line the Cheshires reported that: 'A good many Germans were killed and wounded with the bayonet', but also added that 'many more sent back as prisoners.'[63] This fine example of interpersonal combat, in keeping with the Butterflies' previous combat record, remained a singular observation. Moreover, the second account of actual killing returned the bomb to centre stage. On the following day the North Staffords reported that: 'Enemy snipers very active in front of ODONTO TRENCH and considerably hampered our men from working. A raiding party under 2Lt J. Bell left our lines to clear these snipers out of dugouts, shell holes etc. and other places where they were established. Fifteen of the enemy were actually killed. 5 dug outs bombed and 11 prisoners brought in.'[64]

Even so, these forays still proved to be largely bloodless. The Royal Warwicks, for instance, reported how: 'Enemy snipers from the remains of dug-outs and shell holes in S.E. direction, were active, and inflicted casualties on Coys. Some of these were out-flanked, and half a dozen prisoners including an Officer of the 165th R.I.R. were taken.'[65] Given that these Germans had been inflicting casualties upon their comrades, accepting the surrender seems a remarkably benign act on behalf of these infantrymen.

Thus it is fair to conclude that the Battle of Messines Ridge provided a far lesser challenge to the division's collective combat morale than the battles of 1916. The artillery had blasted away both the enemy's defences and his will to resist. On 7 June artillery really did conquer and the infantry occupy. The autonomous fighting platoon

---

61   Casualties recorded by 19th Division for 7 June were as follows – Loyals: 1 Officer and 'about' 60 ORs; CR of 10% based upon FS 637. King's Own: 8 ORs killed; 5 Officers, 95 ORs wounded; 16 ORs missing; total casualties 124; CR 21% based on FS 598. Worcesters: 9 ORs killed; 2 Officers, 59 ORs wounded; 1OR missing; total casualties 71; CR 11% based upon FS 645. North Staffords: 4 ORs killed; 68 ORs wounded; 4 ORs missing; total casualties 76; CR 11% based upon FS 688. Welch: 23 ORs killed; 4 Officers, 142 ORs wounded; 1 OR missing; total casualties 170; CR 26% based upon FS 681. All figures sourced from battalion diaries. Outstanding reference: WO95/2086 10th Battn. The Worcestershire Regiment War Diary (June 1917) PRO.
62   'Account of Operations carried out by 57th Brigade in the Battle of the Messines Ridge. June 7th – 10th 1917.' WO95/2083 (June 1917), op cit.
63   WO95/2091 (June 1917), op cit. Diary entry 7 June.
64   WO95/2085 'North Staffords' (June 1917), op cit., diary entry 8 June.
65   WO95/2085 'Royal Warwicks' (June 1917), op cit., diary entry 8 June. See also WO95/2085 'North Staffords' (June 1917), op cit.

(and all the connotations of group loyalty and enhanced officer-man relations that this concept involved) awaited its first stern challenge.

The Battle of Pilckem Ridge, 31 July

Having been centre stage on 7 June, the division found themselves pushed out to the wings on 31 July. 'The attack will be carried out by the 56th. Inf. Bde., and 63rd Inf. Bde. (less 2 Battalions) who will form a defensive flank on the right.'[66] This 'defensive flank' had an aggressive edge in the form of a diversionary attack. 'It is the intention that these operations…[56th Brigade stated] should *create the impression* of a serious attempt to capture the WARNETON – ZANDVOORDE Line [my emphasis].'[67] Signalling the BEF's continued tendency towards devolution of command, DHQ requested that 'G.O's C. 63rd and 56th Brigades will forward *their proposals* for the assembly and attack as early as possible…[my emphasis]'[68] Certainly, this apparent autonomy was somewhat circumscribed by the existence of the BEF's prescribed 'art of attack' – *S.S.135* and *S.S.143*. Even so, the division's hand is evident, if with a light touch, in the eventual planning for 31 July.

The 19th Division's orders stated that '56th Bde. will attack with three Battalions in front line and one in support.'[69] Following established practice: 'The advance was to be carried out under a creeping and searching barrage by Artillery and Machine Guns…'[70] Before the attack 56th Brigade stressed that, regarding artillery: 'These are more than were used in the practice barrage' of 22 July.[71] After the event, however, DHQ stated that: 'These guns were required to cover a frontage of 2400 yards, and it was therefore decided that a barrage in depth was impracticable.'[72] This suggests that artillery resources were spread a little thinner than on 7 June, necessitating compromises.[73] This shortfall in artillery was partly compensated for by a increase in the number of machine-guns within the creeping cocktail (totalling 42 guns on 31

---

66 'King's Own Operation Order No. 50', dated 29 July. WO95/2076 (July 1917), op cit.
67 '56th Infantry Brigade Instructions for the Offensive', dated 27 July. Ibid.
68 '19th Division Instructions for the Offensive', written by DHQ 17 July. WO95/2055 (July 1917), op cit.
69 '19th Division Operation Order No. 155', dated 27 July. Ibid. See also 'King's Own Operation Order No. 50', dated 29 July. WO95/2076 (July 1917), op cit.
70 'Narrative of Operations carried out by 19th Division on July 31st, 1917, and following days.' WO95/2055 (July 1917), op cit. See also WO95/2080 (July 1917), op cit.
71 '7th Bn. Loyal North Lancashire Regiment. Instructions for the Offensive', dated 25 July 1917. WO95/2080 (July 1917), op cit.
72 'Narrative of Operations carried out by 19th Division on July 31st, 1917, and following days.' WO95/2055 (July 1917), op cit.
73 For artillery arrangements see '57th Infantry Brigade Operation Order No. 153', dated 30 July. WO95/2084 Headquarters 57th Brigade War Diary (July 1917) PRO.

July).[74] These guns were bolstered by the arrival of the newly formed '246 Company Machine Gun Corps' – 'Strength of Coy 10 Officers 177 ORs.', whose arrival further signalled the growing dominance of sanitised distance weaponry upon the Great War battlefield.[75]

Discussing the plans for 31 July, Maj-Gen. Bridges reiterated to the 'Officers of 56th Brigade' that: 'There are two phases to the attack – 1, getting there, 2, staying there.' In Bridges' opinion, 'there' had changed, and as a consequence: 'The attack in prospect [was] a new proposition for the Brigade. There [was] no position or line of trenches to be attacked, only strong points supporting each other, and an enemy scattered in shell-holes and short lengths of trenches.'[76] This was just the combat scenario platoon tactics had been scripted to overcome – a point not lost upon Bridges. 'The attack on strong points must be organised beforehand…Platoons must help each other, whatever Battalion they belong to, and where one is held up others must push forward and envelop or surround the obstacles, which will then be mopped up by the Units detailed for the purpose.'[77] The subsequently 'organised' formations were based upon the tenets of *S.S.143*. The 'Plan of attack by 7th Bn. N.Lan.R.' (Loyals) stated that: 'The right front section of each platoon in the two first lines will be the rifle section, the left front section, the Rifle Grenade section. The Bombing section will be behind the Rifle section. The Lewis Gun section will be behind the Rifle Grenade section.'[78] The Trench Mortars were to 'assist in the destruction of the enemy strong points', and, as decreed by *S.S.143*, were to be under the control of platoon commanders.[79]

BEF's philosophical approach to combat was also evolving. Messines had persuaded DHQ of the wisdom of eliciting surrenders *en masse*: 'The enemy must be encouraged to surrender and prisoners must be taken [Bridges informed the officers of 56th Brigade]. The German soldier is told by his Officers that the British shoot their prisoners. He must be disabused of this idea for we wish to bring about surrenders on a large scale. Platoon Commanders have been supplied with megaphones. Shouting "Hands up" and "Kamerad" should facilitate this.'[80] Yet, rather dichotomously, this evocation to arrest the German Army went hand-in-hand with an unrelieved scepti-

---

74 'Narrative of Operations carried out by 19th Division on July 31st, 1917, and following days.' WO95/2055 (July 1917), op cit.
75 WO95/2071 246 Company Machine Gun Corps War Diary (July 1917) PRO, diary entry 16 July.
76 'Notes on Conference given by the Divisional Commander to the Officers of 56th Brigade, 26/7/17'. WO95/2076 (July 1917), op cit.
77 Ibid.
78 '7th Bn. Loyal North Lancashire Regiment. Instructions for the Offensive', dated 25 July 1917, WO95/2080 (July 1917), op cit.
79 Ibid. See also '56th M.G. Corps. General Scheme. Operation Order No. 9.B', dated 28 July. WO95/2076 (July 1917), op cit.; 'King's Own Operation Order No. 50', dated 29 July. Ibid.
80 'Notes on Conference given by the Divisional Commander to the Officers of 56th Brigade, 26/7/17.' WO95/2055 (July 1917), op cit.

cism over the Butterflies' 'offensive spirit'. 'Ensure that men use their rifles' remained the concerned entreaty of the division's senior commanders.[81] The philosophical battle between 'bayonet and bomb' also raged unabated; Bridges stressing that: 'They [strong-points] must, if possible, be rushed at the point of the bayonet, and bomb fights should be avoided as they cause delay.'[82]

Bridges' fears over his troops combat morale had, however, attained a new dimension. Successful developments in the creeping barrage had seemingly persuaded Bridges that 'getting there' was relatively unproblematic – it was 'staying there' that now preoccupied the GOC. 'It must be instilled into all ranks that nothing must turn us out of positions we have taken, or drive us from our ground. The falling back of other troops is no excuse. All retrograde movement brings about disaster on a large or small scale. We lose prisoners, generally the best of our fighting troops, and the infantry losses its morale. Battles are won by sticking it out, and we rely on the resolution and fortitude of the junior officers, N.C.Os and men in the front line to hold their ground [original emphasis].'[83]

Bridges' comments on 'losing the best of our fighting troops' are significant here. It correlates that a unit's most committed trench fighters were more likely to 'stick it out' to the last, leaving them far more vulnerable to death or capture. It also correlates that their loss would be detrimental to the 'collective combat morale' of the unit. Once again it is evident that a commander of 19th Division was witnessing – as Lt-Col Sole (CO Worcesters) had done a few months earlier – that combat invariably rested upon 'a few gallant men'. Or, put differently, 'infantry versus infantry' combat invariably centred upon a minority of committed trench fighters.

Events leading up to the planned attack upon Pilckem Ridge had done little to appease the troubled minds of the division's senior commanders. The division had been ordered to execute a 'minor enterprise' in order to advance the 'jumping off' line for 31 July.[84] Over a five day period (17 to 22 July) Junction Buildings (the objective) was three times captured, and three times lost; fully realising Bridge's fears over the infantry's ability to 'sticking it out'.[85] It is unsurprising that this faltering 'minor operation' should spark off the always smouldering philosophical battle between the bomb and

---

81 'General Instructions' issued 24 July. Ibid.
82 'Notes on Conference given by the Divisional Commander to the Officers of 56th Brigade, 26/7/17.' Ibid.
83 Ibid.
84 '58th Brigade Order No 161' issued 17 July. WO95/2091 (July 1917), op cit.
85 See: G.126/15/13 'report on operations carried out by 58th Inf. Bde. from July 17th to July 19th, for the possession of JUNCTION BUILDINGS', written on 20 July by DHQ for IX Corps. WO95/2055 (July 1917), op cit.; 'Report on Operations carried out by 'A' Coy. 7th South Lancashire Reg't 22.7.17', written on 23 July by CO for attention of DHQ. WO95/2081 (July 1917), op cit; 'G.126/15/11/8' report on operations carried out by 56th Inf. Brigade on the evening of the 22nd July, with the object of regaining possession of JUNCTION BUILDINGS', written 24 July by DHQ for IX Corps. WO95/2055 (July 1917), op cit.

the 'rifle and bayonet', and elicit the adjunctive lament over the infantry's (perceived) lack of 'offensive spirit'. The 'bayonet' had again been conspicuous by its absence. Following 'careful enquiries which have been made from Officers and men who took part in the recent operations against JUNCTION BUILDINGS', Brigadier-General. Glasgow drew the following familiar conclusions: 'Men do not yet realise the power of the rifle and bayonet. It should be engrained into every man that his rifle and bayonet are his first weapons. Men still think that once they have got rid of their bombs, they have no weapon of defence left. The fact that men are being bombed by the enemy and have no bombs left to reply with is not sufficient reason for retiring from a position. A resolute bayonet charge by even a few men will almost certainly drive out the hostile bombers.'[86] Glasgow summarised by decrying: 'The spirit of the bayonet is still not what it should be in spite of the extensive training carried out.'[87]

Glasgow and his fellow senior officers frustration was understandable. For it remained evident that their reasoning remained sound: a 'resolute bayonet charge by even a few men' *did* almost always 'drive out' the enemy, *if* distance killers were absent from the conflict. On the eve of Third Ypres the Gloucesters were raided 'by men of the STURMTRUPPE Battalion of the 4th Army; estimated one company strong…' The enemy's attack had been heralded by a lethal cocktail of artillery, trench mortars and gas, leaving 'the post raided…practically destroyed and the old British front line on the right…badly damaged.' Despite 'considerable casualties [caused] by the bombardment' a 'counter attack was immediately organised' by two junior officers, and although 'the supply of bombs was lost in the Melee, a determined bayonet assault was however made which succeeded in turning out the enemy. Several were shot as they withdrew and 9 dead remained round the trench.'[88] Exemplary leadership and (perhaps) desperate self-defence had motivated this group of Gloucesters to attack with cold steel. The unrelenting headache faced by the chain of command was that it took exceptional circumstances (such as the above) to motivate even a small minority of men to attack with the bayonet.

The subsequent Battle of Pilckem Ridge would have been sadly familiar to the veterans of 1916. DHQ's first despatch to IX Corps (rather euphemistically) recorded: 'The general situation may be summarised as that we obtained early our objectives. Later in the day stubborn local counter-attacks in the vicinity of the junctions with the Divisions on our left and right, forced back our flanks to conform with the general

---

86   Both quotes taken from 'No.B.M.2374', dated 22 July. WO95/2055 (July 1917), op cit. It was these 'careful enquiries' that had led Glasgow to lament that the 'spirit of the bayonet is still not what it should be…' The date of the enquiries suggest that the South Lancs were excluded from the inquest. Evidence suggests, however, that nothing occurred during the attack of 22 July to modify Glasgow's chagrin.
87   B.M.2374, dated 22 July. WO95/2088 (July 1917), op cit.
88   'Report on Raid on 8th Gloucester Regt. at 1.25 am 28th July', written by DHQ for attention of IX Corps. WO95/2055 (July 1917), op cit.

situation.'⁸⁹ Under concerted enemy machine-gun fire the newly reconstituted and retrained platoons retraced many of the backward steps of their former incarnation along the combat morale/behaviour spectrum. On occasions isolated feats of remarkably high combat morale by small pockets of infantry resulted. More typically, junior commanders ordered their men to ground, and they dug in where they lay, rather than where the objective lay. Three days of persistent enemy shelling and sniping followed, leaving 56th Brigade with seventy-five percent casualties by their relief on the 3rd.⁹⁰ Confounding an already desperate situation, the weather contrived to rub salt into the infantry's wounds: 'The whole of the battle area was converted into a sea of mud and water [the King's Own recorded]. The conditions under which the men continued to hold the advanced trenches were indescribably bad, and the evacuation of the wounded was rendered extraordinarily difficult.'⁹¹

The first few hours after Zero went almost to plan. 56th Brigade had formed up under the cover of darkness: '7/Kings Own R/L. Regt on the right. 7/N.Lan.R. on left. [7/E.Lan.R in centre] 7/S.Lan.R. in support.'⁹² Assembly had been relatively untroubled; the Loyals reporting 'Coys started to assemble at 11pm. Assembly was complete with two casualties.'⁹³ The initial advance (on the centre and right) was another 'walkover'. The King's Own recorded that 'Zero was fixed at 3.50 A.M. and at that hour the artillery and machine gun barrage opened and the battalion advanced. All objectives were rapidly secured, the enemy offering very little resistance in the first instance.'⁹⁴ The South Lancs noted that: 'His [the enemy] artillery did not reply immediately, and when it did it was weak.' They also reported success, albeit the success of their fellow Lancastrians. 'Message by lamp from B Coy [received 5.50am] said that 7 E Lanc R runners had come in and said their objective taken without much loss. 100 prisoners taken.'⁹⁵ Prisoners were a conspicuous feature of these early successes. The King's Own similarly reported that 'JUNCTION BUILDINGS which had been the scene of desperate fighting in the days before the attack and were expected to give more trouble, fell into our hands quite early and produced 18 men and 3 officers

---

89 'Résumé of Yesterdays Operations', written by DHQ for attention of IX Corps dated 1 August. WO95/2055 (Aug 1917), op cit.
90 DHQ recorded that: 'The casualties sustained by the Division [which effectively meant 56th Brigade plus the Fusiliers] during the above operations, i.e., from noon 30th July to noon August 3rd, were as follows: Officers. K. 13 W. 25 M. 3 Other Ranks. K. 205 W. 566 M. 58. The actual strength of Infantry making the assault was 1160.' This equated to a casualty rate of approximately 75%. Ibid.
91 WO95/2078 (Aug 1917), op cit., diary entry 5 August.
92 WO95/2079 7th Battn. The East Lancashire Regiment War Diary (July 1917) PRO, diary entry 31 July.
93 WO95/2080 (July 1917), op cit., diary entry 30 July.
94 WO95/2078 (July 1917), op cit., diary entry 31 July.
95 WO95/2081 (July 1917), op cit., diary entry 31 July.

prisoners. TINY and SPIDER FARMS were also speedily captured. Each providing its quota of prisoners.'[96]

Reports from the left flank were far less sanguine. The 'general position [the Loyals reported] was that 'A' 'B' & 'C' Coys had been held up 100 yards short of their Objectives with 'C' Coy 150 yards behind echeloned to the left of 'A' Coy.'[97] The left flank of the advance had rapidly descended into a desperately one-sided 'infantry versus machine-gun' conflict; due, the battalion felt, to problems elsewhere: 'The 122nd. Bde. had not taken FORRET FARM & this with several M.G's behind it caused our two left Coys considerable casualties. It was now ascertained that this hostile strong point had held up practically our whole advance by enfilading it from the left. It consisted of a strong concrete dugout & was unapproachable by infantry without strong Artillery support [original emphasis].'[98]

The implications of this closing comment are deeply significant. Platoon tactics – as delivered by 19th Division thus far – could make little impact upon the German's heavily fortified 'strongpoints'. Success, therefore, still rested upon the artillery's ability to deliver a prior knockout blow. Evidently the artillery had failed to 'silence' Forret Farm. Indeed, the Loyals attested to their artillery's general failure to 'silence' the enemy after Zero on 31 July. 'Enemy started to put up a counter-barrage to our Artillery and M.G. barrage about 15 minutes after the attack. The RAVINE was shelled heavily with 4.2's and 5.9's from 3am to midnight 31st.'[99]

With the battlefield alive with shrapnel and bullets, communications soon broke down. The Loyals recorded that: 'It was difficult to get any sort of report from Coys as any movement across the open from O.B.L. to Objective was at once detected by enemy snipers and M.G. Crews.' Consequently, by the time 'Orderlies [did] however manage to reach Bn H.Q. with information' (around midday) the infantry's decision to go to ground was a *fait accompli*. It was a decision taken, at the very least, with the compliance of junior commanders, because the Loyals noted that there 'apparently were…only 2 Officer casualties.' Significantly, it was a decision taken *sometime before* casualties reached the critical ceiling of thirty percent. By nightfall the Loyals: 'Estimated casualties' to be '90 other ranks killed & wounded…', which represented a casualty rate of approximately fifteen percent.[100]

Large cracks were also rapidly developing in the solidity of the advance on the right flank. By early morning (7am) the South Lancs (in support) were finding No Man's Land a far more treacherous proposition than previously encountered. 'Message to say patrols returned. 2 Lt. Parkin and Sgt wounded – they reported patrols held up by

---

96   WO95/2078 (July 1917), op cit., diary entry 31 July.
97   WO95/2080 (July 1917), op cit., diary entry 31 July.
98   Ibid.
99   WO95/2080 (July 1917), op cit.
100 This figure is based upon DHQ's recorded initial fighting strength of 404 rifles. The Loyal's CR did not surpass 30% until 2 August. WO95/2055 (Aug 1917), op cit.

heavy machine gun and snipers, they could not reach forward troops.'[101] Meantime, these forward troops, cut off from support, were being increasingly overrun. The King's Own soon discovered that not all of the enemy had run, surrendered or been killed. A few survivors emerged from un-cleansed dugouts and 'a machine gun opened fire on 'C' Coy from behind whilst they were consolidating.' The King's Own found, however, that the 'bomb' quickly persuaded these distance killers to surrender: 'A bombing party was sent back to mop it up which they did quite successfully, the crew offering very little resistance when attacked.'[102] Indicating, again, that the machine-gun was less of a threat to infantrymen infiltrating from below ground.

The King's Own's troubles were not confined to the rear. Within a few hours of Zero the enemy had counter-attacked and successfully repelled the extreme right of the advance. 'At about 6.30AM [the King's Own recorded] the enemy counter attacked with a force reported to be about 300 strong. The Battalion on our right [4th Middlesex] was driven completely back to its original line of shell holes.' This retreat left the King's Own's right flank exposed to 'heavy rifle and machine gun fire by the enemy from the direction of the WARNETON LINE.'[103] This already fragile situation was compounded by the fact that 'during the advance a gap of some 300 yards was created between the 1 ½ companies of the R.Lancs. Regt. on the right [mostly C Coy] and the remainder of the Battalion.'[104] The enemy were subsequently able to capitalise upon 'C' Companies isolation. DHQ reported that: 'At 7.45am a hostile counter attack developed from the direction of [map ref] towards (FLY BUILDINGS). This was repulsed by the two left companies of the right battalion but apparently made headway against the 1 ½ companies at the divisional boundary for the enemy were seen advancing at this point and a few men were seen to be in the hands of the enemy.'[105] Evidently a number of C Company's infantrymen had responded to isolation and the imminent arrival of the enemy by surrendering. The King's Own later counted 2 officers and 42 Other Ranks 'missing' from amongst the 'very heavy casualties' suffered by the company. Some infantrymen, however, had successfully executed a fighting retreat: 'Our right flank … was completely broken up, one officer, 2/Lt Yacomen and twelve men only succeeded in fighting their way back to TINY FARM where they occupied a strong point constructed by the R.E.' Meantime '*fragments* of A + B Coys [had] held on in the front line and inflicted many casualties on the enemy with rifle and Lewis gun fire.'[106]

---

101 WO95/2080 (July 1917), op cit., diary entry 31 July.
102 WO95/2078 (July 1917), op cit., diary entry 31 July.
103 Ibid.
104 'Narrative of Operations carried out by 19th Division on July 31st, 1917, and following days.' WO95/2055 (Aug 1917), op cit. See also WO95/2078 (July 1917), op cit., diary entry 31 July.
105 'Narrative of Operations carried out by 19th Division on July 31st, 1917, and following days.' WO95/2055 (Aug 1917), op cit.
106 WO95/2078 (July 1917), op cit., diary entry 31 July.

Throughout the morning 56th Brigade had endeavoured to push forward reserves in order to plug the ever widening gaps in the right flank, but to no avail. Lt-Col. Fitzjohn (CO King's Own) recorded how: 'At 8.10AM 'C' Coy 7.S.Lan.R. which had been placed at my disposal and was in position in the Old British Line was ordered to move up and reinforce the front line … If they had been able to do this immediately, the line would have probably been made good, but at 2.30pm I received a report from the officer in command of the company, timed 10.25AM stating that as soon as he attempted to leave the O.B.L. he was met by heavy machine gun fire, suffered heavy casualties and was stopped.'[107]

It is an indication of the communications breakdown that this message took over four hours to traverse the battlefield. By the time Fitzjohn had 'ordered this company of 7.S.Lan.R. to form a defensive flank … the remaining three platoons of 'C' Coy. S.Lancs. [had, at 12 noon' already] advanced to try and drive the enemy from the gap, but met with considerable rifle and machine gun fire which killed or wounded all its officers.'[108] Fitzjohn ventured, quite correctly, that: 'This order apparently never reached the company commander concerned …'[109]

As the fate of South Lancs' 'C' Company indicates, it was the loss of junior officers, rather than overall fighting strength, that was primarily undermining efforts to reinforce the line. Indeed, the South Lancs recorded a total of 74 casualties between 31 July and 3 August – a relatively low casualty rate of twenty two percent.[110] Maj. P.C. Vellacott (CO South Lancs) had reported that: 'Previous to this [the main advance by 'C' Coy] 2 Lt Francombe of the same Company had taken his platoon under orders of the King's Own to try and reinforce the garrison of the Kings Own at TINY FARM strong point which was being hard pressed…2 Lt Francombe however was wounded on the way and his platoon never reached Tiny Farm.'[111]

In an attack, as the Loyals noted, 'against no definite trench system', on a battlefield dominated by enemy machine-gun fire, and in which even the officers considered that: 'Everything seems mixed up', it is no surprise that OR infantrymen, robbed of leadership, should go astray.[112] However, it is worth noting that these platoons,

---

107 Ibid. See also 'Narrative of Operations from 31st July 1917 to 4th Aug.', written by Major P.C. Vellacott CO South Lancs. WO95/2081 (Aug 1917), op cit.
108 WO95/2078 (July 1917), op cit., diary entry 31 July & 'Narrative of Operations carried out by 19th Division on July 31st, 1917, and following days.' WO95/2055 (Aug 1917), op cit.
109 WO95/2078 (July 1917), op cit.
110 'Narrative of Operations from 31st July 1917 to 4th Aug.', written by Major P.C. Vellacott CO South Lancs. WO95/2081 (Aug 1917), op cit. the full breakdown was as follows: 11 ORs killed; 4 Officers, 54 ORs wounded; 5 ORs missing. CR of 22% based upon 'Strength going in on 31st – off 14, OR. 334…'
111 Ibid.
112 WO95/2080 (July 1917), op cit., diary entry 31 July & HWT sent 2.10pm 31 July from Capt. Hammill (OC 'B' Coy. South Lancs) to 56th Brigade. WO95/2076 (July 1917), op cit.

without the guiding voice of command, tended to gravitate away from the ensuing battle. Vellacott reported that: 'Some of the platoon [Francombe's] eventually reached C Coy of the Kings Own on the left of Tiny Farm [away from the contested right flank]. Others of the platoon became scattered and there were a number of casualties…From this time no news was received of C Coys as an organised body.'[113] On the following day, '22 men of this Coy. [had] been collected near Tool Farm', also to the left of the contested right flank.[114] Whether or not these infantrymen were intentional or accidental 'stragglers' cannot be ascertained. However, their experiences further attest that, upon a battlefield once again submerged in the 'fog of war', units of infantrymen could remain at large for over 24 hours, and battalion COs were relatively powerless to intervene.

As the above experiences allude, decision making was largely in the hands of junior commanders on 31 July – a necessity of which platoon tactics aimed to make a virtue of. Events of the afternoon of 31 July suggest that the division's latest draft of junior commanders (or, at least, a number of them) were equal to the challenge. As news of the crumbling right flank filtered back to 56th Brigade, orders were issued to the Fusiliers (temporarily assigned to the brigade) to 'reconnoitre the position… and support by counter attack if necessary.'[115] By mid-afternoon 'C' Company of the Fusiliers had reached the environs of Tiny Farm. Here they met with 'Capt Hammill of B Coy [South Lancs]' who 'had just returned from Tiny Fm by crawling all the way' and reported that 'Tiny Fm was held by 2 Lt Yacomen, Kings Own' and that 'he could not get a platoon up by day.'[116] The arrival of 'C' Coy Fusiliers seems to have persuaded Hammill to take another look. The South Lancs reported at 3pm that 'Capt Hammill [had] gone to reconnoitre with Capt of C Coy RWF where enemy are said to be surrounding flank of King's Own.'[117] Reconnaissance found these rumours to be true. 'The position upon report [the Fusiliers recorded] appeared to be that one Company on the right of the 56th Brigade (i.e. the left Company of the 63rd Bde) had been counter attacked and fallen back to the line they had started from. This movement had left exposed the right flank of the 7th Kings Own and one company (the right one) appears to have been lost entirely at this time. The enemy continued to push on in small parties up hedges and ditches and were undoubtedly threatening the whole of the captured BLUE LINE with envelopment.'[118]

---

113 'Narrative of Operations from 31st July 1917 to 4th Aug.', written by Major P.C. Vellacott CO South Lancs. WO95/2081 (Aug 1917), op cit.
114 HWT dated 1 August from Maj. Vellacott to 56th Brigade. WO95/2076 (Aug 1917), op cit.
115 WO95/2092 'Fusiliers' (July 1917), op cit., diary entry 31 July.
116 WO95/2081 (July 1917), op cit., diary entry 31 July. The South Lancs HQ received this message around 2pm.
117 Ibid.
118 WO95/2092 'Fusiliers' (July 1917), op cit.

Acting upon their own initiative, these two OCs planned, organised and executed a successful counter-attack which (albeit by self-admission) 'saved the day'. 'On arrival they found the enemy moving along the hedges and trying to penetrate between Tiny Farm and the right of C Coy Kings Own and so they decided their upon Capt Hammill's original plan for his own Coy (B), namely to counter attack here and form a defensive flank. They ran back and brought up the Coy of the 9 RWF and 2 platoons of B Coy 7.S.Lan.R. in support, about 50' in rear of 9 RWFs. There was a lot of firing but the enemy who were still creeping up the hedges were driven off and finally they were driven off and the flank saved. The situation here now gradually quietened down as the fight had come to a standstill.'[119] The Fusiliers drew similar conclusions: 'This operation undoubtedly prevented one Company of the 7th Kings Own ... being surrounded and cut off and in all probability prevented the whole line from being pushed out.'[120]

As we determined in the previous chapter, platoon tactics were intended to enhance the BEF's already strong dependence upon leadership and example, and make the platoon commander the major source of his unit's combat morale. Platoon tactics had also, however, proposed that the baton of 'exemplary leadership' in combat should be handed onto NCOs. The actions of Capt. Hammill on 31 July signal that junior commanders could still raise the collective combat morale of a unit, but that example, rather than delegation, remained the primary means of elevation. His CO, Maj. Vellacott, recorded: 'Capt Hammill, the Commander of B Coy, hearing [wrongly] that the enemy held Tiny Fm decided to reconnoitre himself and make sure. He obtained a guide, and by running made a dash for Tiny Fm, fired at the whole time by the enemy. On arrival there Capt Hammill found an officer of the King's Own with a mixed Garrison of about 17 men...The enemy had between 20 and 30 men who were moving about in the open about 300' South of the Farm apparently trying to reconnoitre the position. After rallying the garrison with the help of the King's Own Officer, fire was opened and the enemy driven off.'[121]

It must be remembered that a whole company had previously failed to reach the beleaguered garrison at Tiny Farm. The unwitting testimony of this account is also significant. Given that the enemy was 'moving about in the open' it would seem that the garrison at Tiny Farm, who had earlier 'fought their way back' to the strongpoint, were no longer firing – even with the presence of their own officer. Hammill seems to have reinvigorated the OC, and in turn both officers motivated the garrison to fire upon the enemy, and repulse the mustering counter-attack.

---

119 'Narrative of Operations from 31st July 1917 to 4th Aug.', written by Major P.C. Vellacott CO South Lancs. WO95/2081 (Aug 1917), op cit.
120 WO95/2092 'Fusiliers' (July 1917), op cit.
121 'Narrative of Operations from 31st July 1917 to 4th Aug.', written by Major P.C. Vellacott CO South Lancs. WO95/2081 (Aug 1917), op cit.

But what was the motivation in operation here? There was no 'officer-man relationship' because officers and men belonged to different unit. Four other possible motivational components remained, none of them mutually exclusive. Hammill may have called upon a socially born 'deference in exchange for paternalism' relationship, one that needed no time upon the frontline to mature. The possibility that many officers were now, by mid-1917, 'ranker-officers' suggests, however, that longer standing 'social relationships' were less of a motivational factor. Hammill was also the voice of authority; ORs were trained to obey that authority, and an array of punishments awaited the man who refused to obey that authority. Yet it is hard to imagine how the fear of 'possible' punishment could overcome the very more immediate and real fear of death or wounding; especially when the chances of suffering the only comparable punishment – death by firing squad – were miniscule by comparison.[122] This leaves two, arguably more probable, sources of motivation – knowledge and example. Junior officers were, despite the best efforts of platoon tactics, still the only frontline infantrymen fully versed in the plan; without this knowledge, even men experiencing high 'aggressive' combat morale would struggle to target their willingness to kill. But the evidence collected so far indicates that 'example' was the key to successful leadership. If the person upon whom immediate battlefield authority rested, and within which knowledge of that plan resided, was himself willing to demonstrate the feasibility of that plan, by leading *from the front*, then he stood a fair chance of being followed. In summary, junior commanders brought a small but vital element of calm to the chaos of battle – they knew the plan, and were (invariably) willing to lead in its execution.

The Battle of Pilckem Ridge ended for 19th Division, as a major set-piece attack, on 31 July. For this the Butterflies had their General to thank, who once again showed that he was no 'thruster'. On the evening of the 31st Bridges had rejected a proposed dawn attack upon the surrendered strongpoints, considering 'that it would be probable that a hastily organised attack at this hour might only result in the same experience as the attack this evening …'[123] Holding the line, however, continued to strain the infantrymen's passive combat morale. The effects were soon evident. At nightfall on 1 August the Loyals reported: 'Rain continues to be heavy and conditions are severely taxing the men's physical endurance. 'Trench foot' is making itself evident, and men have to be evacuated through exhaustion …'[124] The Wiltshires reported in a similar vain on the 3rd: 'Men much exhausted and suffering owing to deplorable condition of trenches.' On the 4th '23 NCOs and Men [were] evacuated sick chiefly though exhaustion and exposure', and on the 5th '30 more NCOs and men [were] evacuated

---

122 The division had executed three infantrymen to this date, and would only execute one more before the armistice. Given that details of executions were read out with Battalion Orders, most infantrymen must have had at least a vague awareness of the unlikelihood of suffering death by firing squad.
123 'Text of Messages' received and sent by DHQ on 31 July. WO95/2055 (July 1917), op cit.
124 WO95/2080 (Aug 1917), op cit. See also WO95/2076 (Aug 1917), op cit.

sick, majority of cases through exposure.'[125] The division's disciplinary record shows that any widespread battle-fatigue had not shown itself in the ultimate expression of negative combat behaviour. In the aftermath of the attack only four infantrymen were found guilty of deserting the battlefield – all were reprieved.[126]

In the immediate aftermath of Pilckem Ridge, senior and battalion commanders were faced with the familiar task of explaining partial success. The 56th Brigade traced the origins of the faltering advance back to the retreat of 63rd Brigade. 'The casualties during the operations were light during the first advance but were subsequently much increased owing to the heavy fighting on the right flank after the withdrawal of the 63rd Inf. Bde. and the enemy's very active sniping during the first three days after the attack.'[127] The reports forwarded by the battalions (allowing for the military proclivity towards blaming 'foreign' units) tend to substantiate this claim. Lt-Col. Fitzjohn (CO King's Own) also pinpointed insufficient fighting strength. 'Except on the left where special provisions had been made, the mopping up parties were in no case strong enough to completely carry out their tasks, in spite of the fact that carrying parties were thrown in to assist.'[128] Lt-Col. L.F. Smeathman (CO Fusiliers), however, suggested a broader causation, one that focused upon the nature of the objective itself. 'The 56th Brigade attacked a line known as the blue line…The objective was easily reached with few casualties but as usual in this form of attack when *the object is to simply contain the enemy* heavy casualties occurred in consolidation [my emphasis].'[129] Smeathman considered that the attack had primarily faltered due to the ambiguities inherent in executing, what was essentially, a feint attack. Smeathman did not venture why, but the post-battle accounts, and especially DHQ's comment upon the artillery's inability to provide 'a barrage in depth', point largely in one direction. The division's feint attack had been provided with enough artillery firepower to cover the advance, but not enough to 'silence' the enemy's outlying strongpoints, or protect the task of consolidation.

The 19th Division's experiences at Pilckem Ridge had drawn out the *real* lesson of Messines Ridge. Overwhelming artillery superiority could deliver success at a cost in lives that the infantry could sustain – both materially and morally. Platoon tactics could provide the advantage in localised 'infantry versus infantry' conflicts. But if the infantry were left alone to fight a 'infantry versus machine-gun' or 'infantry versus artillery battle', the outcome was just as it had in 1915 and 1916 – a bloody failure.

125 WO95/2093 'Wiltshires' (Aug 1917), op cit.
126 WO213/16-17 (Aug 1917), op cit.
127 WO95/2076 (Aug 1917), op cit.
128 WO95/2078 (July 1917), op cit., diary entry 31 July.
129 WO95/2092 'Fusiliers' (July 1917), op cit., diary entry 31 July.

Battle of Menin Road Ridge, 20-22 September 1917

As the battle lumbered into autumn the original high expectations of GHQ were again, like their army, taking a battering. Much as the capture of the tiny hamlet of Beaumont Hamel became, in GHQ's mind, a respectable finale to the Somme, so that Passchendaele village would shortly be offered as a suitable dénouement to Third Ypres. The prelude to the 'battle of the mud' saw the division performing their increasingly familiar role of 'securing the flank': 'The IX Corps is to take part in the Second Army Offensive. The main objective of the attack of the IX Corps is to secure the right flank of the X Corps. The attack from the IX Corps front of attack (viz, YPRES – COMINES CANAL to [map ref]) is to be carried out by the 19th Division.'[130]

Planning for the attack signalled the division's continuing journey (under GHQ guidance) towards a tactical doctrine. 58th Brigade, for instance, recorded that: 'All plans for the following offensive will be based upon the instructions contained in the following publications issued by the General Staff at General Headquarters...'[131] Beyond a few amendments and the odd innovation, the broad outline of the plan mirrored those of 7 June and 31 July. Although on the flank, the number of units deployed matched that of Messines: 'The attack was delivered on a two brigade front (58th Bde. on Right and 57th Bde. on the Left) [DHQ later recorded] with 56th Inf. Bde. in reserve. Each attacking Brigade had three battalions in the front line with one battalion in Reserve.'[132] The composition of each attacking battalion mirrored the formation prescribed by *S.S.143*, with one significant exception; there was no differentiation between riflemen and Bombers. 57th Brigade attacked with '3 Battalions in line, each on a 3 company front, of 1 platoon each company. Each platoon in two lines – 1st line 2 Riflemen Sections. 2nd Line Lewis Gun and Rifle Grenade Sections.'[133] Fifteen months after designated 'Bombers' had formed the vanguard of the assault against La Boisselle, this particular specialism was, in line with DHQ's wishes, being democratised – 'everyman' was becoming a 'Bomber'.

The division's specific 'objectives' posed the tactical problems the autonomous fighting platoon had been prescribed to solve; no long lines of trenches, but a plethora of strongpoints and dugouts. For example, 57th Brigade recorded: 'Objectives ... 10th Worc.R to make good WOOD FARM and, after lift of barrage, MOAT FARM.

---

130 '19th Division Instructions for the Offensive', dated 6 September 1917. WO95/2055 (Sept 1917) op cit. See also: '19th Division Operation Order No. 174', dated 17 September. Ibid.; 'Instructions for the Offensive', dated 14 September 1917. WO95/2084 (Sept 1917), op cit.
131 B.M. 3008 '58th Brigade Instructions for the Offensive', dated 8 September. WO95/2088 (Sept 1917) op cit.
132 'Narrative of Operations carried out by 19th Division on 20th September, 1917.' 'Brief Plan of Attack'. WO95/2055 (Sept 1917) op cit.
133 '57th Infantry Brigade Account of Operations September 20th and 21st 1917'. WO95/2084 (Sept 1917), op cit.

172 Killer Butterflies

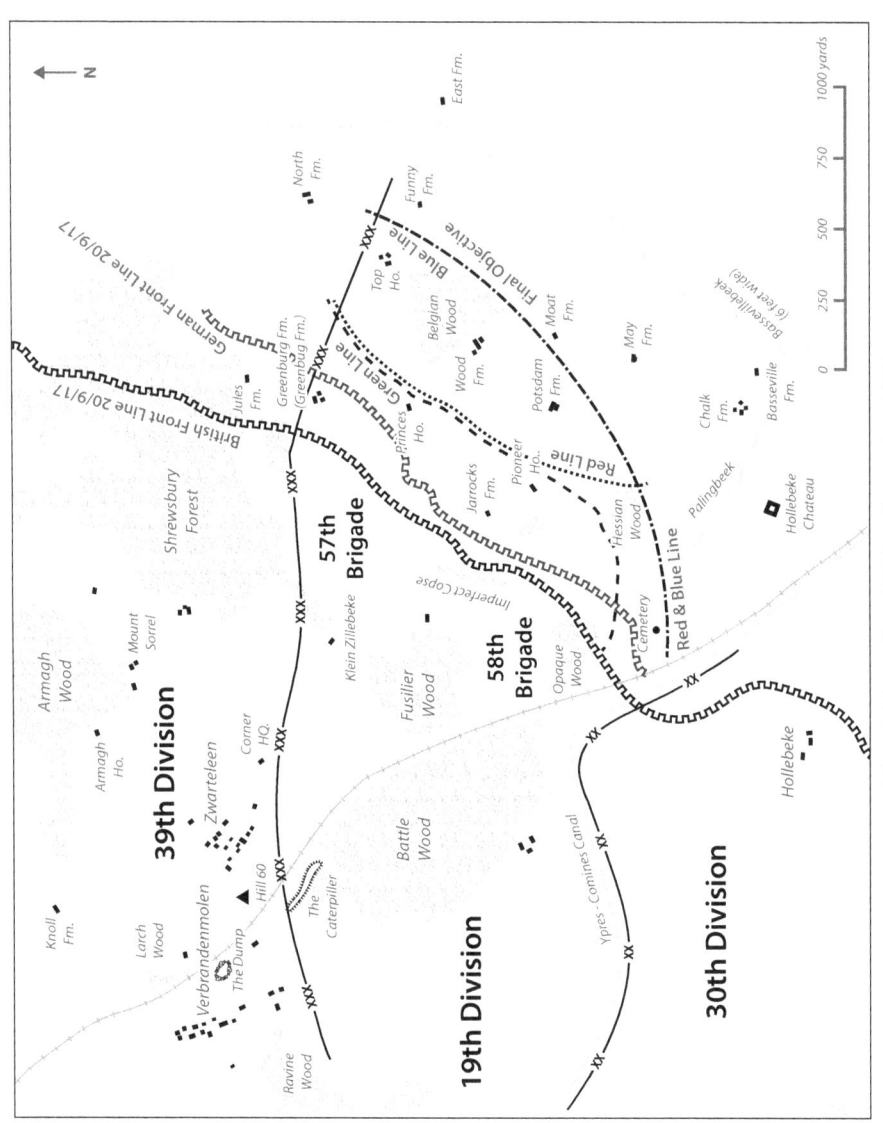

Map 4 Menin Road Ridge, September 1917.

8th Glouc.R. to capture BELGIUM [sic BELGIAN] WOOD. 8th N.Staff.R. to make good TOP HOUSE and, after lift of barrages, dugouts near [map ref].'[134] This collection of fortresses and hideouts did, however, (on paper at least) form into two discernable lines – the Red Line (first objective) and the Blue Line (final objective). Each objective represented an approximate advance of 500 yards.[135]

Artillery support continued to centre upon a 'creeping barrage' that would 'lift' and 'rest' in time with the infantry's advance. Yet this support had grown somewhat in both intensity and scope. For example, DHQ later reported that: 'The artillery barrage, arranged in depth up to 1,000 yards, consisted of guns and howitzers of all calibres. The field guns available gave 2 guns to every 25 Yards in the initial barrage, and one gun to every 17 yards in front of the final objective.'[136] The protective service offered by the artillery had also been extended to cover both 'consolidation' and the 'battle patrols'. DHQ ordered that: 'The creeping barrage – after reaching the final objective – will rest for one hour as a close protective barrage under cover of which dispositions to organize the defence of the position can be made, and consolidation commenced…after this pause of one hour the Artillery will lift…so as to enable battle patrols to move out to clear the immediate foreground and blow up dugouts.'[137]

This creeping projectile mix was complemented by the brigade machine-gunners, who were to perform their familiar role of adding to the ferocity and range of the barrage: '82 machine guns were available for the machine gun barrage to cover the infantry advance [DHQ recorded] … The machine gun barrage was so arranged that the line of the lowest shot in every case fell not less than 300 yards ahead of the artillery barrage line.'[138] Protected by such weighty support, success increasingly hinged upon the infantry's collective willingness to keep time with the barrage. This continuing human 'hinge factor' was not lost upon DHQ, who stressed: 'The chief factor of success and in reducing casualties in the infantry advance is for all ranks to advance close under the Artillery barrage. Failure to dash into the enemy positions the instant the barrage lifts enables the enemy to come out of his shelters and get his machine guns into action.'[139]

Alongside these tactical continuities DHQ introduced a new innovation in the form of a further devolution of battlefield command. Overall command of the post-Zero

---

134   Ibid.
135   WO95/2081 (Sept 1917), op cit., diary entry 20 Sept. Some battalions later signified their first objective as the 'Green Line'.
136   'Narrative of Operations carried out by 19th Division on 20th September, 1917.' 'Brief Plan of Attack'. WO95/2055 (Sept 1917), op cit. See also '19th Division Operation Order No. 174', dated 17th Sept. Ibid.
137   '19th Division Instructions for the Offensive', dated 6 Sept 1917. Ibid.
138   'Narrative of Operations carried out by 19th Division on 20th September, 1917.' 'Brief Plan of Attack'. Ibid.
139   '19th Division Instructions for the Offensive', dated 6 September 1917. WO95/2055 (Sept 1917). Ibid.

battle was placed in the hands of battalion COs acting as 'executive commanders'.[140] 57th Brigade nominated 'Lt. Col. HEATH D.S.O. [who was to] follow the attack and…take up position near or South of the cross roads [map ref] from whence he can observe and control the battle.'[141] Concomitant with the creation of 'executive commanders', control over the deployment of 'reserves' was also been partially devolved to battalion level. DHQ (after the event) explained how: 'Each Company after arrival on the RED LINE had one platoon in reserve, each Battalion had from the outset one company in reserve, and each Brigade had one battalion. The Company, Battalion and Brigade commanders had, therefore, troops at hand to clear up at once 'any positions which were obscure' or reinforce any portion of the attacking troops which had suffered large casualties.'[142]

These command innovations were only rubberstamping the 'unofficial' devolution of command that occurred after Zero. As the division's experiences to date have shown, actual control during the battle usually rested with junior commanders, and little had developed within the realms of battlefield communications to change this situation.[143] Even so, the arrival of the 'executive commander', allied to greater control over reserves, promised to afford the infantry even greater latitude in fighting their battles their way. But if this devolution of battlefield control suggested a growing state of harmony between commanders and commanded during the interregnum between Pilckem and Passchendaele, correspondence between the two parties suggested otherwise. Neither high command nor DHQ were satisfied with the collective combat morale of their troops. The supposed 'sharp end' was, in their minds, still rather blunted. Junior officers lacked the necessary tactical acumen, and their men lacked the necessary 'offensive spirit' to break the new form of 'semi-open' warfare they now witnessed emerging on the Western Front. Underwriting these complaints was the unceasing philosophical battle between the 'bomb and the bayonet'.

Second Army GOC, Gen. Sir Herbert Plumer, found immediate reasons to be dissatisfied with his infantry's performance on 31 July. They had taken too long to capture 'local obstacles [that were] not great', had failed to communicate with either

---

140 57th Brigade recorded that: 'Lieut-Colonel R.M. HEATH D.S.O., 10th R.War.R., was from Zero plus 60' present in executive command of the attacking troops…''57th Infantry Brigade Account of Operations September 20th and 21st 1917'. Ibid. See also B.M. 3008 '58th Brigade Instructions for the Offensive', dated 8 Sept 1917. WO95/2088 (Sept 1917), op cit.
141 'Instructions for the Offensive', dated 14 September 1917. WO95/2084 (Sept 1917), op cit. Heath's role had expanded by the 18th. 'Lt. Col. HEATH D.S.O. is empowered to order the movement of any reserve company of Battalions within that Battalion Area of attack, informing the Battalion Commander simultaneously of his action. He is also empowered to direct movement of part or all of the 10th R.War.R. to any portion of the Brigade Area of attack…' 'Addenda'. Ibid.
142 'Account of the Action' WO95/2055 (Sept 1917), op cit.
143 See G.127/0/27 'Appendix I – Communications, dated 15th September 1917, for details. WO95/2076 (Sept 1917), op cit.

their commanders or one another, and had failed 'to prepare for the counter-attack which might have been considered certain.' At the root of the problem, Plumer considered, lay a changed battlefield which had tripped the infantry up, and exposed a widespread naivety at all levels. '[This battle was] for some Commanders and Staffs the first experience of semi-open warfare carried out on a wide front and they showed clearly that such operations require even more attention to details than those usually described as trench warfare…On our side we have as a rule troops who have only a very limited training and officers and Non-commissioned officers who have not had much experience and who are therefore slow to appreciate the local tactical situation and consequently uncertain as to how it should be dealt with.'[144]

Plumer offered some tactical advice on more efficient 'mopping-up' and improved communications. But his main remedy was the traditional cure – instilling a greater 'offensive spirit', particularly within junior commanders: 'It cannot be too strongly impressed upon young officers and non-commissioned officers who are detached from their superior commanders that it is far better if they are attacked, either to remain in a position if they have been placed in it or to make a bold forward movement. They will thus not only be best fulfilling their instructions but also be more likely to ensure the safety of the men under them than by any withdrawal.'[145] As we have seen, it was often 'to ensure the safety of the men under them', but also because not enough of their men remained with them, that junior officers (and NCOs) often *failed* to act in accordance with Plumer's desired code of combat behaviour.

Meantime DHQ remained preoccupied with the philosophical battle between the bomb and the rifle and bayonet. On the eve of the battle, Bridges repeated the familiar maxim: 'Develop fire power by making men use their rifles and get into good positions for so doing wherever they happen to be. Experience in all recent engagements has shewn [sic] the necessity of consistently impressing on both officers and men that the rifle and bayonet are the first weapons of the infantry soldier and that they have not been replaced by the bomb.[146]

As 19th Division's experiences have indicated, there was no smoke without a degree of combustion – even in the opinions of generals over the fighting acumen of their infantrymen. The infantry did habitually clamour for the bomb, frequently disregarded their rifles, and hardly ever reached for the bayonet. Moreover, as Lt-Col. W. Godfrey (CO Welch) observed (with a rare display of wit) 'non-firing' was even prevalent in self-defence: 'A counter-attack must be expected. Troops will hang on to all ground to be held and will use their rifles freely and immediately…All ranks have

---

144 'Second Army G.72', dated 1 Aug 1917. WO95/2055 (Aug 1917), op cit.
145 Ibid. See also G158/7/3 'Notes on Training' written by DHQ, dated 10 August, for similar complaints from DHQ. WO95/2055 (Aug 1917), op cit.
146 G.127/0/28 'Special Instructions to be Communicated to All Ranks', dated 15 Sept 1917. WO95/2076 (Sept 1917), op cit.

got into a bad habit when they see an enemy of talking about it first. Shoot first and talk afterwards.'[147]

The ongoing remedies that DHQ sought on the training ground represented a development of the ideas outlined during the Spring of 1917. The platoon commander remained pivotal to his unit's combat morale, and he was to be granted more time to 'be taught correct tactical methods and to develop his initiative.'[148] Indicating that these 'tactical methods' were part of a 'self-learning curve', this was to be achieved through: 'Small schemes both with troops and without based upon situations actually met with in recent fighting…', namely: 'Junction Buildings'.[149] Although these 'small schemes' embraced the weaponry and tactical formations outlined in *S.S.143*, DHQ still insisted that the rifle remained the elemental weapon for providing covering fire: 'the platoon commander should be taught to employ in close combination the riflemen, rifle grenadiers, bombers, and Lewis guns but particularly the riflemen. The power of rifle fire to cover movement has been fully exemplified in the recent operations and should be emphasised.'[150]

DHQ recognised that there was two sides to proficient leadership; the leader and the led. The latest drafts of lawless individuals were to be turned into an obedient whole through a combination of habit, trust and loyalty. The methods of inculcation mixed the parade ground with the playing field (and the old with the relatively new). 'The platoon requires to be trained to follow their commander and carry out his orders intelligently … This is a question of discipline, training, and confidence in the commander. Drill and strict attention to detail provide the best means of instilling discipline…Organised games should be instituted for platoons in which the commander leads his men. This helps to increase the powers of leadership of the platoon commander and establish the spirit of trust and affection of the men for their leader.'[151]

Turning this 'sprit of trust and affection' into the prescribed 'offensive spirit' continued to rest upon the 'sprit of the bayonet'. Indeed, the bayonet had been polished-up and rejuvenated in the infantry's latest basic training manual – *S.S.185 Assault Training* (Sept 1917).[152] *S.S.185* left the reader in no doubt: 'It is the spirit of the bayonet that captures the position, and of the bullet that holds it.' Significantly, *S.S.185* overtly stated what the division's own experiences had already hinted at; 'posturing' the act of the bayonet charge was often enough to win the day. 'Two lines advancing against one

---

147 'Operation Orders by Lieut Colonel W. Godfrey D.S.O. Comdg 9th Battalion Welch Regiment' dated 17 Sept 1917. WO95/2092 'Welch' (Sept 1917), op cit.
148 G158/7/3 'Notes on Training' written by DHQ dated 10 August. WO95/2055 (Aug 1917), op cit.
149 Ibid. 'Notes on Training' included a section detailing 'Situation for 1st Exercise. (Junction Buildings Scheme.)'
150 Ibid.
151 G158/7/3 'Notes on Training'. Ibid.
152 *S.S.185* 'Assault Training' Issued by the General Staff, September 1917.

another with the bayonet *will seldom meet*. The one stimulated with the greater fury and confidence, by the force of its determination to conquer, will cause the other line to waver and turn [my emphasis].'[153] Nevertheless, it seems reasonable to conjecture that an advancing line of infantrymen demonstrating 'greater fury' and 'determination' almost certainly contained a number of men willing to execute the act.

A training schedule that aimed at producing such an advancing line of bayonet toting infantrymen was wholly justifiable. If a man was able and willing to kill his adversary close-up with cold steel, then he would be similarly open to killing with a bullet, bomb, machine-gun or rifle grenade. The necessary weapons expertise could be built upon this willingness to kill (at the division's specialist training schools). If, in reality, more infantrymen found themselves willing and able to use weapons that partially sanitised the act of hurting the enemy, then this did not detract from the endeavour to instil the 'spirit of the bayonet'. The problem that continued to hinder the evolution of such a spirit was the majority of infantrymen's evident sustained resistance to inculcation.

The Battle of Menin Road Ridge proved to be a relative success for 19th Division; both objective lines seized and consolidated more-or-less to time. Yet there were times when some familiar spanners threatened to fall into the works. With typically sardonic timing, a determined rain began to fall prior to Zero, turning the battlefield into a mud bath as the day progressed. Cooperation between artillery and infantry suffered accordingly, as a succession of 'halts' and 'lifts' timed for firmer ground left some footsloggers adrift and defenceless against enemy machine-gun and artillery fire. Compounding matters, a number of enemy strongpoints escaped the artillery's attention and added their weight to this already hostile fire, causing the inevitable heavy casualties. But just as a scene from the Somme threatened to replay, two innovations of 1917 stepped forward to rewrite the script. Battalion control over reserves allowed fresh troops to be successfully directed towards the more tenacious enemy strongpoints, whose resilience was then broken by the successful deployment of platoon tactics. The cost in casualties was high: 1933 infantrymen over four days in or around the battle. Yet this represented a 1 in 6 chance of becoming a casualty; good odds on the Salient.[154] One of the 'ones', however, was 'The Divisional Commander, General BRIDGES [who] was severely wounded when visiting Bde. H.Q at Hill 60 about 5pm 20th September.'[155]

---

153 Ibid., p. 8.
154 The full breakdown of casualties suffered between 19 & 23 Sept was as follows: 15 Officers, 325 ORs killed; 58 Officers, 1265 ORs wounded; 1 Officers, 269 ORs missing; total casualties 1933. This represented a approx. 1 in 6 chance of becoming a casualty, based upon a recorded 'Fighting Strength' as of 15 Sept of 10132. WO95/2055 (Sept 1917), op cit.
155 Ibid. Diary entry 20 Sept. Bridges had been hit in the leg, and the wound was severe enough to require amputation. Indicating what a strange breed Great War generals were, Bridges later fed the amputated leg to his pet lion.

Zero was trumpeted by a deluge of rain[156] which caused slippage between the motion of the creeping barrage and the movement of the infantry, undermining this pivotal element in the plan of attack. DHQ recorded that: 'Owing to the state of the ground the troops were unable to keep up to the barrage and casualties were consequently greater than they might have been during the advance to the RED Line.'[157] Yet poor infantry time-keeping caused by poor weather was not the universal experience. For example, DHQ recorded that: 'On the front of the Left Brigade (57th Bde.) the Right Battalion (10th Worc. Regt.) *advanced well under the barrage* and occupied the Red Line in good order although opposition was encountered on their right. The centre and left Battalions (8th Gloucesters and 8th N.Staffs.) were late following the barrage owing to the extremely boggy nature of the ground and consequently suffered heavy casualties from machine gun fire … [my emphasis]'[158]

Neither were all casualties sustained by a failure to keep time with the barrage; it was often the other way around. For example, DHQ recorded that: 'The Right Battalion (Wilts. Regt.) reached their objective to time, but the centre and left Battalions (Welch Regt. and Cheshires) *suffered heavy casualties*, lost touch temporarily on both flanks *and got left behind the barrage* [my emphasis].'[159] An account by the Wiltshires indicates the cause of these heavy casualties. 'At Zero hour 5.40am Battalion advanced to the attack under a heavy Creeping Barrage by our Artillery. Left front Company met with little opposition except for continuous Machine Gun fire from the direction of CEMETERY EMBANKMENT. The machine guns appear to be located *beyond the objective line and to fire through the Barrage* [my emphasis].'[160]

It is apparent that the curtain of fire thrown around the infantry had a number of gaps within it, and these were exploited by unmolested enemy strongpoints. Significantly, keeping good time with the barrage similarly failed to save the Worcesters from enemy fire; 57th Brigade reporting that: 'Considerable casualties were inflicted [on them] by Machine Guns from HOLLEBEKE CHATEAU and WOOD FARM, also when mopping up MOAT FARM.'[161]

A familiar combat scenario had been induced by this piercing enemy machine-gun fire. The sight or notion of one-in-three of their comrades being hit was compelling infantrymen to sacrifice the objective to safety. Any chance of re-igniting the charge was being further dampened by the loss of junior commanders. The Cheshires, for

---

156 See: WO95/2080 (Sept 1917), op cit., diary entry 19 Sept; WO95/2081 (Sept 1917), op cit., diary entry 19 Sept; WO95/2093 'Wiltshires' (Sept 1917), op cit. Diary entry 19 Sept.
157 'Account of the Action' WO95/2055 (Sept 1917), op cit.
158 Ibid. See also '57th Infantry Brigade Account of Operations September 20th and 21st 1917'. WO95/2084 (Sept 1917), op cit.
159 'Account of the Action' WO95/2055 (Sept 1917), op cit. See also WO95/2091 (Sept 1917), op cit. Diary entry 20 Sept.
160 WO95/2093 'Wiltshires' (Sept 1917), op cit. Diary entry 20 Sept.
161 '57th Infantry Brigade Account of Operations September 20th and 21st 1917'. WO95/2084 (Sept 1917), op cit.

instance, reported how 'the remainder of 'D' Coy had to go up to reinforce 'C' Coy [approx. strength 140 ORs] of our own Battn. who had sustained about 50 casualties and were held up by a SNIPERS POST on their extreme right.'[162] Whilst DHQ recorded how 'the Welsh Regt. were still held up in front of HESSIAN WOOD. The Commanding Officer, Major J.A. GIBBS, D.S.O., had been killed and the Battalion had suffered heavy casualties, especially in Officers.'[163] The Welch later recorded that 12 of their 16 officers had fallen casualty.[164]

The opening of the attack had brought about the expected closing of communication channels between the front and rears. Senior commanders were consequently suffering the usual impotency when it came to controlling events upon the battlefield. The South Lancs (in reserve) reported that at '5.40 [am] under the barrage the attacking troops advanced…There was a long wait until any news was received of the doings of the front line.'[165] The communication delay was around 90 minutes, enough for a difficult situation to become critical.[166] It was at this juncture that the empowerment of battalions to deploy their own reserves overcame this communications breech. DHQ detailed how the 'executive commanders' had helped sustain the impetus of the advance: 'In each Brigade a senior Battalion Commander went forward at once to a commanding position on the front of attack from which he could judge the whole tactical situation on the front of the Brigade and was given power to employ any portions of reserve troops as he thought fit without waiting for sanction from Brigade Commanders.'[167]

Although the post-battle reports do not fully illuminate at what level of battalion command decisions over the deployment of reserves were being made, they do shed light upon the resounding success of this newly liberated command process. Moreover, they illustrate that the essential maxim of *S.S.143* had finally been internalised; platoons (or some at least) were now acting 'autonomously'. For example, on 58th Brigade's front the advance by the Welch had ground to a halt, but they were quickly to receive assistance from all three of their fellow battalions. The Wiltshires recorded that: 'On the left the 9th Welch did not reach their objective until 90 minutes after 'C' Coy had began consolidating. To cover his left flank Capt. Williams formed a defensive flank of posts and asked for assistance…one platoon was moved up to assist the left Company to form a defensive flank before the 9th Welch had come into touch and

---

162 WO95/2091 (Sept 1917), op cit. Diary entry 20 Sept. The Cheshires recorded a 'fighting strength' of 20 Officers and 556 ORs. This gave an approximate company strength of 140 ORs. 50 casualties therefore represented a casualty rate of 36%.
163 'Account of the Action' WO95/2055 (Sept 1917), op cit.
164 WO95/2092 'Welch' (Sept 1917), op cit. Diary entry 20 Sept.
165 WO95/2081 (Sept 1917), op cit. Diary entry 20 Sept.
166 The South Lancs recorded '9.15 [am] Another [message] from Bgde informed us that the right Bgde had gained objective at 7.45 am but heavy resistance in HESSIAN WOOD.' Ibid.
167 'Account of the Action' WO95/2055 (Sept 1917), op cit.

later it was reinforced by a second platoon with orders to operate vigorously against HESSIAN WOOD which was believed to be holding up 9th Welch.'[168]

About the same time 'Lt. Col. GODFREY, D.S.O., who had been sent forward to command the Welsh, finding that they were weak and disorganised, moved forward one company of 9th R.W. Fusiliers (Brigade Reserve) to hold the Northern edge of HESSIAN WOOD at 9.10am. The remaining two companies of the 9th R.W.Fus. were moved forward closer to support.'[169] A platoon of Cheshires also came to their aid; their commander evidently acting on his own initiative. '2/Lt. COLVIN, Cheshire Regt. noticing that the Welsh were held up by machine gun fire from the N. corner of HESSIAN WOOD attacked the dugouts there with one platoon from the North and thereby materially assisted their advance, and enabled them to get into the Northern edge of the wood.'[170] A similar flexibility in the deployment of reserves helped deliver the second objective (the task of the Cheshires and Gloucesters). The Cheshires recorded that: 'The advance to the final objective commenced at 6.44am and more resistance was met with. On the left 'A' Coy under Capt H.E. QUAYLE experienced difficulty with machine guns on the ridge in front about MAY FARM, but on receiving a reinforcing platoon from 'B' Coy captured POTSDAM FARM and all their final objectives and established touch with the Worcesters on their left.'[171] After nine months of inculcation, and a number of false starts, the division was finally able to prepare, organise and act as autonomous fighting platoons.

Having subdued the enemy's machine-gun fire, those platoons that pushed-on to their objectives invariably experienced 'little opposition'. The North Staffords recorded that: 'Heavy casualties were inflicted during the advance by enemy machine guns and rifle fire from neighbourhood of [map ref]. Otherwise there was little opposition except from North end of BELGIAN WOOD, TOP HOUSE was occupied without much trouble.'[172] The Cheshires similarly detailed that: 'Other than this [hostile machine-gun fire] no opposition was met with, JARROCKS FARM, PIONEER HOUSE, and the intermediate objective, all being easily carried according to schedule time, only slight casualties were sustained and many GERMANS were killed and captured.'[173] An account given by the Wiltshires suggests that the latter outweighed the former: 'The dugouts in the wood at about [map ref] were dealt with[,] 3 Germans being killed and 19 taken prisoner.'[174] DHQ's overall headcount suggests this was

---

168 WO95/2093 'Wiltshires' (Sept 1917), op cit. Diary entry 20 Sept.
169 'Account of the Action' WO95/2055 (Sept 1917), op cit. It is possible that Godfrey was the 58th's 'executive commander', but no mention was made of this.
170 Ibid.
171 WO95/2091 (Sept 1917), op cit. Diary entry 20 Sept.
172 '57th Infantry Brigade Account of Operations September 20th and 21st 1917'. WO95/2084 (Sept 1917), op cit. See also WO95/2092 'Welch' (Sept 1917), op cit., diary entry 20 Sept.
173 WO95/2091 (Sept 1917), op cit., diary entry 20 Sept.
174 WO95/2093 'Wiltshires' (Sept 1917), op cit., diary entry 20 Sept.

the common experience: 'During the attack 20 Officers and 371 other ranks were taken prisoner.'[175] At the point of capture it would seem that Menin Road Ridge provided a similar combat experience to that of Messines. Outnumbered garrisons, their will to resist battered by unrelenting shell and machine-gun fire, either ran or gave themselves up the moment combat became (or threatened to become) close-up and personal.

How were those enemy soldiers who refused to yield killed? The Butterflies were evidently making proficient use of the distance weaponry afforded by the autonomous fighting platoon. For example, the Wiltshires recorded that: 'As 'D' Coy on the right seemed to meet with considerable resistance Capt WILLIAMS (O.C. 'C' Coy) ordered his right front Lewis Gun to open a brisk fire on the dugouts in front of that Company.'[176] Whilst the North Staffords, endeavouring to overcome one particularly resistive strongpoint, called upon the brigade distance killers temporarily under their command: '2nd Lt. G.S. Carver led D Coy with half of his platoon, two Vickers Guns and a detachment from the 59th M.G. Coy, advanced with the Battn. on the left (16th Notts & Derby) with orders to post his machine guns in a position near NORTH FARM from which he could enfilade our own front. This he did after a short sharp fight in which he captured four M/Guns and 29 prisoners. It was enfilading our left flank.'[177]

But if such accounts offered little to placate senior commanders who wanted to hear more about 'spirit' and less about weapons technology, events elsewhere had evidently provided more satisfying reportage. 57th Brigade unequivocally announced that: 'The rifle and especially the bayonet played a predominant part in the attack. I cannot hear of any bombs having been thrown.'[178] In the mind's eye of the brigade, the philosophical battle between bomb and bayonet was finding some material succour upon the battlefield – the bayonet (and rifle) was winning the day. It is possible, however, that 57th Brigade (and DHQ) were exaggerating the atypical combat behaviour of 20 September because it fitted their vision of a 'soldier's fight'. Only the Gloucesters were reported displaying this much vaunted form of combat behaviour: '8th Glouc.R. were late in following barrage and suffered casualties accordingly, GREEN Line was occupied according to Time Table. Strong opposition was encountered in BELGIAN WOOD, which was cleared by *a determined bayonet attack*. BLUE Line and support posts subsequently occupied [my emphasis].'[179] It would seem inexplicable that infantry

---

175 'Account of the Action'. WO95/2055 (Sept 1917), op cit. See also WO95/2080 (Sept 1917), op cit., diary entry 20 Sept.
176 WO95/2093 'Wiltshires' (Sept 1917), op cit., diary entry 20 Sept.
177 WO95/2085 'North Staffords' (Sept 1917), op cit., diary entry 20 Sept.
178 '57th Infantry Brigade Account of Operations September 20th and 21st 1917'. WO95/2084 (Sept 1917), op cit.
179 '57th Infantry Brigade Account of Operations September 20th and 21st 1917'. WO95/2084 (Sept 1917), op cit. This combat episode unsurprisingly found its way into DHQ's 'Account of the Action', but it was singular. See WO95/2055 (Sept 1917), op cit.

units would enact the bayonet charge (successfully) and then consistently fail to record that they had done their senior commander's bidding. It would seem more probable, therefore, that the Gloucesters (or some of the Gloucesters) alone had summoned up the 'spirit of the bayonet'.

What frontline units *did* consistently continue to record was the high combat morale of a number of junior officers. For example, the Cheshires detailed how '2 Lt. H. COLVIN … had been mainly personally responsible for the clearing of the dug outs in the N.E. corner of HESSIAN WOOD …'[180] Whilst the 58th Machine-Gun Company (indicating that machine-gunners did not always fight a 'distance' war), reported 'Lt CHATER distinguishing himself by single handed attacking 2 enemy machine guns in action, killing one and taking 3 prisoners.'[181]

Two divergent accounts given of the combat behaviour of 19th Division's 'green' troops offer further insights into the influence of leadership upon a unit's collective combat morale. Some of the division's latest drafts were sent to serve as stretcher bearers. 58th Field Ambulance were decidedly unimpressed by their quota. 'The infantry stretcher bearers provided proved most unsatisfactory. There were only 2 Sergeants, 1 Corporal and 5 L/Corporals in a total of 211, and to a great extent these N.C.Os did not know their own men, many of whom stated that they had not been under fire before. It was impossible to keep proper control over them and they avoided their duties whenever possible, hiding in dug-outs and removing their brassards to avoid recognition. The 23 shewn [sic] missing were men who left the forward Bearer Post with cases and did not return.' [The CO went on to recommend that] A proportion of their own officers would probably be a great help in keeping up the morale of the men under fire.'[182]

This was a dangerous task (6 stretcher bearers were killed, and 19 wounded) requiring a high, but totally passive, combat morale.[183] It is doubtful whether any Great War infantryman would want the R.A.M.C. to be his final judge and jury. It may also have been that the Colonel was searching for scapegoats here. This detailed account of the evacuation of wounded seems to have been prompted by complaints from the division's infantrymen that wounded soldiers were not being promptly evacuated.[184] But even if these accusations only held a degree of veracity, they still suggest that many of these 'green' troops were either unwilling or unable to risk their lives to save the lives of others.

New recruits who participated in the attack, however, received a decidedly more glowing report. 57th Brigade considering that: 'The new reinforcements proved

---

180 WO95/2091 (Sept 1917), op cit., diary entry 20 Sept.
181 WO95/2093 '58th Machine-Gun Coy' (Sept 1917), op cit., diary entry 20 Sept.
182 'The Evacuation of Wounded from 19th Division during the Operation of 19th, 20th and 21st September 1917…' written by Lt-Col. Preston dated 24 September 1917. WO95/2072 58th Field Ambulance War Diary (Sept 1917) PRO.
183 Ibid.
184 See ibid.

gallant, but were obviously totally untrained. It is essential that these, when recruits, should reach Battalions much earlier than within 3 or 4 days of a large engagement, as occurred in this case. However, their experience will be of great value to them subsequently.'[185] The inference is that these 'green' infantrymen demonstrated a commendably high passive combat morale (they were gallant', or brave), but were less blessed when it came to aggressive combat morale (they were 'obviously totally untrained', or unable to fight effectively). The missing element between the 'gallant' green infantrymen and the allegedly ungallant 'green' temporary stretcher bearers was *leadership* – primarily that of junior officers, but also that of non-commissioned officers.[186] Significantly, there was no actual *relationship* between leaders and led, because these raw recruits had only just arrived. This suggests again that the other facets underpinning the operation of leadership already outlined – example, knowledge and/or authority – were more important than a formal timeserving relationship.

At midday on the 20th a '19th Div. wire [was] received from IX Corps. Congratulating all ranks of the Div on capture of all objectives.'[187] Part one of the battle was over, part two now began. Whilst the infantry desperately dug-in, the division's own distance killers endeavoured to protect them. DHQ recorded: 'Heavy machine guns fire, particularly from the direction of HOLLEBEKE CHATEAU, interfered with the construction of strong points…The 6 machine guns which had advanced with each Brigade were quickly placed in position in these posts [recently dug], and other guns of the attacking Brigades released from barrage fire were disposed at the points selected as strong-points.'[188]

The recently deposed Germans attempted two counter-attacks during the remainder of the day, but both were repelled by these same distance killers. The South Lancs recorded: '2.17 [pm] Received a message that counter attack had developed all along the line. 3.10 [pm] Heard that counter attack had been dispersed of by S.O.S. barrage.'[189] 57th Brigade recorded how, a few hours later, '57th M.G. Company was moved forward, according to instructions, under the personal direction of Capt. KNOX-LITTLE with remarkable determination and rapidity…The enemy

185 '57th Infantry Brigade Account of Operations September 20th and 21st 1917'. WO95/2084 (Sept 1917), op cit.
186 The group loyalty promoted by platoon tactics could have played no part because these new arrivals had no 'group' to be 'loyal' towards.
187 WO95/2081 (Sept 1917), op cit. Diary entry 20 Sept.
188 'Account of the Action'. WO95/2055 (Sept 1917), op cit. Trench mortars were evidently less effective in this role. DHQ complained that: 'Stokes Mortars proved useless except on the right of the Right Brigade where after the capture of the final objective they could be employed from positions which were almost in our old line and to which communication was good.'
189 WO95/2081 (Sept 1917), op cit., diary entry 20 Sept.

counter-attacked about 400 strong, on the left flank towards 7.20pm. in the direction of NORTH FARM. This attack was annihilated by gun and Machine gun fire.'[190]

But if these accounts underline that part two of the offensive was, like part one, dominated by distance killers, a decidedly 'interpersonal' fight was also being enacted in the endeavour to secure consolidation – a fight between snipers. The Wiltshires recorded how: 'The consolidation was covered by Lewis Guns and the company snipers who were heavily engaged endeavouring to pick off Germans moving down the railway embankment and also in keeping down enemy sniping on the immediate front.'[191] This was a battle between committed trench fighters – two groups of snipers determined to kill or maim their opposition, and thus save the day. But it remained a decidedly marginal combat episode, as the casualty toll of the 56th Brigade attests: 'Total casualties – 14 officers and 342 other ranks – 19th [to] 29th. These were almost entirely due to shell fire[,] 20% being fatal.'[192]

With the battle over, senior commanders reflected upon the division's success in capturing and holding their objectives. 57th Brigade focused upon the barrage, offering qualified praise. 'The artillery barrage was excellent, and all ranks testify to the usefulness of the smoke at the pausing lines. The pace of the barrage was, however, much too fast at first, the left and part of the centre Battalion were quite unable to keep up in the boggy ground during the first 350 yards of the advance. This resulted in many casualties.'[193] The post-battle reports underline the general veracity of this conclusion. The barrage, although imperfect, had allowed enough infantrymen (the majority) to reach their objectives unmolested. On reaching the objective, they invariably found that the intensity of the bombardment ensured that the battered defenders offered 'no opposition'.

For its part, DHQ emphasised the salutary effects of devolving command over reserves. 'The principle of keeping a reserve in the hands of each Battalion and Brigade Commander during the attacks against the present German defensive system proved right.'[194] The post-battle reports have also vindicated this view. However, DHQ also stressed a further cause of eventual success, stating that 'there is no doubt that the policy of having *well trained and fresh troops* for the attack at the expense of preparing the front of attack proved right in this case [my emphasis].'[195] The post-battle accounts have also indicated that being well versed in platoon tactics allowed a number of strongpoints to be overcome; obstacles that, in past experiences, may have held up the advance.

---

190 '57th Infantry Brigade Account of Operations September 20th and 21st 1917'. WO95/2084 (Sept 1917), op cit.
191 WO95/2093 'Wiltshires' (Sept 1917), op cit., diary entry 20 Sept.
192 WO95/2076 (Sept 1917), op cit.
193 '57th Infantry Brigade Account of Operations September 20th and 21st 1917'. WO95/2084 (Sept 1917), op cit.
194 'Account of the Action', 'Comments'. WO95/2055 (Sept 1917), op cit.
195 Ibid.

Messines Ridge and Third Ypres 185

The efficacy of having physically and mentally 'fresh' troops in the advance would seem self-evident. As we have seen, physical and/or mental *fatigue* was a major cause of low combat morale. Following the depression of 31 July, the qualitative accounts forward a tentative case for a rejuvenated 'offensive spirit'. The statistical record supports this impression, and offers some further explanations. The majority of the advancing infantry units suffered a casualty rate just below the thirty percent ceiling.[196] This indicates that Menin Road Ridge did not interrogate the division's morale to the same depths as Pilckem, and, furthermore, provided a comparatively less stern challenge than the previous two year's experiences of major set-piece battles. The Welch shattered the ceiling, suffering a casualty rate of approximately fifty percent, but then only 'D Coy [had] pushed through to the final objective…'[197] Nevertheless, the North Staffords suffered a casualty rate of around forty percent, and still successfully captured their objectives – indicating that the division could still reach the heights of their previously experienced 'collective' combat morale.[198]

The qualitative accounts make no particular mention of the more negative aspects of combat behaviour. There were no reported cases of 'Straggling'. The numbers of reported 'missing' were relatively high though – originally accounting for fourteen percent of the division's total casualties.[199] However, DHQ stressed that: 'Many of the 270 shown as missing are being accounted for daily as having been either killed or wounded and evacuated by other Divisional Field Ambulances. As far as can be ascertained, none of these fell into the hands of the enemy.'[200] The final death toll indicates that, at most, only a handful of infantrymen per battalion surrendered on 20 September.[201] Similarly, 19th Division's disciplinary record shows that only

---

196 The following battalions suffered a casualty rate on or below the 'critical' 30% level. Royal Warwick, FS 628; C 105; CR 17%. Gloucesters, FS 595; C 163; CR 27%. Worcesters, FS 644; C 193; CR 30%. Wiltshires, FS approx. 550; C 152; CR 28%. Fusiliers, FS approx. 550; C 109; CR 20%. Cheshires, FS 576; C 160; CR 28%. Figures taken from: '57th Infantry Brigade Account of Operations September 20th and 21st 1917'. WO95/2084 (Sept 1917), op cit.: WO95/2093 'Wiltshires' (Sept 1917), op cit.: WO95/2092 'Fusiliers' (Sept 1917), op cit.& WO95/2091 (Sept 1917), op cit.
197 Welch, FS approx. 550; C 291; CR 53%. WO95/2092 'Welch' (Sept 1917), op cit., diary entry 20 Sept.
198 North Staffords, FS 660; C 270; CR 41%.
199 WO95/2055 (Sept 1917), op cit., diary entry 20 Sept. To reiterate, the division originally recorded 1933 casualties.
200 'Account of the Action'. Ibid.
201 For example, the full breakdown of casualties for the North Staffords records: 2 Officers, 56 OR killed; 8 Officers, 169 OR wounded; 35 OR missing. *Soldiers Died* records a eventual total of 69 fatalities for 20/21 Sept. If all of these extra fatalities were drawn from the list of missing, then 22 infantrymen were left unaccounted for. This is the highest number throughout the division. '57th Infantry Brigade Account of Operations September 20th and 21st 1917' & *Soldiers Died*, op cit.

smatterings of men were found guilty of deliberately removing themselves from the battlefield.[202]

The 19th Division left the Third Ypres battleground on 24 September, thus ending their participation in the large-scale set-piece battles of 1917. Their final battle of the year had underlined a number of Great War maxims; some of which had been temporarily overlooked on 31 July. Superiority in artillery firepower was *the* essential ingredient in a successful advance. Messines Ridge and Menin Road Ridge had proved the point; Pilckem had shown the folly of compromise. Chose to attack with under-strength, physically (and often mentally) fatigued soldiers, and the chances of a successful advance, even if accompanied by superior artillery firepower, sank like overburdened limbers in the Flanders mud. Remove artillery from the firepower equation altogether and a mercurial contest, one resting upon something as fragile as infantry combat morale, ensued. Yet Menin Road Ridge had also hinted that infantry tactics *could* have agency upon the outcome of a Great War battle. Autonomous fighting platoons, under the overall charge of a frontline commander, could overcome *localised* resistance, and, in doing so, uphold the momentum of the advance. However, if artillery firepower superiority was lost for any period of time then platoon tactics, like any other form of infantry tactics, were destined to fail.

---

[202] In the aftermath of the battle (21 to 30 Sept) 5 soldiers were found guilty of 'absence' or 'ABC', 2 of actual 'Desertion', and 1 of 'Self-Inflicted Wounds'. WO213/17 (Sept 1917), op cit. 57th Brigade recorded that the single case of 'SIW' occurred in the Worcesters. '57th Infantry Brigade Account of Operations September 20th and 21st 1917' & *Soldiers Died*, op cit.

9

The German Spring Offensives

Overview

The 19th Division's arrival in France in July 1915 had coincided with the German Army adopting a defensive attitude upon the British sectors of the Western Front. Consequently, whilst two-and-a-half years of endeavouring to break this stance had bequeathed the division a painfully broad and wide experience of the attack, their collective knowledge of *defending* the line against a similarly concerted enemy incursion was negligible. Like every other soldier in the BEF, the division's newly appointed commander, Maj-Gen. G.D. Jeffreys, (formerly of 57th Brigade) was aware that the Spring of 1918 beckoned the rude awakening of this naivety. He was similarly aware that, due to the high casualties incurred during 1917, and the ever diminishing reserves of 'A1' men available to the BEF, his division would face the expected onslaught shorn of three battalions and populated largely by young and inexperienced conscripts.56th Brigade lost all four of its 1915 battalions and was reconstituted by moving the 8th North Staffs and 9th Cheshires from 57th and 58th Brigades respectively and gaining the 1/4th King's Shropshire from 63rd Division.

On the eve of the German spring offensive, Jeffreys charged his depleted and youthful ranks with the quoted epigraph: there was to be no retreat and no surrender. When the storm finally broke on 21 March, Jeffreys' 'do or die' espousals were soon echoing around a void – the place where his infantrymen had stood. So began a long and relentless twelve week retreat that would see the division taking backward steps across the battlegrounds of their own short history – the Somme and Messines – before being sent South in May, to foreign fields, and to fight alongside a foreign army. It was here, in the region of Champagne, on the suitably momentously named *Montagne de Bligny*, that 19th Division, alongside their French allies, finally made a lasting stand.

The spring of 1918 wrote one more apocalyptical chapter into the 19th Division's bloody history. The '1918 Battle of the Somme', the 'Battle of Lys', and the 'Battle of Aisne-Marne' cost the Butterflies over 8000 casualties – their entire fighting-strength once over. The Butterflies marched onto each battlefield as a division, but returned as a

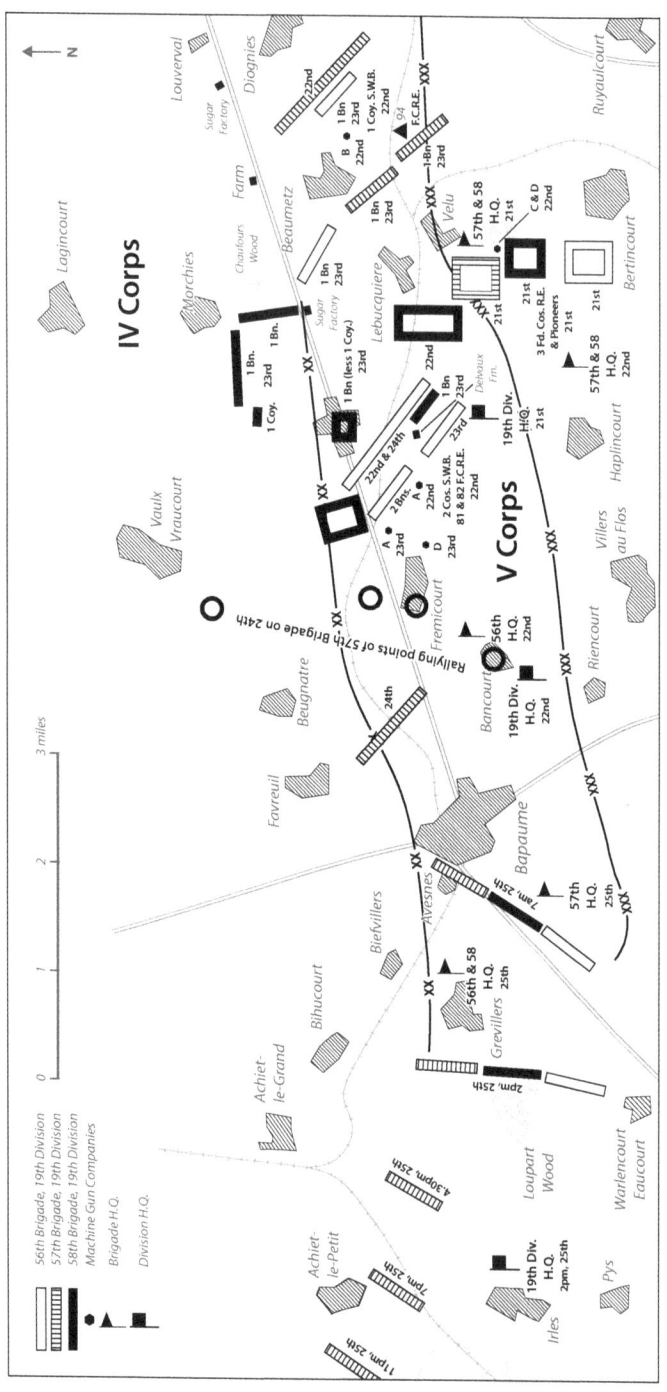

Map 5 Somme, March 1918 (1).

'Composite Brigade'. This endless casualty list was disturbing enough for every officer and man of the division, but it was the *means* by which the ranks were being depleted that was troubling the minds of their senior commanders.

Upward of 4000 Butterflies had been made captive by the German Army. Moreover, many of the division's infantrymen were evading captivity by retreating without orders. Time and time again Jeffreys' found that his earlier demands for martyrdom were falling upon deaf ears. At times units of the division would execute a fighting withdrawal, but at others the retreat threatened to slip into freefall. In June, unaware that the German storm had largely blown itself out against the allied defences, Jeffreys proposed to play the commander's last card in an attempt to steady the fall. The civilised niceties of military law would, in future, be torn up; 'stragglers' would be tried by summarily courts martial as 'deserters', they *would* be found guilty, and summarily executed as an example to the rest.

It took some time for the division's commanders (of all ranks) to recover from the initial shock induced by the German Army's first onslaught. For a while confusion and incredulity reigned, and their only thought was that somebody else had blundered. By the end of the March Offensive the mists were lifting and a clearer narrative had emerged. An almighty lightning barrage concocted of H.E., gas and smoke shells, supported by a blitzing aerial assault, had obliterated the frontline garrisons, leaving the German artillery free to move forward and begin bombarding the support and reserve lines. Under cover of this cocktail of fire and smoke, small parties of elite *Sturm* battalions, armed primarily with machine-guns, probed the support lines searching for weaknesses. Tender points were found and opened up by their persistent jabbing, and then thousands of German *Landsers* poured through the lacerations to outflank the defending infantry and deliver the knockout blow. A domino effect resulted: defending units that had initially repelled the probing *Sturm* suddenly found their flanks exposed, and, hit by enfilading machine-gun fire, outnumbered and outgunned, either fell back or surrendered. Another flank was then exposed and another formerly staunch group of defenders gave way.

By such means the German Army successfully broke the deadlock of trench warfare. 19th Division now found themselves fighting a unfamiliar war of movement – and it was a backward movement throughout the spring of 1918. Yet the naked statistics of attrition remained a paramount factor in deciding ultimate victory or defeat. The German advance may have penetrated deeper and quicker than anything yet delivered by the *Entente* in the West, but each yard of mud and rubble was still brought at an extreme cost in lives and *materiel*. With each battle the German punch grew weaker. Meantime, despite the manpower shortage, each lost infantryman of 19th Division was replaced with a freshly plucked conscript; their artillery gunners were rarely short of shells; their machine-gunners always well stocked with rounds. It was a bloody three month battle for the balance of firepower, but by early June, 19th Division were finding that the coil in the German spring offensive had lost its momentum.

Second Battle of the Somme, 21-28 March 1918[1]

19th Division began March serving in V Corps, Third Army; defending the line between Arras and Cambrai. For some weeks the division's senior commanders had been working on plans to counter the imminently anticipated German attack. Ground was expected to be given, but would be speedily regained through deployment of the 'arts of attack' developed throughout 1917. DHQ noted that: 'These schemes aimed at the recapture of definite localities: HAVRINCOURT. HERMIES. DOIGNIES. LOUVERAL. BEAUMETZ.'[2] These plans for immediate reprisals proved hugely optimistic. As one battalion's fighting travelogue for late March recorded, the eventual battles fought would also include 'MORCHIES, BEUGNY, FREMICOURT, BAPAUME, GREVILLERS, IRLES, HEBUTERNE.'; ruined French hamlets that marked the pitted road back to the battlefields of the Somme.[3]

The storm broke just before dawn on the 21st: 'At 4.50am [DHQ later recounted] a hostile drumfire of terrific violence was opened on our forward trench system and battery positions.'[4] The First and Second Lines soon began to fold, and despite two attempted counter-attacks and a number of 'stands' the division (alongside IV and V Corps) was in full retreat by the evening of the 24th. On the 25th the division ceased to exist as an organised body, disintegrating into ad-hoc units of survivors and stragglers, commanded by any officer who could successfully halt and rally them. A rout briefly threatened; DHQ recording that 'the situation appeared critical. Infantry were reported to be straggling through PUISIEUX and along SERRE Road in thousands...'[5] Enough of these ad-hoc units made a stand to slow the progress of the German hurricane, and allow the remnants of 19th Division to be reorganised for the defence of Hebuterne. Standing less than 2000 strong, with brigades now formed into 'composite battalions', it was fortunate for the division that the German storm briefly subsided on the 26th (allegedly dampened by the booty captured in the fall of

---

1 The British Official History called the first battle of the German spring offensive 'The Battle of Amiens', but 19th Division gave it the nomenclature 'Somme', probably because they were relieved before the fighting reached the outskirts of the aforementioned French city.
2 See: G1091/2 'Action of the 19th Division in the Event of an Attack', dated 7 March 1918 WO95/2056 (Feb 1918), op cit; 'Provisional Operation Order No. 3.B. Attack on Hermies' dated 8 March; 'Provisional Order No. 3.C. Attack on Havrincourt' dated 11 March; 'Provisional Operation Order No. 3.D. Attack on Louverval, dated 12 March. WO95/2084 Headquarters 57th Infantry Brigade War Diary (March 1918) PRO.
3 WO95/2093 6th Battn. The Wiltshire Regiment War Diary (March 1918) PRO. Diary summary for 21–31 March.
4 '19th Division Narrative of Operations. March 21st – 27th 1918' WO95/2056 (March 1918), op cit.
5 Ibid.

Bapaume),⁶ allowing effective artillery cover to be finally established. The firepower balance briefly swung kindly for the infantry and Hebuterne was held.

An army in desperate retreat had little time for studied reflection. Each unit's individual war story was, therefore, necessarily fragmented. Nevertheless, when pieced together, these prosaic accounts afford a reasonably clear picture of German tactics during the opening bouts of the spring offensive. The following report, written by a Captain F.H. Palmer (O.C. C Coy. Cheshires), portrays well the restricted view of the infantrymen at 'the sharp-end'. 'Following a heavy preliminary bombardment of the GREEN LINE lasting two hours, DELSAUX FARM, which I was holding with 'A' Company, was attacked. The S.O.S. which we sent up brought no Artillery fire from our own guns beyond the usual shelling of the BOSCHE assembly position. At the same time my Left flank was in the air through the withdrawal of 'B' Company's advance post and likewise the remainder of 'B' Company. My Right flank was threatened in the same way by the withdrawal of the South Staffs (2nd Div?) on my right. Consequently we were being heavily enfiladed by machine gun fire from both flanks…I, therefore, decided to withdraw to a point a little further back…'⁷

Subjugation to intense lightening bombardments, shortly followed by strafing machine-gun fire, with little or no response from the RFA, were the common lot of the infantrymen caught by the enemy's first blows. It was also typical, as 58th Brigade noted, for only small parties of the enemy's infantry to be observed, and for frontal attacks to be conspicuously absent. 'Between 7am and 8am the enemy opened a heavy bombardment on the 6th Wilts R. and small portions of the enemy could be seen moving across the front of the Wilts to the BAPAUME Road at a range of about 1200 yards. No frontal attack was attempted by the enemy at this time. The shelling in [map ref] and particularly round Bn. H.Q. of the R.W.F. and Wilts became very heavy and machine gun fire swept all the slopes between BEUGNY and MORCHIES making movement very difficult.'⁸

Less commonly observed, perhaps because it was the least effective of the enemy's arsenal of weaponry, was intrusion from hostile aircraft. The Gloucesters, however, were drawn to complain that the enemy 'continued to shell trench system with well directed fire. Our artillery did not respond to S.O.S. at all and enemy aeroplanes

---

6   'Narrative of Operations 57th Infantry Brigade, March 21st to 28th 1918' recorded that on 24 March: 'The enemy followed the Brigade very closely to the Eastern outskirts of BAPAUME but do not appear to have pressed through BAPAUME until the next morning. Possibly looting may have had some attractions for them.' WO95/2056 (March 1918), op cit.

7   'Report on fighting on the morning of the 24th March 1918', written by Capt. F.H. Palmer, O.C. 'A' Coy. Cheshires. This was one of two 'eye-witnesses of the fighting that took place around DELSAUX FARM, on the morning of 24th March 1918', included as an appendix to 'Narrative of Operations carried out by the 56th Infantry Brigade between 21st and 27th March 1918.' WO95/2056 (March 1918), op cit.

8   '58th Infantry Brigade. Narrative of events from March 21st to 28th 1918.' Ibid. Record of events on 23 March.

were flying low over our trenches using M.G.'s with impunity all day.'[9] The frequent accounts of there being: 'Very little artillery support forthcoming' were later given partial explanation.[10] 'Artillery Lessons' candidly admitted that: 'On the 19th Divisional front, only one battery succeeded in hiding itself from the German photographs', and the rest were subsequently 'silenced' by the enemy's counter battery fire.[11]

Captain Palmer's account of exposed flanks forcing a reluctant withdrawal was also the division's universal rationale for retreat. In keeping with military tradition, *someone else* was always to blame; and the more 'foreign' the guilty unit, the better. Group loyalty and/or cap badge loyalty decreed that an officer would rarely admit culpability – however exonerating the circumstances. But pride and honour were not the only reasons for this denial. In the chaos of desperate defence, individual platoons and companies were subsumed by the 'fog of war', and were only conscious of their flank's departure – not their fight. The retreat of a flank must have consequently seemed like something close to betrayal; and hence the implicit bitterness of the post-battle reports.

Whoever had been first to give ground, as the following account by 57th Brigade attests, once the line began to crumble, it was near impossible to stop the rot. A domino effect ensued. 'At about 5.30 to 6pm the troops on the Right in [map ref] began to withdraw, leaving the right flank of 10th R.War.R. completely in the air. A defensive flank was formed along the BAPAUME-CAMBRAI Road, but it was certain that BANCOURT was occupied by the enemy and Very Lights were seen towards BEAULENCOURT. 10th R.War.R. commenced to withdraw at 7pm, 10th Worc.R. owing to their flank being turned from the direction of SAPIONIES had withdrawn half an hour earlier. 8th Glouc.R. held out in the outskirts of BAPAUME until 8pm, when the 10th R.War.R., 8th Glouc.R and a party of 10th Worc.R. withdrew through the S.E. of BAPAUME to a trench system in [map ref]. 10th Worc.R. apparently withdrew with 41st Division round the N. of BAPAUME and rejoined [sic] the Brigade many hours later.'[12]

With the line lacerated, frontal attacks developed: now the massed ranks of the enemy were witnessed. 57th Brigade recorded how: 'Shortly after daybreak [on the 23rd] the enemy shelled the new line very heavily and continued the bombardment until 9am., when hostile infantry advanced to the attack in dense masses … It is estimated that the enemy attacked with a numerical superiority of not less than 9 to

---

9   WO95/2085 8th Battn. The Gloucestershire Regiment War Diary (March 1918) PRO, diary entry 22 March.
10 'Narrative of Operations 57th Brigade, March 21st to 28th 1918'. Ibid. Record of events on 22 March.
11 WO95/2056 (March 1918), op cit. See also 'Narrative of Operations carried out by the 56th Infantry Brigade between 21st and 27th March 1918.' Ibid.
12 'Narrative of Operations 57th Brigade, March 21st to 28th 1918'. Ibid. Record of events on 24 March.

1'[13] Outgunned and outnumbered, the division fell back to escape the ferocity of the storm; actions that were wholly understandable, but nevertheless unpalatable to proud and honourable infantry officers.

A number of officers were able to make more precise observations which began demystifying the tactics driving the German Army's sweeping advances. Captain A. Garthwaite (Wiltshires) reported that 'enemy machine guns were well to the front of each advance and were rapidly in position at each check and materially assisted his advance especially when a cross fire was opened in our positions.'[14] Contrary to official British military thinking, it was not the 'bayonet that captured and bullet that held'. Rather, the *machine-gun* had been the vanguard of the German infantry assault. From the vantage point of DHQ – who were party to the collected wisdom of the retreat – this reliance upon machine-guns took shape as 'infiltration tactics', and were worthy of close contemplation. 'The new German tactics by which small groups of Infantry with light Machine Guns and covered by Trench Mortar and Field Artillery fire work their way forward to positions from which they bring enfilade fire to bear on our front line of forward posts require special study.'[15] Major H. Lloyd-Williams (CO Welch) already had an answer – fight machine-gun fire *with* machine-gun fire – the Major implored the 'urgent necessity for pushing forward Lewis guns to deal with the advanced hostile M.Gs which work from positions well in advance of the leading infantry.'[16]

But at least one officer recognised that it was not so much *subtlety* that had unlocked the British defences, but brute force. Major Monreal (CO 2nd Wiltshires) wrote that:

> To my mind the tactical lessons of the stunt are:
> 1. That no number of lines of trenches is impregnable against a superior enemy determined to pay the price of capture.
> 2. That the defensive values of obstacles has been materially discounted by the latest weapons of demolition.
> 3. That defending infantry unsupported by artillery and aircraft is paralysed in the face of the combined aircraft, artillery and infantry of the enemy.

---

13   Ibid. This estimation was probably an exaggeration, but it did point to the extent to which the German Army held the manpower and firepower upper-hand during the early days of the spring offensive. See also '58th Infantry Brigade. Narrative of events from March 21st to 28th 1918.' Ibid.
14   'Operations 21/28 March 1918', written by Capt. A. Garthwaite on 2 April 1918. WO95/2093 'Wiltshires' (March 1918), op cit.
15   'Lessons from the recent operations of 19th Division South of Arras and Ypres during the period 21st March – 10th April, 1918.' WO95/2056 (April 1918), op cit.
16   'Lessons Learnt' written by Major H. Lloyd-Williams of 9th Welch Regt on 2 April 1918. Included in diary of WO95/2093 'Wiltshires' (April 1918), op cit. See also 'Lessons from the recent operations of 19th Division South of Arras and Ypres during the period 21st March – 10th April, 1918.' WO95/2056 (April 1918), op cit.

4. That machine guns in trenches are doomed to destruction by hostile artillery where the latter has established a superiority over the opposing artillery.[17]

The king of the battlefield – artillery – was still in the counting house. It was the enemy's overwhelming (if localised) superiority in artillery that had ruptured the British frontline – destroying the materiel of the garrison, and the bodies and minds of the soldiers housed within. But 'destruction' still needed to be supported by 'occupation' to deliver victory. And, as Monreal noted, mass infantry advances on the Western Front remained extremely costly endeavours, but, for the moment, the German infantry were willing to pay the price.

Monreal's frequent references to aircraft also identify how technology had eased the deadlock of trench warfare. The infantry were now witnessing a new form of combat – open warfare. But although the German Army were the chief instigators, as DHQ noted, they did not hold all the aces. 'During the afternoon [of the 26th] some excitement was caused by the first appearance of our Whippet Tanks. A Battn. of these was covering the advance of the New Zealand Division and was manoeuvring between BAYENCOURT and COLINCAMPS ... For the first time during the retreat Low Flying E.A. fired M.G.s on our troops but without effect, and they were driven down by heavy rifle and M.G. fire from the ground.'[18] Although the German storm was far from spent, portents of a Summer drought were already on the horizon.

These chinks in the German armour were, as yet, not evident to the infantrymen at 'the sharp end'. Their view was mostly one of death, destruction and constant retreat. Analysing how the infantry responded to the stark choice of fight, flight or submission (there was not much mileage in posturing to a German artillery shell) imparted by the spring Offensive does not afford precision. The tenability of a defensive position could change by the minute, and a committed fighter could find himself detached from his commanders, and counted amongst the stragglers, without his mind ever erring from the task of defence. In particular, the boundaries between different forms of observed combat behaviour are often blurred. The diarist of 19th Machine Gun Corps (perhaps through a slip of the typewriter) described the garrison of Hebuterne as 'stragglers of all battalions', and this would seem a suitable generalisation for the division.[19] Most infantrymen (and artillery gunners) were *struggling* to hold the line: they were either fighting or staying put, and then choosing flight or submission when capture seemed immanent. Nevertheless, within this *struggle*, certain patterns of behaviour emerge, and it is possible to draw some conclusions upon the division's collective combat morale and behaviour during their darkest hour.

17 'Notes from Major Monreal'. WO95/2093 'Wiltshires' (March 1918), op cit.
18 '19th Division Narrative of Operations. March 21st – 27th 1918'. WO95/2056 (March 1918), op cit.
19 '19th Battalion Machine Gun Corps. March 1918. Narrative of Operations'. WO95/2071 19th Battn. Machine Gun Corps War Diary (March 1918) PRO.

The high end of the spectrum can be detected in combat behaviour described by military diarists as 'to the last man'. These were infantrymen who, based upon observable behaviour, *were* 'prepared to die at their posts'. That is, they *intentionally* rejected the chance to withdraw until their options were reduced to capture or certain death. Such actions invariably occurred when battalions were engaged in, what diarists termed, a 'fighting retreat'. The Wiltshires contended that the entire retreat had been 'only one endless and stubborn fight', and that during these 'rearguard action[s]…Many men [were] sacrificing their lives in covering the withdrawal of their comrades.'[20] The division's records make reference to two 'fine' and 'gallant' rearguard actions, and a number of stands 'to the last man' (detailed below). Allowing that, given the nature of lasts stands, many other such acts may have gone unrecorded, the collected narratives nevertheless suggest that the Wiltshires may have attributed the 'many' with the behaviour of the few.[21]

The presence of junior officers remained the essential ingredient in the execution of the fight 'to the last man'. 57th Brigade recorded how, on 23 March: '8th Glouc.R. withdrawal was covered by Capt. JAMES M.C., officers and other ranks of 'A' Company [who] remained at their posts to the last man…Meanwhile Capt. GRIBBLE 'D' Company 10th R.War.R. had remained in his original position in [map ref] after inflicting enormous casualties on the enemy this company was overwhelmed and, as in the case of 'A' Company 8th Glouc.R., fought to the last man.'[22]

It is an indication of how atypical such high combat morale was that both officers were awarded the V.C.[23] This 'stand' of the 23rd finally illustrates how the survival of the lower rings of the chain of command could (sometimes) guarantee that the stubborn demands of senior commanders were obeyed. The Royal Warwicks recorded how: 'The B.G.C. 154 Inf. Bde. [51st Div. had] personally instructed the O.C. 10/R. War.R. that the Battn. was to hold its position to the last'; before the brigadier dutifully retired to Fremicourt and 'no further communication was ever received from the 154th Inf. Bde.'[24] Even though defenceless isolation loomed, Lt-Col. Heath (CO)

20 WO95/2093 'Wiltshires' (March 1918), op cit. Diary summary of action between 21 and 26 March.
21 By its very nature a stand 'to the last man' was liable to going undetected; there being no one left to report their actions. In the five cases cited, however, the actions were either observed by retreating troops, or a small number of men involved later escaped and reported back to battalion H.Q.
22 'Narrative of Operations 57th Infantry Brigade, March 21st to 28th 1918.' WO95/2056 (March 1918), op cit.
23 See Gerald Gliddon, *VCs of the First World War: Spring Offensive 1918* Sutton Publishing (1997), pp. 23-8 (for Capt. James) & pp. 66-8 (for Capt. Gribble).
24 WO95/2085 10th Battn. The Royal Warwickshire Regiment War Diary (March 1918) PRO. See also 'Narrative of Operations 57th Infantry Brigade, March 21st to 28th 1918.' WO95/2056 (March 1918), op cit.

was evidently determined to remain true to the commands of hiserrant brigadier.[25] 'An artillery Officer of 71st Field Battery of 2nd Division reported to O.C. 10/R. War.R. that the artillery Brigade to which his battery belonged were shortly coming into action on the northern slope of ridge to the S. of Bn. Hd. Qrs. The situation as far as was known [that they had been ordered to 'hold the position to the last'] was explained to this officer. About 1 ½ hours later this officer again reported to O.C. 10/R.War.R. with the information that the guns were withdrawing; the O.C. 10/R. War.R. protested on the grounds that artillery assistance was required and that the battalion *had no intention of evacuating their positions*. Apparently these guns fired very little, if at all…Troops of 51st Division on our left [were then] seen withdrawing to S.W…C. Coy. [then] reported situation desperate on our left flank owing to withdrawal of all troops [my emphasis].'[26]

Some needed assistance was now forthcoming from the infantry's own distance killers. 'MAJOR HARCOURT (?) of 51st M.G. Battn, and Capt. KNOX-LITTLE of 19th M.G. Battn. reported to Battn. Hd. Qrs. for instructions and were told that the Battn. was going to hold on, whereupon they returned to their guns in [map ref]. MAJOR HARCOURT and his men appeared to be the only troops of the 51st. Division in this neighbourhood who stood fast.'[27] It was at this juncture that 'D' Company demonstrated their own commitment to their CO's resolve; and paid the price of sacrifice. 'Capt. Gribble D Coy held his original position and was last seen surrounded by Germans at a few yards distance.'[28] Yet it is apparent that the remaining companies did not share Gribble's ultimate determination, having already been 'driven back to the road running E & W through [map ref] where another stand was made.'[29]

As the Royal Warwicks' experiences attest, the spring offensive had thrust the division's Vickers Machine-Gunners (now organised as one single battalion)[30] towards the vanguard of the infantry's defensive operations. As DHQ later recognised, machine-guns were the only effective curative to the German's own forward roaming machine-gunners. Moreover, machine-guns remained the infantry's most effective weapon against a massed frontal assault.[31] A number of the gunners demonstrated a high combat morale commensurate with their new role; losing either their lives or liberty

---

25   At this juncture 57th Brigade had been lent to 51st Division, and the Royal Warwicks were consequently under the command of 154th Brigade.
26   WO95/2085 'Royal Warwicks' (March 1918), op cit.
27   Ibid. We must, of course, be wary of military 'buck passing' in these reports.
28   Ibid. Capt. Gribble (like Capt. James) was taken prisoner. The fate of the surviving ORs went unrecorded. *Soldiers Died* records that Capt. Gribble died in captivity on 25 November 1918.
29   WO95/2085 'Royal Warwicks' (March 1918), op cit.
30   The 19th M.G. Corps totalled 64 guns, 16 per coy.
31   See for example 'Narrative of Operations 57th Infantry Brigade, March 21st to 28th 1918.' WO95/2056 (March 1918), op cit.

in their determination to cover the retreat. The recorded endeavours of 'C' Company on 22 March indicate how lethally effective a unit of machine-gunners could be, but also how covering the retreat of the infantry made them vulnerable to death or capture. 'The enemy was seen to be advancing in large numbers from the direction of MARICOURT and MORCHIES. Eight guns under 2/Lieut B.E. Fowler and 2/Lieut T. Cundall opened fire on the enemy and inflicted heavy casualties. The remaining guns were arranged to cover the retirement of the infantry through the village. On the retirement of the 9th Welch Regiment, these guns duly opened fire. The four guns under 2/Lieut B.E. Fowler were, according to all available information, surrounded and captured, after inflicting extremely heavy losses on the enemy.'[32]

On the same day machine-gunners of 'B' and 'D' Companies made similar stands and suffered similar fates: 'The four guns [of 'B' Coy.] never returned, but were last seen surrounded by the enemy and firing at very close range…Soon afterwards the enemy opened a heavy bombardment, and was seen to be advancing. This section ['D' Coy] under 2/Lieut. G.W. Hargreaves remained at their position until surrounded by the enemy, only one man escaping, who states two guns and teams were knocked out during the bombardment.'[33] Although the presence of junior officers was evidently essential to these stands, the Corps also noted that an NCO of 'C' Company had lived up to the expectations of *S.S.143 (1918)*, and grasped the baton of leadership. 'During the withdrawal 2/Lieut. T.D. Morris was wounded and evacuated. Two guns under Corporal McClean which was situated in an isolated post N.W. of BEUGNY fired until surrounded by the enemy. [T]he gun teams however, succeeded in rejoining [sic] the Company although suffering heavy casualties.'[34]

Accounts of the machine-gunners endeavours on 24 March signal the blurred (perhaps even arbitrary) line between infantrymen executing *intentional* stands 'to the last man' – in the full knowledge that their actions would almost certainly lead to death or capture – and those who may have accepted neither fate, but whose determination to cover the retreat left them snared by the enemy. 'The infantry in the immediate front began to withdraw, and accordingly successive positions were taken up [by 'A' Coy.] to cover the withdrawal of the infantry on to the BAPAUME Line. During this withdrawal considerable casualties were inflicted on the enemy, but as the guns remained firing until it was too late to withdraw, all, except two guns, under Captain

---

32 '19th Battalion Machine Gun Corps. March 1918. Narrative of Operations'. See also WO95/2071 (March 1918), op cit. See also 'Notes on the Operations of the 19th Machine Gun Battalion During the period 21st – 28th March 1918.' WO95/2056 (March 1918), op cit.
33 '19th Battalion Machine Gun Corps. March 1918. Narrative of Operations'. WO95/2071 (March 1918), op cit.
34 Ibid. See also 'Narrative of Operations 57th Infantry Brigade, March 21st to 28th 1918.' WO95/2056 (March 1918), op cit.

L.E. Jones, were eventually knocked out or captured by the enemy.'[35] The machine-gunners lost the better part of two companies to the enemy in similar circumstances later the same day. 'Heavy bombardment commenced [at 8am], and gun positions [of 'C' Coy.] S. of the Road were trench mortared and after covering infantry retirement, the guns found that the enemy had advanced too rapidly, [and] that it was impossible to withdraw and only four men managed to get back. Two of the five guns were put out of action ... 2.30pm. The infantry N. of the Road withdrew. The eight guns [of 'D' Coy.] covered the withdrawal, and were surrounded by the enemy, before they could retire.'[36] The blurred line between *intentional* and *chance* stands 'to the last man' is incidental when we consider the high combat morale demonstrated by all of these infantrymen.

The 19th Division's experiences since 1915 have shown that infantrymen were often more willing to sacrifice their lives to save a comrade than to fire upon the enemy in pursuit of an objective. The March retreat brought the two previously conflicting desires into close harmony. Firing upon the enemy 'to the last man' was both the ultimate act of a soldier defending the line, and the ultimate sacrifice of a soldier wishing to save the lives of his comrades. The close harmony of objective and sacrifice may explain why such behaviour (firing upon the enemy with disregard for personal safety), although still uncommon, was evidently more widely experienced during the retreat than in previous times.

A wider field of combat behaviour and morale lay behind the stand 'to the last man': spanning from units that only withdrew when ordered, and fought all the way; to units who withdrew without orders, with only 'slight' casualties, and fell back without a fight. This mid-range was, however, coloured with one commonality; interpersonal combat was unheard of, and the threat of meeting the enemy close-up always signalled the retreat.

At times, 'fighting retreats' were enacted in response to orders from senior commanders. For example, the Wiltshires recorded how: 'All frontal advances by enemy were repulsed by steady and controlled rifle and Lewis Gun fire. [but] At 2.15pm [on the 23rd] orders received from Bde. to fall back.'[37] Orders for the withdrawal emphasised that infantrymen must not just fall back, but fall back fighting: 'The principle of the retirement [the Cheshires were ordered] will be that no troops in a support or reserve line will vacate their position until they have covered the retirement of and allowed all troops in front of them to pass through.'[38] Orders were also issued which echoed Jeffreys' demand to defend the line *coûte que coûte*. For example, at '10.15am [on the 24th] 57th Bde. [were] ordered by Div. to hold on to the Red Line

35 '19th Battalion Machine Gun Corps. March 1918. Narrative of Operations'. WO95/2071 (March 1918), op cit.
36 Ibid.
37 WO95/2093 'Wiltshires' (March 1918), op cit.
38 HWT from BHQ to Coys., undated. WO95/2079 9th Battn. The Cheshire Regiment War Diary (March 1918) PRO.

at all costs in the event of a withdrawal from the Green Line. Instructions sent out to that effect.'[39]

But communications between the fluid frontline and rapidly retreating brigade and divisional HQs had all but collapsed; only the pigeon and the runner were operating, and neither was making much headway across a battlefield strewn with death and destruction.[40] Consequent upon this void of silence, as the North Staffords noted, 'at times the Commanding Officer became the Brigade Commander to control affairs on the spot...', whilst immediate decisions over fight or flight were often taken by junior officers.[41] For example, 56th Brigade recorded that: 'At 2.30pm our troops were reported retiring from the direction of BEUGNY through [map ref] 3.30pm. It was reported that 2nd Division were retiring to the BAPAUME–LE TRANSLOY Road, and orders were issued to watch the situation and if necessary retire fighting to the line BANCOURT–FREMICOURT [map ref]. The withdrawal actually commenced about 2pm before receipt of this order, and Battalions fell back fighting, through the RED LINE, and were reorganised just E. of BAPAUME by 6pm.'[42] Evidently these companies were fighting their way back regardless of orders – their actions fortuitously corresponding with the wishes of brigade. On at least one occasion a battalion CO intervened to countermand an unofficial order to retire; 56th Brigade recording how, at '2.40pm. [on the 23rd] It was reported that our Infantry had evacuated the GREEN LINE N. of CAMBRAI Road in [map ref] by order of an Officer, they were sent back by O.C. 'A' Coy. 19th Battn. M.G. Corps.'[43] Nevertheless, the decisions of junior officers were invariably decreed a *fait accompli* by the fluidity and confusion of the battlefield.

A report by the Gloucesters hints that an unofficial code of conduct was dictating the decision to withdraw. 'About 7.30am [on the 23rd] left flank withdrew quickly leaving the Battn. in the air. The Battn. therefore was *freed to do the same* and fought a rear guard action [my emphasis].'[44] The implication was seemingly that the battalion's obligation to stand fast had been nullified by the retreat of their fellow flank, regardless of orders to the contrary. Being the first unit to retreat placed a black mark against the honour of the battalion, company, platoon or (post-1918) section – being second

---

39   WO95/2084 (March 1918), op cit.
40   See '9th (S) Bn Royal Welch Fusiliers. Narrative of Events from 21st March 1918 to 29th March 1918', written by the CO on 1 April 1918. WO95/2092 9th Battn. The Royal Welsh Fusiliers Regiment War Diary (April 1918) PRO.
41   WO95/2082 8th Battn. The North Staffordshire Regiment War Diary (March 1918), op cit. Diary entry 24 March. See also WO95/2092 'Fusiliers' (March 1918), op cit.
42   'Narrative of Operations carried out by the 56th Infantry Brigade between 21st and 27th March 1918.' WO95/2056 (March 1918), op cit. See also 'Narrative of Operations 57th Infantry Brigade, March 21st to 28th 1918.' Ibid.
43   'Narrative of Operations carried out by the 56th Infantry Brigade between 21st and 27th March 1918.' Ibid. See also '19th Division Narrative of Operations. March 21st – 27th 1918'. WO95/2056 (March 1918), op cit.
44   WO95/2085 'Gloucesters' (March 1918), op cit.

evidently diluted the taint. But it was not only release from the bonds of honour that was 'freeing' the infantry from the dark waters of the fluid frontline. It is abundantly evident that a less sublime motivation was stimulating the decision to withdraw – fear of interpersonal combat. Certainly, this urge to avoid crossing swords with the enemy was not acting alone. The enemy's preference for flanking operations added the threat of isolation and capture to the infantry's already burdened sack of woes, whilst also tipping the firepower pendulum with enfilading fire.[45] Mounting casualties from hostile shellfire further reduced the infantry's willingness and ability to stand.[46] Even so, the evidence indicates that fear of interpersonal combat was frequently the primary stimulant in deciding the retreat.

If the enemy could be kept at a distance, then, as the following account of 57th Brigade demonstrates, even the experience of heavy casualties would not necessarily undermine the infantry's combat morale. 'Enemy made 3 separate attempts to debouch from the outskirts of DOIGNIES during the morning and afternoon [of the 22nd] but was on each occasion driven back by rifle and M.G. fire of 8th Glouc.R. and 10th Worc.R. and by M.G. fire of 'B' Coy. 19th M'G. Bn. with heavy casualties. 10th Worc.R. suffered heavily from enfilade M.G. and rifle fire in DOIGNIES–BEAUMETZ road from the direction of DOIGNIES, their flank being entirely in the air, but were not shelled, probably owing to the fact that hostile infantry were only 50 yards from their position. They remained in this road throughout the day and inflicted severe casualties on the enemy.'[47] These protracted fire-fights clearly required the involvement of a number of active participants. It has already been suggested that the motivation of 'survival' may have added to the ranks of firers within the division. There are, however, shards of evidence suggesting that not all infantrymen, even in desperate defence, were firing upon the enemy with the aggressive intent of a committed sniper.

The sanitising qualities of the machine-gun (as we have seen) saturated this fluid battlefield, partly (perhaps sometimes completely) negating the need for rifle fire. The following account by the Cheshires further underlines the seminal role of the machine-gun during the fighting retreat: 'by 12 noon [on the 25th] the enemy was seen preparing for his attack on the battalion positions. He gradually worked forward under cover of M.G. and shrapnel fire until contact was made by our troops on the main road at [map ref]. The troops at the latter point, belonging to the Brigade on our left, were withdrawn through GREVILLERS and the enemy thus gained possession of the high ground ... 3 Sections of M.Gs of the 19th M.G. Battn. had taken

---

45 See for example '9th Battn. The Welch Regt – Diary for 21st March to 27th March', written by Major H. Lloyd-Williams on 2 April 1918. WO95/2092 9th Battn. The Welch Regiment War Diary (April 1918) PRO.
46 See for example WO95/2093 'Wiltshires' (March 1918), op cit.
47 'Narrative of Operations 57th Infantry Brigade, March 21st to 28th 1918.' WO95/2056 (March 1918), op cit. See also: '58th Infantry Brigade. Narrative of events from March 21st to 28th 1918.' Ibid.; 'GOC to IV Corps' dated 23 March. Ibid.

up position in the battalion support line and, together with M.G.s established in LOUPART Wood in [map ref], inflicted heavy casualties on the enemy as he endeavoured to force large numbers of troops through over the high ground…'[48]

Yet it would seem that even the infantry's distance killer (and killers)[49] were frequently less effective when the sanitary element of 'distance' was removed from the combat equation. 19th Machine Gun Corps made the following complaint: 'So far as can be ascertained after the first day of the attack the general tendency was to open fire at too long a range, i.e., 1200 to 1500 yards. With a limited supply of bolts fire should be reserved for targets at 500 yards and under … <u>Direct fire at close range is the primary task of M.G's in defence.</u>'[50] 'Targets at 500 yards or under' became increasingly human, and the chances of death by more personal means concomitantly escalated with every yard of the enemy's encroachment.

This reluctance to fire at close-range was also detected amongst the 'every man' specialists of the platoon. Captain Garthwaite (Wiltshires) complained that 'there was a useless waste of S.A.A of Lewis Gun and rifles at long ranges resulting in a serious shortage when the enemy came under short effective ranges.'[51] Major Lloyd-Williams (2nd CO Welch) hinted at a similar problem during 'fighting retreats'; stressing: 'The value of covering-fire and fire control in rear-guard actions. This means accurately sighting of rifles, economy of ammunition in addition to the ordinary meaning of the terms.'[52] Garthwaite went further, indicated that 'non-firing' proliferated during both the initial stand and then the retreat: 'Enemy never faced steady and controlled frontal fire in their advance … [and] the majority of our troops did not understand rearguard and delaying actions and during the early stages of the retirement troops withdrew in bunches no covering fire being brought to bear and no delaying action fought.'[53]

When the once distant target threatened to interlope as a living, breathing adversary, the firing and non-firing Butterflies alike chose flight. The following Cheshires account illustrates how the infantry endeavoured to remain one step away from the enemy. 'By 1.30pm enemy masses were able to approach the trenches and prepare for a heavy assault. The front Companies were consequently withdrawn through the supports under cover of rifle and of M.G. fire from LOUPART WOOD in [map

---

48 WO95/2079 (March 1918), op cit.
49 We must remember that, in addition to the Machine-Gun Corps, half of an infantry platoon were, on paper at least, trained as Lewis Gunners.
50 'Notes on the Operations of the 19th Machine Gun Battalion During the period 21st – 28th March 1918.' WO95/2056 (April 1918), op cit.
51 'Operations 21/28 March 1918', written by Capt. A. Garthwaite on 2 April 1918. WO95/2093 'Wiltshires' (April 1918), op cit. See also 'Narrative of Operations 21 –27 March 1918 – 6th Wiltshire Regt', written by a Captain Alan Garthwaite of the Bn. dated 2 April 1918. Ibid.
52 'Lessons Learnt' written by Major H. Lloyd-Williams of 9th Welch Regt on 2 April 1918. Ibid. The appearance of these post-battle reflections in the Wiltshire's diary indicates their circulation around 58th Brigade.
53 'Operations 21/28 March 1918', written by Capt. A. Garthwaite on 2 April. Ibid.

ref]. This latter fire proved most effective and inflicted very heavy casualties on the enemy, who was seen to fall in large numbers. When the foremost enemy troops were beginning to swarm into the Battalions support positions the remaining Companies withdrew under cover of small rearguards [sic] and formed up on the crest of the rise about [map ref] W. of LOWPART [sic] WOOD.'[54]

The Royal Warwicks recorded two similar occurrences on the 25th. 'The 58th Bde and the 8/Gloucs. then withdrew on our right and the Battn. was then isolated in a position on the high ground just S. of GREVILLERS. The enemy by this time had reached the belt of wire in front of the Battn., and was trying to get through it. He was repeatedly driven off by L.G. and rifle fire but made his way round the left flank into the village. Major WINGROVE [a/CO] therefore ordered all except B Coy. and 1 Platoon A Coy. to withdraw through GREVILLERS to a position near LOUPART Wood.'[55] A few hours later the Royal Warwicks experienced an even closer encounter with the enemy. 'The position was held until 4.30pm in spite of repeated attempts by the enemy to shift us. At this hour the enemy put over some smoke shells, obviously with the intention of rushing our post. The party in the trench therefore withdrew covered by the fire of the two companies 10/Worcs. The enemy was not more than 20 yards away when we left the trench, but the covering fire kept him under. By this time he was coming round the S. side of LOUPART Wood and also down the road. The Worcesters and ourselves therefore retired fighting each party covering the other and successfully joined the rest of the Battalions of the Brigade...'[56] Meantime the Wiltshires were taking similar steps to avoid personal contact with the enemy. 'Eventually the enemy at this point by means of a fold in the ground were able to creep round and assemble for an assault on this position and these troops withdrew in an orderly rearguard action after inflicting heavy casualties on enemy and suffering very slightly themselves.'[57]

Two records of the Shropshires experiences illustrate how the threat of interpersonal combat was probably the decisive factor in deciding the retreat. On the 23rd the near presence of the enemy persuaded the battalion to retreat, seemingly without much of a fight. 'The enemy were seen advancing down the main road and were making steady progress between LEBUCQUIERE and VELU and as the right flank of 1/4th K.S.L.I. was exposed the Battalion withdrew to the GREEN LINE, arriving about 8am....<u>Casualties very slight</u>.'[58] (The underlining belonged to the pen of DHQ, indicating that explanations were in order). Two days later the

---

54 WO95/2079 (March 1918), op cit. Diary entry 25 March.
55 WO95/2085 'Royal Warwicks' (March 1918) op cit.
56 Ibid.
57 'Narrative of Operations 21–27 March 1918 – 6th Wiltshire Regt', written by a Captain Alan Garthwaite of the Bn. dated 2 April 1918. WO952093 'Wiltshires' (April 1918). The record describes events on the 25th.
58 'Narrative of Operations carried out by the 56th Infantry Brigade between 21st and 27th March 1918.' WO95/2056 (March 1918), op cit.

Shropshire's reputation received a restorative. 'At daybreak the enemy commenced to advance, hostile cavalry were reported moving down the BAPUAME-ALBERT Road, and Infantry were seen to be collecting in TILLOY and LE BARQUE… The 1/4th K.S.L.I., who *suffered severe casualties*, put up a protracted fight for some hours, and prevented the enemy from crossing the main road immediately in front of them, they were eventually compelled to withdraw from shortage of ammunition and pressure of the enemy from the direction of WARLENCOURT which threatened their Right flank [my emphasis].'[59] It is telling that the Shropshires were, on this occasion, prepared to execute a prolonged fire-fight and suffer heavy casualties so long as the enemy were kept at some distance. It was only when infiltration threatened (and lack of ammunition, but they still possessed their bayonets) that they chose to retire.

Throughout the retreat 19th Division was not always on the defensive, but attempted (as previously planned) to stem the tide of the German advance through the counter-attack. On 21 March 57th Brigade were ordered to recapture the village of Doignies.[60] The eventual attack was, in the 57th's words, a 'partial success': '8th Glouc.R. penetrated as far as DOIGNIES Church with 2 companies (Capt. JAMES and BOWLES), and 10th Worc.R. gained their objectives, viz. the DOIGNIES – BEAUMETZ Road. 8th Glouc.R. captured 27 prisoners and two M.G's. Both Battalions suffered heavy casualties from Artillery and M.G. fire. 8th Glouc.R. Right Flank was unsupported and severely enfiladed with M.G. fire, Battalion was compelled to withdraw to Third System with outposts in front.'[61]

A battlefield enveloped in shell and machine-gun fire was enough to compel the 57th's to retire, but some of their ranks had met with the enemy, and found him (perhaps after some persuasion) a willing captive. It is a mark of how the first blows of the German spring offensive had rocked the division's collective combat morale that the Butterflies only executed *one* improvised counter-attack during the five day retreat – even though the immediate recapture of lost ground was elemental to the division's defensive strategy.[62] The singular impromptu counter-attack was executed by 'D' and 'A' Companies of the Cheshires on 24 March. 'The battn. was forced out of part of its front line trenches but companies quickly reorganised in their support lines and assisted by D Coy. delivered a counter-attack. This was led by Capts A.D. MILNER ['D' Coy.] and F.H. PALMER ['A' Coy.] and was splendidly carried out – resulting in the re-taking of all the lost trenches and inflicting heavy casualties on the enemy. It was also found that the enemy had suffered heavy casualties during his

---

59 Ibid.
60 See 'Narrative of Operations 57th Infantry Brigade, March 21st to 28th 1918.' WO95/2056 (March 1918), op cit.
61 Ibid.
62 See 57th Inf. Bde. No. G. 190 '57th Brigade Right Brigade Sector Defence Scheme.', dated March 1918.

own attack from our rifle, Lewis gun and machine fire.'[63] (The diarist's slip of the pen – *machine fire* – aptly captured the domination of artillery and machine-gun on the Western Front).

The report clearly indicates that the high combat morale demonstrated by these units was largely dependent upon the exemplary leadership of their junior officers. Captain Milner's 'act of gallantry' was witnessed by a fellow officer, who reported how: 'Under very heavy rifle and machine gun fire Captain MILNER left the Support Line and went over to the Reserve trenches which were above 80 yards in rear and led the Reserve up to counter-attack, in which he was very successful and drove the enemy back to his original position. In leading the men up he was killed.'[64] A report by the 56th Trench Mortars also indicates that this counter-attack was aided by the exemplary leadership of an NCO: 'Enemy attacked right flanks of the Brigade at DELSAUX FARM and captured the front line…NO 2 gun fired 25 rounds at the advancing enemy then the N.C.O. in charge removed the base-cap and along with his team fell back with the infantry. He reported to the nearest infantry officer (Capt. PALMER 9 CHESHIRE.R.) and took his team forward as infantry in the counter attack delivered under that officer's orders. On arrival at his gun position he found the mortar and bombs intact and he immediately replaced the base cap and fired the remaining rounds at the retiring enemy.'[65] We can only postulate the number of similar exemplary acts by the Other Ranks that went unnoticed by the class conscious military diarists. But this singular account does at least signal the possibility that NCOs were also living up to the heightened responsibilities demanded by *S.S.143 (1918)*.

The counter-attack by the Cheshires on the 24th was the last overt show of resistance by the Butterflies until the stand at Hebuterne. For around 36 hours command authority broke down, and the majority of the division's surviving infantrymen were counted as 'stragglers'. Earlier in the retreat neither malady had effected the Butterflies (or at least not to the same degree). For example, after the failed counter-attack of 21 March the 57th Brigade recorded that: 'I am certain that the moral of the Brigade was not impaired by the only partial success of the attack. Both Battalions were re-organised by their Commanding Officers and carefully sorted out from elements of 51st Division in the Third System.'[66] Three days later the integrity of a battalion, as the

---

63 WO95/2079 (March 1918), op cit.
64 Eye-witness account of H.M. Stubbs (rank not recorded), 'D' Coy. Cheshires, writing from 'Liverpool M.M. Hospital' on 28 March 1918. 'Narrative of Operations carried out by the 56th Infantry Brigade between 21st and 27th March 1918.' WO95/2056 (March 1918), op cit. See also 'Report on fighting on the morning of the 24th March 1918', written by Capt. F.H. Palmer, O.C. 'A' Coy. Cheshires. Ibid.
65 WO95/2081 56th Trench Mortar Battery War Diary (March 1918) PRO. Diary entry 24 March.
66 'Narrative of Operations 57th Infantry Brigade, March 21st to 28th 1918.' WO95/2056 (March 1918), op cit.

The German Spring Offensives 205

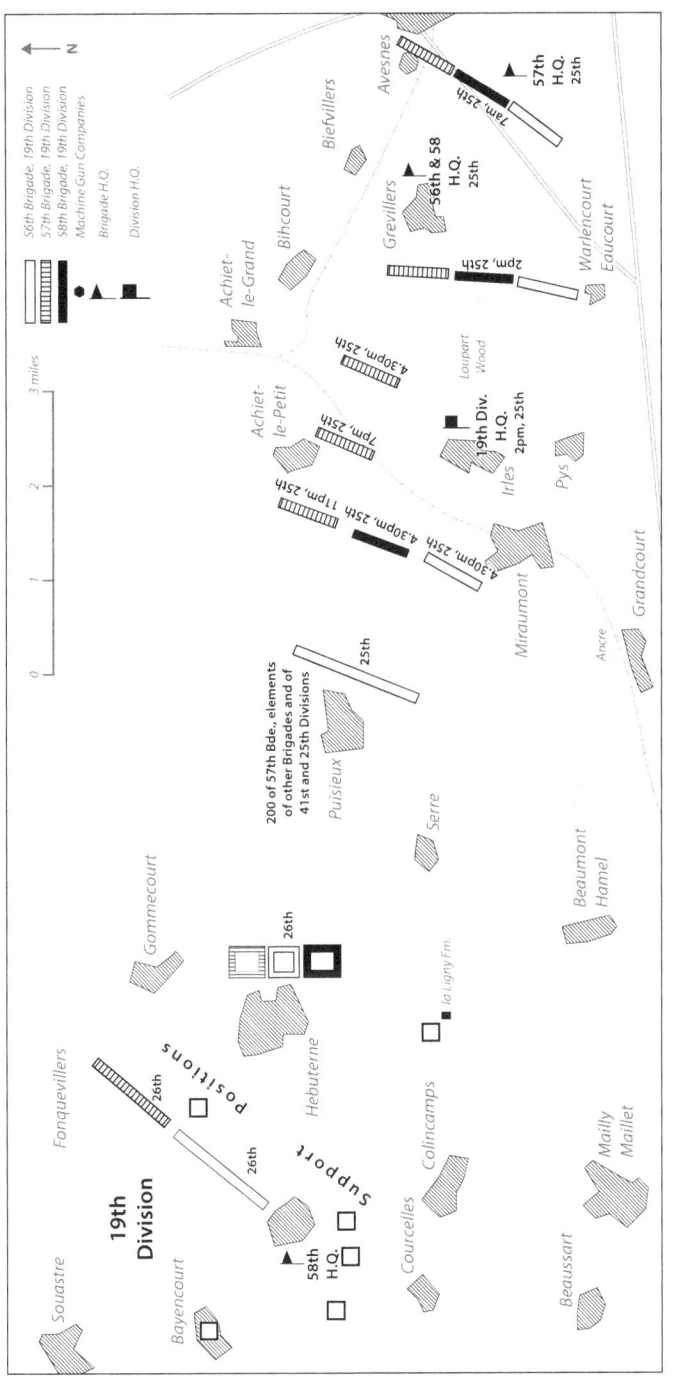

Map 6 Somme, March 1918 (2).

Royal Warwicks discovered, was less easily reassembled. 'The enemy was advancing in masses over the ridge running N & S of FREMICOURT, and continued to advance in spite of M.G., L.G., and rifle fire. A withdrawal to the position supposed to be held by the 56th& 58th Brigades S of BAPAUME was ordered. During this operation, which took place in the dark, the Battn. became very scattered. The enemy followed up very rapidly – in the darkness and confusion the 56th Brigade and 58th Brigade line was not found and the Battn. finally assembled on the BAPAUME-THILLOY Road just W of BAPAUME, about 200 strong…'[67]

The battalion had mislaid around 200 ORs,[68] but was evidently relatively fortunate. The Welch, despite boasting that an 'Excellent and skilful rearguard actions and well controlled covering fire [on the 25th] enabled us to attain the ridge at [map ref] in good order and with very few casualties', later admitted that by dusk 'the battalion was very scattered and numbered hardly more that 25 …'[69] At the same time the Fusiliers confessed that: 'The [58th] Brigade at this juncture was 30 strong with 4 Officers.'[70] 58th Brigade HQ recorded that, even after reinforcement, the headcount still made grim reading. 'The remainder of the Bde. withdrew unmolested from the Eastern Side of BAPAUME and by midnight were re-organised on their new line. Including the reinforcements that had been sent in the whole Bde. at this time did not amount to more than 270 rifles.'[71] By daybreak on the 25th the division – as an operational unit – had dissipated into a collection of Staff HQs and a smattering of infantrymen; senior commanders and battalion COs alike had no idea of the whereabouts of the majority of their surviving infantrymen. For example, 56th Brigade recorded that 'it was not known where the Units of the Brigade had halted for the night [of the 25th]. As many men as possible were collected, and two weak battalions were formed, practically the whole of the 9th Ches. Regt. were unaccounted for.'[72]

The division's chain of command had shattered; but out of the debris the highest links forged with the lowest to (eventually) bar the enemy's path. DHQ first decided to personally intervene and 'halt and rally' their infantrymen during the afternoon of the 25th. 'G.S.O. 3, 19th Division and Capt. H.W. House had been sent with the stragglers collected at PUISIEUX to take up positions W. of ACHIET LE PETIT

---

67   WO95/2085 'Royal Warwicks' (March 1918), op cit., diary entry 24 March.
68   The Royal Warwicks were reinforced late on the 23rd bring their fighting strength up to 15 Officers and 409 ORs. Ibid.
69   '9th Battn. The Welch Regt – Diary for 21st March to 27th March', written by Major H. Lloyd-Williams on 2 April 1918. WO95/2092 'Welch' (March 1918), op cit.
70   '9th (S) Bn Royal Welch Fusiliers. Narrative of Events from 21st March 1918 to 29th March 1918', written by the CO on 1 April 1918. WO95/2092 'Fusiliers' (March 1918), op cit.
71   '58th Infantry Brigade. Narrative of events from March 21st to 28th 1918.' WO95/2056 (March 1918) op cit.
72   'Narrative of Operations carried out by the 56th Infantry Brigade between 21st and 27th March 1918.' WO95/2056 (March 1918), op cit.

and to collect stragglers and form a line. These officers established themselves about [map ref] and halted and reformed all men passing through. There was no panic of any sort, the men of all divisions were quite willing to halt and fight, but as the troops on their right were falling back, and as the difficulty of orders reaching them made them uncertain as to their correct action they fell back slowly and in good order. Once they received some definite orders and came in contact with officers who knew the situation they fell into line and dug themselves in at once.'[73]

At this juncture it is clear that DHQ were relatively sanguine over the existence of a mass army of stragglers, and considered that only *knowledge* (one of the key ingredients of leadership) was missing from the make-up of the infantrymen's combat morale. The rapid collapse of this line and subsequent retreat from Puisieux persuaded DHQ to add a little *authority* to the composition. 'All officers on the staff of, and attached to, Div. H.Q. were summoned to a conference and were divided into parties (with orderlies and police attached) and were sent to different cross roads and likely lines of retreat between the SUCRERIE … and GOMMECOURT with orders to stop all stragglers of any unit, collect them into parties and march them to position of assembly W. of the SAILLY AU BOIS – FONQUEVILLERS ROAD. Arrangements were made for rations to be collected at the positions of assembly so that all men collected might be given a meal. Upward of 4000 of all ranks of various Divisions were collected by this means by dawn – 26th, including about 500 men of the 19th Division.'[74]

The 57th Brigade ventured that the presence of many new recruits had reduced the division's ability to weather the German storm, and had contributed toward the ranks of mass stragglers. 'During the day [the 24th] there were many Stragglers and a good deal of confusion, but it is only fair to suggest that this was inevitable with some 400 new reinforcements, many without Battalion Badges or Shoulder Numerals.'[75] This was the perfect uniform for straggling, and perhaps it wasn't just the absence of the symbols of unity and adherence to authority and leadership that were missing amongst these 'green' troops, but the emotions and thoughts that went with them. DHQ's recognised that there was also an indelible link between shellshock and the retreat, stressing that: 'If the troops are at all shaken strictest discipline must be maintained by all Officers and N.C.Os to prevent the troops who are holding the rearward line in joining in the retirement.'[76]

---

73 '19th Division Narrative of Operations. March 21st – 27th 1918'. Ibid. See also 'Operations 21/28 March 1918', written by Capt. A. Garthwaite on 2 April 1918. WO95/2093 'Wiltshires' (March 1918), op cit.
74 '19th Division Narrative of Operations. March 21st – 27th 1918'. WO95/2056 (March 1918), op cit.
75 'Narrative of Operations 57th Infantry Brigade, March 21st to 28th 1918.' Ibid.
76 'Lessons from the recent operations of 19th Division South of Arras and Ypres during the period 21st March – 10th April, 1918.' Ibid.

It would seem unlikely that a small gathering of MPs and staff officers could turnaround 4000 armed infantrymen, if the majority of these men were not already inclined to halt and rally. Four days of fighting the retreat had not turned the Butterflies into a unruly mob of deserters: most infantrymen were evidently confused and most probably frightened, they had sought sanctuary from the storm, but were not trying to escape the battlefield altogether.[77]

At the bottom of the spectrum lay those infantrymen who willingly surrendered to the enemy without a fight, or escaped the battlefield without any intention to return. Calculating the ranks of the former is problematic. The examples of infantrymen fighting 'to the last man' indicate that being captured by the enemy was far from being a cast-iron symptom of collapsed morale. As the following account by the Fusiliers attests, the rapidity and ferocity of the German advance also combined to snare many unwilling captives. 'Battalion H.Q. of the 6th Wiltshire Regt., 9th R.W.Fus. and the Cheshire Battalion came away at 5pm [on the 23rd] after it became obvious that Companies were endeavouring to withdraw, but very few managed to get through the barrage and undoubtedly many Officers, N.C.O's and men were captured in the Battalion H.Q. Dug-out.'[78] Yet it is the sheer weight of captured men that points towards willing surrendering on a large scale. Of the 4000 plus casualties recorded by DHQ during the March retreat, over half (2300) were labelled 'missing'.[79] A number of these can be accounted for by the fact that, on the 23 March, 'all our wounded, except those walking, had to be abandoned.'[80] Even so, the final casualty toll indicates that a minimum of just under 2000 infantrymen fell into the grasp of the German Army over the five-day retreat.[81] Those willing fighters who, through either wounding or isolation, became unwilling captives, and

77   Gary Sheffield's account of the March retreat also argues that most infantrymen were either exhausted or lost, and were not attempting to flee the battlefield. He also suggests that the greater number of genuine absconders from the battlefield were non-combatants. See Gary Sheffield 'The Operational Role of British Military Police on the Western Front, 1914-18' in Paddy Griffith (ed) *British Fighting Methods in the Great War* Frank Cass (1996) pp. 70-86, pp. 80-1; Gary Sheffield, *The Redcaps: a history of the Royal Military Police and its antecedents from the Middle Ages to the Gulf War* Brassey's (1994) p. 73.
78   '9th (S) Bn Royal Welsh Fusiliers. Narrative of Events from 21st March 1918 to 29th March 1918', written by the CO on 1 April 1918. WO95/2092 'Fusiliers' (April 1918), op cit.
79   The full breakdown was as follows: 15 Officers, 259 ORs Killed; 91 Officers, 1327 ORs Wounded; 47 Officers, 2308 ORs Missing; total casualties 4047. WO95/2056 (March 1918), op cit., diary entry 30 March.
80   'Narrative of Operations 57th Infantry Brigade, March 21st to 28th 1918.' Ibid. See also: WO95/2085 'Gloucesters' (March 1918), op cit.; WO95/2082 (March 1918), op cit.
81   *Soldiers Died* records that 624 ORs of 19th Division were either killed or died of wounds between 21 and 31 March 1918. If the entire difference of 365 infantrymen (between the division's initial calculation and the final toll) is taken from the list of 'missing', and none are taken from the list of 'wounded', then 1943 infantrymen are still left on the captured list.

those who fought to 'the last man' only to suffer a similar fate, can be scratched from the list. This surrender rate of around forty percent nevertheless signals that vast numbers of infantrymen, faced with the stark decision between fight, flight or submission, chose to put their hands up.[82]

The number of infantry choosing flight, and then deciding to continue flying was, according to the division's disciplinary record, almost (perhaps even completely) non-existent.[83] This is not indelible proof of a total abstinence from desertion. How would an errant infantryman be identified amongst the masses of 'missing' and 'straggling' infantrymen? Moreover, at this juncture (as we have seen) DHQ was willing to take a benign view of 'straggling', and may have adopted a similarly lenient view of men found some miles behind the retreating back lines. Even so, the empty column in the division's record of deserters indicates that Boulogne and Calais were almost certainly not overrun with fleeing Butterflies.

If upward of 2000 infantrymen ended the March Offensive occupying the prison cages of the German Army, and therefore the bottom rungs of the combat morale/behaviour spectrum, we should caution against joining the cry of 'bottom of the barrel' at the conscripts that now filled the ranks of 19th Division. Confusion and fear had visited these men on a scale rarely encountered by the division, and never before over such a prolonged period of time. Unsure where the enemy was, uncertain as to where their commanders had gone, surrounded by dead and wounded of any number of units, shells saturating the air, machine-gun fire spitting across the earth, camouflage smoke blinding their eyes and choking the air they breathed, and aircraft strafing the skies; many men choose to give themselves up, or try and find a better place to be. It is perhaps more remarkable that this state of consciousness was not more commonplace. Once the voice of command (and a degree of authority) was restored, most straggling infantrymen willingly returned to the fray – if not always to fight, then at least to stand firm. Even the latter represented courage beyond measure in civilian life, but such a demonstration of combat morale was the least that was expected on the Western Front during March 1918.

---

82   This percentage calculation is based upon a approximate divisional fighting strength of 5000 infantrymen (1500 per brigade and around 500 divisional machine-gunners and brigade Stokes Mortars).
83   There were no infantrymen found guilty of 'Desertion' in the aftermath of the March Offensive, but 6 men were found guilty of 'ABC', including one charge of 'absence' brought in place of 'Desertion'. Prior to this point 5 infantrymen had been found guilty of Desertion during 1918. WO213/19-23 Judge Advocates General's Office: Field General Court's Martial and Military Courts, Registers. (Jan-April 1918) PRO.

The Battle of Lys, 10-18 April

April promised a brief repose; 'the casualties suffered by all units in the Division [DHQ recorded] had been extremely severe and the division was to hold a quiet Sector and recuperate.'[84] 19th Division was duly sent North to join IX Corps (Second Army) at Messines, to be reinforced with large drafts.[85] DHQ recorded that these 'drafts were composed mainly of young and untried troops who had come out to France for their first time.'[86] But the division's planned recuperation inadvertently stumbled across the path of the German Army's own attempt to finally capture Ypres.

The division's first-hand experience of German tactics during the March offensive had brought about some marginal changes in their own defensive preparations. Interwoven lines of isolated posts (in the German mould) were favoured over continuous lines of parallel trenches. DHQ recorded how: 'The Defence of the Divisional Front was organised in three lines of Posts – Front, Support and Reserve. The Reserve Line of Posts was being made a continuous Line of trench.'[87] The German Army, for their part, continued to back the tactics that had pushed the British line back to Amiens, but was yet to secure the breakthrough. The Fusiliers lucidly recorded how the combination of brute force and stealthy infiltration again precipitated the disintegration of the frontline system. 'The barrage was exceedingly heavy and accurate especially on the Left in RAVINE WOOD and all the posts in this wood were ultimately blown in with very heavy casualties, leaving a gap through which the enemy commenced to come. This necessitated the withdrawal of the Posts in ROSE WOOD which took place about 3pm [on the 10th] at the same time touch was lost on the Right with the 6th Wiltshire Regt., and the Right Company also withdrew to the Reserve Line. By 4pm all Companies were occupying the Reserve Line. This was maintained intact until about 7pm when the Right Companies found the enemy behind them in OOSTAVERNE WOOD, presumably owing to the fact that the 6th Wilts. on the right had been unable to maintain their Reserve Line.'[88]

---

84   '19th Division Narrative. Battle of Messines, Wulverghem and early part of Kemmel. April 10th – 19th 1918.' WO95/2056 (April 1918) op cit.
85   The Royal Warwicks fighting strength on 9 April was 29 Officers and 988 ORs. Almost certainly the first time since arriving in France that any unit of the division was at 'full strength'. WO95/2085 'Royal Warwicks' (April 1918), op cit. The Wiltshires had been amalgamated with a battalion of the Wiltshire Yeomanry (now called 6th Wiltshire Yeomanry Battn. The Wiltshire Regiment) and stood at 11 Officers and 580 ORs on 8 April. WO95/2093 'Wiltshire Y' (April 1918), op cit.
86   '19th Division Narrative. Battle of Messines, Wulverghem and early part of Kemmel. April 10th – 19th 1918.' WO95/2056 (April 1918) op cit.
87   '19th Division Narrative. Battle of Messines, Wulverghem and early part of Kemmel. April 10th – 19th 1918.' WO95/2056 (April 1918) op cit See also WO95/2093 'Wiltshires (Y)' (April 1918), op cit.
88   '9th (S) Bn. Royal Welch Fusiliers. Narrative of events from 10-4-18 to 19-4-18.' WO95/2092 'Fusiliers' (April 1918), op cit. See also 'Narrative of Action of 58th Inf.

The German Spring Offensives 211

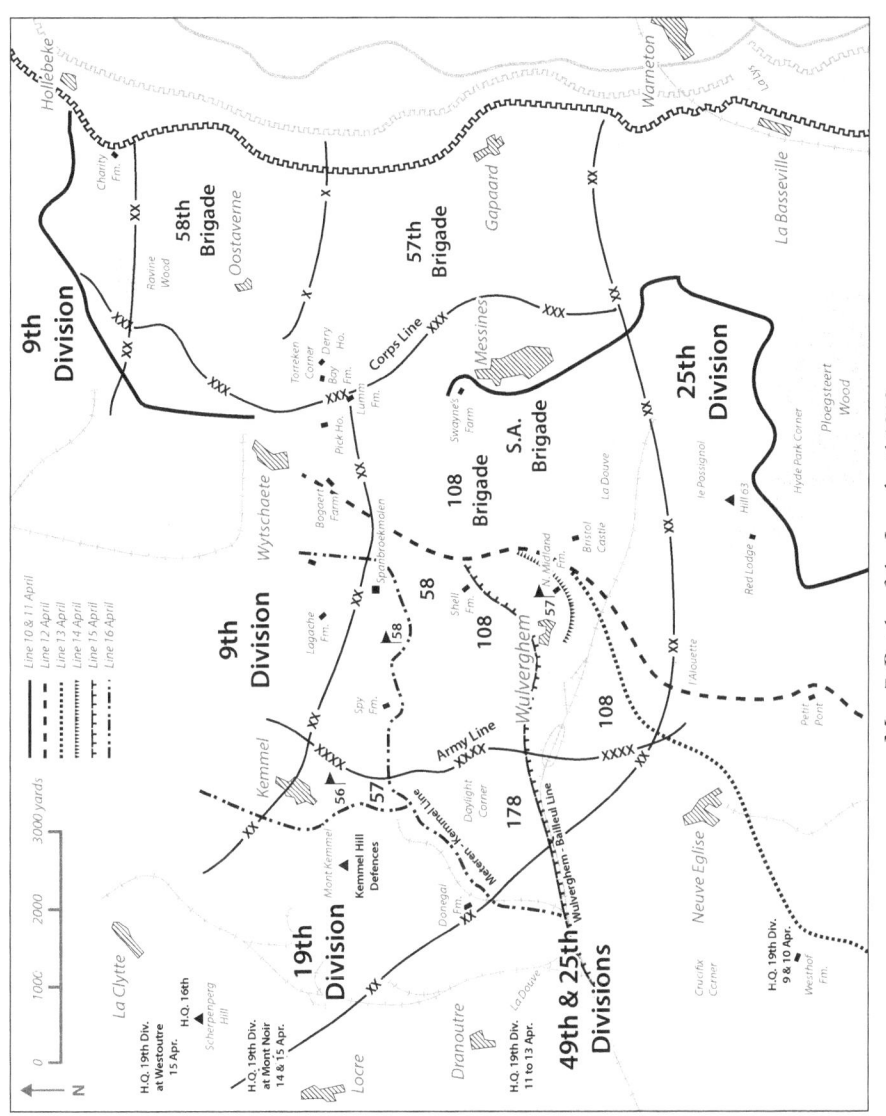

Map 7 Battle of the Lys, April 1918.

The M.G. Corps observed that the German's infiltration tactics had initially received a degree of assistance from the elements; recording that 'nothing was seen of the enemy until he was within close sniping and bombing range of the guns, and most of the guns were attacked at close range from the flanks or the rear by parties of the enemy who had crept through, concealed by the dense mist.'[89] This 'mist' received an artificial stimuli, the Wiltshires recording how: 'About 3.30am [on the 10th] fairly heavy shelling on the whole subsector began consisting of H.E. and gas shells.'[90] But Brig-Gen. Cubitt (GOC 57th Brigade) was certain that the division's new method of defending the line had only served to exacerbate these unpropitious conditions: 'The system of holding a line on a very wide front by unconnected posts is considered to have been proved most unsound. The enemy penetrated, as already stated, in the mist between the posts, attacked them from flank and rear and either killed or captured all the garrisons.'[91]

In response to the April Offensive the division's combat morale/behaviour spectrum showed little change. Three acts were recorded which fell within the high end of the spectrum – fighting 'to the last man'. It was again the defiance of a group of machine-gunners that seized the attention of DHQ. 'A nest of 4 M.Gs. and 25 O.Rs. under 2/Lt. HODGSON M.G.C., belonging to 'B' Coy. 19th Div. M.G. Bn. had been dug in just off the WULVERGHEM–MESSINES Road in [map ref]. During the days of the 10th and 11th this section had rendered great support to the infantry and during the 12th they still remained in their position although in consequence of the withdrawal on the night of 11/12th they were some 600 yds. in front of our front line. The fact that no attack developed against the Bde. on the 12th is[,] it is firmly believed[,] due to the determination and gallantry of this M.G. Section who made the WULVERGHEM–MESSINES Road impassable to any German and killed without exaggeration hundreds of the enemy who attempted to debouch from the village of MESSINES, or cross the MESSINES Ridge. This Section never retired and hung on to the last doing great execution and except in the case of two men who were wounded and got back, the Section never shifted and were killed or taken prisoners at their posts firing to the last.'[92]

This section of machine-gunners had realised the full defensive capabilities of their weapon: if they refused to yield then the advancing infantry could lose tens, maybe

    Bde. from 10th to 20th April, 1918.' WO95/2089 Headquarters 58th Brigade War Diary (April 1918) PRO.
89 'Notes on the operations of the 19th Machine Gun Battalion during the period 9th – 18th April, 1918'. WO95/2056 (April 1918), op cit.
90 WO95/2093 'Wiltshire (Y)' (April 1918), op cit. See also WO95/2079 (April 1918), op cit.
91 '57th Infantry Brigade. Narrative. Battle of Messines – Wulverghem and early part of Kemmel, April 10th – 19th, 1918.' WO95/2084 (April 1918), op cit.
92 '19th Division Narrative. Battle of Messines, Wulverghem and early part of Kemmel. April 10th – 19th 1918.' WO95/2056 (April 1918) op cit.

even hundreds of men to only a small number of opposing gunners. This report also underlines the psychological barriers broken down by the machine-gun. Could 25 ORs and an officer have gone on a three day killing spree with rifle and (especially) bayonet? The accumulated evidence of the past three years suggests a resoundingly negative answer. With the enemy kept, until almost the end, at a impersonal distance, and the fear of being killed kept similarly impersonal, these men fought and killed and maimed for almost three days.

An understanding of the devastating potential of the machine-gun continued to seep into the minds of senior commanders, previously hell-bent on promoting the benefits of the bayonet. Yet the evidence of German successes in the attack, and their own singularly stunning success in the defence, was only stimulating further prevarications. In scripting '19th Division Lessons 10th to 19th April' Brig-Gen. Cubitt tentatively suggested that: '*We might* imitate the enemy in leaving nests of M/guns in front of our own line after withdrawal. One section of 'B' Coy. 19th M/gun Battn. held out…all day on 12th, inflicted the severest casualties on the enemy, and was finally surrounded, but the enemy were completely denied the line of MESSINES – WULVERGHEM Road [-] a very gallant act [my emphasis].'[93] But Cubitt was probably correct in not believing the machine-gun to be the cure-all to the division's defensive troubles. Although teamwork, automation and distance had combined to lift the collective combat morale of these infantrymen, they were still evidently the exception, and exceptional soldiers.

Two other similarly exceptional acts were recorded occurring on 10th April. The Fusiliers recorded how: 'The[ir] Right Company ('D') was surrounded and fought till the last, only about 20 getting away.'[94] Whilst the Wiltshires – in an account which again illustrates the blurred line between *intentional* and *chance* stands 'to the last man' – recorded that: 'About 6pm the enemy organised strong attacks on our right and left flanks – The order to withdraw on to the Reserve Line never reached the front line Coys. so our positions on the support line were held until the enemy had completely surrounded the two front lone Coy. a few elements of which, only, managed to work through to our own lines.'[95] If these isolated groups of infantrymen were *fighting* 'to the last man', it may have been because the option of *submission* (alongside flight) had been removed by the advancing enemy. DHQ recorded how: 'In the enemy's rapid onrush in the mist [on the 10th], the Front and Support Lines of Posts of the 57th Bde. were completely over-run. Practically none of the garrisons were ever seen again and in one case the enemy were seen all round a British post killing off the

---

93 '19th Division Lessons 10th to 19th April', written by GOC 57th Brigade 23 April 1918. Ibid.
94 '9th (S) Bn. Royal Welch Fusiliers. Narrative of events from 10-4-18 to 19-4-18.' WO95/2092 'Fusiliers' (April 1918), op cit.
95 '6th Wiltshire Yeomanry Battn. The Wiltshire Regt. Narrative of events during the operations from April 10th – April 20th 1918.' Written by Maj. H.W. House on 25 April 1918. WO93 'Wiltshires (Y)' (April 1918), op cit.

garrison …'[96] This was a singular account, and it was the enemy's willingness to accept the surrender that had dominated eye-witness reports during their March and April Offensives. But it does suggest that ultimate bellicosity would only elicit a similarly belligerency – the innate demands of survival, so often a force for passivity, *could* become the ultimate force for aggression.

The decision for flight or submission was often delayed if the *fight* could be carried out over some distance. The enemy's frontal attacks proved particularly vulnerable to this form of combat behaviour, as the Wiltshires recorded: 'The Bn. maintained its position everywhere until 4.30pm that afternoon [on the 10th]. At 3.30pm the enemy was massing 2000 yds. east of our front line – and a frontal attack developed, but was unable to materialise owing to our vigorous Lewis…gun and rifle fire…A strong position was then taken up by the two front Coys. on the line of the supporting points. The enemy advanced about 5.30pm to our original front line, but was unable to approach nearer than 600 or 800 yds. owing to our active Lewis gun and rifle fire.'[97]

This willingness to execute fire-fights at impersonal distances could be sustained even in the face of mounting casualties, as the Cheshires reported: 'During the afternoon [of the 11th] the enemy subjected the battalions positions to very heavy shell fire and several times attempted to send forward small attacking parties, these were successfully driven off…Towards evening casualties had increased – the position becoming almost untenable about 4.30pm – being heavily shelled from all directions (it was impossible to tell if our own artillery was shooting short but appearances were strongly in favour of this.) Casualties to other ranks during the day were estimated at 150 … The enemy again put down an exceedingly heavy barrage at 7pm and his infantry attacked about 7.20 – this attack completely broke down under our rifle and Machine Gun fire.'[98]

A singular account from the division's machine-gunners does, however, raise the possibility that the element of 'distance' could be partially removed without infantrymen becoming 'non-firers': 'After the first day, all the forward guns had excellent targets, firing a very large number of rounds, the morale of the men being maintained throughout by their being able to see the enemy actually falling as the result of their fire.'[99]

It is also apparent that the constant exposure to hostile fire was enough to force the retreat without any incursion from the enemy. The Royal Warwick, for instance, reported how: 'Owing to intense and accurate shelling of the PICK HOUSE Line [on

---

96   '19th Division Narrative. Battle of Messines, Wulverghem and early part of Kemmel. April 10th – 19th 1918.' WO95/2056 (April 1918) op cit.
97   '6th Wiltshire Yeomanry Battn. The Wiltshire Regt. Narrative of events during the operations from April 10th – April 20th 1918.' Written by Maj. H.W. House on 25 April 1918. WO95/2093 'Wiltshires (Y)' (April 1918), op cit.
98   WO95/2079 (April 1918), op cit.
99   'Notes on the operations of the 19th Machine Gun Battalion during the period 9th – 18th April, 1918' WO95/2056 (April 1918), op cit.

the 10th] Battn. H.Q. withdrew ... remainder remained under Capt. Brooke in the line just W. of PICK HOUSE until forced to evacuate their position later owing to shelling.'[100] Simply by standing firm and being shelled, without seeing the enemy or returning fire, the battalion was slowly being wiped out, and retreat became the only reasonable action if there was to be anyone left standing by the end of the day. Their diarist hinted that physical casualties from shellfire alone were not forcing the retreat. 'The men by this time were *very exhausted* owing to lack of food, water and sleep, and they had been subjected to heavy and continuous shelling [my emphasis].'[101]

But it was the fall of the flanks – bringing greater exposure to hostile fire, impending isolation, and, most significantly, the threat of interpersonal combat – that remained the primary cause of the Butterflies' flight. The following account by the Cheshires finely illustrates how a frontal attack could be resisted, but threatened incursion from the flanks elicited a quick withdrawal. 'By this time [4pm on the 10th] the enemy's attacking forces had succeeded in forcing their way through into PLOEGSTEERT Wood and were taking the troops in front of the battalion in the rear. These troops fell back fighting into the Battalion line and by 4.30pm the enemy was sighted by our left front Company…By evening the enemy succeeded in bringing up guns and was shelling the front Companies fairly heavily – he also twice attacked, both the attacks were repulsed. However, owing to the situation on the flanks – especially on the right flank, where the enemy was reported to have captured STEENWERCKE – it was necessary to withdraw the front line.'[102]

The following brief account by the North Staffords indicates how the fall of a flank quickly persuaded 'elements' of their infantrymen to retreat: 'About 8pm [on the 11th] withdrawal commenced from the right and elements of A.C. and B. Coys. commenced to withdraw through WULVERGHEM, but this was stopped and the line restored.'[103] The Royal Warwicks reported their own endeavours to stay one step away from the enemy. 'At this time [7am on the 10th] small parties of the enemy were first seen by the Right Reserve Coy to their right front. About ¼ hour later this Coys H.Q. was rendered untenable owing to sniping and M.G. fire…Rt Res Coy engaged small parties of enemy. Enemy continued to work round right flank. O.C. Rt Res Coy withdrew his H.Q. and reported at Bn. H.Q. He reported that enemy were close to Bn. H.Q. and there was a good deal of rifle and M.G. fire directed on Bn. H.Q. from MESSINES. Bn. was evacuated with the exception of a small party who continued to hold a short trench.'[104]

There was, however, one recorded exception to this studied avoidance of interpersonal combat. The Cheshires reported that: 'At dawn [on the 14th] however the

---

100 WO95/2085 'Royal Warwicks' (April 1918), op cit. See also: WO95/2079 (April 1918), op cit.
101 WO95/2085 'Royal Warwicks' (April 1918), op cit.
102 WO95/2079 (April 1918), op cit.
103 WO95/2082 'North Staffords' (April 1918), op cit.
104 WO95/2085 'Royal Warwicks' (April 1918), op cit.

enemy attacked along the valley WATERLOO Road and broke in up the re-entrant to LEWIS FARM. Most effective rifle fire was brought to bear on his troops in [map ref] and heavy losses inflicted on him. Hand to hand fighting ensued however in the neighbourhood of BREEMEERSCHEN [map ref] in which Lt. Col. G.K. FULTON was killed.'[105]

The Cheshires also provided the only recorded occurrence of anything resembling a impromptu counter-attack (the North Staffords was ordered); despite this being elemental to the division's defensive strategy. They found that the enemy was equally desirous of avoiding interpersonal combat. 'About 1pm an enemy M.G. post was located by the Commanding Officer to be in the buildings at BRUNE CAYE. As this was bringing enfilade fire to bare on our own positions a party was sent to turn the enemy out. The party consisted of 1 Officer (2nd Lt STRONG) and 20 men of the 8th BORDER Rgt and 10 men and 1 NCO of the 9th Cheshires. This party approached the building cautiously and then rushed it. 1 Officer and 14 other ranks were taken prisoners.'[106] The composition of the Cheshires' party provides further evidence that the leadership qualities of NCOs and the desired *esprit de section* were occasionally living up to the hopes of *S.S.143 (1918)*.

The very great need to invest responsibility in junior commanders and NCOs was again emphasised by the inevitable breakdown in communications between retreating divisional and brigade HQs and retreating infantry. The Royal Warwicks recorded the immediate severing of the link between front and rears. 'O.C. Left F.L. Coy reported men returning from S.P.s on right [at 6am on the 10th] ... From this time on there was no further communication with either F.L. Coys and lines to Reserve Coys were broken.'[107] Even when the channel remained open, the chaos of the battlefield – now very much exacerbated by units being farmed out to foreign commands – impeded the will of senior commanders. Brig-Gen. R.M. Heath (recently promoted GOC 56th Brigade) made the following barbed report. 'I 'phoned to G.S.O. 1, 25th Division asking if any retirement had been ordered, he replied that there was <u>to be no retirement</u>. 4.50pm O.C. K.S.L.I. 'phoned me that the Wilts. were already coming back over HILL 63, I again instructed him that there was to be no withdrawal, that he was to stop anyone whom he saw retiring, and make such use of them as he could to hold on to the Hill. At 5.50pm I received 25th Division Order No. 289...placing the K.S.L.I. under 7th Infantry Brigade and directing the troops on HILL 63 to retire when 'forced' to do so...As HILL 63 appeared to me to be the key of the MESSINES RIDGE I protested on the 'phone against this order to retire and also against the vagueness of the order which through [sic] the whole onus of the ordering of a withdrawal from this important position on the O.C. K.S.L.I. I also asked if, 'forced' to

---

105 WO95/2079 (April 1918), op cit.
106 Ibid. The number of enemy soldiers captured suggests the whole post surrendered.
107 WO95/2085 'Royal Warwicks' (April 1918), op cit.

withdraw meant 'to die in the last ditch', and was told it did not.'[108] The absence of orders, or, equally, the presence of contradictory orders, essentially empowered (or freed) battalion COs and their juniors to act autonomously. This battlefield, like all its predecessors on the Western Front, was in the hands of infantry commanders.

These commanders remained the beacon of the infantry's collective combat morale. Where the voice of command survived so, invariably, did the infantry's willingness to fight on. The M.G. Corps observed that the presence of an officer ensured firing, whilst, visa-versa, his absence led to non-firing. 'The only guns in the actual sector attacked which are known to have fired for any appreciable time were the two pairs of guns near DESPAGNE FARM and FANNY'S FARM, respectively. The guns of the former were under direct control of an officer and were heard firing quite a considerable time. A pair of guns just on the flank of the sector attacked, near MAHIEU FARM, which were under the direct control of an officer, are known to have put up a splendid fight and to have fired continually for a period of several hours.'[109]

On reflection the Corps decided that 'Guns should be sited in pairs under the actual control of an officer or Sergeant who is on the spot ... owing to lack of control, the vigilance, morale, sanitation and general discipline of the team suffers.'[110] Brig-Gen. Cubitt later contended that the division's defensive strategy itself had undermined the ability to realise this 'control ... A continuous line, even if weakly held, is preferable to scattered posts. Our posts in front of MESSINES were, I fear, mere death traps, many men were netted-in and wired-in. I did not like the camouflage netting nor the all-round wire – especially with our shortage of officers, with attendant impossibility of control, or arrangements for rallying. 10th Worc. R. which was most heavily attacked had only six officers available for 4 companies and occupied 17 posts.'[111]

The following account by DHQ finally illustrates how the reinstatement of leadership could halt a potential headlong retreat. Moreover, it indicates that example, authority and knowledge could act in the absence of 'relationship': the lead being taken by an officer of the RFA, the stand being made by a group of unnamed and unrelated infantrymen who, nevertheless, were prepared to follow. 'Captain E.S. DOUGALL, M.C., R.F.A., who was in command of 'A' Battery, 88th Bde. R.F.A., maintained his guns in action near MESSINES on the 10th April throughout the heavy concentration of the enemy shelling...[Following the infantry's retreat] Captain DOUGALL... assumed control of the situation, rallied and organized the infantry, supplied them with Lewis Guns, and armed as many gunners as he could spare with rifles. With these he formed a line in front of the battery which during this period was harassing the advancing Germans with a rapid rate of fire...Although exposed to both rifle and

---

108 WO95/2077 (April 1918), op cit.
109 'Notes on the operations of the 19th Machine Gun Battalion during the period 9th – 18th April, 1918'. WO95/2056 (April 1918), op cit.
110 Ibid. Recorded under the heading 'The lessons learned in the first phase...'
111 '19th Division Lessons 10th to 19th April', written by GOC 57th Brigade 23 April 1918. Ibid.

machine gun fire Captain DOUGALL fearlessly walked about as though on parade, calmly giving orders and encouraging everybody. His remark to the infantry at this juncture 'So long as you stick to your trenches I will keep my guns here' had a most inspiring effect on all ranks. This line was maintained throughout the day, thereby delaying the enemy's entry into MESSINES for over 12 hours.'[112]

It would seem certain that, with the evident rapid dissipation of organised fighting units, it was commonplace for junior officers to find themselves commanding ad-hoc groups collected from disparate battalions. The Royal Warwicks, for example, noted a 'Report received from O.C. Left Res. Coy. [on the 10th] that he was I/C of a mixed party of 6/Wilts, 9/Welch and his own men, holding a line of posts...about 100 yrds from PICK HOUSE.'[113] In the absence of any 'officer-man' relationship these troops could at least call upon the motivations of group loyalty – whether drawn from *esprit de corps*, *platoon* or *section*. But the desperate need to bolster the fluid frontline with 'Surplus personnel (composed almost entirely of new drafts)' subsequently also diluted the potency of these motivations.[114] Soon after 10 April it would seem likely that many infantrymen were dependent upon leadership and survival alone to bolster their morale, and, as we have seen, survival was very much a double-edged motivation.

Exemplary leadership was, however, far more vulnerable to being silenced than cautious pondering. Capt. Dougall was killed later the same day (and awarded a posthumous VC). The Wiltshires recorded how their CO and second-in-command fell casualty endeavouring to lead from the front. 'Battn. H.Q. Coy. which was utilised in an attempt to strengthen the right rear was also engaged heavily in fighting in which the C.O. Major Monreal was mortally wounded and the 2nd in Command Capt. Garthwaite wounded.'[115] The consequences for the infantry's collective combat morale were severe. DHQ recorded how a temporary 'halt and rally' was precipitated back into headlong retreat by the fall of the Shropshires' CO. 'At 7.10pm [on the 14th] the 1/4th K.S.L.I. reported that troops of the 25th Div. on their right were retiring. Major WINGROVE O.C. 1/4th K.S.L.I. partially succeeded in rallying them but at 8.5pm further reports were received that a lot of straggling was in progress and by 8.15pm it was certain that the line N. of NEUVE ENGLISE was definitely broken and units were in retreat. It subsequently turned out that Major WINGROVE, whose tenacity, gallantry and determination had held the much tried and isolated line up to this time, was wounded and thereupon the line broke.'[116]

---

112 '19th Division Narrative. Battle of Messines, Wulverghem and early part of Kemmel. April 10th – 19th 1918.' WO95/2056 (April 1918) op cit.
113 WO95/2085 'Royal Warwicks' (April 1918), op cit.
114 Ibid.
115 '6th Wiltshire Yeomanry Battn. The Wiltshire Regt. Narrative of events during the operations from April 10th – April 20th 1918.' Written by Maj. H.W. House on 25 April 1918. WO95/2093 'Wiltshires (Y)' (April 1918), op cit.
116 '19th Division Narrative. Battle of Messines, Wulverghem and early part of Kemmel. April 10th – 19th 1918.' WO95/2056 (April 1918) op cit.

It is, however, also evident that the presence of battalion officers was not always enough to lift the spirits of the ORs, because some of the ORs had already melted away. Unless officers of the Royal Warwicks had instigated a new method of command – lead from behind – or had been extremely fortunate in comparison with their ORs, then the following account of their actions is telling. 'At this time [2.30pm on the 11th] Capt. Brooke, 2nd Lt. O'Neill, with 3 Off. and about 50 O.R. was reported to be holding a position between [map ref] with no one on either flank…[a few hours later] Capt Brooke, 2/Lts O'Neill, Wynne, Wright and Mosedale reported with about 10 men.'[117]

With the voice of command either silenced or being ignored, and with the enemy pressing, the propensity to straggle continued. A large number of infantry were retiring when the heat of the battle became too intense, and these men were invariably not obeying orders, rather they were obeying the thoughts, beliefs and emotions that constituted the strength of their combat morale. As we have seen, this was not quite a rout; many men were prepared to halt and rally, or re-join their units once the heat was off. The Wiltshires recorded the gradual return of once errant Butterflies. 'During the night [of the 10th] the survivors of the Battn. rallied on portions of the front between the DAMMSTRASSE and WYTSCHAETE. 75 stragglers were collected and sent up…The remainder of the day was spent in collecting and re-organising the Battn.'[118] This process of netting stray Butterflies was aided by the instigation of 'Stragglers Posts'. DHQ recorded that 'Stragglers' posts were reposted during the morning of the 13th and continued to prove necessary and effective.'[119] Having observed the events of 10 to 18 April, the M.G. Corps again witnessed how susceptible infantrymen were to the herd instinct of survival. 'It is useless to place guns about 500 yards behind the front line…as their fire will be masked by the infantry retiring past them, and they will in all probability be carried away in the general retirement, without firing a shot.'[120] Willing firers would rapidly join the ranks of non-firers if the collective ethos of the infantry had descended into headlong retreat.

How many of these men refused to be halted, or preferred to give themselves up to the enemy, remains ambiguous. The following account by 58th Brigade offers qualitative evidence of a large number of infantrymen falling captive, but also once more suggests that the rapidity and stealth of the enemy's advance may have ensnared a large number of unwilling captives. 'About 7.30pm [on the 10th] O.C. R.W.F. reported that the enemy had got into OOSTAVERNE WOOD apparently behind the Reserve

---

117   WO95/2085 'Royal Warwicks' (April 1918), op cit.
118   '6th Wiltshire Yeomanry Battn. The Wiltshire Regt. Narrative of events during the operations from April 10th – April 20th 1918.' Written by Maj. H.W. House on 25 April 1918. WO95/2093 'Wiltshires (Y)' (April 1918), op cit.
119   '19th Division Narrative. Battle of Messines, Wulverghem and early part of Kemmel. April 10th – 19th 1918.' WO95/2056 (April 1918) op cit.
120   'Notes on the operations of the 19th Machine Gun Battalion during the period 9th – 18th April, 1918'. Ibid.

Line ... The original Front and Support Line Companies were known to have lost heavily during the withdrawal. Elements of them were with the DENYS WOOD Coy but no further information of them could be got and very few of them ever got back...The 6th WILTS had been completely cut off by the enemy's break through from TORREKEN FARM direction. One party of about 50 succeeded in withdrawing Northwards and joined the Coy of the 9th WELCH near PHEASANT WOOD. Elements of the Battn. were believed to be about [map ref] but no formed bodies could be found and only small isolated parties succeeded in getting back through the enemy after dark.'[121] Again, it is the vast numbers of captured men that points towards willing surrendering on a large scale. Of the 3266 casualties recorded by DHQ during the April retreat, 1894 (58 percent) were labelled 'missing'.[122] The final casualty toll indicates that a minimum of just over 1500 infantrymen were captured by the enemy over the eight day battle.[123] A surrender rate of over thirty percent again suggests that the willing greatly outnumbered the unwilling captives.[124]

Desertion, alternatively, remained the act of the very few, with one sentence being passed in the aftermath of the April retreat.[125] The division, abetted by the Military Police, was still faced with the same problems of finding and bringing to trial any would-be escapees, whilst they themselves were still engaged in perpetual retreat. Even so, the leniency with which the lone absconder was treated – 3 years Penal Servitude Suspended – together with one courts martials' willingness to reduce a charge of 'Desertion' to 'guilty-of-absence', suggests that the division's chain of command was yet to feel the strain of mass desertion.[126] This attitude was about to undergo revision.

---

121 'Narrative of Action of 58th Inf. Bde. from 10th to 20th April, 1918.' WO95/2089 (April 1918), op cit.
122 The full breakdown was as follows: 245 Killed; 1127 Wounded; 1894 Missing; total casualties 3266. '19th Division Narrative. Battle of Messines, Wulverghem and early part of Kemmel. April 10th – 19th 1918.' WO95/2056 (April 1918) op cit.
123 *Soldiers Died* records that 515 ORs of 19th Division were either killed or died of wounds between 10 and 19 April 1918. If the entire difference of 270 infantrymen (between the division's initial calculation and the final toll) is taken from the list of 'missing', and none are taken from the list of 'wounded', then 1624 infantrymen are still left on the captured list.
124 This percentage calculation is based upon a approximate divisional fighting strength of 5000 infantrymen (1500 per brigade and around 500 divisional machine-gunners and brigade Stokes Mortars).
125 WO213/21-3 (April/May 1918), op cit.
126 The lone deserter was a private from the South Lancs, suggesting that this wanderer had left the division sometime before GHQ intended him to. See WO213/22 entry 4 May 1918.

Battle of Aisne-Marne, 29 May to 6 June

It was a very 'green' and only partially trained 19th Division that was sent South to Champagne in May 1918 for a second unrealised 'rest'. 'It was intended that the 19th Division should take over a quiet sector in the TAHURE area on the front between RHEIMS and VERDUN [DHQ recorded]. Having suffered extremely heavy casualties in both the SOMME and LYS Battles, the Division was composed almost entirely of new drafts, many of whom were not yet fully trained and some such period of rest or holding the line in a quiet sector seemed essential to enable the Division to recuperate.'[127]

'At 4pm. May 27th', whilst the division was still *en route*, 'information was received that [on] the early morning of that day the enemy had attacked a wide front between RHEIMS and SOISSONS and had penetrated the Allied positions to some considerable depth.'[128] The division duly joined the French Fourth Army in a five day rearguard action (29 May to 2 June) that broadly mirrored the actions and outcomes of the March and April retreats. Two days into the battle Jeffreys received word that his 'green' division lacked the requisite 'fighting spirit'. The 'Message Diary' for 31 May recorded a '5th French Army Commander's letter regarding troops retiring without putting up a fight.'[129] The letter spoke of 'hordes of troops retir[ing] without a real fight.' Jeffreys, with both his national and military pride expectedly offended, responded by telling his troops that he 'relies on 19th Div. to uphold the honour of the British Army by resisting the enemy with the utmost tenacity.'[130]

But by nightfall Jeffries was taking a sterner line. 'Divl. Comdr wishes all ranks to be reminded of the following: (a) They must NOT retire because they see the enemy coming on but must hold their ground and shoot; (b) They must not retire because they see others going back; (c) The sternest measures will be taken to preserve discipline and prevent withdrawals without orders, and to deal severely with stragglers. (d) The word 'Retire' is not to be used and the Divn. must hold its ground at all costs.'[131]

The shortcomings of 'A', 'B', and 'D' had been evident throughout the March and April (and now May) retreats; the martinet response demanded by 'C' had, to date, been conspicuously absent. The events of 1 June did little to cool Jeffreys' temper. 'The A.P.M. report that 50 stragglers of 10th Warwicks were collected today. The G.O.C. regards this number of stragglers in one battalion with displeasure. He directs that strong measures be taken to prevent such straggling. All men who are unable to give

---

127 '19th Division Narrative Marne Operations'. WO95/2056 (June 1918), op cit.
128 Ibid.
129 '58th Infantry Brigade. Narrative of Operations from 1st June to 6th June, 1918', dated 22 June 1918. Ibid.
130 HWT received 31 May, response appended to same telegram. Ibid.
131 'Message Diary' appended to '58th Infantry Brigade. Narrative of Operations from 1st June to 6th June, 1918', dated 22 June 1918. Message timed at 11.30pm and addressed to all brigades. Ibid.

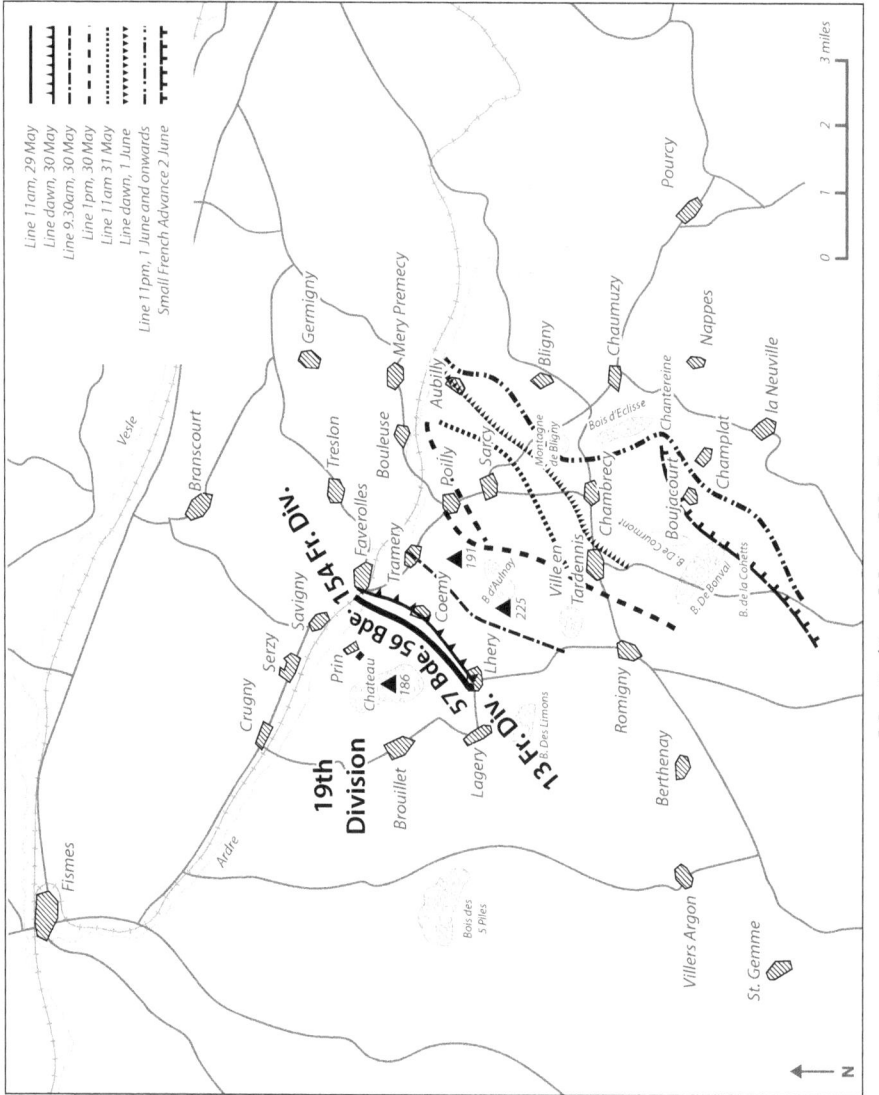

Map 8 Aisne-Marne, May–June 1918.

a satisfactory reason for straggling are to be taken off the leave roster and a proportion tried by court martial. It is to be impressed upon all ranks that straggling is a military offence and offenders are liable to trial by court martial.'[132]

When this order brought no stiffening of 19th Division's collective combat morale Jeffries decided to take the law into his own hands. 'A large number of stragglers have again been intercepted during the last 24 hrs. especially of 10th WARWICKS. For the preservation of discipline an example must be made. All N.C.Os and a proportion of the men will be tried by Court Martial. Where evidence is available such men will be tried for desertion. Where sufficient evidence is not available to support a charge of desertion men will be tried for absence without leave or under Sect 40. F.G.C.M. will be convened under Divl. Arrangements on notification being received of number of cases for trial…Summaries of evidence need not necessarily be taken.'[133] Jeffreys wanted an example set, and to this end was prepared to suspend any deliberation over soldiers' reasons for 'straggling', and arbitrarily choose those who were to face trial. The GOC was proposing to push his division down the dangerous and tumultuous road to kangaroo courts and summary executions.

Jeffreys had already shown his credentials as a martinet during the winter of 1918 when the question of how to lift the combat morale of his troops had again become a point of contention. Jeffrey's answer had been the trench raid. 'The value of a raid', Jeffreys confidently declared, 'apart from securing identification' lies almost entirely in raising the morale of the troops.'[134] During 1917 the division occasionally used raids as an opportunity to practice the newly developing 'art of attack'. Jeffreys did not like this idea; primarily because (as we have also seen) the post-Somme 'art of attack' (if it went to plan) left most of the killing and maiming to the artillery – it was also the German method, and therefore inherently unsound. 'There has been a tendency in some divisions to copy the German method of carrying out a raid; that is to preface the raid with a heavy bombardment, in order to knock out as many men in the front trenches as possible … This is not considered sound. The moral and material effect of a raid which surprises the enemy when he is alive and holding his trenches is far greater than of one carried out on the German plan, where almost everything is done by the artillery.'[135]

This statement is worth dwelling upon. Here we have a senior commander who, in the face of overwhelming evidence that, in the static environs of trench warfare, sound artillery support was the key to a successful infantry assault, wanted his infantrymen to 'practice' attacking the enemy *sans* artillery. This, he thought, would be good for their morale. Fortunately for the infantrymen of 19th Division their battalion commanders

132 Message timed at 11.55pm 1 June, addressed to all brigades. Ibid.
133 Message timed at 2 June, addressed to all brigades. Ibid. The battalion records give no indication that the accused Royal Warwicks were anymore culpable of mass straggling than their fellow Butterflies.
134 'G947 'Some Notes on Raids' issued by DHQ 15February 1918. Ibid.
135 Ibid.

did not agree. Records suggest that over the winter of 1917-18 the division planned and executed *one* raid.[136]

Whether or not the GOC disregarded the civilities of normal military law during the ensuing battle for *Montagne de Bligny* went (understandably) unrecorded. That was the point! Jeffreys did continued to pursue his unequivocal demand for summary executions. Drawing upon the 'Lessons deduced from the Operations ... between 29th May and 6th June 1918', Jeffries insisted that: 'All cases of deliberate straggling should be ruthlessly dealt with by summary court-martial and inflicting of the death penalty as early as possible as a deterrent to others.'[137] Jeffreys later admitted (in the 1930s) that his request for summary executions had been denied by C-in-C Field Marshal Haig. So this would suggests not.[138] A greater number of absconders were certainly tried and convicted through the normal legal channels.[139] Yet the resultant courts martials' reluctance to pass the 'Death' sentence, and High Command's willingness to commute the capital sentences of even multiple offenders, further suggests that commanders on both sides of the chain did not share Jeffreys' views on the efficacy of harsh discipline.[140]

Putting aside the obvious illegality of summary executions, and the dubious morale efficacy of such a policy, it is evident that gross injustices would flow from its implementation. During the offensives of 1916-17 proving 'Desertion' was usually unproblematic; the soldier's unit had advanced, whilst he retreated, often to Boulogne. 'Straggling' was a far more ambiguous piece of combat behaviour. It was hard to

---

136 See 'Report on raid carried out on evening Nov 1st by party of 7th King's own R. Lanc. Regt.' WO95/2055 General Staff 19th Division War Diary (Nov 1917) PRO.
137 'Lessons deduced from the Operations of the 19th Division in the Ardre Valley (S.W. of Rheims) between 29th May and 6th June 1918', written by Lt-Col. H.F. Montgomery (General Staff) on 11 July 1918. WO95/2056 (July 1918), op cit.
138 Gary Sheffield cites correspondence between Jeffries and J.E. Edmonds (official historian) in 1934 in which Jeffries recalled that GHQ had refused a request made in May 1918 to summarily execute 'stragglers'. This refusal did not, however, deter DHQ from writing summary executions into its proposals for future operations. See Gary Sheffield, 'The Operational Role of British Military Police on the Western Front, 1914-18' op cit., p. 77. In his study of the Redcaps Sheffield writes 'Clearly, some summary executions did take place, but it seems that the drastic decision to shoot one's own men was taken only under extreme pressure by harassed officers or NCOs attempting to stem a rout...the author has uncovered no evidence that this practice was officially sanctioned on the Western Front.' Gary Sheffield, *The Redcaps*, op cit., p. 66.
139 Between 5 and 28 June 13 infantrymen of 19th Division were found guilty of Desertion, whilst 3 were committed for 'Absence', and 2 for 'Quitting Post'. None of the recorded Desertions belonged to the Royal Warwicks. WO213/23-4 (June 1918), op cit.
140 Only 4 Death sentences were passed, 3 were commuted to 15 years Penal Servitude (one suspended), and one was not confirmed. One of these 3 included a multiple offender, a private from the Wiltshires. The divisions other serial deserter, a private from the Cheshires, received a sentence of 2 years Hard Labour; an example may have been expected here, given that 7 of the division's 13 absconders were found in this battalion. Ibid.

identify whether 'stragglers' intended to stay with the advance (or the rearguard action), and had got unintentionally waylaid – very easy amongst the smoke and chaos of the battlefield – or had intentionally drifted away from the battle (which could be classified as desertion under the strictures of Military Law).[141] It would seem impossible that Jeffreys' envisaged hastily arranged 'summary' court martials could navigate their way through the ambiguities inherent in the act of 'straggling'. Essentially the GOC wanted to avoid the legal intricacies of Military Law. He wanted a few soldiers shot as an example to the rest.

The justifications for Jeffreys' disciplinarian reactions are questionable. Casualties were slightly less than previously experienced, but upward of 2500 indicates that the objective circumstances of this battle (although waning) still held much of the ferocity of the earlier spring offensives.[142] Calculating the number of captives found amongst this total becomes increasingly difficult for the May/June retreat, because the division collectively stopped breaking down casualties into 'dead', 'wounded' and 'missing' (a strange coincidence for a division under pressure to punish its absconders!). A final death toll of around 300 – approximately twelve percent of all recorded casualties – however, suggests either more wounded or more captured soldiers.[143]

Qualitative accounts once again point to vast numbers of infantrymen falling into the hands of the enemy. 58th Brigade, for example, recorded for 30 May: 'The O.C. 9th Bn. R.W.Fusiliers reported that practically the whole of his Battalion had been cut off and had either been killed or captured only 50 O.R. being left. Later information was received that 3 Companies of the 9th Welch Regt had shared the same fate.'[144] The Fusiliers own account indicates that the battalion 'collectively' did not surrender without a fight. 'By 11am orders were received for a withdrawal to the POILLY – BOIS D'AULNEY Line but by this time the Battalion was engaged in a *hand to hand conflict with the enemy* who had come round on both flanks [my emphasis].'[145] Again,

---

141 See *Manual of Military Law* (1914) IWM, p. 18.
142 The final breakdowns were as follows: 56th Bde. 43 Officers, 871 ORs; 57th Bde. 34 Officers, 893 ORs; Welch 13 Officers, 477 ORs. Total recorded casualties 2331. No record can be found for the casualties suffered by the Fusiliers and the Wiltshires. See WO95/2077 (June 1918), op cit.; '57th Infantry Brigade Narrative of Operations 27th May to 10th June 1918' WO95/2056 (June 1918), op cit; 'Diary of the share taken by the Battalion in the operations between June 1st 1918 and June 8th 1918.' WO95/2092 'Welch' (June 1918), op cit.
143 Soldiers Died records 314 fatalities for the division between 30 May and 6 June 1918. This represented 12% of the total casualties, and would have been lower given the absence of records for two of the battalions. The final percentage of infantrymen killed, compared to wounded or missing, was remarkably consistent during the March and April retreats – totalling 15% and 16% respectively.
144 '58th Infantry Brigade. Narrative of Operations from 28th May to 31st May, 1918', dated 22 June 1918. WO95/2056 (June 1918), op cit.
145 '9th (S) Bn Royal Welch Fusiliers Narrative of Operations' written by CO (no date). WO95/2092 'Fusiliers' (June 1918), op cit.

however, the same conclusions can be drawn from the sheer number of captives suggested by the former account.

Yet it is the stand at *Montagne de Bligny* on 6 June that seemingly refutes any suspicion that 'the class of 1918' had irrevocably surrendered the collective combat morale sustained by their predecessors. The willingness of the infantry to execute countless counter-attacks in an endeavour to regain the hill, bares testimony to a remarkably high offensive spirit. DHQ recorded the tenacity of 56th Brigade: 'Another counter-attack was immediately organized and the 1/4th KING'S SHROPSHIRE LIGHT INFANTRY were brought forward for the purpose. This counter-attack was quickly planned and most brilliantly executed by the 1/4th KING'S SHROPSHIRE LIGHT INFANTRY and the remnants of the 9th CHESHIRE Regt. who gallantly advanced to counter-attack for the second time, being carried forward by the magnificent dash and spirit of their comrades. The enemy appeared to be taken by surprise, as having warded off one counter-attack he apparently considered himself immune from further attacks for some hours. By 12.15pm the MONTAGNE DE BLIGNY was again in our hands and the enemy driven well down the forward slopes of the hill. 1 officer and 33 O.R.s were taken prisoner in this counter-attack and many of the enemy were killed.'[146]

The Welch recorded their (ultimately faltering) contribution. 'The [enemy] attack was repulsed and three times he was driven back by our L.Gun and Rifle fire. His losses were very heavy… The remainder of the support platoon was then ordered for counter-attack and endeavour[ed] to regain the wood and secure the position on the right flank of the 9th Welch. They attacked three times but each time [were] repulsed by heavy machine gun fire from the CHAMBRECY – SARCY road. At 5pm The 9th Cheshires counter-attacked and retook the crest of the hill but the wood on the Western slope was still in the hands of the enemy who was holding it with about eighty men. The remaining 9th Welch reserves then attempted to retake the wood. They made 3 counter-attacks with covering Machine Gun Fire but were unable to obtain a foot hold in the wood owing to heavy casualties caused by hostile shelling and Machine Guns.'[147]

These were not the actions of infantrymen suffering from a diminished combat morale. Moreover, the bayonet charge executed by the remnants of 58th Brigade,

---

146 'Operations of the 19th Division in the Battle of Aisne-Marne, May – June 1918.' WO95/2056 (June 1918), op cit.
147 'Diary of the share taken by the Battalion in the operations between June 1st 1918 and June 8th 1918.' WO95/2092 'Welch' (June 1918), op cit. The Welch claimed that the Cheshires had originally been to blame for the loss of the crest of the hill. 'At 10am the enemy delivered a strong attack in the direction of BLIGNY and at the same time he commenced shelling the 9th Welch posts causing considerable casualties…At 1pm the 9th Cheshires on the right withdrew to the BLIGNY – CHAMBRECY road. The enemy thereupon advanced to the crest of the MONTAGNE DE BLIGNY and commenced to dig himself in without opposition.'

mostly the Wiltshires,[148] was even more indicative of a group of infantrymen whose willingness to kill or be killed was touching the high end of the combat morale/behaviour spectrum. DHQ recorded how: 'A Composite Bn. of the 58th Bde…were holding this line and immediately opened a brisk rifle and L.G. fire on the advancing enemy and a large number were seen to fall. The remaining enemy continued to advance whereupon the defenders got out of their trenches and rushed at them with fixed bayonets. The enemy broke and attempted to escape but very few succeeded in doing so.'[149]

First news of this action suggests that 'posturing' the act was enough to win the day. 58th Brigade telegrammed to the 56ths reporting that: 'Wilts Company and Battn. HQ hold their original front others also believed holding. Enemy attacked and was met in the open by our men with the bayonet. Enemy ran. Bugle sent herewith was captured please retain for us. Our casualties slight.'[150] The singularity of this combat episode, however, again underlines how rare the (potential) crossing of swords was between these two armies. If the combat morale of 19th Division had not greatly diminished since 1916-17, then their disinclination to engage in interpersonal combat remained similarly obdurate. Nevertheless, this singular act does also indicate the possibility that infantrymen were (relatively) more willing to fight with the bayonet when being attacked, rather than attacking.

If the class of 1918 had occasionally betrayed faltering combat morale, then a number of extenuating circumstances can be offered in their defence. DHQ admitted that these 'green' and youthful infantrymen were, at best, half trained. Any resultant lack of weapons competence would have hindered their ability to fight, regardless of their morale state. Soldiers who were yet to learn the 'habit' of obedience may have also found the presence of *authority* less inspiring. These troops had also been denied the opportunity to learn the ropes of trench warfare. Perhaps most crippling of all, little time had elapsed in which to meld the bonds of officer-man relations and loyalty to the primary group. As it was, these bonds, however well formed, were often shattered by the ferocity of the German assault, leaving ad-hoc units to fight where once a organised unit had stood. The following account by the Cheshires well illustrates the 'temporary' nature of the units fighting for Montagne de Bligny: 'The Commanding Officer…organised two parties to attack this left flank; one was led, very gallantly, by 2nd Lieut JONES (9th Welsh Rgt) but was unsuccessful, the officer being wounded; the other[,] Captain Griffiths[,] himself led and succeeded in capturing a small portion of the trench, killing several of the enemy and wounding others – the remainder fled. The attacking party, oddments of all units, remained in occupation of this post.'[151]

---

148 The 6th Wiltshire (Yeomanry) had been absorbed by the regiment's 2nd Battalion, but came under the command of 19th Division.
149 'Summary of Operations on 19th Divisional Front on 6th June 1918'. WO95/2056 (June 1918), op cit.
150 HWT received by 56th Brigade at 6.15am 6 June. WO95/2077 (June 1918), op cit.
151 WO95/2079 (June 1918), op cit. Diary entry 6 June.

Why did these infantrymen, bereft of many of morale defences enjoyed by their processors, fight on? Exemplary leadership, with or without the presence of a relationship, clearly remained inspirational to many men, and inspirational leaders could still be found in abundance. It would also seem possible that a rapidly formed *esprit de section*, or perhaps simply the comforting presence of fellow infantrymen, particularly a comrade who was firing, provided a adequate substitute for more longer standing group loyalties. It may have also been that in these straitened circumstances, the naked motivation of survival often became a force for *fight* rather than *flight*. If the *fear of being killed* possibly acted as a resistant to killing during the offensive, then when fighting with their backs to the wall, and with few means of escape, the tables were turned, and killing may have become a means of *avoiding being killed*. Finally, perhaps the youth and inexperience of these troops acted as an aid to combat, not a resistant. They were certainly not fatigued or ground down by years (even months) of trench warfare. Neither had they much time to imbibe any of the values and mores of the frontline infantryman that occasionally usurped the plans of senior commanders (studiously avoiding trench raids, sacrificing the objective to safety and so forth).

Whatever the components of their combat morale, the adolescent conscripted Butterflies had proved that they were good enough to repel all that the German Army could concentrate upon a divisional frontage. On 6 June, with their backs against the wall of Montagne de Bligny – Jeffreys' chosen *Voie Sacrée* – the remnants of the division mustered enough fighting spirit to repel the enemy's last throw. The spring storm had finally blown itself out against the allied defences. All that remained was to win a war.

10

The Last Hundred Days

Overview

The autumn of 1918 witnessed the realisation of a great deal that *S.S.143* (both 1917 and 1918) had aspired towards: autonomous platoons (and sections), acting on their own initiative, and utilizing all the weaponry of the infantry, successfully overcoming the enemy through a succession of 'infantry versus infantry' conflicts. The war's final movements, moreover, were largely orchestrated by battalion COs and their juniors, now *officially* granted control over this most fluid of battlefields. 19th Division as a whole were also making further ascents along the learning curve. The deployment of forward probing 'Vanguard' battalions – composed of every branch of the division's armoury, and charged with spearheading a passage through the enemy's withering defences – endeavoured (albeit with mixed success) to raise all-arms cooperation to previously unimagined heights.

Yet any account of this fairly momentous turnaround in infantry combat behaviour must be delivered with a number of caveats. With the shackles of trench warfare now irrevocably broken, and the domination of defence giving way to a war of movement, the Western Front provided a far more propitious stage upon which to perform platoon tactics. 'Infantry versus infantry' conflict had previously been conducted as a relative sideshow to the mammoth 'artillery versus artillery' battle. But with the power of artillery partially subdued by the fluidity of this battlefield, the actions of infantrymen held more agency over success or failure. Of greater moment, however, was the morale, manpower and *materiel* strength of the division's adversary. By mid-autumn the Butterflies were no longer engaging in *attacks* or *advances* against the enemy, but were in perpetual *pursuit* of an army in headlong retreat. This statement does not intend to detract from the achievements of the 19th Division of late 1918. Their collective combat morale, like that of their predecessors, proved *good enough* for the challenges they faced. It is simply to suggest that their predecessors – the original volunteers who had advanced against hopeless odds at Loos, or who had attacked time and again on the Somme, those who had struggled to learn the lessons of these

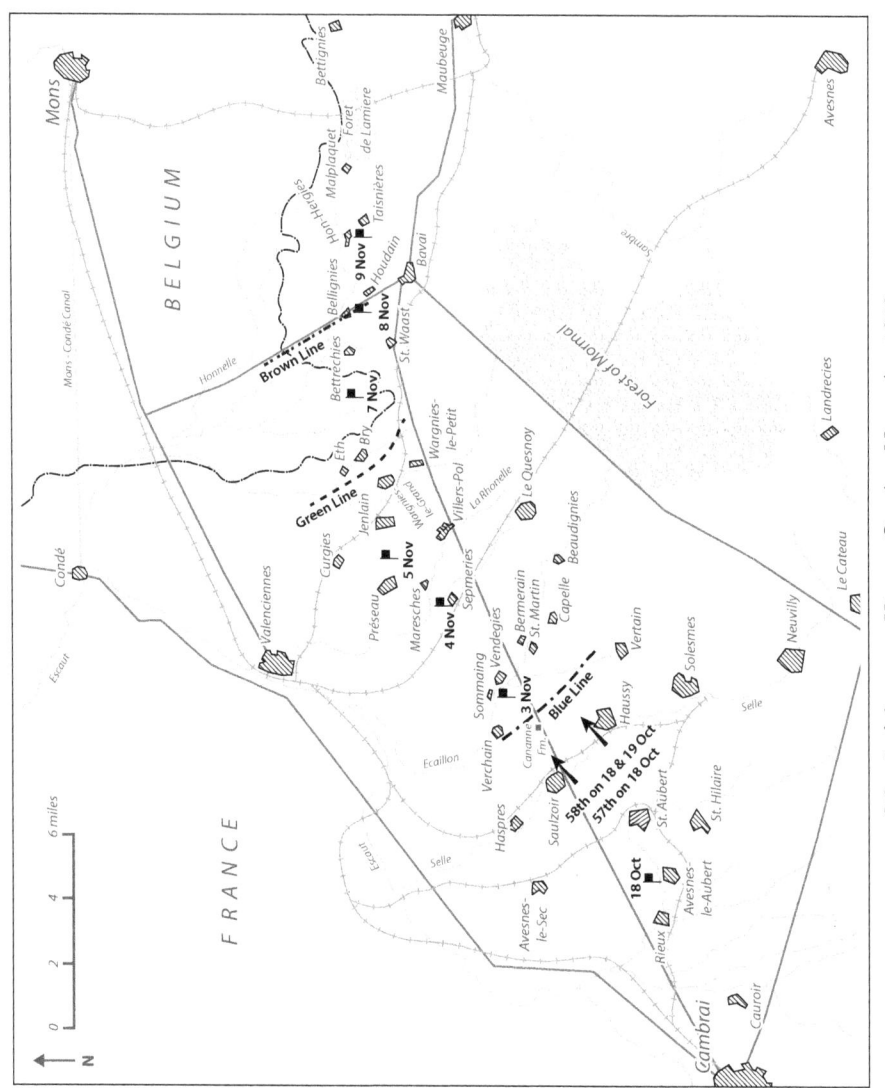

Map 9 Advance to Victory, October–November 1918.

faltering advances, with success at Messines, but with ultimate failure during Third Ypres, and the conscript army that fought, with ultimate success, to quell the ferocity of the German Spring Offensives – would have all willingly swapped their German adversary for the pallid incarnation of late 1918.

The Last Hundred Days

The summer of 1918 finally brought 19th Division the respite from battle they had sought without satiation for four long months. Much of July was spent training and refitting at Rumilly. August saw a return to frontline duty and the revisiting of some familiar haunts: Bethune, Croix Barbee, Richebourg St Vaast and other French hamlets where the division had, three years earlier, first learnt the ropes of trench warfare.

Signs that the fortunes of war had turned in the BEF's favour were immediately detected; 57th Brigade reporting: 'A withdrawal by the enemy discovered during the day [of 5 August], followed up closely by 3rd Worc.R. ... a total advance of 1,000 yards. Little resistance was met with.'[1] Similarly favourable portents had been sensed during February 1917 when the German Army retreated behind the ramparts of the Hindenburg Line, but this time they were to prove anything but chimerical.

Through a succession of 'minor operations', punctuated by a number of larger set-piece attacks, 19th Division pushed the enemy from Neuve Chapelle and beyond (3 to 25 September),[2] through Cambrai (17 to 23 October),[3] and towards the outskirts of Mons (3 to 9 November);[4] before the armistice brought an unexpected end to what had appeared a pursuit without end.

During this chase, reports of: 'The enemy put[ting] up practically no resistance and all objectives [being] gained with slight casualties' were not uncommon.[5] Yet there

---

1   WO95/2084 Headquarters 57th Brigade War Diary (Aug 1918) PRO. See also: '19th Division Intelligence Summary No. 7 from 6am 12/8/18 to 6am 13/8/18'. WO95/2057 (Aug 1918), op cit.;
2   See: '19th Division Order No. 236' dated 2 Sept 1918. WO95/2057 (Sept 1918), op cit. '19th Division Intelligence Summary No. 28 (from 6am 2/9/18 to 3/9/18).' Ibid. '19th Division Order No. 238', dated 17 Sept 1918. Ibid.
3   See: '19th Division Order No. 245' dated 9 Oct; '19th Division Order No. 247' dated 18 Oct; '19th Division Order No. 248' dated 21 Oct. WO95/2057 (Oct 1918), op cit.; 'Narrative of Operations of 57th Infantry Brigade from 17th October to 23rd October inclusive.', written by (or on behalf of) GOC dated 29 Oct 1918. WO95/2084 (Oct 1918), op cit.; WO95/2085 8th Battn. The Gloucestershire Regiment War Diary (Oct 1918) PRO, diary entry 23 Oct.
4   See '58th Infy. Bde. Order No. 285', dated 3 Nov. WO95/2089 (Nov 1918), op cit.; '57th Infantry Brigade Order No. 257' dated 6 Nov.; '57th Infantry Brigade Order No. 258' dated 7 Nov; '57th Infantry Brigade Order No. 259' dated 8 Nov. WO95/2084 (Nov 1918), op cit.
5   WO95/2086 3rd Battn. The Worcestershire Regiment War Diary (Sept 1918) PRO, diary entry 3 Sept. The 10th Worcesters had been absorbed by the 3rd Battalion of the regiment, who joined the division.

were enough black days in the division's diary (particularly 20 September)[6] to remind the infantry that, should the enemy chose to fight, hostile artillery and machine-gun fire could still inflict the severest casualties. The enemy's collective response was, however, rarely strong enough to challenge the division's collective combat morale. The final week of the war saw an advance of over 14 miles, and by 9 November the Welch could report entering 'villages…full of civilians who were very enthusiastic at the return of the British Troops.'[7]

The 19th Division had finally realised the objective they were sent to France and Flanders to achieve; they had become an army of liberation. This hundred day pursuit of the enemy forced the division's senior commanders to comprehend a number of tactical changes; some old, some borrowed and some new. The creeping barrage, and its latest evolution, the 'jumping barrage' (designed to counter the enemy's more disparate lines of defence), remained the hinge of the set-piece attack until November.[8] From this point on DHQ considered that: 'Creeping Barrages take a long time to arrange, tend to restrict the élan of the Infantry and are the cause of delays inseparable to the transport of the large amount of ammunition required', and such fulsome preparations were henceforth deemed prohibitively time consuming and largely redundant.[9] Heavy preliminary bombardments were also no longer considered *de rigueur*. Technical evolutions in the laying of artillery fire (primarily sound ranging and aerial photography), together with the fluidity of the battlefield (less fixed lines of defence), had tipped the delicate balance between destruction, and warning the enemy of imminent attack. From hereon, all barrages began at 'Zero hour'.[10]

The infantry advancing behind these 'creeping barrages' continued to be arranged in platoon formations prescribed by *S.S.143 (1917)*;[11] the succeeding 'fighting patrols', however, had evolved considerably since their first appearances in 1917. This latest guise had evidently been inspired by (uncomfortably) close observation of German

---

6   See: '19th Division Intelligence Summary No. 46 (from 6am 20/9/18 to 6am 21/9/18).' WO95/2057 (Sept 1918), op cit.; 'Narrative of Operations on 20-9-1918' written by CO 21 Sept 1918. WO95/2085 10th Battn. The Royal Warwickshire Regiment War Diary (Sept 1918) PRO.
7   WO95/2092 9th Battn. The Welch Regiment War Diary (Nov 1918) PRO.
8   For details of the 'jumping barrage' see '56th Infantry Brigade Operation Order No. T.E.1.' (orders for a training exercise), dated 30 Oct. WO95/2077 Headquarters 56th Brigade War Diary (Nov 1918) PRO. See '57th Brigade Order No. 258', dated 7 Nov. for details of proposed artillery free advances. WO95/2084 (Nov 1918), op cit.
9   'GA 382/73 'Some Lessons Learnt and Emphasised from the Operations of 19th Division During the Period Oct. 20th – Nov 9th 1918' 'CREEPING BARRAGES. WO95/2057 (Nov 1918), op cit.
10 See for example '56th Infantry Brigade Operation Order No. 155', dated 3 Nov. WO95/2077 (Nov 1918), op cit.
11 See for example: '57th Infantry Brigade Order No. 232', dated 2 Sept. WO95/2084 (Sept 1918), op cit.; WO95/2089 (Sept 1918), op cit. Appended to diary without Order No.

infiltration tactics. 'If some opposition is encountered [DHQ ordered], strong fighting patrols covered by artillery fire will advance and establish themselves at selected points on or near the objective, and will then work their way outwards towards the flanks so as to cut off any pockets of Germans still remaining…the object being <u>deliberately to establish ourselves in salients</u> at certain points in the German outpost screen, and thus compel him to fall back from the remainder of the line if he is to avoid being cut off. Such tactics were very successfully employed against us by the enemy in his recent offensives in March and April of this year.'[12]

As can be determined, the British derivative intended to deploy infiltrating 'fighting patrols' *after* the main attack, as a means of lacerating deeper into the enemy's lines, rather than as the spearhead of the attack. But this diversification was primarily due to the German preference for defending their line in depth, rather than holding the frontline as the main line of resistance.

The 19th Division had also finally been driven to adopt, having dallied throughout the Spring, the German's bold use of forward roaming machine-gun sections (although this particular influence was less overtly stated). Plans for August, for instance, stated that: 'The O.C. 19th M.G. Bn. will arrange to send forward 'Forward Guns' to cover the infantry in their new positions and to assist them in the capture of any small enemy rearguard posts.'[13] Whilst plans for 6 November similarly ordered that: 'Two Sections of M.G's will go forward with the leading Battalions…'[14]

The battlefield innovations of late 1918 were not, however, all inspired by the enemy. By mid-October 19th Division was introducing a method of infiltration that went some way beyond the original German model; proposing to spearhead the advance with an all-arms 'Vanguard' unit. 'From all information to hand the enemy is carrying out a retirement on a large scale. A vigorous pursuit had been ordered along the whole Army front [a plan dated 10 October stated]…the Vanguard will probably consist of the following troops, the whole under the command of the O.C. Battalion: 1 Battalion. 1 Sec. T.M.B. 2 Sec R.F.A. 1 M.G. Coy. 1 Sec. 94th Field Coy. R.E. Divl. Mounted Detachment (less I section)…The Vanguard must act with the greatest vigour and boldness. Its duty is to drive in weak forces of the enemy and so avoid delaying the Main Guard.'[15] The rigid formation of the division, suitable for the largely static trench warfare, would be stripped down and mobilised for a far more fluid battlefield. The development of the 'Vanguard' remained in its infancy, however; not being deployed until the last days of the war.[16]

---

12 '19th Division Order No. 236' dated 2 September. WO95/2057 (Sept 1918), op cit.
13 '19th Division Order No. 232' dated 7 August. Ibid.
14 '57th Infantry Brigade Order No. 257', dated 6 November. WO95/2084 (Nov 1918), op cit.
15 '58th Infantry Brigade Order No. 277', dated 10 October. WO95/2089 (Oct 1918), op cit.
16 The 'Vanguard' was not overtly evident in planning until November 7th. See '57th Brigade Order No. 258', dated 7 Nov. WO95/2084 (Nov 1918), op cit.

The placement of a battalion CO in charge of the proposed 'Vanguard' signals the degree of devolution forced upon the division by the fluidity of the Western Front by autumn 1918. By late September DHQ was proposing that decision making over possible objectives should be devolved entirely to battalion commanders. 'It is essential that every Battalion and Company Commander should have a definite scheme of advance, with a definite objective to gain without waiting for orders from anyone, and that he should communicate his action immediately to Battalions and Companies on his flanks, and to Brigade Headquarters, who will at once inform flank Brigades and Divisional Headquarters. The artillery, also, must be on the alert to change their S.O.S. line immediately to suit the new conditions.'[17]

Such weighty devolution of command was not realised until November, when the fluidity of the battlefield swept away any attempts by senior commanders to hold onto the reigns of command. By 3 November DHQ was offering a 'guide' to possible objectives. 'The lines showing objectives [on maps appended with orders] are purely diagrammatical, the Tactical features in the neighbourhood form the real objectives. Similarly Boundary lines are intended as a guide to frontages. They may always be crossed for tactical purposes …'[18] By 5 November the final decision evidently belonged to the assaulting units – there were no imposed limits. The Fusiliers' CO recorded how 'verbal orders were received that … the Battalion was to … push forward as far as possible without limit. Three objectives were chosen to be taken successively …'[19] All the 'musts' and 'will nots' had been erased from the script; independence and intuition were (literally) the orders of the day. The infantry were now required to think and act on their own volition; not just when it came to rejecting the objective (a decision they had always taken autonomously), but on matters of finding it, and working out how to capture it.

It was not just in matters of command that the infantry now carried a greater weight of responsibility. With the effectiveness of artillery being steadily nullified by the enemy's increasing lack of organised (and therefore detectable and destroyable) defence systems, more of the burden of combat was passing onto the infantry's shoulders. The rapid evolution of the 'fighting patrol' bore testimony to this expanding combat role. The division's senior commanders were again thinking the previously unthinkable; that enemy wire and machine-gun fire were not necessarily the responsibility of the artillery. In firming up plans for the October offensives, DHQ ordered that: 'Once a machine gun post has been located, every endeavour will be made to outflank it and kill or capture the hostile detachment. Full use will be made of all the weapons with which the infantry are provided, and covering artillery and machine gun fire

17 '19th Division Order No. 243', dated 29 September. WO95/2057 (Sept 1918), op cit.
18 '58th Infy. Bde. Order No. 285', dated 3 November. WO95/2089 (Nov 1918), op cit.
19 'Short account of Operations undertaken by the 9th (S) Bn Royal Welch Fusiliers from Nov: 3rd to Novr: 9th 1918.' Written by CO. WO95/2092 'Fusiliers' (Nov 1918), op cit. See also '10th (S) Bn. The Royal Warwickshire Regiment. Narrative of Operations from 7th to 9th Nov. 1918', written by CO. WO95/2085 'Royal Warwicks' (Nov 1918), op cit.

should be employed whenever practicable. Subordinate commanders are not to wait for the machine gun to retire of its own accord or for orders from higher authority. Concentrated machine gun fire is of the utmost value to make the enemy keep under cover, and smoke rifle grenades [another recent innovation] are useful to blind the enemy and conceal the attacking infantry.'[20] Never before had the division's senior commanders made such an overt call for the execution of platoon tactics, and all that this method of fighting entailed.

The call was evidently answered. With the battlefield open and fluid, the dominance of artillery quelled, and the ground not torn asunder by years of trench warfare, there was much greater latitude for the kind of 'minor operations' that had, during the years of trench deadlock, often seemed pointless, wasteful, and consequently worth undermining. Small skirmishes between sections or platoons of 19th Division and equivalent German *Gruppen* continued throughout August. It was here, on the battlefield, that the tenets of platoon tactics, and their adaptation to the 'fighting patrol', were honed and (according to later accounts) near perfected.

The number of infantry involved in these 'fighting patrols', and the degree of 'all-arms' cooperation enlisted, depended upon whether the intention was to raid or capture the enemy's post(s). The raid typically called upon the services of a section of infantry, commanded by a junior officer. The flowing account by DHQ records the near perfect application of platoon tactics by a section of the Shropshires. 'A fighting patrol of 8 men under the command of 2nd Lieut. CLAYTON 1/4th K.S.L.I. immediately went out with the object of surrounding the house [an earlier 'forward patrol' had established that the house was occupied by the enemy] A Lewis Gun was placed on the right flank about [map ref]. Rifle bombers worked round to the left flank… and opened fire on the house, under cover of which the rifle section worked straight forward to the house. The explosion of the bomb brought one of the Officers to the door of the house and he was shot by one of the rifle section. The remaining officer and orderly tried to bolt but the Officer was killed by the Lewis Gun on the flank; the orderly escaped.'[21]

Capturing a post typically required a near platoon strength 'fighting patrol' supported by 'all-arms' of the division. For example, 56th Brigade ordered that: 'A party of the 1/4th Shrops L.I. consisting of 1 Officer and 19 Other Ranks will attack this post on the evening of the 28th August, with the objective of capturing and occupying the post…The attacking party will advance under cover of the barrage and at

20 '19th Division Order No. 243', dated 29 September. WO95/2057 (Sept 1918), op cit. See also '56th Infantry Brigade Operation Order No 154', dated 26 September. WO95/2077 (Sept 1918), op cit.
21 '19th Division Intelligence Summary No. 7 from 6am 12/8/18 to 6am 13/8/18'. Ibid. See also '19th Division Intelligence Summary No. 9 from 6am 14/8/18 to 6am 15/8/18' Ibid.

Zero hour will attack the enemy post. A Lewis Gun team will be held in readiness to occupy the post as soon as it is captured.'[22]

The operation of 'fighting patrols' were then integrated, with an apparent degree of seamlessness, into the division's execution of set-piece attacks. For example, the Welch reported how: 'During the night 3rd/4th [September] orders were received that the 58th Bde would push…fighting patrols out under a barrage at 6am on 4th, with their objective the B line (Old British Support Line). These patrols were to be followed by the remainder of their Coys. A and D Coys therefore pushed on and captured this line without difficulty and they were then ordered to push forward to the OLD BRITISH FRONT LINE.'[23] Whilst a similar operation was executed to advance the line following the set-piece attack of 20 October. 'At midnight 21st/22nd [57th Brigade recorded] a minor operation was carried out to secure the Bridgehead across the River HARPES at [map ref] and to capture the FERME DE RIEUX which had been reportedly occupied by the enemy with a Machine Gun. A fighting patrol was assembled in the ditch at [map ref] and advanced under cover of a trench mortar barrage which was fired from the pit at [map ref]. The patrol found the farm unoccupied as the enemy had hurriedly evacuated the position when the barrage opened. A post was immediately established East of the River.'[24] 'Fighting patrols' were to remain integral to the division's art of attack during the November 'pursuit'.[25]

The successful execution of platoon tactics, in the form of 'fighting patrols', would seem to have required more infantrymen taking an active part in combat. It was certainly feasible that these 'fighting patrols' were formed out of a vanguard of 'committed fighters', as had occurred during the reign of the Bomber in 1916. But the impression given by the evidence is that the burden of combat fell upon whichever platoon(s) happened to be holding the line. The abundance of distance and/or sanitising weaponry (particularly the Lewis Gun) that now dominated the platoon's armoury provides one explanation for any potential increase in active participation.[26] However, these weapons had been in place since 1917 with no significant impact. With the enemy's artillery frequently silent, and his infantry disinclined to fight, the fear of being killed had certainly been substantially erased from the equation. There is, perhaps, one further explanation (one that has occasionally cropped up throughout the division's active service) – a greater tendency to fire upon a retreating enemy.

22 '56th Infantry Brigade Operations Order No. 143', dated 28 Aug. WO95/2077 (Aug 1918), op cit.
23 WO95/2092 'Welch' (Sept 1918), op cit. Diary entry 4 Sept.
24 'Narrative of Operations of 57th Infantry Brigade from 17th October to 23rd October inclusive.', written by (or on behalf of) GOC dated 29 Oct 1918. WO95/2084 (Oct 1918), op cit.
25 For example see 'Narrative of Operations Nov. 3rd – Nov 9th' WO(5/2057 (Nov 1918), op cit.
26 The Royal Warwicks, for example, reported on 19 October 'Trench strength – 22 Officers, 465 O.R. 33 Lewis Guns.' WO95/2085 'Royal Warwicks' (Oct 1918), op cit.

The execution of 'fighting patrols' provided one recorded example. A unnamed 'officers patrol' had stumbled across 'a hostile post', reinforcements were sent for: 'The post [was] now rushed by the patrol. The hostile M'G. [sic] was captured together with four prisoners (one wounded). Two of the enemy who would not come out were killed. In addition it is estimated that at least four more of the enemy who attempted to escape from a post just in rear were killed by L.G. and rifle fire.'[27] This singular account was replicated twice during the set-piece attacks of the last hundred days. For example, the Wiltshires detailed how: 'Patrols again pushed forward and opposition again encountered but not so serious as yesterday. 'C' Coy pushed forward on the right in the attempt to clear a group of houses which had harboured enemy machine guns. With the assistance of T.M's and rifle grenades they made about 7 bosche [sic] run from one house and a Lewis Gun opening on them caused at least 5 to fall as casualties.'[28] This evidence suggests that a retreating enemy may have removed a significant barrier to 'firing'.

The above accounts indicate the domination of 'sanitising' weaponry during these combat episodes, although there is also some evidence of interpersonal combat. The 'fighting patrols' carried out during August, provided one account of unmitigated interpersonal combat. The Wiltshires reported how: 'In the early morning [of the 10th] a forward patrol under 2nd LT SILLARS located enemy machine gun post in field S. of VERT BOIS FARM. Leaving a portion of his patrol to keep touch with enemy 2nd LT SILLARS returned to Company H.Q. to organise the attack. Under covering fire of a Lewis Gun on his right flank and 4 rifle bombers firing No. 36 R.B. from the cup dischargers on his left flank 2nd LT SILLARS accompanied by 2nd Lt STOTHERS led the rifle section to the attack and rushed the post. The enemy fought stubbornly and refused to surrender – 12 of them were killed and 2 taken prisoner, none escaping. While it lasted the fight was fierce. Several of the enemy were knocked on the head with rifle butts. He [presumably 2nd Lieut. Sillars] displayed considerable skill both in the tactical disposition of his small force and in the intelligent use of the various platoon weapons at his disposal. Both 2nd Lt SILLARS and 2nd Lt STROTHERS led the men with great courage and dash and much needed and valuable identification was secured…Both Officers were unfortunately wounded.'[29]

This account offers a fine illustration of how a classic execution of platoon tactics depended largely upon distant and/or sanitary weaponry. But it also vividly demonstrates the nature of combat should one side refuse to take flight or submit. It is worth noting that the 'rifle butt' was apparently used in preference to skewering the enemy. But this is small beer given the amount of interpersonal combat that evidently took

---

27 '19th Divisional Intelligence Summary No. 8 from 6am 13/8/18 to 6am 14/8/18'. WO95/2057 (Aug 1918), op cit.
28 WO95/2093 (Sept 1918), op cit, diary entry 3 Sept. See also WO95/2085 'Royal Warwicks' (Oct 1918), op cit.
29 WO95/2093 (Aug 1918), op cit.

place. The most telling qualification is, once again, derived from its uniqueness. Interpersonal combat remained atypical, and even allowing for the raised chances of its executioners becoming lost to posterity, the fact that senior commanders wanted to read of 'severe hand-to-hand fighting', and a 'real soldiers fight', and the fact that they rarely did, still indicates that the exceptions very much proved the rule.

The set-piece attacks likewise only produced one recorded account of (potential) interpersonal combat. This singular piece of combat behaviour occurred on the 25 September, as the Worcesters successfully recaptured the lost objectives of the 20th. 'A and B Coys attacked taking SHEPHERD'S REDOUBT and the DISTILLERY. All objectives captured, about 80 prisoners and 10 machine guns captured. Our casualties slight … 10th Royal Warwickshire Regt. were unable to conform to our movements on the left, and A Coy had to form a defensive flank, but were able to hold on to their line…6pm Very heavy barrage put down just behind our front line. Enemy immediately attempted to counter-attack, but was scattered by our rifle and Lewis gun fire. *Our men advanced from their trenches to meet the enemy and to escape the barrage. Our line absolutely intact* [my emphasis].'[30]

Comparisons with the combat behaviour of the Worcesters' flanks are telling. The Royal Warwicks, in explaining the 'Reasons for Non-Success', attributed, quite reasonably: 'The heavy shelling of our positions throughout the day and the weight of the counter-attack.'[31] The Worcesters, however, rather than be pushed back by the former, were compelled to advance and thus repelled the latter. Of course, the actions of the Royal Warwicks were the norm, and the behaviour of the Worcesters the exception: as was underlined by the praise heaped upon them by both their brigadier and general. 'Please convey my hearty congratulations to Lt Col. WHALLEY and all ranks of the [3rd] Worcestershire Regiment [Jeffreys effused] on their fine performance in capturing SHEPHERD'S REDOUBT and the DISTILLERY and holding then against all counter attacks'[32]

The above combat episodes aside, the set-piece assaults were evidently bereft of interpersonal combat. Yet the inclinations of the Butterflies were not the lone causation; the enemy themselves (as we have seen) almost always chose flight or submission as the advancing infantry neared. The trend was set on 9 September when 'the 8th GLOUCESTERSHIRE Regt. (57th Bde.) attacked and captured the enemy's front line from [map ref] None of the enemy were encountered and it is thought that he must have evacuated the area as soon as our barrage started.'[33] The attacks of 20 and 25 September reaped a bounty of prisoners; '79 prisoners were captured and several M.Gs'[34] by 57th Brigade on the former, '82' prisoners by the Royal Warwicks during

30 WO95/2086 (Sept 1918), op cit.
31 WO95/2085 'Royal Warwicks' (Sept 1918), op cit.
32 Telegram from Maj-Gen. Jeffreys to Worcesters dated 26 September. WO95/2086 (Sept 1918), op cit.
33 WO95/2057 (Sept 1918), op cit. Diary entry 9 November.
34 WO95/2084 (Sept 1918), op cit. Diary entry 20 Sept.

the latter.³⁵ Similarly: 'The first objective was gained [by the Royal Warwicks] without encountering the enemy' on 20 October, and '1 Officer and 55 other ranks prisoners' secured on the 23rd.³⁶

Evidently the 19th Division's infantry were willing to accept the enemy's surrender: civilian mores and values were being speedily re-established on what was, admittedly, a comparatively benign battlefield. However, the fragile codes of submission were (allegedly) violated by the enemy on 23 October. A 'Coy. Commander of 8th Glouc.R.' reported how: 'Having completed the consolidation of my Company on the Objective about 6.30am I proceeded to my Coy. H.Q. slits about [map ref], a short while after my arrival here the sentry called attention to a party of the enemy who appeared on the Sandpits about [map ref] wearing soft caps, holding up their hands, waving their hands and caps and shouting to attract attention. – presuming they wished to surrender I advanced with two signallers and two runners to bring them in. The enemy immediately opened very heavy fire from two M.G's and also rifle fire on us. We succeeded in regaining our slits. I dealt with the party by means of rifle grenades and the rifle fire of my signallers and runners driving them in a South Easterly direction…in an endeavour to regain their own lines through our new front line, we followed them up and drove them on to the various front posts, who killed or wounded the whole party. I am satisfied that the enemy intended to fire on us after he induced us to approach, their guns were properly mounted and laid, after firing on us they sent up double Green Verey Light Signals and when they eventually withdraw endeavoured to carry away their guns. I estimate their strength at about thirty (30).'³⁷ Here magnanimity quickly disappeared, replaced by incredulity and a spirit of revenge, and the culprits paid for their deception with either their lives or limbs.

Yet a spirit of magnanimity prevailed (suggesting this was an isolated incident of deception) and prisoners continued to flood in into November. 56th Brigade reported 321 captives, 270 taken by the Cheshires,³⁸ whilst the Wiltshires reported a single 'mopping up' operation yielded '50 prisoners being captured from the chateau'.³⁹ Meeting the enemy under any circumstances became an increasing novelty. DHQ recorded for the 4th that 'considerable Machine Gun fire was encountered but was overcome without great difficulty, the German gunners, in most cases, abandoning

---

35   WO95/2085 'Royal Warwicks' (Sept 1918), op cit. Diary entry 25 September.
36   Ibid. Diary entries 20 and 23 October.
37   'Report on action of party of enemy, left in Sandpits about [map ref] after our attack in the early morning of 23rd', written by 'a Coy. Commander of 8th Glouc.R.' WO95/2084 (Oct 1918), op cit.
38   '56th Infantry Brigade Narrative of Operations 3rd to 9th November 1918' written by (or on behalf of) Brig-Gen. R.M. Heath, and dated 23 November 1918. WO95/2077 (Nov 1918), op cit.
39   WO95/2093 (Nov 1918), op cit.

their guns and running away before our infantry could come to close quarters.'⁴⁰ 56th Brigade added that the 'objective was gained with few casualties…The enemy apparently ran as soon as the barrage opened.'⁴¹ The enemy continued to decline interpersonal combat on the 8th, 57th Brigade reporting that: 'A patrol of the enemy was encountered in the village of MALPLAQUET by the 10th R. War. R. This patrol hastily retreated when in close contact with our troops, leaving one prisoner in our hands.'⁴² By the 9th the only mark the enemy was leaving upon the battlefield was his retreating tyre tracks; the Gloucesters reporting that: Enemy machine-guns fired at intervals but withdrew directly our line approached…On the evidence of the inhabitants it appears that many of the enemy departed by motor car just prior to our attack.'⁴³ Brig-Gen Heath's reflection that 'we were now fighting against a beaten and partly demoralised enemy who was weak in effectives and therefore not likely to put in any strong or determined attack to regain ground lost' was seemingly borne out by the Butterflies experiences of the war's last days.⁴⁴

When resistance *was* experienced by the pursuing infantry during set-piece attacks, it was often overcome by a fine demonstration of platoon tactics. Although the Royal Warwicks were subsequently counter-attacked and repulsed on 20 September, the initial capture of 'The Distillery' had drawn from the wisdom of *S.S.143*. 'The final objective along the LA BASSEE Road was gained at 7am. The chief centres of resistance were the DISTILLERY and the cross roads at [map ref]. The DISTILLERY was captured by an encircling movement from both flanks. Here the enemy held strong positions with machine guns. Active bombing took place until the enemy was finally cleared. Many were killed and three M.Gs captured.'⁴⁵

During the set-piece attacks of October, the Royal Warwicks similarly adeptness for the tenets of *S.S.143*. On the 20th local resistance was overcome by autonomous platoons helping one another out. 'On the left of the Final objective … a pocket of about 30 of the enemy held out for some time and were hampering the progress of the left Coy. The two left platoons of this Coy were attracted by this resistance and were knowingly diverted from their correct direction. After killing three of the enemy and taking 19 prisoners these platoons returned to their correct position

---

40 'Narrative of Operations Nov. 3rd – Nov 9th' WO95/2057 (Nov 1918), op cit. See also 'Narrative of Operations from 3rd to 9th [Nov] 1918' WO95/2089 (Nov 1918), op cit.
41 '56th Infantry Brigade Narrative of Operations 3rd to 9th November 1918' written by (or on behalf of) Brig-Gen. R.M. Heath, and dated 23 November 1918. WO95/2077 (Nov 1918), op cit.
42 '57th Infantry Brigade Narrative of Operations from 3rd – 9th November 1918' WO95/2084 (Nov 1918), op cit.
43 WO95/2085 'Gloucesters' (Nov 1918), op cit. Diary entry 9 November.
44 '56th Infantry Brigade Narrative of Operations 3rd to 9th November 1918' written by (or on behalf of) Brig-Gen. R.M. Heath, and dated 23 November 1918. WO95/2077 (Nov 1918), op cit.
45 'Narrative of Operations on 20-9-1918' written by CO 21 Sept 1918.' WO95/2085 'Royal Warwicks' (Sept 1918), op cit.

on the Final objective.'⁴⁶ Whist success was realised on the 23rd partly because the battalion had covered their advance with Lewis Gun fire. 'Enemy points of resistance were easily overcome where our Lewis Gun teams afforded covering fire for the other section which actually attacked the enemy.'⁴⁷ A similar feat was achieved by the North Staffords on 4 November; only, on this occasion, against a rare protracted barrage of hostile fire. 'Almost immediately very heavy Machine Gun Fire was met from the Red Line, and in a short time close 'Pip Squeak' Fire from a Battery just behind BRY. In spite of this the leading Coys. pushed on in admirable fashion by rushes as far as the ridge 250 yards W. of Track to BRY, in [map ref], covering each other by Lewis Gun and Rifle Fire. There was no cover of any description. Going over the ground afterwards I [the CO] counted 7 M.G. position close to WARGNIES-LE-GRAND BRY Road alone, each with a large pile of empty cases.'⁴⁸

The pursuit of November also witness the kind of intuitive display by a junior commander that was vital if the tenets of platoon tactics were to be fully accomplished. DHQ recorded that: 'Meanwhile the 24th Division had been held up [on the 4th] and were unable to reach the GREEN LINE. Realising that the right flank of the Division was exposed to enfilade fire from the Southern portion of WARGNIES LE GRAND, a Company Commander of 9th Cheshire Regt. with his Company mopped up the remainder of the village and attacked and captured a nest of Machine Guns near [map ref]. A considerable number of prisoners were taken in the village and platoon Posts were established.'⁴⁹

Reflecting upon the events of November, DHQ praised the tactical acumen of his junior officers, stating: 'There were many cases where the value of recent training was very clearly shown, and where subordinate Commanders actually put into practice with excellent results the lessons they had been taught.'⁵⁰ The Cheshires' CO was equally fulsome in extolling tactical successes of both leaders and the led, observing that: 'The Battalion profited greatly by recent training. All Infantry and Machine Gun opposition was quickly dealt with by supporting sections pushing round the enemy's flank, whilst the sections held up gave covering fire. These tactics were invariably successful.'⁵¹ It would seem evident that a final victory for the BEF was, to some extent, achieved through a victory for *S.S.143*, and the *esprit de platoon/section*.

---

46 'Narrative of Operations of 10th (S) Bn, The Royal Warwickshire Regiment, from 18-10-18 to 24-10-18', written by CO 26 Oct 1918. Ibid.
47 Ibid.
48 '8th (Service) Battalion North Staffordshire Regiment An account of operations from Nov. 2nd to Nov 9th.' Written by CO. WO95/2082 8th Battn. The North Staffordshire Regiment War Diary (Nov 1918) PRO.
49 'Narrative of Operations Nov. 3rd – Nov 9th' WO95/2057 (Nov 1918), op cit.
50 'GA 382/73 'Some Lessons Learnt and Emphasised from the Operations of 19th Division During the Period Oct. 20th – Nov 9th 1918'. Ibid.
51 Appendix untitled narrative written by CO dated 17 November, comments made under the heading 'chief lessons learnt or emphasised'. WO95/2079 9th Battn. The Cheshire Regiment War Diary (Nov 1918) PRO.

One previously common complaint was noticeable by its absence in the reflections of senior and battalion commanders – 'non-firing'. Indeed, the Cheshire's CO observed that the opposite had been true during the November pursuit. 'Importance of men using their rifles. enemy machine gun and rifle fire was *silenced by our rifle fire*. Rifle bombs were carried and all men were practiced in their use, but they were not fired. I think they might have been used with advantage on several occasions [my emphasis].'[52] Clearly this was not a commander who wanted to denigrate every modern 'sanitising' weapon, which adds further veracity to his claim. We can again postulate that a retreating enemy, and/or a lessened fear of death or injuring, had contributed to this observed increase in active participation in combat. However, the absence of a single reference to the 'bayonet' points to its final death knell in the philosophical battle with the 'bomb' (and every other sanitising weapon that now proliferated upon the battlefield).

Reflections over the operations of the 'Vanguard' were decidedly more ambivalent. Despite the exultations of senior commanders, comprehensive artillery protection remained *sine qua non* against any serious enemy resistance. For example, a 'small stunt' planned by the Wiltshires' CO with the intention of 'bring[ing] the right flank to a suitable jumping off line' for the attack of 20 September, failed when it 'was badly held up by a thick belt of wire which was mostly covered with vegetation [and] Hostile machine guns prevented [the OC] cutting the wire and he was forced to withdraw.' A quickly convened 'Brigade Conference' 'finally decided to postpone it (with sanction from division) until the heavy artillery and trench mortars had cut the enemy's wire and smashed in his concrete machine gun emplacements.'[53] Even during the November pursuit it was occasionally necessary to order comprehensive artillery cover. For example, 58th Brigade recorded how: 'Attempts to push on over this crest [on the 5th] to the spur in [map ref] and the village of BETTRENCHIES were stopped by heavy machine gun fire from a number of machine guns firing from the spur in [map ref]...As soon as it was quite dark two strong patrols were sent forward to try and effect a footing on the Ridge in [map ref]. They were fired at from machine guns all along this Ridge and were unable to get on to it. It was therefore decided to put down a barrage and continue the advance at Dawn.'[54]

A number of battalion COs felt that the 'Vanguard' had proved no substitute for the established pattern of artillery/infantry cooperation. The general complaint being that the artillery had failed to keep pace and, as a consequence, were as likely to shoot their own infantrymen as the enemy's. The Cheshires' CO, for instance, stressed: 'The importance of artillery keeping in touch with progress of Battalions. Throughout operations [of November] the Battalion was hampered and casualties caused by our own artillery. If the artillery have not the time to ensure a reasonable degree of

52 Ibid.
53 WO95/2093 (Sept 1918), op cit., diary entry 19/20 Sept.
54 'Narrative of Operations from 3rd to 9th [Nov] 1918' WO95/2089 (Nov 1918), op cit.

accuracy they had better not fire at all.'⁵⁵ The Royal Warwicks' CO also noted that the artillery were not lone culprits: 'No artillery *or machine gun support* was given [on the 8th] as the guns had not been able to keep pace with our advance [my emphasis].'⁵⁶ However, if the infantry's own distance weapons struggled to realise their role within the 'Vanguard', then battalion COs were partly to blame. It is evident that attached sections of the Machine-Gun Corps were not always deployed 'boldly' (as requested), but used primarily for consolidation purposes. For example, 58th Brigade recorded that the: 'Eight machine guns allotted to the Battalion for this attack [on the 5th] were used partly to protect the Left flank and partly to cover the Eastern slopes of the valley of the HOGNEAU after the capture of the village.'⁵⁷ The Trench Mortars, meantime, were apparently even more underused; 56th Battery complaining that: 'The sections took part in the attack and capture of JENLAIN [on the 4th], but no call was made for their services, although they were well supplied with ammunition.'⁵⁸ The North Staffords' CO, in a rare moment of praise, did, however, record that on the 6th: 'Two Sections F.A. and 8 Vickers were sent up in Support and gallantly took up exposed positions on the ridge…'⁵⁹

DHQ's own somewhat circumspect appraisal of the 'Vanguard' seemed to reflect, albeit with less malignance, the doubts of their battalion COs: 'Forward guns were usefully employed, but the lesson is that training and experience are required to synchronise the action of Infantry in working round strong points and machine gun nests, such as houses, while direct fire is brought to bear on them from forward sections. Co-operation between the Artillery and the front line Infantry in an advance is not easy and requires practice.'⁶⁰

GOC 56th Brigade was, alternatively, fulsome in his praise for the 'Vanguard', and especially the artillery's role in its success; stressing the: 'Very great usefulness of forward guns – throughout the operations of 3rd to 6th November their services were characterised by conspicuous dash and courage. Great keenness to get forward to a position to fire from open sights was shown and every effort was made by the artillery

---

55 Appendix untitled narrative written by CO dated 17 November 1918, recorded under the heading 'chief lessons learnt or emphasised'. WO95/2079 (Nov 1918), op cit. See also: 'Short account of Operations undertaken by the 9th (S) Bn Royal Welsh Fusiliers from Nov: 3rd to Novr: 9th 1918.' Written by CO. WO95/2092 'Fusiliers' (Nov 1918), op cit.; '8th (Service) Battalion North Staffordshire Regiment An account of operations from Nov. 2nd to Nov 9th.' Written by CO. WO95/2082 (Nov 1918), op cit.
56 '10th (S) Bn. The Royal Warwickshire Regiment. Narrative of Operations from 7th to 9th Nov. 1918', written by CO. WO95/2085 'Royal Warwicks' (Nov 1918), op cit.
57 'Narrative of Operations from 3rd to 9th [Nov] 1918' WO95/2089 (Nov 1918), op cit.
58 WO95/2082 56th Light Trench Mortar Battery War Diary (Nov 1918) PRO.
59 WO95/2082 'North Staffords' (Nov 1918), op cit. '8th (Service) Battalion North Staffordshire Regiment An account of operations from Nov. 2nd to Nov 9th.' Written by CO.
60 'GA 382/73 'Some Lessons Learnt and Emphasised from the Operations of 19th Division During the Period Oct. 20th – Nov 9th 1918'. WO95/2057 (Nov 1918), op cit.

to help and coordinate with the movements of the infantry. Further facilities for working with artillery during training would make this cooperation more perfect.'[61]

It is possible that Brig-Gen. Heath had been driven to defend the role of the division's artillery by the vitriol of his battalion COs. As we have frequently seen, especially in the war's last year, as consequence of the desperate circumstances they invariably fought under, the view of the Great War soldier was often myopic in the extreme, with no empathy or understanding for the troubles faced by other branches. On this occasion, Heath almost certainly supplied a necessary corrective.

If the tactical capabilities of 19th Division was being severely challenged during the war's last months, then it is evident that their morale strengths were given a comparatively (in respect to previous set-piece battles) light examination.[62] Subsequent reports of 'no opposition' and hordes of 'prisoners' all point to waning enemy resistance. The infantrymen of 19th Division were wise enough to realise that the German Army was not the foe of old. The Fusiliers' CO perceptively observed that: 'The country in this area [around Maubeuge and Mons] was wooded and full of steep valleys with small streams through them and would, *had the enemy meant to fight seriously*, have been most difficult and costly to capture [my emphasis].'[63] The casualty rates suffered during the period underline the impression given by the qualitative accounts that the German Army had, especially into November, rarely offered a 'serious fight'. The Worcesters experienced an approximate casualty rate[64] of fifteen percent during the set-piece attack 25 September,[65] whilst 57th Brigade as a whole recorded approximate rates just

---

61 'Lessons Learnt' section of '56th Infantry Brigade Narrative of Operations 3rd to 9th November 1918' written by (or on behalf of) Brig-Gen. R.M. Heath, and dated 23 November 1918. WO95/2077 (Nov 1918), op cit.
62 The word 'comparatively' must be stressed here, and the notion of comparison was almost certainly motivating the use of words such as 'easy' to describe the fighting of the war's last days. See for example '8th (Service) Battalion North Staffordshire Regiment An account of operations from Nov. 2nd to Nov 9th.' Written by CO. WO95/2082 'North Staffords' (Nov 1918), op cit.
63 'Short account of Operations undertaken by the 9th (S) Bn Royal Welch Fusiliers from Nov: 3rd to Novr: 9th 1918.' Written by CO. WO95/2092 9th Battn. The Royal Welsh Fusiliers Regiment War Diary (Nov 1918) PRO.
64 Only the Royal Warwicks gave a detailed account of fighting strengths during the war's last months, recording that the 'Fighting Strength at which the Battn went into the line [on 18 October] was 21 Officers. 482 Other Ranks.' 'Narrative of Operations of 10th (S) Bn, The Royal Warwickshire Regiment, from 18-10-18 to 24-10-18', written by CO 26 Oct 1918. W)95/2085 'Royal Warwicks' (Oct 1918), op cit. A fighting strength of around 500 had represented the lower end of a battalion's composition prior to a set-piece attack throughout 1916-18, and has been taken as the mean in all subsequent calculations for this period.
65 The complete breakdown for the 25Sept was recorded as follows: 12 ORs killed; 1 Officer, 65 ORs wounded; 1 OR missing; total casualties 79. This represented a CR of around 15% based upon a approx. FS of 500. Only 19 casualties were suffered on the 20th. WO95/2086 (Sept 1918), op cit.

below thirty percent in total for the two set-piece attacks of October.⁶⁶ 56th Brigade, who bore the brunt of the November pursuit, suffered an approximate casualty rate of just under thirty percent over seven days of combat in this month,⁶⁷ whilst 57th Brigade suffered less than ten percent casualties between the 7th and 9th.⁶⁸

We should therefore expect to find many less infantrymen occupying the lower rungs of the combat behaviour/morale spectrum during the last months of the war. Only on one occasion – the Royal Warwicks on 20 September – did the division record infantrymen 'missing' on a scale which indicates a noticeable degree of surrendering.⁶⁹ The 'exhaustion' noted by many diarists by 7 November was probably, for the most part, 'physical'; brought on by 'troops at this period [being] sopped to the skin and tired out having come approximately 14 miles since the 3rd Nov … and had practically no hot food during the whole period.'⁷⁰ Even so, the Royal Warwicks' conscientiously maintained headcount of shellshock victims indicates that, even during the comparatively 'easy' fighting of November, a few infantrymen became so obviously incapacitated that they had to be sent away from the lines.⁷¹ There were, however, no recordings of 'stragglers'. The gradual decline 'Desertion' experienced by the division

---

66 The complete breakdown for 20 and 23 Oct was recorded as follows: Royal Warwicks 8 Officers, 116 ORs; Gloucesters 9 Officers, 126 ORs; Worcesters: 2 Officers, 89 ORs. This represented CRs of 25%, 27% and 18% respectively based upon a FS of 500. 'Narrative of Operations of 57th Infantry Brigade from 17th October to 23rd October inclusive.', written by (or on behalf of) GOC dated 29 Oct 1918. WO95/2084 (Oct 1918), op cit.
67 The full breakdowns were recorded as follows. Cheshires: 1 Officer, 12 ORs killed; 8 Officers, 110 ORs wounded; 12 ORs missing; total casualties 143, approx. CR 29%. Shropshires: 2 Officer, 16 ORs killed; 2 Officers, 104 ORs wounded; 13 ORs missing; total casualties 137, approx. CR 27%. North Staffords: 4 Officer, 21 ORs killed; 7 Officers, 101 ORs wounded; 9 ORs missing; total casualties 142, approx. CR 28%. '56th Infantry Brigade Narrative of Operations 3rd to 9th November 1918'written by (or on behalf of) Brig-Gen. R.M. Heath, and dated 23 November 1918. WO95/2077 (Nov 1918), op cit.
68 The full breakdowns were recorded as follows. Royal Warwicks: 3 Officer, 11 ORs killed; 1 Officers, 35 ORs wounded; 13 ORs missing; total casualties 63, approx. CR 13%. Gloucesters: 0 Officer, 1 ORs killed; 0 Officers, 5 ORs wounded; 0 ORs missing; total casualties 6, approx. CR 1%. Worcesters: 0 Officer, 5 ORs killed; 2 Officers, 35 ORs wounded; 4 ORs missing; total casualties 46, approx. CR 9%. '57th Infantry Brigade Narrative of Operations from 3rd – 9th November 1918' WO95/2084 (Nov 1918), op cit.
69 The final breakdown of casualties was as follows: 9 ORs killed; 4 Officers, 46 ORs wounded; 56 ORs missing; total casualties 119. *Soldiers Died* records a final toll of 15 ORs killed on 20 Sept. It would, therefore, seem that upward of 50 infantrymen may have surrendered during this action. 'Narrative of Operations on 20-9-1918' written by CO 21 Sept 1918. WO95/2085 'Royal Warwicks' (Sept 1918), op cit.
70 'Short account of Operations undertaken by the 9th (S) Bn Royal Welch Fusiliers from Nov: 3rd to Novr: 9th 1918.' Written by CO. WO95/2092 'Fusiliers' (Nov 1918), op cit.
71 The Royal Warwicks reported 2 shell shocked infantrymen amongst their daily casualties for both 6 and 7 November. '10th (S) Bn. The Royal Warwickshire Regiment. Narrative of Operations from 7th to 9th Nov. 1918', written by CO. WO95/2085 'Royal Warwicks' (Nov 1918), op cit.

further underlines, moreover, that the fluid Western Front of late 1918 was not a battlefield many infantrymen felt compelled to escape from.[72]

72 FGCM sentenced 6 infantrymen of 19th Division for 'Desertion' during Aug 1918. Respective numbers for Sept were 1 Oct 0 Nov 3 and Dec 3. One infantryman was found guilty of the rarely recorded crime of S.18 (SIW) in August. Sentencing remained compassionate and seemingly not driven by the demands of example. 7 of the 13 deserters received non-capital sentences, whilst the remaining 6 all had their original 'Death' sentences commuted, including a Private who had absconded from the 3rd Worcesters on three separate occasions. See WO213/24-7 Judge Advocates General's Office: Field General Court's Martial and Military Courts, Registers. (August to December 1918) PRO.

11

Lessons Learnt

Overview

This final chapter will consider the typicality of 19th Division's experience of war, and the wider implications that can be drawn from the study. To achieve these objective it will compare and contrast the findings of the study with the literature first outlined in Chapter One, whilst also examining the findings of similar 'small unit studies' into the experiences of the allied forces.[1] This synthesis of historical understanding will be arranged around the key themes examined by the study, but will also include a discussion of the light cast by the study on the distinct theme of the allied forces' tactical development, and its part in final victory in late 1918.

Paddy Griffith has demonstrated that generalisations between units over issues of training and tactics are always tentative because, despite the monolithic appearance of the BEF's command structure, subordinate commanders were able to exercise some autonomy.[2] Even so, it is evident from a review of the salient literature that 19th Division's ascent of the tactical and technological learning curve was largely in step with the broad experiences of the allied forces. This study's closer focus upon the *human element* within this learning curve – the subtle interplay between tactics, weapons and the soldiers who were charged with both firing and surviving them – suggests, however, that 'friction' caused by the infantrymen's interaction with certain weapons often hindered the climb. In particular, 'lessons learnt' in late 1916 were not fully implemented upon the battlefield until the autumn of 1918. Moreover, 19th Division's experiences suggest that throughout the war 'infantry verses infantry' conflicts were often sideshows to the more decisive 'artillery verses artillery' duels, and consequently *the* critical learning curve was that ascended by the artillery. It will

---

1   The term 'allied forces' will be used to denote British and Dominion forces serving on the Western Front.
2   Paddy Griffith, *Battle Tactics of the Western Front: The British Army's Art of Attack 1916-18* Yale University Press (2000) 1st ed 1994, p. 29.

be suggested that both apparent facets of the tactical and technological learning curve have been somewhat underplayed by the literature to date.

The allied forces were comprised of human beings who shared the same fragile physiological makeup, and therefore generalisations regarding reactions to combat are perhaps more defendable. It has been outlined in the Methodology that 19th Division's recruitment background and war experiences open the door to guarded generalisations regarding combat behaviour and morale. This study has found that episodes of non-firing, or battlefield pacifism, occurred throughout the war within the ranks of 19th Division and incidences of interpersonal combat were rare. Many infantrymen found themselves either unwilling or unable to execute the soldiers' fundamental role – to kill or maim the enemy, especially at close range.

It could be argued that this was symptomatic of a generally poor fighting unit. This was almost certainly *not* the case. For instance, the division rarely received any complaints regarding its fighting performance from the legion of Corps and Army commanders they served under. GHQ's deployment of its divisions (which offers a tentative guide to a unit's soldierly worth) seems to indicate that 19th Division were at the very least considered 'dependable'. 19th Division were rarely called upon to spearhead an attack, which may indicate that the Butterflies were not considered in the same league as, say for example, the much used Dominion formations, or 2nd and 9th Divisions of the BEF.³ But they do seem to have been considered a reliable unit to flank an attack – an important battlefield role. The division's overuse during the spring of 1918 was, according to their own accounts, an unfortunate accident. But their continued deployment during the last hundred days suggests that GHQ's generally good regard of 19th Division remained untainted by events earlier in the year.

Establishing that 19th Division's infantry were not 'duds' and/or considered a 'line holding unit' certainly aids the forwarding of potential generalisations over their combat behaviour and morale. But what if it could be established that 19th Division were an 'elite' unit? Such an appraisal would surely hold deep implications for the potential widespread typicality of the division's experiences of battlefield pacifism. Both Griffith's and Peter Simkins' comparative analyses of the combat performance of allied forces on the Western Front confer a guarded 'elite' status upon 19th Division.⁴ For example, Simkins finds that the division was one of only two (the other being 66th Division) that enjoyed a one hundred percent success rate in the twelve 'attacking operations' carried out between August and November 1918. They were also one of five units (9th, 16th, 19th, 25th and 66th) that, by Simkins' criteria, outshone the undeniably successful Dominion units. 19th Division's position on this spectrum of combat performance seems all the more credit worthy when we consider that they

---

3   See Paddy Griffith op cit., p. 81.
4   Ibid., p. 80; Peter Simkins, 'Co-Stars or Supporting Cast? British Divisions in the 'Hundred Days', 1918' in Paddy Griffith (ed) *British Fighting Methods in the Great War* Frank Cass (1996), pp. 50-69, p. 56.

were one of only five units involved in the last hundred days to have fought in all three of the defensive battles of the previous spring.[5] Thus, the findings of this study raise the possibility that even amongst elite units many soldiers may have found themselves unable to break the civilian and religious codes of 'thou shall not kill'.

Combat Behaviours and the Learning Curve

In 1996 Peter Simkins decried what he perceived as the continuing reluctance of military historians to witness the great tactical and operational advances made by the BEF between 1914 and 1918. 'Sadly, the hundreds, if not thousands, of after-action reports and narratives contained in the army, corps, divisional, brigade and battalion war diaries – which clearly demonstrate that a great deal of post-battle analysis and evolution was, in fact, carried out by the officers of the BEF – remain unfamiliar territory for all too many writers on the conflict.'[6] Simkins' words have proved more of a rallying cry than a lament. Since the early 1990s a number of studies have emerged which have, in academic circles at least, finally laid to rest the notion that British generalship on the Western Front was dominated by 'Donkeys'[7] and 'Butchers and Bunglers',[8] and that innovation and intuition were the sole preserve of the German Army, or the late arriving American forces.[9] It is now overwhelmingly evident that the BEF and Dominion forces learnt from and adapted to the problems raised by superior defensive firepower and the subsequent emergence of trench warfare (dominated by the defensive triad of artillery, barbed wire and machine-guns). Where there remains lively debate is over the origins and subsequent trajectory of the various forces' 'learning curves'.

As the BEF ascended the learning curve so the anticipated role of the infantryman evolved. According to Desmond Morton in his groundbreaking study of the Canadian Expeditionary Force (CEF): 'The fifty months from August 1914 to November 1918 witnessed a remarkable transformation in almost everything that affected the soldiers.'[10] Richard Holmes uses the analogy of the difference between a 'gamekeeper' and an 'industrial worker' to illustrate the deep impact of technological and tactical changes upon the soldiers' experience.[11] The experiences of 19th Division, however, caution against any notion that Great War infantrymen responded to new weapons

---

5   Peter Simkins op cit., pp. 55-6.
6   Peter Simkins op cit., p. 51.
7   Alan Clarke, *The Donkeys* Pimlico (2000) 1st ed 1961.
8   John Laffin, *Butchers and Bunglers of World War One* Sutton Publishing (1992) 1st ed 1988.
9   For a recent exposition of this thesis see John Mosier, *The Myth of the Great War: A New Military History of World War One* Profile Books (2001).
10 Desmond Morton, *When Your Number's Up: The Canadian Soldier in the First World War* Random House of Canada (1993), p. viii.
11 Richard Holmes, *Tommy: The British Soldier on the Western Front 1914-1918* Harper Collins (2004), pp. 365-7.

and tactics like automata. Weapons have a psychological impact upon their users that sometimes usurp the best laid plans of commanders. Throughout the war the 'friction' caused by the division's interaction with certain weapons (along with other factors) ensured that the division's 'learning curve' was often rather more undulating than the current historiography sometimes suggests.

The Butterflies of 1915 were unlikely to handle any weapon beyond the rifle and bayonet. By the eve of the Somme, however, the BEF's policy of specialisation and centralisation had turned upward of thirty five percent of infantrymen into 'specialists' – handling either a machine-gun, trench mortar or bomb – most operating under the command of brigade. Meantime, the BEF's attendant policy of 'cumulative aggression', whilst flawed in its belief that the balance of firepower could be mastered through 'minor operations', bequeathed the infantry a dependence upon the bomb, and the specialist role of the 'Bomber'. Consequently, throughout the Somme offensives, the division's infantry attacked with a diminutive sharp end and a hefty tail; with Bombers at the head, supported by brigade specialists, and supplied by the remaining riflemen. This devotion to the 'bomb' was common to all allied forces at this time.[12] Paddy Griffith describes a 'cult of the bomb' spreading throughout the BEF.[13] Similarly, Bill Rawling, in his own study of the CEF, states that 'the British Army expected troops to take trenches in hand-to-hand fighting. The Canadian infantry, however, much preferred using bombs.'[14] However, Rawling also indicates that the CEF never embraced 'specialisation' with the same commitment as the BEF; bombing was encouraged as a universal art by late 1915, and efforts were made to familiarise all troops with emerging automatic weaponry such as the Lewis Gun.[15]

The failure of the Somme Offensive to break the German Army led to a tactical rethink that significantly advanced the 19th Division's expected combat role. It was primarily motivated by the acceptance that senior commanders could not control the post-zero battlefield; particularly after the German Army's adoption of 'defence in depth' tactics. A solution was sought in the more mobile and flexible 'autonomous fighting platoon', armed with every weapon currently available to the infantry, and all under the immediate charge of a junior infantry commander. Not only did 'platoon tactics' make junior officers more elemental to success or failure, but the NCOs and men of the platoon also had to display a tactical acumen and weapons expertise largely unknown to the original volunteers. In particular, three-out-of-four other ranks were

---

12 A.D. Harvey illustrates the ubiquity of the 'hand grenade' during the Great War by showing how seventeen percent of all commemorative acts of bravery involved the use of this weapon: 'No other weapon, not even the rifle, was instrumental in the winning of so many VCs.' A.D. Harvey, 'The Hand Grenade in the First World War' in *R.U.S.I. Journal* Vol. 138 No. 4 (1993) pp. 44-47, quote p. 44.
13 Paddy Griffith op cit., p. 68.
14 Bill Rawling, *Trench Warfare: Technology and the Canadian Corps, 1914-1918* University of Toronto Press (1992), p. 72.
15 Ibid., p. 58.

now expected to handle specialist weaponry (Lewis Gun, rifle grenade or bomb), whilst increasingly, 'everyman' was expected to be a *pro tempore* specialist, especially in the arts of the machine-gun.

All allied forces sought a solution to the deadlock of trench warfare through the reinvigoration and improvement of small unit tactics. Morton describes how: 'In the months after the Somme, Canadian infantry battalions rediscovered platoons…A permanently constituted platoon with four specialized sections represented a fighting team that an officer might be able to control … Leaders and men would know each other and, through briefings and rehearsals, all would know what to do. It had taken a long time, but Canadian infantry would be organized and trained to fight their own battles and not to be patriotic automata.'[16] Rawling concurs, stating that: 'Various tactical developments [within the CEF] led to a different way of waging war, relying on fire and movement and the actions of small units.'[17] Glyn Harper details similar evolutions within the New Zealand forces: 'Infantry tactics had also been modified as a result of the slaughter on the Somme in 1916. Infantry units now advanced across no-man's land in smaller, nonlinear columns with emphasis on the technique of fire and movements.'[18] In delineating developments within the BEF, Griffith argues that the emergence of platoon tactics represented a watershed in the art of war. 'SS. 143 may be seen as a vital milestone in tactics, marking a change-over from the Victorian era of riflemen in lines to the twentieth-century era of flexible small groups built around a variety of high-firepower weapons.'[19]

We should not, however, expect to find it possible to draw a uniform learning curve from the experiences of the allied forces, because much of this learning process was a 'bottom up' development; hence why this study has often applied the phrase *self-learning curve*. 19th Division scripted its own *Standard organization* in response to the lessons learnt on the Somme, but the close similarities with the official dictums of *SS 143* and *SS 135* place large question marks over the division's claims to originality. Nevertheless, the development of a 'Divisional School', and the growing ethos of disseminating 'lessons learnt' between battalions (via the columns of the post-battle reports), does indicate a degree of divisional level autonomy in the learning process. Griffith suggests that this balance between autonomy and uniformity was quite common throughout the BEF, resulting in the emergence of a loose 'doctrine'.[20] Morton places greater emphasis upon the bottom-up process, stating that: 'Since GHQ and its army headquarters offered little more than grand directives and windy principles, corps and divisions had to develop specific tactics for the tough problems

---

16 Desmond Morton op cit., pp. 163-4.
17 Bill Rawling op cit., p. 6.
18 Glyn Harper, *Massacre at Passchendaele: The New Zealand Story* Harper Collins (2000), p. 20.
19 Paddy Griffith op cit., p. 78.
20 Paddy Griffith, 'The Extent of Tactical Reform in the British Army' in Paddy Griffith (ed – 1996) op cit., pp. 1-22, esp. pp. 3-4.

the Germans regularly created.'²¹ Rawling is rather more charitable over the role of GHQ, suggesting the wide net thrown out by the Canadians in search of tactical advances enmeshed some of the wisdom of *SS 143*, along with catches from the French experiences at Verdun, and observations of German methods on the Somme.²² Clearly tactical development upon the Western Front could not take place within a vacuum, and 19th Division's experiences of a *two-way* learning process would seem to have been reasonably typical.

Yet the adoption of a plethora of semi-automatic weapons and emergence of the autonomous fighting platoon did not fundamentally change the Butterflies behaviour in combat during 1917. It could be argued that this delay in realising the potential of platoon tactics places 19th Division amongst the slow learners upon the Western Front. For example, Rawling argues that the CEF's successful deployment of small unit tactics was instrumental in the capture of Vimy Ridge, 9 April 1917.²³ Whereas the first signs that platoon tactics had infiltrated the Butterflies was not until that autumn on the Menin Road, and they were not instrumental in success until the following autumn. It was the 'class of late 1918', the young 'green' conscripts of 19th Division, more so than the 'class of 1917', who finally enacted the combat roles scripted by platoon tactics. However, Rawling's own delineation of the CEF's achievements at Vimy Ridge allows that platoon tactics could not overcome German concrete strongpoints untouched by artillery fire: 'platoon tactics could not come into play until troops were within Lewis-gun and rifle grenade range of the enemy (about 100 yards), and to get there they needed artillery to pound strong points and keep defenders away from the parapets.'²⁴ Indeed, Morton's retelling of the same battle argues that it was primarily improvements in artillery, especially in counter-battery work, that led to the Canadian's successes.²⁵ 19th Division's experiences would seem to attest that the key to success or failure on the battlefields of the Western Front lay largely beyond the infantry's grasp, and in the hands of the artillery. Dale Blair's close longitudinal study of the 1st Battalion Australian Imperial Force (AIF) offers credence to this vision of a continued subordinate role for the infantry. In Blair's retelling, artillery remained king, and the digger's primary role was to 'occupy' the enemy's blown out trenches and then steel himself to survive the inevitable counter-bombardment; a role that left very little room for his alleged individualism or initiative.²⁶

The essential infantry lesson to learn, therefore, was *good artillery cooperation*. The nature of infantry/artillery cooperation within 19th Division also underwent considerable evolution. The simple maxim that artillery would conquer and infantry occupy

---

21 Desmond Morton op cit., p. 162.
22 Bill Rawling op cit., esp. pp. 8-36, p. 47 & p. 97.
23 Ibid., p. 114.
24 Ibid., p. 128.
25 Desmond Morton op cit., p. 168.
26 Dale Blair, *Dinkum Diggers: An Australian Battalion at War* Melbourne University Press (2001), p. 107.

gave way to a new principle: the artillery, primarily through a 'creeping barrage' (increasingly complimented by brigade machine-gunners and trench mortars) would 'neutralise' the enemy's fire sufficiently long enough to allow the infantry to advance unscathed and fight the enemy in his trenches. Griffith's account of the evolving 'creeper' indicates that the division's experiences were fairly typical. The artillery's primary role shifted from destruction to 'neutralization' during 1916, with the journey beginning after the failed assault of 1 July, and increasing reliability being achieved throughout 1917.[27] Rawling indicates, however, that the 'creeping barrage' made its debut at Neuve Chapelle in March 1915, where the artillery protected the infantry advance through a series of 'lifts', albeit at some distance ahead of the advancing troops.[28] Reliance upon the 'creeper' nominally left the task of injuring the enemy to the infantry, but in reality the Butterflies found that defenders who had been battered for hours by artillery fire, and/or forced to keep their heads down until the advancing infantry were upon them, often chose flight or submission over fight. Consequently, the battles of 1917, if the artillery performed their protective role successfully, invariably unravelled into two part performances; 'getting there', and 'staying there' – the latter often proving decidedly more troublesome than the former.

Blair's account of the 1st Battalion AIF's attack on Pozières demonstrates the common experience, by mid-Somme campaign, of the 'two part attack', and how the infantry's aggressive part in this form of combat was often minimal. The Australian infantry advanced without much opposition, and then were strafed mercilessly until relief; during this time each side's infantry fired hardly a shot at one another, and the diggers main task became mentally and physically surviving the incessant bombardment.[29] The 19th Division experiences suggest that 'part two' of the battle – consolidation – invariably hinged upon the counter-battery work of the artillery. Despite major evolutions in the infantry's combat role, therefore, the decisive battle upon the Western Front remained 'artillery versus artillery'.

From Civilian to Soldier

On the evidence of 19th Division's experiences, infantry training methods underwent a less elevated learning curve. Eric Leed offers a fine summation of the essential goal of military training: 'The purpose of training is to identify the soldier as an aggressor and to get the soldier to accept that identification.'[30] Put differently, military training aims to strip the soldier of his civilian mores and values. The division were the recipients of a number of stimuli designed to persuade the civilian to adopt a soldiery

---

27 Paddy Griffith (1996) op cit., p. 10.
28 Bill Rawling op cit., p. 27.
29 Dale Blair op cit., pp. 108-119.
30 Eric Leed, *No Man's Land: Combat and Identity in World War I* Cambridge University Press (1979), p. 105.

mentality: obedience, weapons competency, conditioning, loyalty to a cause or body higher than oneself, threat of punishment and leadership.

Obedience remained the first priority, particularly for the 'green' recruit, and parade ground 'Drill' the preferred manner of delivery. This was common to all allied forces. Morton, for instance, states that: 'Training [in the CEF] continued as it had been. Traditions and past practices were hard to change…Parade-square and 'eyewash' were almost as conspicuous in 1918 training programs as they had been in 1915.'[31] This fixation with 'Drill' was founded partly upon the belief that obedience would become habit, and subsequently, amidst the chaos of the battlefield, the infantryman would fire his weapon when ordered; like an automaton. Given this conviction, it is understandable why so much effort was expended over 'Drill'. Add a degree of weapons *competency* (which was delivered through rifle-range musketry, with additional specialist classes, which grew in profusion as the number of specialists increased) and the ingredients were in place for the perfect combat soldier. Leed's understanding of how Drill functioned is rather more simplistic and brutal. The drill sergeant oppressed the young recruit to the point where, desiring to become the oppressor rather than the oppressed, he took his revenge upon the enemy.[32] This was certainly not the BEF's official dictum, and not a method ever recorded by 19th Division. Indeed, it would seem to fit better with the armies of Nazi Germany and Imperial Japan in the next war.[33]

Leed's analysis also misses the mark because obedience did not function in isolation; not least of all because, in 19th Division's experience, the BEF invested a great deal of time and energy in a number of other stimuli. One significant area of investment remained battlefield *conditioning*. Conditioning the soldier to kill rested primarily upon the 'Bayonet'. The BEF steadfastly believed that skewering a sandbag with a bayonet would naturally inspire and inure the infantryman towards skewering his fellow man. With absolute justification, this prioritising of the bayonet was based upon the belief that a man willing and able to kill his adversary close-up with cold steel should suffer no barriers to any other form of combat. 19th Division's experiences indicate, however, that parade-ground bayonet drill failed to deliver an army of interpersonal killers.

Within the ranks of 19th Division the stimuli of *loyalty to a cause or body higher than oneself*, alternatively, underwent considerable transformation in both source and method as the war ground on. The instigation of platoon tactics in 1917 witnessed a seismic shift in the source of *esprit de corps*; descending from the regiment to *esprit de platoon*, and encompassing *esprit de section* from 1918 onwards. John Bourne has suggested that, what later armies would call 'loyalty to the primary group', had working-class civilian roots, being derived from the 'mutuality' of the workplace, and

---

31   Desmond Morton op cit., p. 92.
32   Eric Leed op cit., p. 105.
33   See for example Omar Bartov, *Hitler's Army: Soldiers, Nazis, and War in the Third Reich* Oxford University Press (1991).

the BEF were the accidental beneficiaries of its morale potency.[34] It was certainly the case that the 19th Division embraced loyalty to the primary group because of continuing concerns over battlefield command, more so than over their infantry's morale. The devolution to platoon tactics naturally suggested a concomitant emphasis upon the morale of the platoon (and later section), rather than a recognition that comradeship could provide a potent morale force upon the battlefield. The BEF could also not convincingly claim (although they tried) to have initiated the means by which this newly discovered loyalty to the primary group would be engendered and quickly cultivated. It was on the playing field that *esprit de platoon/section* was planned to ignite, the preferred torch being the working man's favourite pastime, football. As John Fuller has argued, this transposition of working-class cultural norms from civilian to military life was a largely bottom-up process, and one that the BEF initially tried to scupper.[35]

If all other stimuli should fail, then there was always the threat of *punishment* to bolster the infantryman who found his combat morale wavering. Coercive discipline does not appear to have been the primary stimuli within 19th Division's motivational locker. At most, it seems to have functioned as a silent menacing presence, a malevolent safety-net should all else fail. Gerald Oram has demonstrated that death sentences within the BEF tended to increased on the eve of major battles, suggesting the ultimate example was used as a pre-emptive bolster to morale, but there appears to have been no similar correlation within 19th Division.[36] During the German Spring Offensives, when DHQ certainly feared that all else was failing, the threat of punishment momentarily took on a far more forceful presence. However, the role of compulsion diminished along with the threat of impending German victory.

The various strands of combat stimuli were brought together in the division's junior battalion commanders. The junior officer oversaw all modes of training, was the other rank's immediate source of authority (allowing for the role of NCOs), his first point of contact with military discipline, and the beacon of primary group loyalty. But it was his exemplary role that the division's senior and battalion commanders lauded above all other stimuli. The belief that *exemplary leadership* by junior battalion commanders would infuse those he led remained a cornerstone of the division's thinking throughout the war. The democratisation of the officer-class from 1917 onwards had little effect upon the division's ability to find exemplary leaders. And although the chain of command also dallied with passing the baton of exemplary leadership on to NCOs, it never brought itself to fully enact this seismic shift in battlefield inspiration. There

---

34 John M. Bourne, *Britain and the Great War 1914-1918* Edward Arnold (1989) esp. Chap. 9 'Comradeship, Discipline and Morale' pp. 199-224 & John Bourne, 'The British Working Man in Arms' in Hugh Cecil & Peter H. Liddle, (eds) op cit., pp. 336-352.
35 John G. Fuller, *Troop Morale and Popular Culture in the British and Dominion Armies, 1914-1918* Clarendon Press (1990).
36 Gerald Oram, *Worthless Men: Race, Eugenics and the Death Penalty in the British Army During the First World War* Francis Boutle Publishers (1998).

was nothing unique in 19th Division's heavy dependence upon the exemplary qualities of its temporary junior officers. Holmes illustrates the BEF's continued dependence upon the exemplary leadership of its junior commanders, but adds that this reliance wasted the leadership potential of its non-commissioned ranks.[37] Morton's summary of the qualities required of a Canadian junior officer indicates similar dependence within the CEF: 'they gave leadership, took responsibility, and set an example, if necessary, by dying.'[38]

Trench Raiding

From late 1915 onwards the conviction spread throughout the BEF that the brittle cast of training ground fighting spirit could only be beaten into a finely honed sharp-end through mild exposure to the 'real thing'. Consequently, for the remainder of the war, a much more direct form of battlefield conditioning was attempted through the policy of 'trench raiding'. The earlier literature unequivocally condemned the notion that raiding could raise the confidence, and thus the morale, of fledgling soldiers. Charles Moran called upon the full might of his weighty prose to denounce trench raiding for 'dissipat[ing] like a spendthrift not only the lives but the moral heritage of the youth of England.'[39] Along with most things concerning the allied forces, this outright condemnation has undergone revision. Amongst the historians of tactics and technology trench raiding is generally witnessed as an important factor within the learning curve – although most writers add the caveat that raids were rarely popular with soldiers. For example, Simkins states that: 'Despite their unpopularity with the troops themselves, such operations…made a substantial contribution to the BEF's tactical education.'[40] The 19th Division's experiences indicate that raiding during the early part of 1916 may have helped the infantry develop the arts of the bomb fight, and, to some extent, all-arms cooperation. During 1917, raids also provided a (albeit often barren) practicing ground for platoon tactics. The Butterflies' continued disinclination towards raiding, however, suggests that the policy remained similarly unpopular within the ranks of 19th Division.

The morale qualities of raiding have also experienced a minor revision in some quarters. Peter Liddle's and Keith Simpson's recasting of the 'average' British infantryman into a keen and committed trench fighter essentially portrays trench raiding as a necessary outlet for the pugnacious drives of the British Tommy.[41] Because most historians

37 Richard Holmes op cit., pp. 537-8.
38 Desmond Morton op cit., p. 107.
39 Lord Moran, *The Anatomy of Courage* The Keynes Press (1984) 1st ed 1945, p. 53.
40 Peter Simkins op cit., p. 52. See also Paddy Griffith (1994) op cit., p. 62; Bill Rawling op cit., pp. 48-9.
41 Peter Liddle, 'British Loyalties: The Evidence of an Archive' in Hugh Cecil & Peter H. Liddle, (ed) op cit., pp. 523-38, p. 525. See also Peter H. Liddle (1985) (ed) *'Home Fires and Foreign Fields'* op cit; Peter H. Liddle, *The 1916 Battle of the Somme: A Reappraisal* Leo

do not share this vision of the aggressively inclined footslogger, the morale efficacy of raiding remains largely doubted. Both Rawling and Morton share this study's view that, 'since only the best from the battalion volunteered for such operations', raiding always carried the unwanted caveat of losing a unit's most committed trench fighters before the main event; which did little for the collective morale of a unit.[42] This study has also argued that there was a fine line between useful conditioning and the first descents towards battle fatigue. Significantly, Blair reveals that the AIF's policy of 'peaceful penetration' (a rather euphemistic term for the continuous execution of small raids) during the period April to July 1918, whilst achieving its battlefield objectives, resulted in a near epidemic of psychological breakdowns.[43] Blair is also quick to dispel the 'myth' that the Australians gladly embraced raiding: 'It has been suggested that the Australians actually enjoyed raiding and patrolling, viewing that mode of warfare as an exciting but deadly game. The suggestion that the men enjoyed such operations has little credibility.'[44] Tim Bowman's largely quantitative analysis of the disciplinary record of Irish regiments during the Great War has concluded that: 'There seems to be little evidence, however, that trench raids did anything to raise morale. Equally, in terms of discipline, it is noticeable that units which actively engaged in trench raids, such as the 9th Battalion, Royal Irish Rifles, often had poor disciplinary records.'[45] It would seem, therefore, that this study's conclusion that trench raiding was a flawed policy, insofar as morale was concerned, is in keeping with the general thrust of the literature.

The Committed Few

The occurrence of non-firers, or battlefield pacifism, remains a hidden history of the First World War. The hardships and the sufferings of the frontline soldier have (quite rightly) been well documented, but his behaviour in combat has received comparatively little academic interest. This has resulted in the largely unquestioned assumption that

---

Cooper (1992); Peter Liddle, 'Passchendaele Experienced: Soldiering in the Salient during the Third Battle of Ypres' in Peter H. Liddle, (ed) *Passchendaele in Perspective: The Third Battle of Ypres* Leo Cooper (1997) pp. 305-323; Keith Simpson 'The British Soldier on the Western Front' in Peter H. Liddle (ed) op cit., pp. 135-158.

42 Bill Rawling op cit., p. 47. Morton acknowledges that, alongside the Scots and Australians, the Canadians have a reputation for being the most committed raiders on the Western Front, but remains ambivalent over their worth, suggesting raids 'brought some individuality and adventure to an otherwise 'industrialized' war, but at a high price…heavy losses [which] included the infantry's most enthusiastic officers and soldiers…' Desmond Morton op cit., p. 127.
43 Dale Blair op cit., pp. 146-7.
44 Ibid., p. 139.
45 Tim Bowman, *The discipline and morale of the British Expeditionary Force in France and Flanders 1914-18, with particular reference to Irish units* Ph.D. thesis University of Luton (1999), p. 334.

most men tried to fulfil the fundamental role of the combat soldier – to kill or maim the enemy. It is clear that the evidence is out there – hiding in the complaints of senior commanders, the post-battle reports of junior officers, the 'lessons learnt' columns, the battle narratives of the war diaries, and in the lists of casualties (or rather, the 'non-battlefield casualties') – but the historian must be willing to forgo their heavy dependence upon personal sources, particularly post-war memoirs, and the narratives of 'good soldiers' that tend to dominate the archive. More fundamentally, the historical enquiry into the soldiers' experiences of the Great War must first recognise the historical phenomenon of non-firing; we may then find that even the historian of experience's traditional sources are replete with hints and inferences of battlefield pacifism.

A close examination of 19th Division's official archive reveals that battlefield pacifism, although rarely widespread, was a common occurrence amongst the ranks of the Butterflies. The chain of command lauded the 'rifle and bayonet' for much the same reasons the Victorians lauded piety; not because its use was prevalent throughout their society's ranks, but because they wished it was. It was commonplace for only 'a gallant few' to take an active part in endeavouring to kill or maim the enemy. From the trench raids of early 1916 emerged the committed trench fighters, those infantrymen willing and able to execute (something appropriating) interpersonal combat. Their ranks were replenished, but rarely swelled, as the war ground on. They were joined by a greater number of infantrymen willing and able to fight the enemy with semi-automatic weaponry such as machine-guns and rifle grenades; but even this conclusion is based upon the guarded assumption that most operators of semi-automatic weapons were firing with intent to hit the enemy. Making 'everyman a specialist' from 1917 onwards did not compel every man to take an active part in combat. It is probable, however, that the two divergent circumstances of 1918 – desperate defence (the German Spring Offensive) and fighting a defeated enemy (the last hundred days) – increased the number of infantrymen taking an active part in combat.

Nevertheless, throughout the war many of 19th Division's infantrymen remained committed non-firers. The belligerent trench fighter of Keith Simpson's and Peter Liddle's depiction was clearly a marginal figure within the ranks of the division. The same can be said of potential recruits for Joanna Bourke's army of wanton killers. Volunteers there were, but in truth it was a very small band of men, often drowned out by the marching beat of the more pacifistic majority.[46] On the evidence of these findings, David A. Grossman's reluctant combative, unable to overcome the inhibitors of either social learning or innate programming, was a far more common soldier on the division's sector of the Western Front.[47]

46 Joanna Bourke, *An Intimate History of Killing: Face-to-Face Killing in Twentieth-Century Warfare* Granta Books (1999),esp. pp. 13-16.
47 Dave Grossman, *On Killing: The Psychological Cost of Learning to Kill in War and Society* Little, Brown & Company (1995).

Significantly, an understanding of the potential ubiquity of non-firing has recently emerged from two studies into the Dominion soldier's experiences. The 'digger myth' portrays the Australian infantryman as a superhuman combat soldier; very much at odds with the reconstructed infantrymen of this study. Blair's interpretation of the Australian infantrymen's combat behaviour and morale brings the digger more into line with the Butterfly. During the fighting at Gallipoli 'inertia' (giving up the option of fighting), straggling, and the disorderly rout, were all modes of combat behaviour enacted by the 1st Battalion at Anzac Cove.[48] Blair concludes that '*some of its men* had displayed exceptional courage, and in accordance with the Division's pre-battle instructions, had attempted to 'push on at all costs'; *some, not all* [my emphasis]'[49] In summarising the Diggers performance upon the Western Front, Blair similarly concludes that most Australian infantrymen played a supporting role to the minority of 'desperate fighters' whose actions determined success or failure.[50] Blair borrows the phrase from Morton's summation of the Canadian infantrymen's combat behaviour under fire: 'Terrified soldiers forgot how to use their rifles or to pull the pin from a grenade. Finding themselves alone in the terrible din, brave men panicked, fled, and then returned, weaker than ever, for a second try ... *Most soldiers*, laden down with weapons, ammunition, and kit, *were supporting players for the minority of desperate fighters* [my emphasis].'[51]

Strangely, neither author makes any further comment upon on this facet of combat behaviour they deem 'typical'. In particular, Blair does not attempt to link the Australian's battlefield pacifism into the 'digger myth' he seeks to expose. But it must surely be telling that two armies commonly regarded as comprising some of the best soldiers on the Western Front should allegedly contain so many combat passengers. Both studies undoubtedly add credence to the potential typicality of 19th Division's widespread experiences of non-firing.

Like most studies of the soldiers' experience, Morton's delineation of discipline and morale identifies the *fear of being killed* as the main force wearing away at the 'soldier's heart'. No mention is made of the act of killing, nor any problems associated with the act; despite Morton's delineation of the 'desperate' few.[52] Griffith, in a rare contemplation of the psychological impact of weaponry, offers a human explanation into the 'cult of the bomb', but it rests exclusively upon a fear of being killed: 'the frontal assault with the rifle is doubtless the best approach; but…the frontal approach may very well easily turn out to be suicidal. However uncertain his progress, the bomber working his way forward from one shell hole to another, or from one traverse to another, may well have the better part of the bargain.'[53]

---

48 Dale Blair op cit., pp. 80-2.
49 Ibid., p. 86.
50 Ibid., p. 108.
51 Desmond Morton op cit., p. 158 & p. 180.
52 Ibid., pp. 227-259.
53 Griffith (1994) op cit., p. 69.

What is generally missing from deliberations on the psychological impact of combat on the soldier, and particularly the psychological impact of weaponry, are explanations that goes beyond a fear of being hurt. A fear of being killed or wounded, particularly at close quarters, was almost certainly a major cause of the Butterflies' disinclination towards combat. Survival was the dominant instinct upon the battlefield, and as the battles of autumn 1918 demonstrated, when the fear of being harmed subsided, the likelihood of infantrymen taking an active part in combat rose. But a *fear of killing* almost certainly helped influence this widespread battlefield passivity. This is signalled by the Butterflies' willingness to risk their lives and limbs to save a comrade's life long after they had surrendered the objective to safety.

Greater understanding of the impact of a *fear* upon a soldier's actions, and in particular, *a fear of killing*, calls for a re-evaluation of weapons use upon the Western Front; one that goes beyond explanations centred upon tactical utility. Such an understanding makes it clearer why the use of semi-automatic weaponry was far more prevalent than the rifle, and certainly the much vaunted bayonet. The typical use of the machine-gun and trench mortar called upon the infantryman to fight an unseen enemy over considerable distances. Teamwork and automation may have also eased the burden of killing, but evidence of non-firing at closer ranges suggest that *visual distance* was the most significant sanitising element to this form of combat. It is similarly apparent why, when the distance between foes diminished, those few who continued to fight invariably reached for the bomb rather than the bayonet. The bomb allowed the combatant to fight the enemy from a distance of up to ten yards, and often from behind some form of barricade; two lines of trenches, the outside of a dugout and so forth. Consequently, the adversary was often a shadowy figure whose fate could only be guessed at; thus also giving to the bomb a mild dose of the sanitising element of visual distance. The threat of unmitigated interpersonal combat almost always persuaded one or other adversary to choose flight or surrender. This was particularly true of the exceptional circumstances in which swords were drawn; the very sight of a bayonet charge usually being sufficient to persuade the adversary to retire or throw their hands up. Indeed, both sides' general willingness to accept the surrender indicates how speedily civilian mores and values were re-established when combat became altogether more human. This was a most impersonal battlefield upon which artillery and machine-gun fire predominated, and the cause of death was rarely seen.

Command Authority

One commonplace aspect of the Butterflies' combat behaviour that has similarly been neglected by the literature is the soldiers' 'collective' ability to hold some agency over their battlefield fate. The volunteers and conscripts of 19th Division were not always the innocent victims of trench warfare prescribed by the poets and writers of 'disenchantment'. Not so much because they were willing and aggressive participants, but because they were sometimes able to tacitly subvert the more extreme expectations of the chain of command. This vital element of battlefield control took a very basic form;

infantrymen going to ground during an advance, and thus sacrificing the objective to safety. This decision was usually taken by the officer in immediate command of the attack, either in defence of his men's welfare, or in response to their actions, or was collectively taken by the other ranks, in response to the death or wounding of their commander. In outlining the options available to the advancing soldier besides 'fight', Morton indicates that 'going to ground' was a common behaviour enacted by soldiers of the CEF who did not want to risk death or maiming in combat; but he sees this as a dead-end piece of combat behaviour. 'A soldier whose courage failed faced a few desperate options. He could run, hide, or even give himself the 'Blighty' for which so many soldiers yearned. More soldiers dropped on the battlefield than were ever knocked over by enemy shells or bullets, but a defender's artillery and machine-guns swept no man's land, and there was little added safety in falling behind the line of attack.'[54]

The 19th Division's experiences suggest that many soldiers were able to safely return from the battlefield, having 'fell behind' the advance, and avoided censure from the chain of command – it was *the* most effective way an infantryman could limit his commitment to the objective. The 'fog of war' that hung across the Western Front with a stolid permanence obscured evidence of such acts from senior commanders long enough to deem their actions a *fait accompli*. The cumulative outcome of this combat behaviour was consequently far-reaching; throughout the war it remained infantrymen who decided when an engagement was over, not generals. Even during the German spring offensives – when this tacit subversion became too overt, and jarred too heavily with the demands of the chain of command, eliciting the threat of summary executions – it remained the humble footslogging Butterfly who essentially decided where and when 19th Division would make its stand.

It is understandable that this facet of the infantrymen's combat behaviour has escaped the literature. Traditional sources have offered little evidence of its operation. To the individual infantryman any notion of 'control' may have been beyond recognition. Each time he went over the top he witnessed comrades being killed or maimed by machine-gun bullets and artillery shrapnel. As time went on, the future increasingly promised the same grim end. Why should he write about 'control'? Yet the findings of this study indicate that each time an infantryman went to ground endeavouring to avoid this fate, his junior officer (if still standing) responded to his actions by calling a temporary halt to the advance, and the chain of command, having found that the consequences of these actions had already taken effect, invariably called the attack off and began making alternative arrangements.

Tony Ashworth has persuasively delineated the infantrymen's ability to impose his generally pacifistic will upon episodes of 'trench warfare', but has rather uncritically

---

54 Desmond Morton op cit., p. 249.

assumed that the post-Zero battlefield was beyond his control.⁵⁵ The findings of this study indicate that this element of control did not terminate at Zero-hour. Rather, they suggest that the tacit renegotiation of proportionality that Leonard V. Smith found endemic within the French Army may well have permeated the British Army's command structure between 1914 and 1918.⁵⁶ The sources examined have not shed light on whether these episodes of tacit renegotiation resulted in any permanent change in the expectations of the chain of command (and this was not an objective of the study). However, the gradual post-1916 devolution of 'official' battlefield command to the infantry, and the granting of a greater degree of latitude over plans for the attack, are at least suggestive of a lasting impact upon command authority within the British Army.

It is no coincidence that Smith's findings were the consequence of a 'small unit study' (the French Fifth Infantry Division), and one that analysed the official documentation generated by that unit. Studying whole armies does not evidently allow a subtle enough investigation to reveal the constant negotiation process that accompanied army command authorities bending under the weight of an influx of civilian soldiers. McCartney's small unit study of the Liverpool Rifles and Liverpool Scottish also finds that pre-war civilian mores and values survived the mud and shelling and significantly impacted upon the way the Liverpool Rifles and Scottish fought their war: 'utilizing strategies for negotiation borrowed from civilian life, and supported by Territorial traditions and their links with home, the citizen soldiers were able to retain a degree of control over their military service.'⁵⁷ This 'control' stretched to 'the men influence[ing] the level of violence on their section of the front.'⁵⁸ McCartney witnesses that a soldier could materially improve or change his immediate situation through the non-verbal communication channel of behaviour. What she does not recognise is the possibility that he was able to modify his commitment to combat through his behaviour *upon the battlefield*; by such means as 'going to ground' or 'straggling'. The Territorial's limits of tacit (and not so tacit) forms of negotiation took place, according to McCartney, only prior to jump-off.⁵⁹ It is perhaps differing methodologies that underlie these variant understandings. Ashworth rejected war diaries unequivocally, McCartney uses them only as a complementary source. Solid evidence of a continually negotiated boundary of proportionality may possibly only be found within the official correspondence and communications between frontlines and rear.

55 Tony Ashworth, *Trench Warfare, 1914-1918: The Live and Let Live System* MacMillan (1980).
56 Leonard V. Smith, *Between Mutiny and Obedience: The Case of the French Fifth Infantry Division during World War I* Princeton University Press (1994).
57 H.B. McCartney, *The 1/6th and 1/10th Battalions of the King's (Liverpool) Regiment in the period of the First World War* Ph.D. thesis Cambridge (2001), abstract & p. 173, quote from abstract.
58 Ibid., p. 203.
59 Ibid., pp. 239-242.

Bomb and the Bayonet

Tim Travers has persuasively argued that the prewar Edwardian army (like most of the major armies of pre-war Europe) was dogged by an 'unrealistic cult of the offensive'; borne of a desire to realise the age-old goal of a *decisive battle*, upon a battlefield increasingly saturated with industrially manufactured machine-gun bullets and shell fire, and fought by an industrially produced proletarian army of doubted morale worth. Travers contends that: 'The British army recognised and accepted the emergence of fire-power as a major factor in modern warfare, but reacted by overemphasizing the offensive just because of the very difficulty of troops crossing the deadly and terrifying fire-swept zone and still continuing the assault.'[60] This growing belief in the 'cult of the offensive' exacerbated the pre-existing 'amateurism' of the British officer corps, which tended to stress human qualities of initiative, self-discipline and courage, over developing tactical and technological answers to the problems posed by increased firepower. Travers suggests that the British Army's devotion to the 'cult of the offensive' was never wholly shattered by exposure to the full destructive realities of industrialised warfare. As the war unfolded two competing approaches to overcoming the stagnation of trench warfare did battle. Until mid-1917 the 'human-centred' 'breakthrough concept' predominated, in which the aim was to achieve decisive victory through mass attacks, the capturing of consecutive lines of enemy trenches, routing the enemy, restoring mobility and sending in the cavalry. After this point the 'weapons-centred', artillery dominated, 'bite and hold' method of attack gained increasing favour, without ever fully achieving predominance. The former vision of battle belonged to the school of the 'cult of the offensive', the latter to the rarer group of technologically minded professional soldiers who had 'come to the conclusion that artillery and not manpower was the key.'[61]

Morton similarly witnesses the endurance of a 'cult of the offensive' amongst the combatants on the Western Front. The consequences, he suggests, were catastrophic. 'Put to the test of actual war, most theories of the offensive failed. The French doctrine of attack *à l'outrance* cost them 110,000 dead and 175,000 wounded or captured, and hurled their armies into full retreat. The German search for flanks ended with the Ypres *Kindermord*. The British 'muddle through' approach was drowned in their men's blood at Neuve Chapelle in March 1915, and again at Loos the following September. The Canadians practiced their own version of the 'spirit of the bayonet' with disastrous results at Kitchener's Wood on the night of 23 April 1915, and again in assaults at Festubert and Givenchy a few weeks later.'[62] Morton largely concurs with this study's conclusion that infantry morale could not overcome superior firepower. The

---

60   Tim Travers, *The Killing Ground: The British Army, the Western Front and the Emergence of Modern Warfare, 1900-1918* Routledge (1987), p. 37 & pp. 37-8.
61   Ibid., pp. 38-55. quote p. 55.
62   Desmond Morton op cit., p. 149.

key to unlocking the deadlock of trench warfare did not lie with such quixotic notions as élan and offensive spirit. He suggests that 'generals were reluctant to admit that, to penetrate enemy trench systems, heavy artillery and engineers could accomplish more than infantry, and cavalry were virtually useless.'[63]

This volume, in congruence with Travers and Morton, has understood the desire for the 'offensive spirit' and the evolution of weapons technology as two principles often in conflict. Albert Palazzo, in what might be the stiffest defence of the British way in war since the drafting of Sir Douglas Haig's final despatches, has questioned this understanding. He argues that the two ideals were complementary within the BEF's understanding of warfare. This was because, unlike the French and Germans, the pre-war British army did not witness morale alone as the solution to superior defensive firepower. A dependence upon the 'offensive spirit' was only one part in three elements that made up the pre-war army's principles of warfare; the other two being manoeuvre and firepower superiority. 'The British concentrated on three areas in the struggle to wrest from the defender the ability to control the outcome of battle. Their effort took the form of an emphasis on morale, a determination to employ manoeuvre, and a pursuit of technological superiority in the application of firepower. Through a combination of these factors the British gradually built up the advantages necessary for ending the stalemate on the western front.'[64]

Palazzo argues that the officer corps was willing to embrace any technological evolution that would overcome the enemy's original superiority in defensive firepower, and marry that technology with the high morale and discipline of its soldiers.[65]

The 19th Division's experience of a continued (what this study has termed) *psychological battle between the bomb and the bayonet* seemingly indicates that this marriage was not always as harmonious as Palazzo suggests. Brigadiers and generals remained concerned that too greater reliance upon weapons technology would dampen the ardour of their infantrymen. We must recall that GOC Jeffries even wanted to limit the use of artillery during raids to allow the infantry to experience more of the fight. It is evident that behind the major confrontation between, what Travers identifies as, the 'psychological battlefield' and the 'technological battlefield' continued a related small scale offensive between the 'technological' bomb and the 'psychological' bayonet.

The malady surfaced in the wake of the Somme offensive, where it became quite evident that infantrymen preferred to fight with the bomb rather than the bayonet. The enemy's subterranean labyrinth of dugouts and bunkers certainly recommended the bomb, but the chain of command feared that this predilection for the weapon was symptomatic of the infantrymen's disposition rather than any tactical decision. The answer to this prejudice against the bomb (and other semi-automatic weapons) was

63 Ibid., p. 150.
64 Albert Palazzo, *Seeking Victory on the Western Front: The British Army and Chemical Warfare in World War I* University of Nebraska Press (2000), p. 18, pp. 30-1, quote p. 30.
65 Ibid., p. 4.

that the division's pre-war regular officers feared the infantryman's (supposed) traditional fighting spirit was being superseded by this growing impedimenta of industrial killing machines. Every failed or faltering operation during 1917 and 1918 sparked off this always smouldering philosophical battle. Even when the German Spring Offensives proved beyond doubt that it was *not* the 'bayonet that captured and bullet that held', but, insofar as the infantry were concerned, the machine-gun that handled both combat episodes, the chain of command continued to insist that the rifle and bayonet were the first weapons of the infantryman. So with one hand 19th Division's senior commanders granted its infantrymen a plethora of semi-automatic weapons, whilst placing the other across its head and despaired at the consequences of their actions.

This psychological conflict between bomb and bayonet was evidently a common malady throughout the allied forces. Rawling delineates how the 'Canadian soldiers rarely used their rifles', preferring the bomb, and indicates that even the far-sighted Currie engaged in a prolonged campaign to promote use of the rifle and bayonet.[66] Griffith outlines a similarly protracted psychological battle within the BEF. In Griffith's terms, this battle becomes one of a 'post-modernist' reaction against the 'modernist bomber'. 'It seemed to many that the cult of the bomb could only too easily be used as an excuse for the timid soldiers who wanted quietly to forsake the offensive and revert to the 'Live and Let Live System'. The bomber's contract seemed to include too much emphasis on 'not exposing oneself', and too little on such things as 'capturing the enemy's trench'. Far from storming forward, in fact, such troopers were now perceived as preferring to cower behind a traverse.'[67]

Griffith suggests that the pre-war commander's distrust of the offensive spirit and tactical acumen of the New Army remained unalleviated throughout the war.[68] Griffith also provides evidence that the psychological battle between the bomb and the bayonet would have predated the arrival of the New Army, were it not for the pre-war regular commander's tendency to don rose tinted monocles when evaluating the 'Old Contemptibles'. He argues that the regular army of 1914 never had the opportunity to demonstrate the 'fire and movement' they were later to become famed for, because the battles of 1914 were mostly defensive engagements. He also says that they embraced the bomb with a similar enthusiasm as the New Army, when they could lay their hands on one.[69] It is possible, therefore, that the Butterflies' interaction with the weaponry of trench warfare, and their reactions to combat, may not only have been common to many volunteer and conscripted troops throughout the allied forces, but also may have been shared by many pre-war regulars.

66   Bill Rawling op cit., p134.
67   Paddy Griffith (1994) op cit., p. 68.
68   Ibid., p. 13.
69   Ibid., p. 51.

Morale

We are left with the question that has preoccupied the literature since the late 1920s – was the morale of the BEF's infantrymen sustained throughout the Great War? The initial answer, given by the poets and writers of 'disenchantment', was that the morale of the British Tommy did not survive the summer of 1916, let alone the war. The Somme turned wide-eyed enthusiasm into a thousand yard stare of cynicism, and that was the end of the story. The first serious academic attempts at recording everyman's view of war made few amendments, but did admit that a 'brotherhood of the damned' had allowed the infantry's morale to scrape and crawl its way through the Somme and Flanders mud towards eventual survival. The revisionist canon of the past twenty years or so, whilst differing over the reasons, has spoken with one voice in disclaiming this despairing tale. The morale of the BEF's infantry remained remarkably resilient in the face of the undeniable hardships of static trench warfare, and whilst not always soaring, spent far less time wallowing in the depths of despair than previously imagined.

The findings of this study broadly agree with the revisionist canon – but also add a number of significant caveats. The collective combat morale of each 'class' of recruits within 19th Division displayed a notable continuity. The young and hastily trained conscripted 'class of late 1918', like the volunteering 'class of 1914-15', surrendered the objective to safety when casualties threatened to surmount one-in-three of their comrades. There were fluctuations between individual units during individual combat episodes, but the thirty percent casualty rate ceiling remained the norm. Given that the chain of command was generally satisfied with this level of commitment and that it was often enough to achieve success, it would seem reasonable to suggest that this thirty percent casualty rate offers a dependable guide to 'good enough' combat morale.

Thus, it would seem defendable to argue that the combat morale of the Butterflies was, for the most part, 'good enough', and on occasions deserved the prefix 'high'. However, there were some steep, if narrow, downturns. The muddy denouement to the Somme and the worse days of Third Ypres pushed the infantry's endurance towards the edge, whilst the German Spring Offensives of 1918, at times, pushed it over the precipice. During these dark days casualty rates fell away, and increasingly infantrymen took backward steps along the combat morale/behaviour spectrum; swelling the ranks of stragglers, captives and deserters. Yet these collapses were always transient, a brief period of rest and recuperation and an intake of fresh drafts was usually enough to reinvigorate morale.

Peter Simkins' analysis of troop postal censorship delineates a similar morale graph for the last two years of the war, concluding that 'despite the low point of late 1917 and the crisis of March-April 1918, British units and soldiers remained committed to winning the war – a vital element in their performance in the latter half of 1918.'[70]

---

70 Peter Simkins op cit., p. 60.

Blair's delineation of the Diggers offensive spirit during the latter periods of the Somme indicates that the Australian infantry's morale had hit rock bottom by the winter of 1916.[71] Harper's study of the New Zealanders at Passchendaele contends that GHQ's decision to continue the 'battle of the mud' after 4 October effectively surrendered British and Dominion morale, and gave the German morale a much needed fillip. 'The British armies were worn down after the fourth, and, as a result, German morale rose while that of the attackers – British, Australian and New Zealand – plummeted to the depths of despair ... The disasters at Passchendaele caused the British army, the New Zealand Division included, to lose its confidence and optimism. Its good spirits were replaced by a "deadly depression".'[72]

Few would dispute that Third Ypres severely challenged the morale of the attacking armies on the Western Front. But it is perhaps Harper's focus upon a single battle that leads to such a forlorn conclusion. 19th Division's experiences, supported by Simkins and others, indicate that the morale of an army could go *up*, and well as *down*. The British and Dominion armies on the Western Front demonstrated a remarkable ability to recover form the hammerings they often experienced during major set-piece attacks.

Yet the evidence of this study indicates that high or even 'good enough' morale did not always equate to high *active* participation. In this increasingly industrialised war, fought between mass armies of civilian soldiers, the active participation in combat of perhaps less than half the 'fighting strength' was often enough to make a unit an effective fighting force. The Western Front was often a crowded and claustrophobic battlefield, but it was populated by civilian soldiers, and civilian mores and values often survived amidst the mud and the shelling. This significant caveat to arguments over the morale of frontline soldiers has been almost completely overlooked by both revisionists and the earlier literature alike.

Civilian Soldiers

So we find that our grandfathers and great grandfathers displayed resilience and courage beyond measure in civilian life, but commonplace upon the Western Front, and made sacrifices that post-1945 generations have increasingly found beyond their realm of comprehension. It is this understanding of sacrifice and courage that subsequent generations have been charged with remembering – 'least we forget'. But we can also see a lesser known and perhaps more uplifting narrative emerging from the volunteer and conscript infantrymen's experiences of the Great War. These men were not always the powerless victims of trench warfare. Some went to war to kill, and endeavoured to execute this fundamental role of the combat soldier. Others took active steps to modify the best laid plans of generals, and in doing so, wrestled back a

---

71 Dale Blair op cit., p. 123.
72 Glyn Harper op cit., pp. 93-4.

degree of control over their battlefield fate. But perhaps the most uplifting narrative of all can be found in the undying humanity of human nature. Amidst all the carnage and destruction inflicted by distant killing machines, many men discovered they were not killers. As Thomas Paine understood; 'Man is naturally the friend of Man, and human nature is not in itself vicious.'

Bibliography

I. PRIMARY SOURCES

1: Unit Histories
Becke, Maj. A.F. (comp) *History of the Great War: Order of Battles of Divisions, Part 3A New Army Divisions (9-26)* H.M.S.O. (1938).

Jeffreys, Maj.-Gen. G.D. *A Short History of the 19th (Western) Division 1914-18* John Murray (1919).

Wyrall, E. *The History of the 19th Division 1914-18* Edward Arnold & Co (1939).

2: Official Military Documents

(Housed at the National Archives/PRO (Kew))

2a: Military Courts Martial Records

WO213/4 to WO213/29 Judge Advocates General's Office: Field General Court's Martial and Military Courts, Registers. (July 1915-May 1919).

WO90/6 & WO90/8 Judge Advocates General's Office: General Court's Martial Registers, Abroad. (1900-1943)

WO86/63 to WO86/65 Judge Advocates General's Office: District Court's Martial Registers, Home and Abroad. (Aug 1914-July 1915)

WO71/608, WO71/569, WO71/464, & WO71/521: Trial Papers pertaining to soldiers of the 19th Division executed under orders of the Army Act.

2b: Unit War Diaries

Corps
WO95/1090 General Staff Indian Corps War Diary (June-Dec 1915)
WO95/639 II Corps General Staff War Diary (Oct-Nov 1916)
WO95/672-3 General Staff III Corps War Diary (May-July 1916)
WO95/717 General Staff IV Corps War Diary (March 1918)
WO95/747-9 General Staff V Corps War Diary (1916-18)
WO95/833-5 General Staff IX Corps War Diary (1916-18)

WO95/852 X General Staff X Corps War Diary (April/May 1917)
WO95/880-1 General Staff XI Corps War Diary (Sept 1915 – May 1916)

19th Division
WO95/2052-7 General Staff 19th Division War Diary (1915-19)
WO95/2071 19th Battn. Machine Gun Corps War Diary (March 1918-19)
WO95/2071 246 Machine Gun Corps War Diary (July 1917-Feb 1918)

56th Brigade
WO95/2075-7 Headquarters 56th Brigade War Diary (1915-19)
WO95/2082 56th Light Trench Mortar Battery War Diary (June 1917-19)
WO95/2082 56th Machine Gun Company War Diary (March 1916-Feb 1918)
WO95/2072 57th Field Ambulance War Diary (1915-19)
WO95/2078 7th Battn. King's Own (Royal Lancaster Regiment) War Diary (1915-Feb 1918)
WO95/2078 1/4th Battn. Kings Shropshire Light Infantry Regiment War Diary (March 1918-19)
WO95/2079 7th Battn. The East Lancashire Regiment War Diary (1915-Feb 1918)
WO95/2079 9th Battn. The Cheshire Regiment War Diary (March 1918-19)
WO95/2080 7th Battn The Loyal North Lancashire Regiment War Diary (1915-Feb 1918)
WO95/2081 7th Battn. The South Lancashire Regiment War Diary (1915-Feb1918)
WO95/2082 8th Battn. North Staffordshire Regiment War Diary (March 1918-19)

57th Brigade
WO95/2083-4 Headquarters 57th Brigade War Diary (1915-19)
WO95/2086 57th Light Trench Mortar Battery War Diary (June 1917-19)
WO95/2086 57th Machine Gun Company War Diary (March 1916-Feb 1918)
WO95/2072 58th Field Ambulance War Diary (1915-19)
WO95/2085 8th Battn. The Gloucestershire Regiment War Diary (1915-19)
WO95/2085 8th Battn. The North Staffordshire Regiment War Diary (1915-Feb 1918)
WO95/2085 10th Battn. The Royal Warwickshire Regiment War Diary (1915-19)
WO95/2086 10th Battn. The Worcestershire Regiment War Diary (1915-May 1918?)
WO95/2086 3rd Battn. The Worcestershire Regiment War Diary (May 1918-19)

58th Brigade
WO95/2087-9 Headquarters 58th Brigade War Diary (1915-19)
WO95/2093 58th Light Trench Mortar Battery War Diary (June 1917-19)
WO95/2093 58th Machine Gun Company War Diary (March 1916-Feb 1918)
WO95/2073 59th Field Ambulance War Diary (1915-19)
WO95/2090-1 9th Battn. The Cheshire Regiment War Diary (1915-Jan 1918)
WO95/2092 9th Battn. The Royal Welch Fusiliers War Diary (1915-19)

WO95/2092 9th Battn. The Welch Regiment War Diary (1915-19)
WO95/2093 6th Battn. The Wiltshire Regiment War Diary (1915-May 1918)
WO95/2093 2nd Battn. The Wiltshire Regiment War Diary (June 1918-19)

2c: Training Manuals and Manuals of Military Law

(Housed at the Imperial War Museum, London (IWM))
British Trench Warfare 1917-1918: A Reference Manual The Imperial War Museum (1997). Originally compiled by the General Staff, War Office.
Manual of Military Law War Office (1914).
Infantry Training 1914 General Staff War Office H.M.S.O.
S.S.391 *Field General Courts-Martial: Notes for Guidance of Presidents* (printed March 1916) & *'Circular Memorandum on Courts-Martial: For the use of Convening and Staff Officers, and Officers giving instructions on this subject'* (Printed April 1916).
S.S.135 *Instructions for the Training of Divisions for Offensive Action* Issued by the General Staff (Dec 1916). Reprinted with Amendments, Aug 1917.
S.S.135 *The Training and Employment of Divisions, 1918* Issued by the General Staff (Jan 1918).
S.S.143 *Instructions for the Training of Platoons for Offensive Action, 1917.* Issued by the General Staff (Feb 1917).
S.S.143 *The Training and Employment of Platoons, 1918* Issued by the General Staff (Feb 1918).
S.S.185 *Assault Training* Issued by the General Staff (Sept 1917).
(Housed at the Worcestershire Regimental Headquarters (WRHQ))
Field Service Regulations Part II: Organisation and Administration War Office (1909) Reprinted 1914.

2d: Records Pertaining to Casualties

(Housed at University College Worcester)
Soldiers died in the Great War, 1914-19: A complete and searchable digital database [CD ROM] Naval & Military Press (1998).

II. SECONDARY SOURCES

1: First World War

1a: Books

Ashworth, T., *Trench Warfare, 1914-1918: The Live and Let Live System* Pan Books (2000) 1st ed 1980.
Audoin-Rouzeau, S., *Men at War 1914-1918: National Sentiment and Trench Journalism in France during the First World War* Berg (1992).

Babington, A., *For the Sake of Example: Capital Court Martial 1914-18. The Truth* Leo Cooper (1993) 1st ed 1983.
Baynes, J., *Morale: A Study of Men and Courage – The Second Scottish Rifles at the Battle of Neuve Chapelle 1915* Cassell (1967).
Bet – El, I.R., *Conscripts: Lost Legions of the Great War* Sutton Publishing (1999).
Blair, D., *Dinkum Diggers: An Australian Battalion at War* Melbourne University Press (2001).
Bourke, J., *Dismembering the Male: Men's Bodies, Britain and the Great War* Reaktion Books (1999) 1st ed 1996.
Bourne, J.M., *Britain and the Great War 1914-1918* Edward Arnold (1989).
Brown, M., *The Imperial War Museum Book of the Somme* Pan Books (1996).
Brown, M., *The Imperial War Museum Book of 1918* Pan Books (1998).
Brown, M. & Seaton, S., *Christmas Truce* Pan Books (1999) 1st ed 1984.
Clark, A., *The Donkeys* Pimlico (1991) 1st ed 1961.
Cook, T., *No Place to Run: The Canadian Corps and Gas Warfare in the First World War* UBC Press (1999).
Dallas, G. & Gill, D., *The Unknown Army: Mutinies in the British Army in World War I* Verso (1985).
DeGroot, G.J., *Blighty: British Society in the Era of the Great War* Longman (1996).
DeGroot, G.J., *The First World War* Palgrave (2001).
Dyer, G., *The Missing of the Somme* Penguin (1995).
Eksteins, M., *Rites of Spring: The Great War and the Birth of the Modern Age* Bantam Press (1989).
Ellis, J., *Eye-Deep in Hell: Trench Warfare in World War I* Purnell Book Services (1976).
Ferguson, N., *The Pity of War* Penguin (1999) 1st ed 1998.
Fox, J., *Forgotten Divisions: The First World War from both sides of No Man's Land* Sigma (1994).
Fuller, J.G., *Troop morale and popular culture in the British and Dominion armies, 1914-1918* Clarendon Press (1990).
Gliddon, G., *VCs of the First World War: The Somme* Sutton Publishing (1991).
Gliddon, G., *VCs of the First World War: Spring Offensive 1918* Sutton Publishing (1997).
Griffith, P., *Battle Tactics of the Western Front: The British Army's Art of Attack 1916-18* Yale University Press (2000) 1st ed 1994.
Groom, W.H.A., *Poor Bloody Infantry: A Memoir of the First World War* William Kimber (1976).
Gudmundsson, B.I., *Stormtroop Tactics: Innovation in the German Army, 1914-1918* Praeger (1989).
Harper, G., *Massacre at Passchendaele: The New Zealand Story* Harper Collins (2000).
Harris, J.P., *Amiens to the Armistice: The BEF in the Hundred Days' Campaign, 8 August – 11 November 1918* Brassey's (1998).

Holmes, R., *Tommy: The British Soldier on the Western Front 1914-1918* Harper Collins (2004).
Hynes, S., *A War Imagined: The First World War and English Culture* Bodley Head (1990).
Keegan, J., *The First World War* Pimlico (1999) 1st ed 1998.
Laffin, J., *British Butchers and Bunglers of World War One* Sutton Publishing (1997) 1st ed 1988.
Leed, E.J., *No Man's Land: Combat and Identity in World War I* Cambridge University Press (1979).
Liddell Hart, B.H., *Liddell Hart's History of the First World War* Book Club Associates (1973) 1st ed 1970.
Liddle, P.H., *The 1916 Battle of the Somme: A Reappraisal* Leo Cooper (1992).
Macdonald, L., *They Called it Passchendaele: The Story of the Third Battle of Ypres and of the men who fought it* Penguin (1993) 1st ed 1978.
MacDonald, L., *Somme* Penguin (1993) 1st ed 1983.
MacDonald, L., *1915: The Death of Innocence* Penguin (1997) 1st ed 1993.
MacDonald, L., *To the Last Man: Spring 1918* Penguin (1999) 1st ed 1998.
Marwick, A., *The Deluge: British Society and the First World War – 2nd Edition* Macmillan (1991).
Mead, G., *The Doughboys: America and the First World War* Allen Lane (2000).
Middlebrook, M., *The First Day on the Somme* Penguin (1984) 1st ed 1971.
Mitchinson, K.W., *Gentlemen and Officers: The Impact and Experience of War on a Territorial Regiment 1914-1918* Imperial War Museum (1995).
Moore, C. *Trench Fever: An Intimate Story of The First World War* Abacus (1998).
Moorhouse, G., *Hell's foundations: A town, its Myths and Gallipoli* London : Hodder & Stoughton (1992).
Moran, Lord, *The Anatomy of Courage* The Keynes Press (1984) 1st ed 1945.
Morton, D., *When Your Number's Up: The Canadian Soldier in the First World War* Random House of Canada (1993).
Mosier, J., *The Myth of the Great War: A New Military History of World War One* Profile Books (2001).
Neillands, R., *The Great War Generals on the Western Front 1914-1918* Robinson (1999).
Oram, G., *Worthless Men: Race, eugenics and the death penalty in the British Army during the First World War* Francis Boutle Publishers (1998).
Palazzo, A., *Seeking Victory on the Western Front: The British Army and Chemical Warfare in World War I* University of Nebraska Press (2000).
Penn, A., *Targeting Schools: Drill, Militarism and Imperialism* Woburn Press (1999).
Pugsley, C., *On the Fringe of Hell: New Zealanders and Military Discipline in the First World War* Hodder & Stoughton (1991).
Putkowski, J. & Sykes, J., *Shot at Dawn: Executions in World War One by the authority of the British Army Act* Leo Cooper (1996) 1st ed 1989.
Rawling, B., *Trench Warfare: Technology and the Canadian Corps, 1914-1918* University of Toronto Press (1992)

Reader, W.J., *'At Duty's Call': A Study in Obsolete Patriotism* Manchester University Press (1988).
Richter, D., *Chemical Soldiers: British Gas Warfare in World War I* Leo Cooper (1992).
Rhodes-James, R., *Gallipoli* Pimlico (1999) 1st ed 1965.
Schreiber, S., *Shock Army of the British Empire: The Canadian Corps in the Last 100 Days of the Great War* Preager (1997).
Sheffield, G.D., *The Redcaps: a history of the Royal Military Police and its antecedents from the Middle Ages to the Gulf War* Brassey's (1994).
Sheffield, G.D., *Leadership in the Trenches: Officer-Man Relations, Morale and Discipline in the British Army in the Era of the First World War* Macmillan (2000).
Sheffield, G., *Forgotten Victory: The First World War Myths and Realities* Headline (2001).
Simkins, P., *Kitchener's Army: The Raising of the New Armies, 1914-16* Manchester University Press (1988).
Simpson, A., *Hot Blood and Cold Steel: Life and Death in the Trenches of the First World War* Tom Donovan (1993).
Smith, L.V., *Between Mutiny and Obedience: The Case of the French Infantry Division during World War I* Princeton University Press (1994).
Stephen, M., *The Price of Pity: Poetry, History and Myth in the Great War* Leo Cooper (1996).
Taylor, A.J.P., *English History 1914-1945* Oxford University Press (1992) 1st ed 1965.
Terraine, J., *Impacts of War 1914 & 1918* Hutchinson (1970).
Terraine, J., *White Heat: The New Warfare 1914-1918* Leo Cooper (1982).
Travers, T., *The Killing Ground: The British Army, the Western Front and the Emergence of Modern Warfare, 1900-1918* Routledge (1987).
Warner, P., *The Battle of Loos* Wordsworth Editions (2000) 1st ed 1976.
Warner, P., *Passchendaele* Wordsworth Editions (1999) 1st ed 1987.
Wilks, J. & Wilks, E., *The British Army in Italy 1917-1918* Leo Cooper (1998).
Winter, D., *Death's Men: Soldiers of the Great War* Allen Lane (1978).
Winter, D., *Haig's Command: A Reassessment* Penguin (2001) 1st ed 1991.
Winter, J., *The Great War and the British People* MacMillan (1985).
Winter, J., *Sites of Memory, Sites of Mourning: The Great War in European Cultural History* Cambridge University Press (1998) 1st ed 1995.

1b: Articles

Beckett, I., 'The Territorial Force in the Great War' in Liddle, P.H. (ed) *Home Fires and Foreign Fields: British Social and Military Experience in the First World War* Brassey's Defence Publishers (1985) pp. 21-37.
Beckett, I.F.W., 'The Singapore Mutiny of February, 1915' in *Journal of the Society for Army Historical Research* Vol. 62 (1984) pp. 132-153.

Bond, B., 'British "Anti-War" writers and their critics' in Cecil, H. & Liddle, P.H. (ed) *Facing Armageddon: The First World War Experienced* Leo Cooper (1996) pp. 817-30.

Bourke, J., 'Effeminacy, Ethnicity and the End of Trauma: The Suffering of "Shell-shocked" Men in Great Britain and Ireland, 1914-39.' in *Journal of Contemporary History* Vol. 35(1) (2000) pp. 57-69.

Bourne, J., 'The British Working Man in Arms' in Cecil, H. & Liddle, P.H. (eds) *Facing Armageddon: The First World War Experienced* Leo Cooper (1996) pp. 336-352.

Davidian, I., 'The Russian Soldier's Morale from the Evidence of the Tsarist Military Censorship' in Cecil, H. & Liddle, P.H. (ed) *Facing Armageddon The First World War Experienced* Leo Cooper (1996) pp. 425-433.

Ekins, A., 'The Australians at Passchendaele' in Liddle, P.H. (ed) *Passchendaele in Perspective: The Third Battle of Ypres* Leo Cooper (1997) pp. 227-254.

Englander, D. & Osborne, J., 'Jack, Tommy, and Henry Dubb: The Armed Forces and the Working Class' in *The Historical Journal* Vol. 21 No. 3 (1978) pp. 593-621.

Gooch, J., 'Morale and Discipline in the Italian Army, 1915-1918' in Cecil, H. & Liddle, P.H. (eds) *Facing Armageddon: The First World War Experienced* Leo Cooper (1996) pp. 434-447.

Griffith, P., 'The Extent of Tactical Reform in the British Army' in Griffith, P. (ed) *British Fighting Methods in the Great War* Frank Cass (1996) pp. 1-22.

Harvey, A.D., 'The Hand Grenade in the First World War' in *R.U.S.I. Journal* Vol. 138 No. 4 (1993) pp. 44-47.

Hughes, C., 'The New Armies' in Beckett, I.F.W. & Simpson, K. (eds) *A Nation in Arms: A Social Study of the British Army in the First World War* Tom Donovan (1990) 1st pub 1985 pp. 100-126.

Latter, E., 'The Indian Army in Mesopotamia 1914-1918' in *Journal of the Society for Army Historical Research* Vol. 72 (1994) pp. 232-246.

Lee, J., 'The British Divisions at Third Ypres' in Liddle, P.H. (ed) *Passchendaele in Perspective: The Third Battle of Ypres* Leo Cooper (1997) pp. 215-226.

Lee, J., 'Some Lessons of the Somme: The British Infantry in 1917' in Bond B. et al, (eds)*'Look To Your Front': Studies in the First World War by The British Commission for Military History* Spellmount (1999) pp. 79-87.

Liddle, P., 'British Loyalties: The Evidence of an Archive' in Cecil, H. & Liddle, P.H. (ed) *Facing Armageddon: The First World War Experienced* Leo Cooper (1996) pp. 523-38.

Liddle, P., 'Passchendaele Experienced: Soldiering in the Salient during the Third Battle of Ypres' in Liddle, P.H. (ed) *Passchendaele in Perspective: The Third Battle of Ypres* Leo Cooper (1997) pp. 305-323.

Mosse, G.L., 'Shell-shock as a Social Disease' in *Journal of Contemporary History* Vol. 35(1) (2000) pp. 101-108.

Noon, G., 'The Treatment of Casualties in the Great War' in Griffith, P. (ed) *British Fighting Methods in the Great War* Frank Cass (1996).

Oliver, D., 'The Canadians at Passchendaele' in Liddle, P.H. (ed) *Passchendaele in Perspective: The Third Battle of Ypres* Leo Cooper (1997) pp. 255-271.

Oram, G., 'Pious Perjury: Discipline and Morale in the British Forces in Italy, 1917-18' in *War in History* Vol. 9 No. 4 (2002) pp. 412-430.

Peaty J., 'Capital Courts-Martial during the Great War' in Bond B. et al *'Look To Your Front': Studies in the First World War by The British Commission for Military History* Spellmount (1999) pp. 89-104.

Pugsley, C., 'The New Zealand Division at Passchendaele' in Liddle, P.H. (ed) *Passchendaele in Perspective: The Third Battle of Ypres* Leo Cooper (1997) pp. 272-291.

Putkowski, J., 'The Kinmel Park Camp Riots 1919' in *Flintshire Historical Society* Vol. 32 (1989) pp. 55-107.

Scott, P., 'Law and Orders: Discipline and Morale in the British Armies in France, 1917' in Liddle, P.H. (ed) *Passchendaele in Perspective: The Third Battle of Ypres* Leo Cooper (1997).

Sheffield, G., 'Officer-Man Relations, Discipline and Morale in the British Army of the Great War' in Cecil, H. & Liddle, P.H. (ed) *Facing Armageddon: The First World War Experienced* Leo Cooper (1996) pp. 413-424.

Sheffield, G., 'The Operational Role of British Military Police on the Western Front, 1914-18' in Griffith, P. (ed) *British Fighting Methods in the Great War* Frank Cass (1996) pp. 70-86.

Sheffield, G., '"A very good type of Londoner and a very good type of colonial": Officer-Man Relations and Discipline in the 22nd Royal Fusiliers, 1914-18' in Bond B. et al *'Look To Your Front': Studies in the First World War by The British Commission for Military History* Spellmount (1999) pp. 137-146.

Simkins, P., 'Co-Stars or Supporting Cast? British Divisions in the "Hundred Days", 1918' in Griffith, P. (ed) *British Fighting Methods in the Great War* Frank Cass (1996) pp. 50-69.

Simpson, K., 'The British Soldier on the Western Front' in Liddle, P.H. (ed) *Home Fires and Foreign Fields: British Social and Military Experience in the First World War* Brassey's Defence Publishers (1985) pp. 135-158.

Spiers, E.M., 'The Regular Army in 1914' in Beckett, I.F.W. & Simpson, K. (ed) *A Nation in Arms: a social study of the British Army in the First World War* Tom Donovan (1990) 1st pub 1985 pp. 38-62.

Strachan, H., 'The Morale of the German Army, 1917-18' in Cecil, H. & Liddle, P.H. (ed) *Facing Armageddon: The First World War Experienced* Leo Cooper (1996) pp. 383-398.

Wawro, G., 'Morale in the Austro-Hungarian Army: The Evidence of Habsburg Army Campaign Reports and Allied Intelligence Officers' in Cecil, H. & Liddle, P.H. (ed) *Facing Armageddon: The First World War Experienced* Leo Cooper (1996) pp. 399-412.

2: Other Conflicts

2a: Books

Addison, P. & Calder, A., (ed) *Time to kill : the Soldier's Experience of War in the West, 1939-1945* Pimlico (1997).
Bartov, O., *Hitler's Army: Soldiers, Nazis, and War in the Third Reich* Oxford University Press (1991).
Bourke, J., *An Intimate History of Killing: Face-to-Face Killing in Twentieth-Century Warfare* Granta Books (1999)
Clausewitz, Carl von, *On War* Penguin (1968), 1st ed 1832.
Ellis, J., *The Sharp End: The Fighting Man in World War II* Pimlico (1990) 1st ed 1980.
Graham, D., *Against Odds: Reflections on the experiences of the British Army, 1914-45* MacMillan Press Limited (1999).
Ginzberg, E., *The Lost Divisions* Greenwood Press (1975) 1st ed 1959.
Hess, E.J., *The Union Soldier in Battle: Enduring the ordeal of combat* University of Kansas Press (1997).
Holmes, R., *Acts of War: The Behavior of Men in Battle* The Free Press (1986).
Hynes, S., *The Soldier's Tale: Bearing Witness to Modern War* Pimlico (1998) 1st ed 1997.
Keegan, J., *The Face of Battle* Pimlico (1999) 1st ed 1976.
Linderman, G.F., *Embattled Courage: The Experience of Combat in the American Civil War* The Free Press (1987).
MacKenzie, S.P., *Politics and Military Morale: Current-Affairs and Citizenship Education in the British Army, 1914-1950* Clarendon Press (1992).
Marshall, S.L.A., *Men Against Fire: The Problem of Battle Command in Future War* Peter Smith (1978) 1st ed 1947.
McPherson, J.M., *For Cause and Comrades: Why Men Fought in the Civil War* Oxford University Press (1997).
Moskos, C.C., *The American Enlisted Man: The Rank and File in Today's Military* Russell Sage Foundation (1970).
Schrijvers, P., *The Crash of Ruin: American Combat Soldiers in Europe during World War II* MacMillan Press (1998).
Stouffer, S.A. et al, *The American Soldier: Adjustment During Army Life – Volume I* Princeton University Press (1949).
Stouffer, S.A. et al, *The American Soldier: Combat And Its Aftermath – Volume II* Princeton University Press (1949).
Strachan, H., *European Armies and the Conduct of War* Routledge (1983).
Van Creveld, M., *Fighting Power: German and U.S. Army Performance, 1939-1945* Arms and Armour Press (1983).

2b: Journal Articles

Bartov, O., 'Daily Life and Motivation in War: The Wehrmacht in the Soviet Union' in *Journal of Strategic Studies* Vol. 12 (1989) pp. 200-214.

Ellis, J., 'Reflections on the "Sharp End" of War' in Addison, P. & Calder, A. (ed) *Time to Kill: The Soldier's Experience of War in the West 1939-1945* Pimlico (1997) pp. 12-18.

French, D., '"Tommy is No Soldier": The Morale of the Second British Army in Normandy, July-August 1944' in *The Journal of Strategic Studies* Vol. 19 No. 4 (Dec 1996) pp. 154-178.

French, D., '"You Cannot Hate the Bastard Who is Trying to Kill You...": Combat and Ideology in the British Army in the War Against Germany, 1939-45' in *Twentieth Century British History* Vol. 11 No. 1 (2000) pp. 1-22.

Grant, S.M., 'For God & Country: Why Men Joined up for the US Civil War' in *History Today* (July 2000) pp. 21-27.

Hart, S., 'Montgomery, Morale, Casualty Conservation and "Colossal Cracks": 21st Army Group's Operational Technique in North-West Europe, 1944-45' in *The Journal of Strategic Studies* Vol. 19 No. 4 (Dec 1996) pp. 134-153.

Holden Reid, B., 'What Made American Civil War Soldiers Fight?' in *The Journal of Strategic Studies* Vol. 22 No. 4 (Dec 1999) pp. 131-138.

Little, R.W., 'Buddy Relations and Combat Performance' in Janowitz, M. (ed) *The New Military: Changing Patterns of Organization* Russell Sage Foundation (1964) pp. 195-223.

Sheffield, G., 'The Shadow of the Somme: the influence of the First World War on British Soldiers' Perceptions and Behaviour in the Second World War' in Addison, P. & Calder, A. (ed) *Time to Kill: The Soldier's Experience of War in the West 1939-1945* Pimlico (1997) pp. 29-39.

Shils, E.A. & Morris Janowitz, M., 'Cohesion and Disintegration in the Wehrmacht in World War II' in *Public Opinion Quarterly* 12 (Summer 1948) pp. 283-86.

Spiller, R.J., 'S.L.A. Marshal and the Ratio of Fire' in *R.U.S.I. Journal* Vol. 133 pt. 4 (winter 1988), pp. 63-71.

Strachan, H., 'The Soldier's Experience in Two World Wars: Some Historiographical Comparisons' in Addison, P. & Calder, A. (ed) *Time to Kill: The Soldier's Experience of War in the West 1939-1945* Pimlico (1997) pp. 369-378.

3: Combat Psychology and Psychiatry

3a: Books

Binneveld, H., *From Shellshock to Combat Stress: A Comparative History of Military Psychiatry* Amsterdam University Press (1997).

Dinter, E., *Hero or Coward: Pressures Facing the Soldier in Battle* Frank Cass (1985).

Dixon, N., *On the Psychology of Military Incompetence* Pimlico (1994) 1st ed 1976.

Gabriel, R.A., *No More Heroes: Madness and Psychiatry in War* Hill and Wang (1987).
Gabriel, R.A., *The Painful Field: The Psychiatric Dimension of Modern War* Greenwood Press (1988).
Grossman, D., *On Killing: The Psychological Cost of Learning to Kill in War and Society* Little, Brown & Company (1995).
Kellett, A., *Combat Motivation: The Behaviour of Soldiers in Battle* Kluwer-Nijhoff Publishing (1982).
Leese, P., *Shell Shock, Traumatic Neurosis and the British Soldiers of the First World War* Palgrave Macmillan (2002).
Shalit, B., *The Psychology of Conflict and Combat* Praeger (1988).
Shephard, B., *A War of Nerves: Soldiers and Psychiatrists 1914-1994* Jonathan Cape (2000).
Watson, P., *War on the Mind: The Military Uses and Abuses of Psychology* Hutchinson (1978).

3b: Articles

Belenky, G. & Jones, F.D., "Introduction: Combat Psychiatry – An Evolving Field" in Belensky, G. (ed) *Contemporary Studies in Combat Psychiatry* Greenwood Press (1987) pp. 1-7.
Kellett, A., "Combat Motivation" in Belensky, G. (ed) *Contemporary Studies in Combat Psychiatry* Greenwood Press (1987) pp. 206-32.
Swank, R.L. & Marchand, W.E., "Combat Neuroses: Development of Combat Exhaustion" in *Archives of Neurology & Psychiatry* (1946) Vol. 55 pp. 236-247.

4: Theses

Bowman, T., *The discipline and morale of the British Expeditionary Force in France and Flanders 1914-18, with particular reference to Irish units* Ph.D. thesis University of Luton (1999).
McCartney, H.B., *The 1/6th and 1/10th Battalions of the King's (Liverpool) Regiment in the period of the First World War* Ph.D. thesis Cambridge (2001).

III: PUBLISHED MEMOIRS

Blunden, E., *Undertones of War* Penguin (1982) 1st ed 1928.
Coppard, G., *With Machine Gun to Cambrai* Cassell (1999) 1st paperback ed 1968.
Downing, W.H., *To the Last Ridge* Grub Street (2002) 1st ed 1920.
Dunn, J.C., *The War the Infantry Knew 1914-1919* Abacus (1987) 1st ed 1938.
Graves, R., *Goodbye to All That* Penguin (1960) 1st ed 1929.
Jűnger, E., *Storm of Steel* Penguin (2004) 1st ed 1920.
Masefield, J., *The Old Front Line* Pen and Sword ((2003) 1st ed 1917.
Remarque, E.M., *All Quiet on the Western Front* Vintage (1996) 1st ed 1929.

Sassoon, S., *Memoirs of a Fox-Hunting Man* Faber & Faber (1975) 1st ed 1928.
Sassoon, S., *Memoirs of an Infantry Officer* Faber and Faber (2000) 1st ed 1930.
Sherriff, R.C., *Journey's End* Penguin (1983) 1st ed 1929.
Terraine, J. (ed), *General Jack's Dairy: War on the Western Front 1914-1918* Cassell (2000) 1st ed 1964.

Index

Absence 44, 49-50, 62, 65, 115, 121, 126, 162, 186, 207, 209, 217-218, 220, 223-225, 242
Aircraft xiii, 191, 193-194, 209
Ancre 81, 115, 118-119, 122-125, 150
Arras 190, 193, 207
Artillery xiii-xv, 57, 59-60, 64-66, 68-70, 73-76, 80-81, 83-84, 87, 97-99, 101-102, 104-107, 112-113, 116, 120, 124, 128, 130-131, 138, 141, 146, 148-149, 155-156, 158-159, 162-164, 170, 173, 177-178, 184, 186, 189, 191-194, 196, 203-204, 214, 223, 229, 232-236, 242-244, 247, 249, 252-253, 260-261, 263-264
Artois 53, 56, 64
Australian Imperial Force 252-253, 257

Backhouse, Second Lieutenant H.H. 140, 143, 151
Baillescourt Farm 117, 120-121, 125
Bapaume 84, 104, 107, 190-192, 197, 199, 206
Bayonets i, xiii-xiv, 32, 43, 55-57, 67, 72, 75, 78, 83, 86, 102, 117, 124, 130, 132, 136, 138-139, 142-143, 146, 148, 150-151, 158, 161-162, 174-177, 181-182, 193, 213, 226-227, 242, 250, 254, 258, 260, 263-265
Beaumetz 190, 200, 203
Berners, Lieutenant Colonel R.A. 89, 91, 93, 95, 102-103
Beugny 190-191, 197, 199

Bombers/bombing parties 22, 41, 60, 65, 72, 74-77, 79, 83, 85, 87-89, 91-103, 110, 112, 117-118, 120, 129, 131-134, 139, 143, 162, 165, 171, 176, 235, 237, 250
Bridges, Major General G.T.M. 64, 66, 106, 124, 134-135, 139, 146, 160-161, 169, 175, 177
British Army, Armies:
  First Army 51, 53, 57, 64, 78-79, 84
  Second Army 49, 171, 174-175, 210
  Fourth Army 84-85, 104, 111, 221
British Army Corps:
  II Corps 115, 117-118
  III Corps 47, 56, 81, 84-85, 87-88, 100-101, 103-106, 111-114
  IX Corps 116, 144, 148, 151-152, 155-156, 161-163, 171, 183, 210
  X Corps 148, 171
  XI Corps 64, 66, 68, 73-75, 79, 84
  Indian Corps 51, 53-54, 56-57
British Army Divisions:
  2nd Division 53, 56-57, 59, 155, 196, 199
  19th Division i, v, viii, xiii-xv, 38, 42-43, 47-48, 51-54, 56-59, 63-64, 66-67, 70, 72-73, 75, 78-81, 84-87, 89-90, 101, 103-107, 111, 115-118, 121-122, 125-126, 128-129, 133-137, 139-140, 144, 148-150, 154-161, 164-166, 169-171, 173, 175, 177, 182-183, 185-187, 189-190, 193-194, 198-199, 203, 206-210, 212-214, 217-221, 223-224, 226-227, 229, 231-235, 239, 241, 243-244, 246-256, 258-261, 264-267

British Army Brigades:
  56th Brigade 54, 56-57, 66-67, 71, 78, 85, 87, 91, 93, 96-103, 107, 109, 112, 117, 119, 144, 146, 151, 159-161, 163, 166-167, 170-171, 184, 187, 191-192, 199, 202, 204, 206, 216, 225-227, 232, 235-236, 239-240, 243-245
  57th Brigade 47, 54, 56-57, 72, 75, 81, 86-88, 91, 93, 95-96, 98-99, 107-109, 111-112, 117-119, 121-125, 135, 140, 149, 152-155, 157-159, 171, 174, 178, 180-187, 190-192, 195-200, 203-204, 207-208, 212-213, 217, 225, 231-233, 236, 238, 240, 244-245
  58th Brigade 51, 53, 55, 57, 59-63, 67, 73, 85, 89, 91-95, 101-103, 105, 116-117, 135, 143, 151-152, 155-156, 161, 171, 174, 179, 191, 201, 206, 210, 219, 225-227, 242-243
British Army Regiments:
  Cheshire 58-59, 61, 63, 65, 74, 88-92, 94-96, 104-105, 111, 118-119, 123-125, 136, 150, 152-153, 157-158, 178-180, 182, 185, 187, 191, 198, 200-201, 203-204, 214-216, 224, 226-227, 239, 241-242, 245
    9th Btn: 61, 88, 92, 94-95, 187, 216, 226
  East Lancashire 54-55, 69, 92-94, 99-100, 107, 109-110, 118, 120-121, 125, 142-144, 150, 152, 163
  Gloucestershire 70, 89, 95, 107, 110, 114, 118, 121, 125, 150, 162, 178, 180-182, 185, 191, 199, 208, 240, 245
    8th Btn: 173, 181, 192, 195, 200, 203, 239
  North Staffordshire 70, 75-76, 79, 85-88, 91, 93-96, 102, 104-106, 111, 119, 122, 125-126, 153-155, 158, 180-181, 185, 199, 215-216, 241, 243-245
  Royal Warwickshire 67, 95, 106-108, 110, 112-114, 119, 121-122, 125, 135, 141-142, 150, 152-154, 158, 185, 195-196, 202, 206, 210, 214-216, 218-219, 223-224, 232, 234, 236-241, 243-245
  King's Shropshire Light Infantry 202-203, 218, 235, 245
    4th Btn: 202-203, 218, 235
  South Lancashire 48, 68, 73-74, 89, 91, 97-99, 105, 107-110, 118-121, 125, 139-140, 142, 150, 152, 162-164, 166-168, 179, 183, 220
  Royal Welsh Fusiliers 47, 199, 244
  Welch Regiment 58, 72, 91, 102, 152, 176, 197, 200, 232
  Wiltshire 59, 75, 86, 91-92, 94, 102-104, 150, 152, 169-170, 178-181, 184-185, 190, 193-195, 198, 200-202, 207, 210, 212-214, 218-219, 224-225, 227, 237, 239, 242
    6th Btn: 117, 191, 201-202, 208, 210, 220
  Worcestershire 47, 76, 86, 88, 95, 105-106, 108, 111, 114-115, 118, 122, 125, 135, 140-141, 143-144, 150, 153, 158, 161, 178, 180, 185-186, 202, 231, 238, 244-246
    10th Btn: 88, 125, 171, 192, 200, 203, 231
British Army, Other:
  Machine Gun Corps 42, 150, 160, 194, 196-199, 201, 212, 217, 219

Cambrai 190, 192, 199, 231
Canadian Expeditionary Force 249-252, 254, 256, 261
Champagne 53, 187, 221
Civilian soldiers iv, xi, xiii-xv, 42, 50, 262, 267
Combat psychology vii, x-xi, 27-28, 33, 36, 43, 79
Conscripts i, xii, 21, 38, 42, 189, 231, 267
Contalmaison 81, 84, 100-104
Cubitt, Brigadier General T.A. 155, 212-213, 217

Desertion 38, 49-50, 115, 126, 157, 186, 189, 208-209, 220, 223-225, 245-246, 266

Index 283

Doignies 190, 200, 203
Drill xiv, 28, 85-86, 136, 176, 254

Esprit de corps vii, 23, 128, 137, 218, 254

Fasken, Major General Charles Grant Mansell 51, 62, 64, 66
Field General Courts Martial 49-50, 126, 246
Fitzjohn, Lieutenant Colonel Tudor 71, 74, 78, 111, 166, 170
Fog of war xiv, 57, 65, 73, 91, 93, 119-120, 167, 192, 261
Fremicourt 190, 195, 199, 206
French Army 26, 221, 262

Garthwaite, Captain A. 193, 201-202, 207, 218
German Spring Offensives vii, xv, 134, 187, 231, 255, 261, 265-266
Godfrey, Lieutenant Colonel W. 142-143, 175-176, 180
Grandcourt 81, 116-118, 120-121, 125
Grevillers 190, 200, 202

Haig, Sir Douglas 29, 47, 67, 84, 224, 264
Haking, Lieutenant General Richard 64-66, 68-73, 79
Heath, Lieutenant Colonel R.M. 174, 195, 216, 239-240, 244-245
Hebuterne 129, 190-191, 194, 204

Jeffreys, Major General G.D. xiii, 51, 53, 59-60, 66, 118-120, 122, 124-125, 187, 189, 198, 221, 223-225, 228, 238
Junior officers 39, 71, 100, 108, 119-120, 124, 129, 137, 142, 235, 255-256, 261

Kitchener, Lord xii-xiii, 19-21, 23, 51, 53, 263
Kitchener's Army xii, 20, 23, 51

La Boisselle 72, 81, 83, 86-88, 90-96, 98-99, 101-102, 106, 115, 139, 171
Last Hundred Days vii, xv, 229, 231, 237, 248-249, 258

Learning curve xiii-xiv, 81, 128, 134-135, 146, 176, 229, 247-251, 253, 256
Lewis Gun 67, 85, 110, 129, 132-134, 142-143, 150, 160, 165, 171, 181, 198, 201, 204, 214, 235-238, 241, 250-251
'Live and Let Live' system 26, 44, 55, 69, 262, 265
Loos vii, xiii, 47, 51, 62, 73, 95, 107, 229, 263
Lys viii, 81, 187, 210-211, 221

Machine-guns i, 32, 43-44, 53, 58, 64, 76, 79, 89, 93, 98-100, 105-108, 110, 114, 121, 138, 149-150, 163-166, 170, 177-178, 180-182, 189, 191, 193, 200-201, 203-204, 209, 213, 232-234, 243, 250-251, 260-261, 263, 265
Mackenzie-Stuart, Brigadier General D. 62, 66, 141
Menin Road Ridge viii, 146, 171-172, 177, 181, 185-186
Messines Ridge vii, xv, 140, 146, 148-155, 157-158, 170, 186, 212, 216
Military Law 50, 189, 224-225
Mines xiii, 70, 76, 150-152
Montagne de Bligny 187, 224, 226-228
Morale v, xii, xiv-xv, 19, 23-26, 28-29, 38-40, 44-45, 48-49, 53-56, 59-64, 75, 77, 80, 83, 90-91, 93, 95, 99-100, 102, 104, 106-109, 111, 113-115, 122-127, 131, 136-138, 141, 148, 150, 157-158, 161, 163, 168-169, 174, 176, 182-183, 185-186, 194-196, 198, 200, 203-204, 207-209, 212-214, 217-219, 223-224, 226-229, 232, 244-245, 248, 255-257, 259, 263-264, 266-267
Moran, Lord Charles 19-20, 39, 256

Neuve Chapelle 19, 53, 64, 231, 253, 263
New Zealand Division 194, 267

Onslow, Brigadier General C.C. 66, 86, 91, 96
Oosttaverne 148, 153-154, 156
Ovillers 87, 90, 95

Pacifism xi, 18, 36, 48, 248, 257-259
Palmer, Captain F.H. 191-192, 203-204
Passchendaele xii, 22-23, 41, 171, 174, 251, 256, 267
Pilckem Ridge 146, 159, 161-162, 169-170

Rifle Grenades 129, 133, 160, 171, 177, 251-252

Self-Inflicted Wounds 38, 49-50, 186
Semi-automatic weapons xiv, 252, 258, 264-265
Serre 84, 129, 190
Shellshock xi, 29, 34, 36, 50, 96, 207, 245
Snipers 41, 55, 62, 87, 89, 91, 94-95, 97, 103, 114, 120, 132, 158, 164-165, 179, 184
Sole, Lieutenant Colonel D.M. xii, 140-141, 144-145, 161, 249
Somme vii-viii, xiii, xv, 21-22, 42, 64-65, 79, 81-83, 86, 101, 106, 115-116, 123, 125-126, 133, 135, 143, 146, 148, 151, 171, 177, 187-188, 190, 205, 221, 223, 229, 250-253, 256, 264, 266-267

Stragglers 123, 167, 189-190, 194, 204, 206-207, 219, 221, 223-225, 245, 266

Tanks xiii, 117, 130, 150, 194
Third Ypres vii, xv, 41-42, 140, 146, 148, 162, 171, 186, 231, 266-267
Trench mortars 65-66, 76, 83, 87, 99, 112, 117, 129, 132, 152, 155, 160, 162, 183, 204, 242-243, 253

Volunteers i, xiii, 17, 21-23, 38-39, 42, 45, 72, 265, 267

Watts, Lieutenant 61, 63, 95, 157
Winser, Lieutenant Colonel C.R.P. 74, 89, 91, 97-99, 105, 108
Worgan, Lieutenant Colonel R.B. 88, 91-92, 94-96
Wulverghem 210, 212-215, 218-220
Wytschaete 81, 129, 148, 219

Ypres vii, xv, 22, 41-42, 129, 140-141, 146, 148, 162, 171, 186, 193, 207, 210, 231, 256, 263, 266-267

Lightning Source UK Ltd.
Milton Keynes UK
UKHW022236091222
413685UK00006B/38